NATIONAL SECURITY, CIVIL LIBERTIES,

AND THE

WAR ON TERROR

NATIONAL SECURITY, CIVIL LIBERTIES,

AND THE

WAR ON TERROR

EDITED BY

M. KATHERINE B. DARMER AND RICHARD D. FYBEL

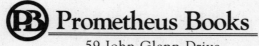 Prometheus Books

59 John Glenn Drive
Amherst, New York 14228–2119

Published 2011 by Prometheus Books

Cover image © 2011 PhotoDisk, Inc.
Cover design by Grace M. Conti-Zilsberger

Inquiries should be addressed to
Prometheus Books
59 John Glenn Drive
Amherst, New York 14228–2119
VOICE: 716–691–0133
FAX: 716–691–0137
WWW.PROMETHEUSBOOKS.COM

15 14 13 12 11   5 4 3 2 1

Library of Congress Cataloging-in-Publication Data

National security, civil liberties, and the war on terror / by M. Katherine B. Darmer and
Richard D. Fybel, eds.
        p. cm.
    Includes bibliographical references.
    ISBN 978–1–61614–396–1 (pbk.)
        1. War and emergency powers—United States. 2. Civil rights—United States.
3. Terrorism—Prevention—Law and legislation—United States. 4. War on Terrorism,
2001–2009. I. Darmer, M. Katherine B. II. Fybel, Richard D., 1946– III. Title.

KF5060.N38 2011
343.73'1—dc22

2011007362

CONTENTS

CONTENTS

PART TWO: INTERROGATION PRACTICE:
FROM TORTURE TO *MIRANDA* WARNINGS?

A. Torture

CONTENTS

CONTENTS

CONTENTS

PART FIVE: DETENTIONS AND THE CONSTITUTIONAL BALANCE OF POWER

CONTENTS

ACKNOWLEDGMENTS

M. Katherine B. Darmer wishes to acknowledge the helpful research assistance of Tiffany Chang (Chapman University School of Law JD, 2010), Lisa Mahlum and Tyler Schoenberg (Chapman JD candidates) as well as the extensive administrative support of Maria Sanchez (Chapman).

Both editors also wish to acknowledge the helpful editing of Brian McMahon at Prometheus Books.

INTRODUCTION

M. Katherine B. Darmer

As galley proofs for this volume were being finalized, President Obama announced that American special forces had killed the terrorist Osama bin Laden on May 1, 2011. The editors join other Americans in a sense of profound relief that bin Laden was brought to justice. And yet, as President Obama noted, "[t]he cause of securing our country is not complete."

When this volume's precursor, *Civil Liberties vs. National Security in a Post-9/11 World* was published in 2004, the editors noted that "[a]fter September 11, for our country at least, that line became the demarcation point: before and after. The world as we knew it changed, irrevocably, on that day in history."[1] In the immediate aftermath of 9/11, Congress passed the USA PATRIOT Act and the executive branch acted aggressively in an effort to preempt any further attacks. In the ensuing decade, the executive, legislative, and judicial branches of government have continued to wrestle with the challenges to national security. With more time for reflection, with a well-developed post-9/11 jurisprudence, and with an extensive body of information about the tactics our country has used, this volume poses continuing questions about national security, civil liberties, and the War on Terror. I note that while the current administration has moved away from using the term "war on terror," the term has been used so widely that it seemed appropriate for this volume.

As was true with the precursor volume, in an effort to present a balanced analysis, we publish competing views on the issues related to civil liberties and national security. Nevertheless, this book is not designed to be a comprehensive analysis of the "war on terror." In particular, the military dimensions of that war are only touched upon. Moreover, we leave aside the currently raging battle over Arizona's new immigration law, SB 170, and the ensuing federal challenges, as well as the recent efforts to curtail the right to birthright citizenship. While acknowledging the role that concerns about national security play in the debates surrounding these initiatives, we also believe that they implicate broader concerns and are worthy of fuller treatment than we can provide in this volume. We do, however, include one selection addressing immigration from a historical perspective.

As a former assistant United States attorney who left the government before 9/11, my views are necessarily shaped by my experiences as a Department of Justice employee. After 9/11, I shared the view that Osama bin Laden posed a substantial and ongoing threat and that the threat was "unique." On the other hand, the notion that the threat is "unique" has led to the use of tactics that I view as deplorable. Others disagree, and we have included their views in this book. Thus, situating the War on Terror in historical context is one of the aims of this book.

My coeditor, Justice Richard Fybel, brings a particular historical perspective to this project, and I have welcomed his insights in structuring this volume on national security and the War on Terror. Not only is Fybel a respected jurist, but his family fled Nazi Germany and Lithuania after facing persecution. He has personally contributed to this volume an original essay on the role of the judiciary in the Nazi regime. Part one of this volume is titled "Framing the War on Terror: History and Context," and Justice Fybel's essay, "The Absence of Judicial Ethics and Impartiality: The German Legal System, 1933–1945," is the first selection. His essay traces the increasing restrictions on individual rights in the Nazi regime, the coordination of the judiciary into the regime, and the ethical corruption of the German judges. Indeed, he points out that what the Nazis did between 1933 and 1945 was "legal" under the German legal system. In that situation, the "rule of law" did not provide protections, even against mass murder.

The second chapter is from the late Chief Justice William Rehnquist's book, *All the Laws but One: Civil Liberties in Wartime*. Written three years before the terrorist attacks of September 11, Rehnquist's book addresses such issues as President Lincoln's suspension of the writ of habeas corpus during the Civil War and the internment of Japanese Americans during World War II. In his chapter excerpted here, bearing the Latin phrase *Inter Arma Silent Leges* ("In time of war the laws are silent"), Rehnquist argues that, inevitably, the government is less deferential to civil liberties in times of war. Yet his message is ultimately one of optimism that the courts are equipped to balance the government's claimed need to protect security with competing claims for civil liberties.

The next chapter is a limited excerpt from Ernesto Hernandez-López's comprehensive 2009 article "*Boumediene v. Bush* and Guantá-namo, Cuba: Does the 'Empire Strike Back'?" Hernández-López takes a postcolonial perspective and situates recent events at Guantánamo Bay in a historical framework. He provides important background regarding the lease agreement at Guantánamo and argues that, rather than being an aberration, Guantánamo's "legal anomaly" serves the strategic interests of the United States.

The next two selections offer profoundly different views of the trade-offs between liberty and security in the War on Terror. In Marjorie Cohn's "Trading Civil Liberties for Apparent Security Is a Bad Deal," she argues that the distinction is a false one. She argues that the Bush administration, like prior wartime administrations, was guilty of overreaching. She addresses issues of surveillance, detentions of people of color, and torture, concluding that citizens have a duty to protest when "our government fails to live up to our principles."

Robert J. Pushaw Jr. takes a contrasting view in "Justifying Wartime Limits on Civil Rights and Liberties," wherein he argues that the Constitution contemplates expansive powers for the president during wartime. In assessing the current antiterrorism effort, he defends such measures as the USA PATRIOT Act, noting that President Bush enjoyed wide popular support for his policies until initiating the war in Iraq. He concludes that "War is hell" and that presidents faced with national emergencies are often called upon to take drastic action.

Part one concludes with an assessment of recent history: the policy shift from the Bush to the Obama administration with regard to countering terror. In "Broken Promises or Unrealistic Expectations?: Comparing the Bush and Obama Administrations on Counterterrorism," Tung Yin describes the difference between the criminal prosecution and the military force paradigms, ultimately concluding that both are necessary in the War on Terror. In addressing indefinite detentions, military commissions, and the use of lethal aerial drone strikes, Yin concludes that Obama's policies have been largely consistent with those of his predecessor.

One area in which Obama has tried to take a sharp turn away from the Bush administration is with regard to the use of torture. Obama, for example, has renounced the use of waterboarding. Part two, titled "Interrogation Practice: From Torture to *Miranda* Warnings?" seeks to address such issues. Perhaps no topic considered by this book has generated more controversy than the tactics used during the interrogation of terrorist suspects. Views differ widely. While some believe that full protections such as those provided in *Miranda* should apply to all suspects, others believe that even torture is justified in some situations. This book seeks to give voice to those vastly competing viewpoints. We note that even Obama's condemnation of torture does not foreclose the possibility of a future administration taking a different direction. Studies suggest that there is wide popular support for the use of torture in extreme circumstances.

An excerpt from my own 2009 essay "Reliability, Waterboarded Confessions and Reclaiming the Lessons of *Brown v. Mississippi* in the Terrorism Cases" is included in section A of part two. The essay argues that the historic case of *Brown*, which unequivocally condemned the use of torture in a unanimous 1936 Supreme Court opinion, serves as an important starting point in current conversations about torture. *Brown* emphasized that tortured confessions are absolutely unreliable, but the Court's later shift away from a concern with reliability has left troubling "protection gaps" for suspects. In *Brown*, the Court recognized that torture offends due process not only when inflicted by law enforcement, but also if relied upon later at the "pretense" of a trial. To the extent that the modern torture debate has sought to ask the question whether torture "works," we are at risk of failing the lessons of *Brown*.

We then include a brief excerpt of the August 1, 2002, Department of Justice ("DOJ") Memorandum regarding "Standards of Conduct for Interrogation," sometimes referred to as the "torture memorandum," and which I have referred to elsewhere as the BYTAP ("Bybee-Yoo Torture and Power") Memo. While signed by Jay Bybee, who now sits as a Ninth Circuit Court of Appeals judge, the memo was primarily authored by John Yoo, a former DOJ employee and a tenured law professor at the University of California at Berkeley. The BYTAP Memo suggests that only the harshest of interrogation methods are banned by statutes and treaties proscribing torture, such as the Geneva Convention, and argues further that the president may not be bound even by limits on torture. It also argues that the defenses of necessity and of self-defense may be available to officials accused of torture. The memorandum has garnered substantial notoriety since it was leaked to the press in 2004. While it was repudiated even under the Bush administration, many have argued that the memorandum set the stage for substantial abuses of detainees, including "waterboarding." Accordingly, I believe an understanding of the memo is important in contextualizing the ongoing debate about interrogation practice.

The next selection is an excerpt from Jeremy Waldron's article "Torture and Positive Law: Jurisprudence for the White House." Waldron argues that the prohibition on torture is not just an ordinary rule but also a legal "archetype." Waldron offers a powerful indictment of BYTAP and similar efforts to justify coercive interrogation techniques and also criticizes the position famously advanced by Alan Dershowitz that courts should be authorized to issue "torture warrants."

The next selection presents a middle view. In "Interrogating Suspected Terrorists: Should Torture Be an Option?" Professors John T. Parry and Welsh S. White argue that torture is and should be illegal but that any law enforcement agent who uses torture should be able to defend the "necessity" of his actions in a particular case. Thus, in a "ticking time bomb" scenario, a law enforcement agent would not be authorized to use torture, but he would have a defense if his actions were criminally prosecuted.

When the precursor volume to this book was published, the term "waterboarding" had not entered the popular lexicon. We know now that this practice has been used on terrorism suspects. We sought to include John Yoo's recent defense of such practices in a 2009 *Wall Street Journal* op-ed, but Professor Yoo declined permission. That op-ed is addressed, however, in an excerpt of my own 2009 article, "Waterboarding and the Legacy of the Bybee-Yoo 'Torture and Power' Memorandum: Reflections from a Temporary Yoo Colleague and Erstwhile Bush Administration Apologist," which describes BYTAP and canvasses the extensive academic criticism of that memorandum, concluding that waterboarding does, indeed, constitute torture. This subsection then concludes with a brief editorial from the *New York Times*, which addresses the torture issue.

The second part of our consideration of interrogation practices then turns to questions about *Miranda* and terrorism cases. We excerpt my 2003 article "Beyond *Bin Laden* and *Lindh*: Confessions Law in an Age of Terrorism," which argues that *Miranda* both under-regulates and over-regulates in the terrorism context. The article advocates for exceptions to *Miranda* in the terrorism cases, building on the current "public safety" exception to *Miranda*, but also argues that truly compelled statements should never be admissible.

The next three selections are short pieces that provide different views on legislation proposed in 2010 to modify *Miranda* in terrorism cases and/or discuss *Miranda* warnings in the context of the recent case of Faisal Shahzad, the "Times Square bomber" and Umar Farouk Abdulmutallab, the so-called Christmas Day bomber. On October 21, 2010, the Department of Justice issued new guidelines stating that "agents should ask any and all questions that are reasonably prompted by an immediate concern for the safety of the public or the arresting agents without advising the arrestee of his *Miranda* rights" and then, with some exceptions such as the necessity for gathering intelligence, provide the rights once initial safety questions have been resolved. In a *Los Angeles Times* editorial dated April 4, 2011, these guidelines were praised as striking a "good balance between the needs of law enforcement and the rights of suspects," but the editorial also noted a divergence of views on the contentious issue of providing warnings to terrorism suspects. Questions regarding the use of *Miranda* in the terrorism context continue.

Part three of the volume then turns to issues of immigration and racial profiling.

Jennifer Chacón provides a historical perspective on immigration, noting that while immigration was freely allowed during the early days of our nation's history, it was later used to control the racial makeup of the population. Modernly, she argues, issues of immigration, crime control, and national security are conflated. The notion of "criminal illegal aliens" resonates in popular culture but is in fact grossly distorted.

Stuart Taylor's piece, "The Skies Won't Be Safe Until We Use Commonsense Profiling," concedes that the chances that any Middle Eastern passenger on an airplane is a terrorist are "tiny." He argues nonetheless that the odds that future al Qaeda terrorists will be Middle Eastern make it critical not to ignore apparent national origin in airline screening. He warns that future terrorists may provide no behavioral clues to their intentions, suggesting that profiling may be the only tool that could work to prevent acts of terror by perpetrators who appear innocent.

Taylor's selection is followed by an excerpt from a recent article by John Tehranian detailing ways in which those of Middle Eastern descent are subject to profiling and arguing against its use.

Part four then addresses issues of secrecy and surveillance, including the "state secrets" doctrine and the Foreign Intelligence Surveillance Act (FISA). In chapter twenty, we include an excerpt from Sudha Setty, which traces the historical origins of the state secrets act, explaining the courts' treatment of the doctrine in recent cases and arguing for its modification. When the government relies upon the state secrets doctrine, parties may be unable to proceed in court with claims against the government because information necessary to make their claims may be deemed "state secrets."

We then include David Cole and Martin S. Lederman's introduction to a law review symposium addressing the warrantless wiretapping program undertaken by the National Security Agency. In that introduction, Cole and Lederman describe various key documents in the debate about the lawfulness of the program, including the Bush administration's defense of the program and contrary arguments maintaining that such wiretapping violates FISA.

We next include a district court opinion that arises at the intersection of the state secrets privilege and FISA. In that 2010 case, the court found that, without relying upon classified information, the plaintiffs had marshaled adequate publicly available information to proceed with a case in which they alleged that they had been subjected to wiretapping in violation of FISA.

We then include a *New York Times* op-ed related to FISA and a recent op-ed by Dean Erwin Chemerinsky, sharply criticizing a Ninth Circuit Case in which the court agreed that the state secrets doctrine barred a lawsuit alleging torture.

Finally, in part five, we turn to questions concerning the balance of powers, specifically the tug-of-war between the president, Congress, and the courts regarding the rights of terrorist detainees. The Supreme Court has decided four important cases dealing with the rights of so-called enemy combatants and habeas corpus review: *Hamdi v. Rumsfeld* (addressing due process rights of citizens deemed "enemy combatants"), *Rasul v. Bush* (providing constitutional protections to detainees at Guantánamo), *Hamdan v. Rumsfeld* (striking down military commissions because of violations of the Uniform Code of Military Justice and the Geneva Convention), and *Boumediene v. Bush* (finding unconstitutional Congress's effort to limit judicial review of "enemy combatant" designations and finding review an inadequate substitute for habeas corpus). Excerpts from the first and last of those opinions are included as chapters 25 and 28.

Those cases are the subject of vastly different interpretations. We return in this section to the competing views of Marjorie Cohn and Robert Pushaw, who, in other sections of their articles excerpted in part one, address these decisions from different perspectives, with Cohn largely supporting the role of the Court in limiting the executive branch and Pushaw arguing that the cases are a departure from the Court's traditional deference to wartime presidents.

Finally, we include a recent DC Circuit case *Al Maqaleh v. Gates*, which ordered the dismissal of habeas petitions brought by Bagram detainees. That case also provides a helpful summary of the Supreme Court cases dealing with habeas review. Finally, we include an *LA Times* editorial that questions the practice of holding terrorism suspects without trial.

While acknowledging that our treatment of this topic is not comprehensive, we do hope that readers who want to critically assess the important issues involving liberty and security trade-offs will get a working start with the materials in this book. Finally, I note that the inclusion of any particular piece in this volume in no way implies either editor's endorsement of the views expressed therein.

Editors' Note: Because of the scope of the topics covered in this volume, many selections have been heavily edited, with virtually all footnotes eliminated from law review articles and legal cases. Readers are encouraged to consult the original sources for the citations to supporting authority contained therein. With the exception of minor style changes introduced by the publisher, including to court decisions, all other changes to the selections are generally indicated with ellipses and alteration with brackets. Where footnotes are included, the publishers have endeavored to conform the footnotes to the Chicago Manual of Style. In some instances, however, not all information required by the Chicago Manual was readily available. Information provided in footnotes in those instances is consistent with information required by the Blue Book for Legal Citations, though footnotes still appear in the style of the Chicago Manual.

PART 1

FRAMING THE WAR ON TERROR
History and Context

THE ABSENCE OF JUDICIAL ETHICS AND IMPARTIALITY
The German Legal System, 1933–1945

Richard D. Fybel

I.

INTRODUCTION

Immediately after I took the oath as an Associate Justice of the California Court of Appeal, my mother Ruth, a refugee from Lithuania to America in early 1939, said to my wife, "This is my revenge against Hitler." On the morning after *Kristallnacht* in November 1938, in her hometown of Memel, sixteen-year-old Ruth Benjamin was barred from entering her school because she was Jewish. A few months later, with a visa to America clutched in her hand, she was able to flee from Lithuania with her mother. Ruth graduated from high school in Los Angeles and worked as a seamstress in a factory during the war. She met and married my father Ernest, who in July 1938 had escaped from Germany via Holland together with his parents and brother.

Everything the Nazis did from 1933 through 1945, including mass murder and deprivation of all individual rights, was legal under the German legal system. This essay describes how Germany legalized murder and other criminal acts, and focuses on the acts of the judiciary and individual judges.[1]

The German judiciary from 1933 through 1945 was ethically corrupt with its judges playing integral roles in the legal system of Germany and its occupied countries. The lessons of this "legal barbarism" confirm the importance of the hallmarks of our American judiciary and its judges: impartiality, the rule of law based on our constitution, protection of individual liberties from government intervention, and the rendering of equal justice to all.

II.

THE GERMAN LEGAL SYSTEM, 1933–1945

A. Chronological Summary of Destruction of Legal Rights Under Law.[2]

From 1933 through 1945, the Nazis murdered millions of people throughout Europe, including 1.5 million Jewish children. To grasp the magnitude of this number of children, recall that it is the same amount in the throng on the Capitol Mall at the inauguration of President Obama. How were millions of lives destroyed and freedoms stolen as an official policy and practice of a state in the civilized world in the twentieth century? What were the roles of the judiciary and of individual judges?

In January 1933, Germany had a civil code enacted in 1898 and an established and well-organized legal system. Hitler was legally appointed chancellor by the president of the republic. Between 1933 and 1945, the Nazis enacted anti-Jewish laws enabling the state—essentially the Nazi party and the police—to ignore all individual liberties. The Nazis recognized and emphasized reliance on their written laws as a source of state authority. They acted to establish their rule "within the framework of traditional law."[3] It is instructive to analyze these step-by-step, incremental, but fundamental, changes to the legal process in Germany.

On February 28, 1933, relying on a provision in the German constitution, President von Hindenburg and Chancellor Hitler had issued an emergency decree "for the Protection of the People and the State." The decree was made as a "defensive measure against communist acts of violence endangering the state" and suspended sections of the constitution affecting freedom of the press and individual rights.[4]

Although many rights were in suspense, Germany still had a constitution. But article 76 of the constitution permitted it to be changed by a two-thirds vote of a quorum of the national legislature, the elected Reichstag. The Enabling Law of March 23, 1933, passed by the Reichstag, empowered Hitler as the executive to enact legislation deviating from the constitution for four years and to do so without the approval of the Reichstag. The Reichstag effectively voted itself out of existence and gave Hitler dictatorial powers. Eighty-four courageous members of the Reichstag voted against the act. By virtue of this Enabling Law, the executive was given unlimited "legislative power" and its stated basis was "for the Recovery of Germany."

On August 1, 1934, hours before the death of President Von Hindenburg, the offices of president and chancellor were merged, effective at the moment of the president's passing. On August 2, when Von Hindenburg died, Hitler became Führer, the "Leader and Reich Chancellor." The law was ratified by a nationwide plebiscite on August 19.[5]

On August 20, 1934, German judges began taking an oath to follow Hitler. The new oath eliminated the former oath's reference to their country's constitution. Both oaths maintained a judge's duty to observe (or be obedient to) the law.[6]

In 1933 and 1934, by executive decree and emergency legislation, all public assemblies in Germany were subject to prior police approval. All public assemblies which could pose a potential threat to public order and security were prohibited. What happened to freedom of the press? A ban was placed on publications whose content was likely to endanger public security and order. All rights under the German Constitution were suspended by law and replaced by a new law directed against "treacherous acts against the Government of the National Revolution."

Also, in 1933, cities started proclaiming and enforcing their own laws excluding Jews from public life in Germany. In Berlin, Jewish lawyers and notaries were no longer allowed in court. Cologne decreed that Jews could not be employed in municipal offices. Munich prohibited Jewish doctors from treating non-Jewish patients in city hospitals.

In 1933 and 1934, decrees from national, state, and local governments barred Jews from professions (including legal and medical), jobs, and education. Hitler called for a boycott of Jewish-owned businesses and marking those shops with the word "Jude." What was the reaction of the judiciary after this boycott was announced and implemented? According to Rabbi Leo Baeck, the leader of Berlin's Jewish community: "The universities were silent, the courts were silent. . . ."[7] Books by Jewish authors were burned in mass rallies.

In September 1935, the "Nuremberg Laws" were passed by the Nazi Party Congress. This "Reich Citizenship Law" deprived German Jews of citizenship, limiting German citizenship to persons of German or "kindred blood." An intricate set of rules set forth who had Jewish "blood." This law defined a Jew based on the religion of his or her grandparents. The civil and other legal rights of Jews were cancelled and their voting rights were abolished. By December 1935, a decree ordered dismissal of all Jewish professors, teachers, physicians, lawyers, and notaries—even those previously exempt because of military service to Germany in World War I. These laws also prohibited intermarriage and "extramarital relations" between Jews and non-Jews. The penalty? Death sentence.

THE ABSENCE OF JUDICIAL ETHICS AND IMPARTIALITY

Throughout 1936 and 1937, all of these laws were enforced by the police. As we shall see, the judiciary and judges fully cooperated in these actions. Indeed, in December 1936, the Supreme Court of Germany interpreted and enforced the Nuremberg Race Laws broadly and aggressively.[8]

In 1938, even more decrees were issued from the Reich ministries covering everything from organizing *Kristallnacht* in November 1938 to forbidding Jews from attending theaters and movies, to expelling all Jews from German schools, to freezing all Jewish property and assets. During this time, the Nazis also persecuted Sina-Romas (gypsies), Jehovah's Witnesses, the mentally and physically disabled, and homosexual persons.

On November 8, 1938, all Jewish newspapers and magazines were ordered to stop publication; all Jewish cultural activities were suspended indefinitely; and all Jewish children were ordered out of elementary schools. On November 10, it became a crime for a Jew to possess a weapon.

On the evening of November 9, 1938, and in the early morning hours of November 10 and throughout that day, known as *Kristallnacht*, the Nazis organized and caused the burning of over 1,000 synagogues throughout Germany.[9] Jewish-owned shops were destroyed, and the police rounded up and took about 30,000 Jewish men from their homes and off the streets of their hometowns and sent them to concentration camps. Over one-fourth of all Jewish men in Germany were sent away to camps over just a few days.[10]

As written in "Kristallnacht: Prelude to Destruction," by Sir Martin Gilbert, these actions were not spontaneous but instead were a "coordinated, comprehensive rampage" organized by the Nazi Party and the government itself.[11] These actions went beyond Germany itself and were repeated in all the countries in German-occupied territory. In Vienna (under Nazi rule since March 1938), most of the city's 95 synagogues were partially or totally destroyed.[12]

B. The Judiciary

1. The VGH

On April 24, 1934, the Nazis created a special court, the National Socialist Peoples Court, or *Volksgerichtshof* (VGH), in which the judge became the state's investigator and prosecutor. This court initially had jurisdiction over the crime of treason, broadly defined to include political prisoners. Judges were appointed because of their "loyalty to the National Socialist state."[13] By 1936, the VGH's status changed from a special court to a regular one.[14] In 1936, if a person was acquitted by the court, the Gestapo would rearrest him or her; if a person was convicted, the Gestapo would take the person into "protective custody" and send him or her to a concentration camp. As early as March 1936, a state secretary had stated that "'it was the Führer and only the Führer' who decided on legal matters."[15]

By 1939, the judiciary's own acknowledged purpose was not to dispense justice but, in the words of a state prosecutor, "to annihilate the enemies of National Socialism."[16] The VGH had jurisdiction over Germany and all annexed and occupied territories.[17] Indeed, by 1938, judges were compliant within this system and by 1939, the VGH had become "a direct tool of the state executive" and completely subservient to the Gestapo.[18] The Gestapo itself "never bowed to the principle of control of police action by the courts."[19] By mid-1941, alleged offenders were handed over to the Gestapo even before judgment had been passed.[20]

In June 1942, the German Ministry of Justice announced that the Führer had the right to intervene in all judicial rulings "over and above all existing formal arrangements."[21] From late 1942, Jews were not subject to its jurisdiction because they were all deemed to be "inferior people," "not worthy of the rule of law."[22]

THE ABSENCE OF JUDICIAL ETHICS AND IMPARTIALITY

2. The Rationale of the Judiciary

What was the underlying rationale that supported the judiciary's role as an instrument of Nazi state power?

According to scholar Diemut Majer, "[t]here were essentially three principles that were held to be axiomatic for the entire field of administration as well as the judiciary: the principle of absolute rule by a leader (the Führer principle), the principle of authority of the party over the state, and the influence of race as the fundamental principle guiding affairs of state ('racial inequality')."[23] Historian Richard J. Evans agrees: "The purpose of the law, in the eyes of the Nazis, was not to apply long-held principles of fairness and justice, but to root out the enemies of the state and to express the true racial feeling of the people."[24]

Key elements of Nazi rule confirm these conclusions:

- The oath of lawyers and judges was to Hitler, not to the constitution.
- Special legislation and decrees administered laws for "inferior races"—such as Jews and Poles—not for justice but instead as an instrument to ensure Germany's so-called "racial purity."
- Any semblance of a judiciary independent from the executive or the legislature was obsolete. The law applied only in the interest of the party—not of the individual.

According to one historian, "the first and foremost task of the judiciary was to subordinate itself to the totalitarian will of National Socialism."[25]

3. Individual Judges

We have observed the coordination of the entire judiciary into the Nazi system. What was the role of individual judges? As early as 1942, according to author H. W. Koch, the "German legal profession, above all judges, had fully succumbed to the power of corruption, not in the material but in the ethical sense."[26] As Koch describes, the judges entered a "moral abyss."[27] According to Evans, "[t]he judiciary and legal and penal administrators were happy to co-operate in this whole process of subversion of the rule of law."[28]

The most comprehensive study of this question concluded that "not a single judge appears to have resigned in protest."[29] Indeed, no author I have discovered has confirmed the resignation of any German judge in protest of the acts of the Nazis, or to protest the "coordination" of the judiciary into the Nazi state.[30] One judge did complain to authorities about "injustice . . . masquerading in the form of law" and he was allowed to quietly retire in late 1940 with a pension.[31] In addition, one source quotes Listgard Wundheiler who recalled that her father, a judge in Marburg, Germany, refused to join the Nazi Party in 1936, and, as a result, he "was summarily dismissed from the judiciary but managed to land a job as a court messenger."[32]

Whether the number of judges who resigned or retired in protest was none, one, or two, the total is meager.[33] The German judges who continued to perform their jobs without question did the work of the Nazis. The president of the VGH, Roland Freisler, declared as early as 1935 that "[t]he German judicial system can take pride in being the first branch of government in the Third Reich to carry out in its personnel policies, throughout the Reich and at all levels of civil service, the principle that the movement, the people, and the state are one."[34]

Holocaust scholars agree that the "judiciary largely contributed to its own demise."[35] In particular, it "actually promoted [its own] takeover by close cooperation with the police."[36] The judiciary complied with the Nazis with "zeal."[37]

Dr. Meinecke, a historian at the United States Holocaust Memorial

Museum in Washington, DC, makes the following two important points in his lectures on Nazi judges. First, he states that with few exceptions, the German judges before Hitler came into power were the same people who continued as judges after he became Führer. Second, a judge with a conscience should have and could have made a difference in many lives long before he was faced with a decision whether to resign. Dr. Meinecke validly points out that judges did not protest the emergency decrees in 1933 and in many cases thereafter judges interpreted ambiguous laws in the broadest possible way to enforce the "intent" of the Nazi racial purity laws.

A question that naturally arises is: *why* did the German judges so willingly coordinate themselves in the Nazi system and enforce its doctrines?

A key scholar argues: As Nazis, they "believed that a state was not only empowered but also obliged to override individual civil rights in the interest of creating an ethnically homogeneous nation."[38] In *The Nazi Conscience*, Claudia Koonz describes how the Nazis "denounced the idea of universal human rights, saying: Not every being with a human face is human."[39] As she describes, "[t]his belief expressed the bedrock of Nazi morality."[40] This "morality" was a combination of "biological theories and racist passions."[41] "[E]thnic Germans were exhorted to expunge citizens deemed alien and to ally themselves only with people sanctioned as racially valuable. The road to Auschwitz was paved with righteousness."[42] Koonz argued that Germans' "pretensions to ethnic virtues created the conditions within which evil metasticized."[43]

Koonz's explanation joins many other theories on why Nazi civil servants coordinated themselves with the Nazi system. Why would the same people who were judges before Hitler make decisions according to Nazi doctrine? Were their actions driven by nationalism or racial pride? Were they afraid their careers were threatened? Did they want to advance their own careers? Were they afraid of the Nazis for the safety of themselves and their families? Were they just following orders? According to Dr. Meinecke, German judges after the war claimed they were victims too and were only following the "law." Those judges argued they did not have the power of "judicial review" of executive and legislative acts and their only job was to follow and "interpret" the law.

Whatever the reason or combination of reasons, it is manifestly true that the German judges coordinated themselves into the Nazi system and were ethically corrupt. As succinctly stated by a leading scholar, Majer, the "principle of [the] rule of law [is] not compatible with that of authoritarian leadership."[44] As observed by Majer, judges became *immediately answerable to the Führer.* This reality "represented the climax of the destruction of judicial independence."[45]

It is important to pause here to emphasize that it would be a serious mistake to assume that judicial independence alone is an answer to totalitarianism. Independence of the judiciary is generally defined as the "freedom from influence or controls other than those established by law."[46] In the context of the judicial system in Germany, this independence, in my view, would be from the Führer because the "law" permitted the judges to act as they did. The judiciary and judge—independent from the executive and legislative branches as they may be—still must be fair and impartial, follow the law, and have integrity. This lesson is dramatically illustrated by the example of Hans Frank, Hitler's personal lawyer and an early member of the Nazi Party.

Frank "insisted upon the necessity for and the proper scope of an independent judiciary."[47] Frank declared in 1941: "No Reich without law—not even ours! No law without judges—not even in Germany! No judge without real power—not even the German one!"[48] He spoke out against the rule of the Security Service (the SS) and the police and urged a "new legal code for Germany."[49]

Yet this is the same Hans Frank who, after Germany conquered

Poland, "became the governor-general there, ruling from Kraków. Known as the 'Butcher of Kraków,' he set out to kill Jews, intellectuals, and professionals and to make the rest of Poland a source of slave labor."[50]

The new German colony was ruled by Hans Frank. During his first month in office, Governor-General Frank declared that "any Jews leaving the district to which they have been confined" would be killed, as would "people who deliberately offer a hiding place to Jews. . . . Instigators and helpers are subject to the same punishment as perpetrators; an attempted act will be punished in the same way as a completed act."[51] Hans Frank was a defendant in the main Nuremberg trial and was sentenced to death and executed for his crimes.[52]

In Case No. 3 at the Nuremberg trials, in the American zone after the main trial, members of the Reich Ministry of Justice, judges of the VGH, and prosecutors were tried for war crimes and crimes against humanity "by using the legal process for 'enslavement and extermination on a vast scale.'"[53] In the "Justice Case," the defendants were sixteen officials of the Reich's judicial system.[54] They were tried for abuse of the judicial process and the administration of justice. Prosecutor Telford Taylor described their crimes: "The dagger of the assassin was concealed beneath the robe of the jurist."[55] US state court trial judges heard these cases. Of fourteen defendants who remained through judgment, four were acquitted and ten were convicted, with sentences ranging from life to time served.[56] These are the cases depicted in the movie and play *Judgment at Nuremberg*.

C. The Wannsee Protocol of January 1942

A historic meeting in a palace in Wannsee, a suburb of Berlin, took place on January 20, 1942. The meeting is significant because the decisions to implement the Final Solution—the mass murder of millions of Jews—

were made there. The summary minutes of the meeting dramatically reveal the absence of any concern that the courts or the judges would do anything to stop the planned mass murder.

The meeting was convened at the request of, and chaired by, Reinhard Heydrich of the SS. He reported directly to Heinrich Himmler, head of the SS. Heinrich Müller and Adolph Eichmann were in charge of the meeting. Müller was head of the Gestapo, part of the SS.[57] Eichmann was also an officer of the SS; he became "notorious for his role in the wartime extermination of Europe's Jews."[58] Those attending included lawyers, state ministers, and police. Of the fifteen participants at Wannsee, many had advanced law degrees.[59] They decided, according to their written minutes, on the "final solution" of the Jewish question.

These minutes of the Wannsee Protocol of January 20, 1942, consist of eight neatly typewritten pages.[60] They show the assignment of bureaucratic and operational responsibility for the extermination of all the Jews of Europe.

Those attending the meeting decided upon the "final solution of the Jewish question in Europe." This "solution" was to be accomplished "without regard to geographic borders." The minutes declared that "[t]he aim of all this was to cleanse German living space of Jews in a legal manner." They left no question of the magnitude of the goal: "Approximately 11 million Jews will be involved in the final solution of the European Jewish question. . . ." The minutes then listed thirty-five countries, territories, and regions with their corresponding numbers of Jews totaling eleven million.

The scope of the "final solution" detailed in the minutes is breathtaking. The terms "final solution of the Jewish question" or "final solution" are used ten times. Yet, the words "murder," "kill," or "exterminate" are never mentioned.

So we have a meeting of high-ranking Nazis, including lawyers, in early 1942, deciding on the mechanism for murdering millions of people. Throughout the minutes, there is not a single reference to the courts or judges as even a potential obstacle to the implementation of the Final Solution. What better evidence could there be of the total coordination of judges and the judiciary into the Nazi system?

In Eichmann's trial in 1961, he testified that those at the meeting discussed the methods of killing the Jews. At its conclusion, the leaders drank cognac to celebrate. The meeting lasted all of one and a half hours and succeeded in coordinating the mechanics of murdering the Jews of Europe.

LESSONS, GRATITUDE, AND CONFIDENCE

The judiciary in America strives to achieve the goal of "Equal Justice Under Law" as etched on the building of the United States Supreme Court. I have researched and written this essay because we can learn important lessons from the catastrophic ethical corruption of the German judicial branch and its individual judges from 1933 through 1945.

When my mother and father were onboard ships entering the harbor of New York City, I imagine each of them thought, in Yiddish, they were arriving in *der goldenach medinah*, the golden land, America. As their son, I am grateful to our nation and the opportunities it has afforded to me and my family. As a judge, I am confident our judiciary and its judges will continue to uphold our Constitution and the values of due process of law, liberty and equal justice.

INTER ARMA SILENT LEGES
(1998)

William H. Rehnquist

The United States has been engaged in several armed conflicts since the end of World War II, but in none of them has Congress declared war on another nation. Recent presidents have been eager to establish their authority to engage United States troops in foreign military operations without such a declaration, and Congress has never declared war without having been requested to do so by the president. When North Korea invaded South Korea in 1950, President Truman relied on a United Nations resolution to commit US troops to fight in Korea. When the war in Vietnam escalated during the mid-1960s, President Lyndon Johnson similarly relied on the Gulf of Tonkin Resolution, enacted by Congress in 1964, for similar authority. Before the Gulf War in 1991, President Bush received approval to use armed force against Iraq from both houses of Congress. In each case, Congress has appropriated the necessary funds for the military effort, but in none was there a declaration of war.

Without question the government's authority to engage in conduct that infringes civil liberty is greatest in time of declared war. . . . In *The Prize Cases*,[1] decided in 1863, the Supreme Court held that an insurrection could be treated by the government as the equivalent of a declared war.

There are marked differences between the government's conduct during the Civil War, during World War I, and during World War II.

One of the main differences is that in the Civil War, the Lincoln administration relied on presidential authority or on the orders of military commanders to curtail civil liberties, while in the twentieth-century wars, the executive branch resorted much more to laws passed by Congress. Neither Lincoln's original suspension of the writ of habeas corpus, nor Stanton's order for the trial of civilians by military commissions, was authorized by Congress. The same was true of Postmaster General Montgomery Blair's suspension of the mailing privileges of New York newspapers. Those privileges were suspended during World War I by Postmaster General Albert Burleson, but he acted under a provision of the Espionage Act passed by Congress. President Roosevelt authorized the internment of west coast Japanese during World War II, but Congress immediately ratified his action.

It may fairly be asked by those whose civil liberty is curtailed, whether they are any better off because Congress as well as the executive has approved the measure. As a practical matter, the answer may be no, but from the point of view of governmental authority under the Constitution, it is clear that the president may do many things in carrying out a congressional directive that he may not be able to do on his own. Justice Robert Jackson, in his now authoritative concurring opinion in the Steel Seizure cases decided during the Korean War, observed:

> When the President acts pursuant to an expressed or implied authorization of Congress, his authority is at its maximum, for it includes all that he possesses in his own right plus all that Congress can delegate. In these circumstances, and in these only, may he be said (for what it may be worth), to personify the federal sovereignty. If his act is held unconstitutional under these circumstances, it usually means that the Federal Government as an undivided whole lacks power.[2]

It should be added that Congress may not always grant the president all of the authority for which he asks. It refused, for example, President Wilson's request for censorship authority during World War I.

The second notable difference in the treatment of civil liberty is the increasing resort to the courts since the Civil War. This is partly because of the very limited jurisdiction of the lower federal courts in the 1860s. They could issue writs of habeas corpus, and a defendant might raise a constitutional claim as a defense. But for someone who had neither been detained nor sued but wished to challenge an action taken by the government, the only practical remedy was to sue in the state courts. Not until 1875 did Congress grant lower federal courts authority to hear cases where the plaintiff based his lawsuit on a violation of the federal Constitution. Thus, the publishers who were denied mailing privileges by Blair would have found it difficult, if not impossible, to assert any constitutional claim in a federal court. By the time of World War II, [those subject to Japanese internment orders] were able to initiate claims of constitutional violation as plaintiffs in federal court.

There were no similar limitations on state courts, but many of these courts were neither experienced in, nor hospitable to, claims arising under the United States Constitution.

But an even more important reason for court involvement was increasing reliance by the government on prosecution in the federal courts for acts which had been made criminal by congressional legislation. In the Civil War, Clement Vallandigham was tried before a military commission, not for an offense against a law passed by Congress, but for violation of an order issued by the commanding general of a military department. During World War I, there were no such prosecutions; those who violated the Espionage Act were tried in civil courts by juries. In these prosecutions, the defendant was able to urge constitutional claims before judges who, if not particularly sympathetic, were far more neutral and detached than the members of a military commission. The result of these trials and appeals from them was the development by the Supreme Court of a body of case law interpreting the First Amendment.

A third great difference between the Civil War and the later conflicts was the extent to which the government sought to suppress public criticism of the administration's war effort. During the Civil War, the government used a heavy-handed, blunderbuss approach; local agents in the field would seize newspapers and confiscate the presses of those who opposed its policy. There was simply no federal challenge to these gross violations of the First Amendment. During World War I, Burleson successfully suppressed radical criticism of the administration, but at least his actions were subject to review by the courts. During World War II, there was no overt effort by the government to suppress public criticism of government war policy. Some of this change may have been due to the fact that the United States' entry into World War II was a defensive reaction to the Japanese bombing of Pearl Harbor and the German declaration of war. There was much less opposition to that war than to either the Civil War or World War I. But part of the change also resulted from the fact that the First Amendment had come into its own.

Despite this generally ameliorative trend, however, there remains a sense that there is some truth to the maxim *Inter arma silent leges*, at least in the purely descriptive sense. *Quirin*,[3] decided during the darkest days of World War II, actually cut back on some of the extravagant dicta favorable to civil liberty in *Milligan*.[4] Of the three Japanese internment cases, only *Endo*,[5] decided near the end of World War II, represented even a minor victory for civil liberty. And as for *Duncan*,[6] the good news for the people of Hawaii was that the Court held that martial law there during World War II had been unlawful; the bad news was that the decision came after the war was over, and a year and a half after martial law had been ended by presidential order. Again, part of the delay in such decisions is endemic to the legal process; given a hierarchical system of courts, a decision by the Supreme Court usually occurs months, if not years, after the lawsuit was begun. But there is also the reluctance of courts to decide a case against the government on an issue of national security during a war.

Is this reluctance a necessary evil—necessary because judges, like other citizens, do not wish to hinder a nation's "war effort"—or is it actually a desirable phenomenon? Judicial reluctance can manifest itself in more ways than one. A court may simply avoid deciding an important constitutional question in the midst of a war. . . . A court may also decide an issue in favor of the government during a war, when it would not have done so had the decision come after the war was over. Would, for example, *Duncan* have come out the same way in 1943 as it actually did in 1946?

Viewed as a matter of legal or constitutional principle, the law governing a particular set of facts—in *Duncan*, for example, whether a stockbroker could be tried for fraud by a military court in Hawaii in 1943—should not be different in 1946 than three years earlier. But one need not wholly accept Justice Holmes's aphorism that "the life of the law has not been logic, it has been experience" to recognize the human factor that inevitably enters into even the most careful judicial decision. If, in fact, courts are more prone to uphold wartime claims of civil liberties after the war is over, may it not actually be desirable to avoid decision on such claims during the war?

Lambdin Milligan, imprisoned after his trial before a military commission, surely would answer no to this question. While the body of case law might benefit from such abstention, those who are actually deprived of their civil liberties would not. But a decision in favor of civil liberty will stand as a precedent to regulate future actions of Congress and the executive branch in future wars. We must also ask whether in every case a ruling in favor of a claimed civil liberty is more desirable, more "just," than a contrary result.

The answer to this question will depend, in turn, on just what is meant by *civil* liberty. It is not simply "liberty" but civil liberty of which we speak. The word "civil," in turn, is derived from the Latin word *civis*, which means "citizen." A citizen is a person owing allegiance to some organized government, and not a person in an idealized "state of nature" free from any governmental restraint. Judge Learned Hand, in remarks entitled "The Spirit of Liberty," delivered during World War II, put it this way: "A society in which men recognize no check upon their freedom soon becomes a society where freedom is the possession of only a savage few."[7]

. . . .

In any civilized society the most important task is achieving a proper balance between freedom and order. In wartime, reason and history both suggest that this balance shifts to some degree in favor of order—in favor of the government's ability to deal with conditions that threaten the national well-being. It simply cannot be said, therefore, that in every conflict between individual liberty and governmental authority the former should prevail. And if we feel free to criticize court decisions that curtail civil liberty, we must also feel free to look critically at decisions favorable to civil liberty.

Was the dictum in the *Milligan* case, for example—saying that Congress could not authorize trials of civilians by military tribunals where civil courts were functioning and there was no invasion by hostile forces—a wise exercise of judicial power? The reasoning of the majority in that case would rule out not merely trials of civilians by military commissions but trials of civilians by a duly appointed federal judge without a jury. One may fully agree with the rather disparaging but nonetheless insightful argument of Jeremiah Black in the *Milligan* case—soldiers are no more occupationally trained to conduct trials than are sailors or sheep drovers—and yet believe that Congress should be able to provide for trial of defendants by a judge without a jury in a carefully limited class of cases dealing with national security in wartime.

The foregoing discussion deals with the judicial treatment of civil liberty claims. But this is only one part of the story during wartime. The . . . statement of Francis Biddle about Franklin Roosevelt's support for the internment of Issei and Nisei during World War II bears repeating here: "Nor do I think that the Constitutional difficulty plagued him. The Constitution has not greatly bothered any wartime President. That was a question of law, which ultimately the Supreme Court must decide. And meanwhile—probably a long meanwhile—we must get on with the war."[8]

Some executive actions in time of war will be reviewed by the courts only after the fact, if at all. Lincoln believed that the very survival of the Union could depend on getting troops from the northeast to Washington in April 1861. He also believed that the suspension of the writ of habeas corpus was necessary to guard against further destruction of the railroad route through Baltimore used to transport these troops. Should he have carefully weighed the pros and cons as to whether he was authorized by the Constitution to do this before acting? Should he, to paraphrase his own words, have risked losing the Union that gave life to the Constitution because that charter denied him the necessary authority to preserve the Union? Cast in these terms, it is difficult to quarrel with his decision.

But the same degree of necessity surely did not obtain in the suppression of the New York newspapers, or the trial of the Indianapolis defendants by a military commission. It is all too easy to slide from a case of genuine military necessity, where the power sought to be exercised is at least debatable, to one where the threat is not critical and the power either dubious or nonexistent.

One would think it likely, of course, that a Roman legal maxim which originated two millennia ago in a legal system with no written constitution, would have only the most general application to America. But the fact that the phrase *Inter arma silent leges* is quoted by modern writers suggests that it has validity at least in a descriptive way. As such, it may have several different levels of meaning. It speaks first simply as a truism: in time of war the government's authority to restrict civil liberty is greater than in peacetime. . . . But at another level, the maxim speaks to the attitude of wartime presidents such as Lincoln, Wilson, and Franklin Roosevelt, so well captured in Biddle's phrase "the Constitution has not greatly bothered any wartime President." Quite apart from the added authority that the law itself may give the president in time of war, presidents may act in ways that push their legal authority to its outer limits, if not beyond. Finally, the maxim speaks to the timing of a judicial decision on a question of civil liberty in wartime. If the decision is made after hostilities have ceased, it is more likely to favor civil liberty than if made while hostilities continue. The contrast between the *Quirin* and the Japanese internment decisions on the one hand and the *Milligan* and *Duncan* decisions on the other shows that this, too, is a historically accurate observation about the American system.

An entirely separate and important philosophical question is whether occasional presidential excesses and judicial restraint in wartime are desirable or undesirable. In one sense, this question is very largely academic. There is no reason to think that future wartime presidents will act differently from Lincoln, Wilson, or Roosevelt, or that future justices of the Supreme Court will decide questions differently from their predecessors. But even though this be so, there is every reason to think that the historic trend against the least justified of the curtailments of civil liberty in wartime will continue in the future. It is neither desirable nor is it remotely likely that civil liberty will occupy as favored a position in wartime as it does in peacetime. But it is both desirable and likely that more careful attention will be paid by the courts to the basis for the government's claims of necessity as a basis for curtailing civil liberty. The laws will thus not be silent in time of war, but they will speak with a somewhat different voice.

BOUMEDIENE V. BUSH AND GUANTÁNAMO, CUBA
Does the "Empire Strike Back"?
(2009)

Ernesto Hernández-López

Lando Calrissian: Lord Vader, what about Leia and
the Wookiee?

Darth Vader: They must never again leave this city.

Lando Calrissian: That was never a condition of
our agreement . . .

Darth Vader: Perhaps you think you're being
treated unfairly?

Lando Calrissian: No.

Darth Vader: Good. It would be unfortunate if I
had to leave a garrison here.

—*The Empire Strikes Back*

"[E]ven if we do not own the island, we are
responsible for its conduct . . . and the just and
equitable treatment of foreigners residing
thereunder."

—General Leonard Wood
(US Military Governor of Cuba, 1900–02)

NATIONAL SECURITY, CIVIL LIBERTIES, AND THE WAR ON TERROR

I. INTRODUCTION

Following over six years of detention and over seven hundred detainees at the US Naval Station at Guantánamo Bay, Cuba ("Guantánamo"), Supreme Court opinions in *Boumediene v. Bush* refer to the base as a "quirky outpost" with a "unique and unusual" jurisdiction. Critics call it the "gulag of our time" and a "legal black hole," where detention includes torture, indefinite confinement, no charges or court proceedings, and violations of individual rights guaranteed by the Constitution, Geneva Conventions, and international humanitarian and human rights law. The base's "quirky" location in Cuba, which the United States considers part of an "Axis of Evil," facilitates this type of detention. Agreements between the United States and Cuba shape this anomaly. A 1903 agreement states that Cuba has "ultimate sovereignty" over the base and that the United States has "complete jurisdiction and control." Between sovereignty-and-jurisdiction and Cuba-and-United States, legal norms ambiguously check military authority on the base. Gerald Neuman describes this as an anomalous legal zone, with "legal rules" fundamental to larger policies "locally suspended" in a geographic area.[1] Perceived as far from checks in constitutional or international law, Guantánamo was chosen as a detention center to benefit from this uncertainty. Examining the legality of this detention, *Rasul v. Bush* (2004), *Hamdan v. Rumsfeld* (2006), and *Boumediene v. Bush* (2008) address this anomaly.

This article makes three general arguments about how US law has determined what norms apply to Guantánamo. First, Guantánamo's legal anomaly is not an aberration, but instead is a precise objective of US foreign relations since Cuban independence in 1898. This anomaly is the product of legal determinations in the Platt Amendment from

1901, which limited Cuba's foreign relations power, provided the United States with a "right to intervene" in Cuba, and required that Cuba provide the United States bases on Cuban territory. Second, four legal objectives concerning US influence overseas frame this anomaly, historically and presently. These are that the United States avoids sovereignty abroad, limits incidents of sovereignty for foreign states, avoids constitutional limits for its overseas authority, and protects strategic overseas interests (geopolitical, economic, and legal). With the Platt Amendment securing influence over Cuba by limiting its sovereignty, these objectives characterized US-Cuba foreign policy. Specific to Guantánamo, these objectives appear in bilateral agreements, which provide the United States infinite control over the base without formal sovereignty, while Cuba has "ultimate sovereignty" and no power to end US occupation. Outside US territorial sovereignty, Guantánamo is perceived to be beyond the Constitution's application. *Boumediene* addresses this anomaly with these four legal objectives. Specifically, to hold that the Constitution's Suspension Clause has extraterritorial effect, the Court makes significant determinations regarding sovereignty on the base and the Constitution's limited application overseas. Objectives regarding United States and Cuban sovereignty, limited rights protections, and strategic overseas goals are highly influential in the Court's reasoning. These objectives are central to legal reasoning supporting base occupation in 1903, as well as *Boumediene*'s holding in 2008. Third, tracking the relationship between legal norms, base occupation, and base detention, a postcolonial analysis of US foreign relations suggests how current legal doctrine evades individual rights protections with overseas authority. This illuminates how, capitalizing on legal determinations since 1898, the United States attempted to create a rights-free zone overseas in 2002. . . .

As illustrated below, *Boumediene* examines the law in a postcolonial situation. "Postcolonialism" refers to the effects of colonization and imperial influence on a society's culture or political structures. Examining overseas authority and the historic doctrine supporting it, *Boumediene* answers a postcolonial legal question: Do constitutional habeas corpus rights extend to nonsovereign territory under United States control? This is often presented as a constitutional, national security, or international law issue. The decision relies on legal doctrine from American informal imperial influence over the Caribbean, Cuba, and Guantánamo. This is intrinsically postcolonial, because it examines what happens after imperial influence, i.e., after US overseas authority in the region commenced in 1898.

The phrase "The Empire Strikes Back" exemplifies the significance and ambiguity of what happens "after the empire." For this article, the phrase questions how overseas power influences a central authority or its subjects overseas. . . . Describing the uniqueness of literatures from decolonized countries, which are wrongly labeled English literature, Salman Rushdie explains "the empire writes back with a vengeance."[2] In his book *The Empire Writes Back*, Bill Ashcroft examines how variations in language and representations are central to Eurocentric assumptions in literature.[3] In the movie *Star Wars V: The Empire Strikes Back*, the Empire hunts down rebel Jedi Luke Skywalker and tries to indefinitely detain his friends Princess Leia and Chewbacca in the protectorate of Cloud City. City administrator Lando Calrissian asks how an agreement with the Empire provides for detention. These examples point to imperial rule's long-term and structural effects, whether it is resisting this power or eliminating this resistance. Law, whether it is constitutional or international, supports this overseas authority, past and present. Focusing on US influence over Cuba and Guantánamo, this article highlights the significance of postcolonial legal methodologies. It asks whether there is a postcolonial response, i.e., "does the empire strike back," when the law examines detention on overseas nonsovereign territory under US control? Postcolonial inquiry analyzes how legal instruments (doctrine, reasoning, treaties, and adjudication) developed during prior relationships of empire or colonialism and how these instruments influence current legal reasoning.

This article is not an exhaustive normative, doctrinal, or empirical study of Guantánamo detention litigation, which has been extremely complex and evolving. This litigation includes military commissions, Combatant Status Review Tribunals (CSRTs), appeals to the United States Court of Appeals for the District of Columbia, and district court habeas proceedings. Adding to this, in an executive order, President Obama ordered the base detention program to end by January 2010. From a policy perspective some things appear certain, i.e., base detentions will end. [Editors' Note: As discussed in chapter 6, however, detentions did not end by January 2010.] Similarly, some legal issues on the base have become clearer, since *Boumediene* affirms base detainees have constitutional habeas rights. Much uncertainty remains regarding what law, whether in terms of individual rights protections or checks on executive authority, actually applies to the base. Litigation since *Boumediene* in response to court orders to release Guantánamo detainees has been the most dramatic. Similarly, the January 2009 executive order stopped many military commissions, which had been conducted in response to the *Rasul* and *Hamdan* decisions and provided detainees some rights protections. The order also claimed that it creates no individual rights. It set a date to end detention but leaves the state of rights protection uncertain. Rights protections on the base remain anomalous, but perhaps judicially moot with detention ending.

With so much uncertainty about the law's present and future, this article is a limited analysis of habeas corpus jurisdiction on the base, as seen from a postcolonial lens concerning the base's legal history. As such,

Boumediene is merely one judicial step, beginning in 2002, recognizing that the right of habeas extends to the base and finding procedural substitutes for habeas inadequate. With such uncertain and developing jurisprudence, this article offers a researched suggestion on postcolonialism's relevance regarding international and constitutional law and how they are intertwined, even when the mix is foreign in a "domestic sense."

This article describes US-Cuba relations and US foreign relations after the Spanish-American War of 1898 (the War). From these events, legal instruments were developed to extend US influence overseas, avoid US *de jure* sovereign authority abroad, limit sovereignty for foreign states, and evade constitutional limits in US foreign relations power. After the War, the US occupied Cuba until 1902. Devised during occupation, the Platt Amendment provided that the United States had a "right to intervene" in Cuba, control Cuba's foreign relations, and most importantly (for this inquiry) it provided a right to put US bases on Cuban soil. The Platt Amendment made Cuba a US protectorate. During this period, the United States continually exercised informal imperial influence over Cuba. Reflecting this, a lease agreement in 1903 set the terms of base occupation at Guantánamo.

This lease begins to frame present legal anomaly. Referring to base territory, it provides Cuba with "ultimate sovereignty" and the United States with "jurisdiction and complete control." This unclearly demarcates which norms apply on the base and whether "ultimate sovereignty" has any significance before US occupation ends. The lease ambiguously designates legal obligations on the base, but clearly provides the United States indefinite control. This anomaly has facilitated "War on Terror" detention, because the base escapes limits in constitutional and international law. Those who support the current detention policy argue this.

This article correlates norms in recent base detention with norms developed during prior foreign relations. In both contexts, US law has endorsed overseas authority, i.e., over the protectorate of Cuba and over the base at Guantánamo. To make these connections, this article follows insights from postcolonial scholarship. Defining the terms postcolonialism, empire, and informal empire is important to this inquiry. They show analytical links between recent jurisprudence and history. Postcolonialism examines "the effects of colonization on cultures and societies."[4] It assumes that these effects do not require formal colonial relationships; influences may be *de facto* or informal, and they occur in cultural, economic, political, or social realms. Postcolonial scholarship identifies how Western or European perspectives use discourses, narratives, representations, or language to exclude the non-Western or the less powerful actor, e.g., a state. This article examines US legal doctrine as such a discourse, with its assumptions and exclusions endorsing Guantánamo detention.

Definitions of empire or imperialism deepen these perspectives. Edward Said defines imperialism as "the practice, the theory, and the attitudes of a dominating metropolitan center ruling a distant territory."[5] Michael Doyle describes empire as "a relationship, formal or informal, in which one state controls the effective political sovereignty of another political society. It can be achieved by force, by political collaboration, or by economic, social, or cultural dependence. Imperialism is simply the process or policy of establishing or maintaining empire."[6] Informal empire is the practice of overseas control, without formal political control, between politically independent states, often with the dynamics of free-trade economics and superior military power.

Informal imperial control over Cuba from 1898 to 1934 crafted the base's anomalous jurisdiction. Since 2002, Guantánamo detention litigation has addressed this legacy. This situation is intimately postcolonial. First, the base is a remnant from when the United States sought naval superiority in the Caribbean. The postcolonial condition is that a base which served regional geopolitical and economic interests historically now serves detention objectives. Second, US influence over Cuba was imperial, using Said and Doyle's definitions. This created a need for legal anomaly.

. . . .

Building on these arguments, this article contains five parts. Part I introduces the article's subject. Part II elaborates on postcolonial theory as applied to foreign relations and international and constitutional law. These theories show how legal reasoning endorses overseas authority and rights exclusion, pointing to how the law is central to postcolonial contexts. Generally, narratives in legal doctrine exclude populations from sovereignty, create "ambivalence in the rule of law," and limit constitutional protections for overseas US territories such as Puerto Rico, Guam, and other locations. Part III, "Guantánamo's Anomalous Past," examines the base's historic anomaly in legal approaches to Cuban independence in 1898, the Platt Amendment in 1901, and agreements for base occupation in 1903. For each period, the mentioned four objectives shaped the legal anomaly. Part IV, "Guantánamo's Anomalous Recent Past," examines how this anomaly and the four objectives shaping it influence recent detention litigation. It describes *Boumediene's* holding that the writ of habeas corpus in the Constitution's Suspension Clause applies to base detention, as an example of the law addressing postcolonial anomaly. The decision does not question the legality of base occupation. Importantly, it finds that the United States has de facto sovereignty over the base and that prudential factors determine if the Constitution has extraterritorial application on the base. Part V, "Empire's Anomalous Future," describes how despite *Boumediene's* holding and an Executive Order to end base detention, individual rights protections on the base continue to be a legal anomaly. Even if base detention ends for the remaining 242 persons, much uncertainty remains for rights protections in extraterritorial contexts. As such, US law may apply similar anomalous reasoning to create other rights-free zones. Given the extensive US network of bases worldwide in over ninety-eight countries and the "War on Terror" presented as global, the Guantánamo experience could be replicated. The conclusion, Part VI, presents these examples as suggestions for further postcolonial inquiry on constitutional and international law endorsing overseas authority.

II. THE POSTCOLONIAL IN GUANTÁNAMO: SOVEREIGNTY DENIED, OVERSEAS AUTHORITY, AND RIGHTS EXCLUSION

For the purposes of this article, a postcolonial perspective analyzes how prior foreign relations practices of empire or colonialism (with one state controlling an overseas population or territory) resonate in current international affairs. This perspective identifies how imperial practices continue and how they presently pose important limits. Postcolonialism examines how political institutions, economic relations, or social constructs in the international system are inherited from imperial or colonial relationships. These legacies influence current circumstances. Postcolonial legacies are often *de facto*, economic, political, or cultural, not necessarily requiring *de jure* control. Such control would entail a relationship of a colonizing population and colony, or of one state having formal political control of a colony.

Applied to this article's subject, a postcolonial perspective generally argues that foreign relations between Cuba, globally powerful states, and the international system developed the legal structures that facilitate current overseas detention by the United States on Guantánamo. The United States would be the most influential state in these relations as Cuba's neighbor, the most powerful regional state, and its former protector, but relations with Spain, the Soviet Union and other socialist states, Europe, and Western Hemispheric states would also be influential. The United States first occupied Guantánamo during the war for Cuba's independence from Spain in 1898. Following four years of occupation, Cuba was made a US protectorate, with the United States seeking a right of intervention and significant influence in Cuban affairs. In 1903, base occupation was legally sanctioned with lease agreements between the United States (protector/occupier/lessee) and Cuba (protectorate/host state/lessor). These agreements delineate the terms of Guantánamo's legal anomaly.

. . . .

. . . US constitutional law has a long history and current practice of denying statehood to territorial possessions overseas, consequently excluding rights protections for their populations. Beginning with the *Insular Cases* (1901–1922) and still governing territorial possessions, constitutional law endorses overseas authority while selectively applying constitutional limitations to political authority and individual rights protections on these territories.[7] Territorial examples include insular possessions in the Caribbean Sea and in Asia acquired as a result of the Spanish-American War, and island possessions in the Pacific Ocean acquired during the twentieth century (e.g., the Northern Mariana Islands, American Samoa, Guam, Puerto Rico, and others). With these possessions, the United States values strategic and geopolitical objectives in the Caribbean and Pacific theatres over republican and self-determination goals for these populations. Alternatively, the United States could make these territories states in the Union or relinquish sovereign control over them.

These relationships shed some theoretical light onto Guantánamo's current anomaly. Foreign relations objectives motivated the creation of an anomalous legal zone on the base. Specifically, as a territorial space controlled by the United States, Guantánamo was purposefully excluded from US sovereign authority, territorially classified as exogenous to many constitutional rights, and ambiguously placed between Cuba's sovereignty and US control. This was done to avoid checks on overseas authority in international and constitutional law. This anomaly is a product of early twentieth-century foreign relations. These perspectives on international and constitutional law provide theoretical guidance to pose postcolonial questions about present US authority over Guantánamo.

A. Postcolonial Theory Sheds Light on Informal Empire and Its Current Influence

Applied to a range of disciplines, postcolonial perspectives ask how international structures of empire and colonialism influence present circumstances. For the sake of simplicity, the postcolonial school of thought gained popular academic appeal in the United States with Edward Said's *Orientalism*, published in 1979.[8] Basically, Said argued that false assumptions held by European and Western academics about the Middle East; painting the foreign as an "Other," exotic, or irrational; sustained a discourse whereby Middle Eastern populations or perspectives were denied, excluded, and/or rejected. These assumptions were central to characterizations by Western academics and policymakers and were self-perpetuating by denying alternative perspectives. European perspectives were able to exclude alternative visions by presenting themselves as a scientific, positivist, or objective voice. Like with many postcolonial scholars, Said suggests examining how this exclusion occurs, what discourse is used to justify it, and what assumptions are needed for this exclusion.

Postcolonial scholars build on these viewpoints by arguing that exclusion or domination of subaltern populations or states occurs by a discourse built on false assumptions or misstated "objective," universal, or scientific conclusions. Said initially examined Western scholarship on the Middle East, but his insights have been applied to other regions, such as Africa, South Asia, Asia, Oceania, and Latin America.

Postcolonial perspectives are quite varied and are not necessarily in agreement on many issues concerning definitions, causations, and future options.... Post-colonialism generally argues that prior events frame how current circumstances develop and what options presently exist to confront these predicaments. This can be labeled as historical appreciation in postcolonial scholarship. Likewise, from a transnational vein, these scholars argue that events and actors abroad heavily influence local contexts. Local or domestic circumstances are not determined solely by local or domestic actors or events. These insights help explain why Guantánamo's present legal anomaly is framed by events and actors influential in Cuba's history.

. . . .

B. International Law Facilitates Overseas Authority by Excluding Territories and Populations from Sovereignty

International law had a central role in extending imperial and postcolonial control around the globe. International law seeks to order the obligations and rights in foreign relations belonging to states and individuals. With states extending their influence overseas, this set of legal doctrines alternatively justified, facilitated, or resisted imperial influence. Postcolonial perspectives critically examine both international law's assumptions and its limitations (past, present, and future). Norms and doctrines in international law are based on previous state practices. These practices are often an outgrowth of European states, or more powerful states, expanding their influence worldwide and seeking economic and territorial gain. From its genesis, international law developed from these contexts of empire, colonization, and protectorates.

. . . Antony Anghie . . . argues that the discipline and practice of international law possessed a "civilizing mission" in which Western mindsets classified the Orient or non-European as "the Other." Legal determinations of "cultural difference" repeatedly classified societies as "civilized" or "uncivilized." Foreign relations practice claimed that law created by "civilized" perspectives was "universal," while "uncivilized" perspectives on the law were instead particular. Race-based reasoning motivated legal determinations of civilized versus uncivilized persons.[9]

Through this process, native or non-Western populations were denied international sovereignty. Sovereignty provided recognized final authority in the international system, which was vital to protect any state independence from foreign powers. To have influence in this international system, many non-European societies found accommodating Western pressure necessary, which led to relationships as colonies or protectorates. Economically and militarily powerful states extended their governmental authority overseas to attain colonies, extend empires, establish protectorates, and lease territories.

Peter Fitzpatrick and Eve Darian-Smith present another postcolonial insight into international law: the "ambivalence in the rule of law." Fitzpatrick and Darian-Smith examine how law is at the forefront of the West's relations to its "others." They explain how European or Western structures seek to exclude non-Western identities as "others," savages, or barbarians, and even those in the West who are "less occidental than they should be." This is antithetical to international law's claims of universalism because it rejects while it simultaneously claims to be inclusive or all-encompassing. This produces an "irresolute identity," wherein the West is excluding yet encompassing its "others."[10] ...

....

C. Constitutional Law Excludes Overseas Territories and Populations from Sovereignty and Individual Rights Protections

....

The *Insular Cases* [discussed by the Supreme Court in *Boumediene*] provided constitutional law the first opportunity to answer the question: "What rights protections and political deference extend to territories overseas under US sovereignty?" ...

....

Popular culture of the period presented the *Insular Cases*' constitutional concerns as whether "the Constitution follows the flag," asking if individual right-protections in the Constitution extend to places where the United States governs. The effective answer from the *Insular Cases* was "yes, but not fully." Describing reaction to *Downes v. Bidwell*, newspapers reported Secretary Elihu Root as saying: "as near as I can make out the Constitution follows the flag—but doesn't quite catch up with it."[11] Constitutional application did not miss the territories, nor did it stop at the continental states, but similarly not all rights in the Constitution were protected overseas. Approving overseas authority in a "Constitution-light" fashion, the *Insular Cases* legally endorsed an informal overseas empire in constitutional law. Informal empire and US overseas expansion relied on a legal sensibility denying sovereignty to overseas populations and avoiding constitutional limits.

This article argues that recent Guantánamo detention cases ask whether limits in constitutional or international law follow US authority on leased overseas territory outside US sovereignty. Colloquially, this asks: "Does the Constitution or international law follow the flag flown over detention camps at Guantánamo?" . . .

III. GUANTÁNAMO'S ANOMALOUS PAST: CUBA AS A PROTECTORATE AND A LEASED BASE

. . . .

A. Dancing Around Cuban Sovereignty, the United States Enters War and Peace in 1898

The American occupation of Guantánamo is a by-product of the long and complex process of Cuba's independence from Spanish rule. United States Marines first landed on Guantánamo on June 10, 1898, to fight Spanish troops for one month. Guiding the campaign against Spain, US objectives were to avoid sovereign control but retain influence over Cuba, while protecting strategic and economic interests on the island and in the Caribbean. US interests in the region were expanding in intensity and scope with diplomacy and overseas investments. By 1902, Congress eagerly supported prospects for an Atlantic-Pacific Ocean Canal in Panama, which became a prime regional concern for the United States. It could protect access to a canal and regional markets with influence over Cuba and a base on the eastern end of the island.

The US military campaign of the "Spanish-American War," with

Cubans and Americans fighting against Spain, started in April of 1898 and ended quickly by August. . . .

. . . .

On December 10, 1898, in Paris, Spanish and US representatives signed a peace treaty, providing the United States with territories in either sovereign control or in military occupation. Cuban representatives did not participate in discussion of the treaty terms. In article I, the treaty provided that "Spain relinquishes all claim of sovereignty over and title to Cuba" and the United States shall occupy the island with obligations under international law "for the protection of life and property." In articles II and III, it ceded the Philippines, Puerto Rico, Guam, and the Mariana Islands to the United States.

This cessation resulted in the United States having territorial possessions over which it maintained sovereignty but of which it did not intend to make states in the Union. Because these possessions had sovereign authority but not statehood, the legal controversies in the *Insular Cases* arose, which attempted to generally resolve questions about what legal norms applied to territories within US sovereignty but not incorporated as states into the Union. Cuba, though, was firmly regarded under US law as independent, not to be annexed or incorporated. Congressional resolution, executive objectives, international treaty negotiation, and even the Supreme Court affirmed Cuba's formal independence.

B. Avoiding Sovereignty, the Platt Amendment Makes Cuba a Protectorate and Provides a Base at Guantánamo

The American occupation of the base at Guantánamo began with the Platt Amendment, which was initially conceptualized in 1901 by US

Secretary of War Elihu Root. It was included in congressional military appropriations for 1902. Senator Orville Platt of Connecticut introduced the bill, providing for its common reference as the "Platt Amendment." The amendment has been extremely controversial in Cuban, Latin American, and international law debates, because it secured for the United States a "right to intervene" in the independent state of Cuba. It also initiated the United States move to legally occupy bases in Cuba. The Amendment was not limited to just military appropriations; instead its provisions were also included in Cuba's Constitution of 1901 and in a 1902 treaty between Cuba and the United States. For this reason, this article refers to it as the "Amendment" (for the sake of simplicity) or as the "Amendment process" (to highlight its inclusion in American, Cuban, and international law). Importantly, the Amendment served US goals by avoiding sovereignty over Cuba (i.e., it was not annexed or made a colony) and providing Cubans formal independence from Spain. It secured naval bases to patrol US interests in the Caribbean and recognized a "right of [ ] intervention" in case the Cuban government could not fully protect US investments. . . .[12]

. . . .

Historical analysis of Cuban politics shows the Amendment was an enormous destabilizing force for Cuban democracy. It created a constant threat of US intervention. Likewise it created an incentive for Cubans to see the United States as an overseer or guardian. Domestic decisions on Cuban debt and foreign relations were legally tied to the objectives of partisan US politics in Congress, foreign policy led by the US president, and a foreign country representing different cultural attitudes on religion, "civilization," and expanding international economic interests. Ultimately, the United States did intervene in Cuba with military occupation from 1906 to 1909, with troops combating domestic insurrection in 1912 and 1917, troops stationed in Cuba during World War I, and a military presence seeking financial and political reforms during 1921 to 1923. Guantánamo was used by US troops for the 1906 occupation.

The Amendment offered a legal basis in American, Cuban, and international law, for base occupation on Cuban soil. It directly led to the United States occupying the base at Guantánamo. But more conceptually, the Amendment reflected American legal objectives regarding sovereignty. The United States avoided sovereignty over Cuba, but Cuba's sovereignty was also mitigated. It applied key foreign relations objectives to the base's legal context. This sowed the doctrinal seed for the current legal anomaly. The Amendment reflected four objectives concerning legal approaches to US-Cuban relations. These are that the United States avoids sovereign control, denies incidents of this control for foreign states, avoids constitutional limitations in this overseas authority, and protects strategic interests overseas. The Amendment provided the United States with nonsovereign control over Cuba. Cuba remained formally independent, but with its sovereignty checked. The Amendment mitigated Cuba's sovereignty by taking away key foreign relations powers, such as the power to enter into treaties and to allow another state to intervene militarily. The Amendment protected US investments by providing the "right of intervention" and minimizing the risk of Cuban public debt default.

Incidentally, the Platt Amendment avoided the complex constitutional debates regarding US territories such as Puerto Rico, where the United States retained sovereignty, but did not incorporate the territories into the Union. In other words, the Amendment provided control, but it did not result in the protracted constitutional law debates evident in the *Insular Cases*.

C. Agreements Frame Guantánamo's Legal Anomaly, Providing the United States Complete but Non-Sovereign Control

. . . .

. . . [A]greements carve out for the United States an anomalous legal zone at Guantánamo, which originally served foreign relations goals for the early twentieth century, but now serves overseas detention goals. The initial agreement states the United States has "complete jurisdiction and control" and Cuba has "ultimate sovereignty." . . .

Recent jurisprudence on base detention refers to both "jurisdiction" and "sovereignty," illustrating how contemporary legal reasoning addresses historically created "ambivalences in the rule of law." These disputes decide whether US jurisdiction permits or requires constitutional limitations on the base. Similarly, these inquiries examine if sovereignty, belonging to Cuba and/or denied to the United States, precludes the base from limitations in constitutional or international law. These two doctrinal concepts, jurisdiction versus sovereignty, cloud detention litigation and reify the base's anomalous legal quality.

Taken in their entirety, the 1903 agreements are simple and do not address many issues. They definitely do not refer to the controversies regarding individual rights protections in American or international law, which have basically been at issue since the detentions began in 2002.

Importantly, the United States does not have a Status of Forces Agreement (SOFA) regarding Guantánamo, as it does with most overseas bases. These agreements serve as references for courts to determine what obligations and rights protections—in American, international, or municipal law—apply on a base. With other overseas bases, the United States and a host-state positively articulate in a SOFA what law governs the actions of base employees, stationed military personnel, and host-state nationals. A unique aspect of Guantánamo occupation is the absence of a SOFA. The United States occupied the base with informal imperial control when Cuba's consent or conditions were less important to the United States. Interestingly, until recently the only other US overseas bases without a SOFA were in Iraq, which the United States occupied from March 2003 to June 2004.

The lack of a SOFA with Cuba coupled with the lack of diplomatic relations between America and Cuba creates a complex situation wherein occupation and a legal anomaly persist. Specifically, many of the legal concerns of an overseas base (or of having a foreign base on domestic territory) are left unanswered by any agreement. In a different scenario, a SOFA may provide more guidance between lessor (Cuba) and lessee (United States) and on how jurisdiction is characterized between Cuban, American, and international law.

The February 1903 lease first refers to the Platt Amendment provisions, in US appropriations and the Cuban Constitution, requiring Cuba to "sell or lease lands necessary for coaling or naval stations." It mentions that the base provides for the maintenance of Cuban independence, protection for Cubans, and the United States' own defense. In article I, it states that the duration of the lease is "for the time required for the purposes." There is no further elaboration on this in either 1903 agreement. In fact, the duration of base occupation is not addressed until the 1934 treaty. The February 1903 agreement reports on the base's exact location and coordinates. Article II refers to the use of water adjacent to the land. The July agreement requires fences or enclosures to mark base boundaries. It states the United States will not permit any "commercial, industrial, or other enterprise" on the base. Lastly, article V regards vessels entering the bay as "subject exclusively to Cuban laws," except for vessels carrying materials for base use. The 1934 treaty makes base occupation effectively indefinite by requiring the United States either to stop occupation unilaterally or to agree to end the lease terms.

The United States has continued to occupy the base pursuant to these three agreements. However, US-Cuba relations changed after the 1959 revolution; and with the intensification of American fear of states becoming socialist, especially for those states in close proximity to the United States, Cuba questioned the legality of the lease agreements. After 1961, Cuban civilians and American military personnel ceased to move freely between the base and nonoccupied Cuban soil. Ultimately, Cuba stopped providing water treatment services after 1961, forcing the base to become self-sufficient.

At times, academics have challenged the validity of the lease on international law grounds such as *rebus sic stantibus*. This principle in international law permits an agreement to be terminated if there has been a fundamental change in circumstances which were essential to the agreement-consent or which radically transforms agreement obligations. It is doubtful that changed circumstances may be sufficiently claimed to nullify the treaty. A court may easily see that the 1934 treaty theoretically provides a method to change the lease terms and that changes since 1961 still permit the base to be used by the United States for defense purposes and Cuba to be remunerated. Creatively, Kal Raustiala argues that the lease text of "ultimate sovereignty" may be interpreted as providing Cuba with reversionary or residual sovereignty. This, coupled with the "complete jurisdiction and control" and practical understanding of the authority exercised by the United States on the base, makes this territory "American territory as Puerto Rico."[13]

Despite academic or diplomatic claims that the 1903 lease and 1934 treaty are inconsistent with international law, states have traditionally used such leases to exercise indirect control over foreign territories. After 1898, a consistent US foreign policy goal for the Caribbean and Central

American region was to exercise indirect control. This was not only specific to Cuba, but generally exercised in the region. Leases or servitudes provided the United States a legal instrument to control the strategically valuable bay at Guantánamo. Relevant to Guantánamo's history and current legal anomaly, leases provided two significant benefits for lessee-states. First, they conferred a way to control territory without annexing it. Second, sovereignty would remain in the lessor/host-state. This restriction for the lessee made these agreements a servitude because the restriction was tied to the territory. Leases developed in international law after prior common practices of attaining bases by simple occupation and flying a national flag.

Lease agreements commonly laid out two important sets of rights. First, for the lessee, there was a grant of authority to occupy and use the delineated area. Second, there was a description of jurisdictional rights and duties between the host/lessor and lessee states. Within the second set of stipulations, the agreement would describe how the host/lessor's sovereignty was restricted. This was invariably determined by the specific relations and contexts of the two states at that period in time. This includes history, relative political power, and domestic politics.

Editors' Note: The portion of the author's article analyzing the *Boumediene* case is not included because of space constraints. The *Boumediene* case itself is excerpted in part five, as are the sections of this author's article addressing post-*Boumediene* developments.

TRADING CIVIL LIBERTIES FOR APPARENT SECURITY IS A BAD DEAL
(2009)

Marjorie Cohn

Framing the discussion as a tradeoff between civil liberties and security creates a false distinction. This discourse is not new in the United States. Benjamin Franklin warned, "They who can give up essential liberty to obtain a little temporary safety, deserve neither liberty nor safety."[1] Throughout our history, we have grappled with this apparent tension.

Unfortunately, all too often, we have lost our liberties—with no tangible benefit. It has been primarily the executive branch that has overreached beyond the lines that separate our three branches of government. Under the guise of his "Global War on Terror," former president George W. Bush arrogated to himself a level of presidential authority that violated the Constitution and made us less safe.

As US military leaders said, the two things that have posed the biggest threat to our soldiers in Iraq are Abu Ghraib and Guantánamo, which have served as recruitment tools and have become the symbols of American cruelty and hypocrisy.

I. LINCOLN'S SUSPENSION OF CIVIL LIBERTIES

President Abraham Lincoln also put civil liberties on hold in an effort to preserve the Union when he suspended the writ of habeas corpus without congressional approval after anti-Union riots occurred in Baltimore. But then, as now, suspension of the Great Writ was used as a tool to suppress dissent.

Lincoln ignored court orders and congressional laws that sought to limit his power to incarcerate citizens without giving them access to courts. People were arrested not for what they had done, but "for what probably would be done." Lincoln said arrestees would include the "man who stands by and says nothing when the peril of his Government is discussed," or one who "talks ambiguously—talks for his country with 'buts' and 'ifs' and 'ands.'"[2]

Lincoln also imposed martial law and used military force in areas of the North where there was strong Confederate sympathy. In violation of congressional legislation, Lincoln authorized military trials, convictions, and punishment of civilians who were accused of aiding the South. Tens of thousands were arrested by military authorities and several thousand were tried by military commissions even though civil courts were functioning. In *Ex parte Milligan* (1866), the Supreme Court declared military trials of civilians, where civil courts were available, to be unconstitutional.

Many Northerners suspected of treason were tortured and some were handcuffed and suspended by their wrists. Water torture was routinely used and people were doused with strong streams of water until their skin broke.

As historian James G. Randall said, "No president has carried the power of presidential edict and executive order (independently of Congress) so far as [Lincoln] did . . . It would not be easy to state what Lincoln conceived to be the limit of his powers."[3]

But while Lincoln rationalized his usurpation of power as a temporary remedy, expecting an early end to the conflict—he called it medicine prescribed during an illness—Bush's "war on terror," on the other hand, is slated to last for years, perhaps forever.

The danger of presidential overreaching was anticipated by the Founding Fathers. James Madison, in *The Federalist*, no. [47], wrote: "The accumulation of all powers legislative, executive, and judiciary in the same hands...may justly be pronounced the very definition of tyranny."[4]

Former Attorney General John Ashcroft painted the defenders of civil liberties as anti-American fear-mongers when he said on December 6, 2001, "To those who scare peace-loving people with phantoms of lost liberty; my message is this: Your tactics only aid terrorists—for they erode our national unity and diminish our resolve. They give ammunition to America's enemies, and pause to America's friends."[5]

II. THE US GOVERNMENT'S HISTORY OF SUPPRESSION OF CRITICISM

But surveillance in this country has historically been aimed at slaves, immigrants, political radicals, suspected lawbreakers, the poor, workers, and anyone with a credit card or a computer. It has frequently been used by the government to stifle criticism of its policies.

. . . .

According to Professor Michael Kurt Curtis, "Military suppression of reactionary, anti-war speech during the Civil War may well have paved the way for civil suppression of socialist and other anti-war speech during World War I."[6]

Subsequent examples of repressive legislation passed and actions taken as a result of fear-mongering during periods of xenophobia are the Espionage Act of 1917, the Sedition Act of 1918, the Red Scare following World War I, the forcible internment of people of Japanese descent during World War II, and the Alien Registration Act of 1940 (the Smith Act).

During the McCarthy period of the 1950s, in an effort to eradicate the perceived threat of communism, the government engaged in widespread illegal surveillance to threaten and silence anyone who had an unorthodox political viewpoint. Many people were jailed, blacklisted, and lost their jobs. Thousands of lives were shattered as the FBI engaged in "red-baiting."

COINTELPRO (counter-intelligence program) was designed to "expose, disrupt and otherwise neutralize" activist and political groups.[7] In the 1960s, the FBI targeted Dr. Martin Luther King Jr. in a program called "Racial Matters." King's campaign to register African American voters in the South raised the hackles of FBI director J. Edgar Hoover, who disingenuously said King's organization was being infiltrated by communists. In fact, the FBI was really concerned that King's civil rights and anti-Vietnam War campaigns "represented a clear threat to the established order of the US."[8] The FBI wiretapped King's telephones, securing personal information which it used to try to discredit him and drive him to divorce and suicide.

In response to the excesses of COINTELPRO, a congressional committee chaired by Senator Frank Church conducted an investigation of activities of the domestic intelligence agencies. The Church Committee concluded that "intelligence activities have undermined the constitutional rights of citizens and ... they have done so primarily because checks and balances designed by the framers of the Constitution to assure accountability have not been applied."[9] The committee added, "In an era where the technological capability of Government relentlessly increases, we must be wary about the drift toward 'big brother government'.... Here, there is no sovereign who stands above the law. Each of us, from presidents to the most disadvantaged citizen, must obey the law." The committee stressed that the "advocacy of political ideas is not to be the basis for governmental surveillance."[10]

III. THE FOREIGN INTELLIGENCE SURVEILLANCE ACT

Congress established guidelines to govern intelligence gathering by the FBI. Reacting against President Richard Nixon's assertion of unchecked presidential power, Congress enacted the Foreign Intelligence Surveillance Act (FISA) in 1978 to regulate electronic surveillance while protecting national security.

FISA established a secret court to consider applications by the government for wiretap orders. It specifically created only one exception for the president to conduct electronic surveillance without a warrant. For that exception to apply, the attorney general must certify under oath that the communications to be monitored will be exclusively between foreign powers, and that there is no substantial likelihood that a United States person will be overheard.

The FISA court rarely denied a wiretap request by the executive. But in 2002, in direct violation of FISA and the Fourth Amendment, Bush signed an executive order establishing his Terrorist Surveillance Program. It authorized the National Security Agency to wiretap people within the United States with no judicial review. The NSA has eavesdropped on untold numbers of private conversations. It has combed through large volumes of telephone and Internet communications flowing into and out of the United States, collecting vast personal information that has nothing to do with national security. Whistleblower Russell Tice, a former US intelligence analyst, recently said that most journalists in the US have been subjected to surveillance.[11]

Electronic surveillance was first used during the Holocaust when IBM worked for the Nazi government organizing and analyzing its census data. Death camp barcodes—linked to computerized records—were tattooed onto prisoners' forearms.

The advent of digital technology has raised surveillance to a new level. Social security numbers, credit cards, gym memberships, library cards, health insurance records, bar codes, GSM chips in cell phones, toll booths, hidden cameras, workplace identification badges, and the Internet all provide the government with effective tools to keep track of our finances, our politics, our personal habits, and our whereabouts through data mining. The Privacy Foundation determined in a 2001 survey that one-third of all American workers who use the Internet or e-mail on the job are under "constant surveillance" by employers.[12]

IV. CIVIL LIBERTIES SUPPRESSION AFTER 9/11

One month after the terrorist attacks of September 11, 2001, Ashcroft rushed the USA PATRIOT Act through a timid Congress. The act lowered the standards for government surveillance of telephone and computer communications, and placed in effect, "an FBI agent behind every mailbox."[13] It created a crime of domestic terrorism targeting political activists who protest government policies, which was so broadly defined as to include even environmental and animal rights groups.

After September 11, 2001, hundreds of people of color, particularly those of Middle Eastern descent, were detained in US prisons. Most were suspected of no crime or connection to the events of 9/11; yet they were held incommunicado, in indefinite, preventive detention, many subjected to abusive treatment, in violation of the Constitution.

Rabih Haddad, a Lebanese immigrant, described the conditions of his confinement. Strangely reminiscent of the prisoners in Guantánamo, he described his 6′ by 9′ solitary cell, the camera permanently fixed on him, his lack of exercise, and "waves of cockroaches" in his cell at night.[14]

These roundups were evocative of our government's excesses during World War II, when it interned thousands of Japanese Americans in a shameful and racist overreaction. In 1944, the Supreme Court upheld the legality of the Japanese internment in *Korematsu v. United States*. But Justice Robert Jackson warned in his dissent that the ruling would "lie about like a loaded weapon ready for the hand of any authority that can bring forward a plausible claim of an urgent need."[15]

That day came with the decision of a New York federal judge, dismissing a case that challenged the detention of hundreds of Arab and Muslim foreign nationals shortly after 9/11. None was convicted of any crime involving terrorism. US District Judge John Gleeson ruled in *Turkmen v. Ashcroft* that the roundup and indefinite detention of foreign nationals on immigration charges based only on their race, religion, or national origin did not violate equal protection or due process. This is not surprising in light of the anti-immigrant hysteria sweeping our country today.

Three developments on Bush's watch had a chilling effect on protected First Amendment activity: 1) the shift from reactive to preemptive law enforcement; 2) the enactment of domestic antiterrorism laws; and 3) the relaxation of FBI guidelines on surveillance of Americans.

Like Bush's "preemptive" or "preventive" war strategy, which led us into Iraq in violation of the United Nations Charter, law enforcement in the United States moved from reaction to "preemption," in violation of the Constitution.

Collective preemptive punishment against those who seek to exercise their First Amendment rights has taken several forms: content-based permits, where permission to protest is screened for political correctness; pretextual arrests in anticipation of actions that haven't yet occurred (like Lincoln); the setting of huge bails of up to $1 million for misdemeanors; the use of chemical weapons; and the employment of less lethal rounds fired without provocation into crowds. Protestors were painted by the government and the mainstream media as violent lawbreakers.

In his 1928 dissent in *Olmstead v. United States*, Justice Louis Brandeis cautioned, "The greatest dangers to liberty lurk in insidious encroachment by men of zeal, well-meaning but without understanding."[16] Seventy-three years later, former White House spokesman Ari Fleischer warned Americans that "they need to watch what they say, watch what they do." ...

V. A POLICY OF TORTURE

For more than seven years, pursuant to Bush's "war on terror," the US government has held up to 800 foreign-born men and boys prisoner at Guantánamo Bay, Cuba. No charges have been filed against most of them, and, until the Supreme Court decided *Boumediene v. Bush* (2008), all had been denied access to any court to challenge their confinement.

Prisoners released from Guantánamo report being tortured. They describe assaults, prolonged shackling in uncomfortable positions, and sexual abuse. There are reports of prisoners being pepper-sprayed in the face until they vomited, fingers being poked into their eyes, and their heads being forced into the toilet pan and flushed. Prisoners who engaged in hunger strikes were brutally force-fed, a practice the United Nations Human Rights Commissions called "torture." Dozens of videotapes of American guards brutally attacking prisoners are reportedly catalogued and stored at the Guantánamo prison. Thirty-two attempted suicides took place in an eighteen-month period.

As evidence of torture leaked out of Abu Ghraib prison, a Guantánamo-Iraq torture connection was revealed. General Geoffrey Miller, implicated in setting torture policies in Iraq, had been transferred from Guantánamo to Abu Ghraib specifically to institute the same harsh interrogation procedures he had put in place at Guantánamo.

The interrogation policy that permitted torture and abuse came from the top. Former Vice President Dick Cheney recently admitted that he authorized waterboarding. It is well-established that waterboarding constitutes torture. Torture is considered a war crime under the US War Crimes Act. Bush's National Security Council's Principals Committee, consisting of Vice President Cheney, National Security Adviser Condoleezza Rice, CIA Director George Tenet, Secretary of Defense Donald Rumsfeld, Attorney General John Ashcroft, and Secretary of State Colin Powell, participated in the sanctioning of "enhanced interrogation techniques"; Bush admitted that he approved. Lawyers from the Department of Justice's Office of Legal Counsel rewrote our laws on torture to facilitate the commission of war crimes and immunize Team Bush from prosecution.

Those who carried out the torture and abuse did so in secret, accountable to no court or public scrutiny. Guantánamo was, according to a spokeswoman from the International Committee of the Red Cross, "a legal black hole."[17]

The Convention against Torture and Other Cruel, Inhuman or Degrading Treatment or Punishment, a treaty the United States has ratified, which makes it US law under the Constitution's Supremacy Clause, declares, "No exceptional circumstances whatsoever, whether a state of war or a threat of war, internal political instability or any other public emergency, may be invoked as a justification of torture." Its language is unequivocal. Furthermore, torture doesn't work. The person being tortured will say anything to make the torture stop; his information is unreliable.

Editors' Note: Because of space constraints, section VI addressing rendition, is not included. Section VII, addressing recent Supreme Court opinions, is contained in part 5 of this volume.

VIII. CITIZENS' DUTY TO RESIST GOVERNMENT LAWBREAKING

The Bush administration capitalized on the 9/11 attacks to try to maintain members of Congress and the American people in a state of fear; this enabled the White House to enact several repressive measures, which did not make us safer. Bush's Defense Department claimed that as many as sixty-one ex-detainees from Guantánamo had returned to the battlefield of terror. That claim, however, was roundly debunked by reports from Seton Hall School of Law.[18]

It is our duty as citizens in a democracy to speak out when our government fails to live up to our principles and follow the law. We must refuse to trade our liberties for vague promises that it will protect our democracy and make us safer. The Obama administration should bring those to justice who have committed crimes; nobody is above the law. This includes the former Department of Justice lawyers such as John Yoo and Jay Bybee, who gave the Bush officials "legal" cover to commit their crimes. The US government should disclose the identities, current whereabouts and fate of all persons detained by the CIA or rendered to foreign custody by the CIA since 2001. Those who ordered renditions should be prosecuted. And the special task force should recommend, and Obama should agree to, end all renditions.

We cannot gain civil rights by sacrificing civil liberties—they are not mutually exclusive. Our best bet is to uphold the rule of law.

JUSTIFYING WARTIME LIMITS ON CIVIL RIGHTS AND LIBERTIES
(2009)

Robert J. Pushaw Jr.

Many law professors and commentators condemned the Bush administration's "War on Terrorism" as involving unprecedented assertions of Article II power that sacrificed constitutional rights and liberties for no purpose, as America actually became less safe.... [My] historical perspective casts doubt upon the conventional wisdom that the War on Terrorism has caused unique harm to the Constitution's structure and the individual rights it guarantees.

. . . .

Initially, it is impossible to say with any certainty whether or not presidents like Abraham Lincoln and Franklin Roosevelt had to infringe constitutional liberties the way they did in order to win their wars. Perhaps they could have achieved the same results with fewer intrusions. But maybe greater solicitude for personal freedoms would have led to defeat, or to a victory that exacted a far greater cost in blood and money. Speculating about such matters is an academic exercise. All we know for sure is that these presidents took the actions they deemed necessary to prevail, and they did. For better or worse, the Constitution commits to the president almost unbridled discretion to determine what must be done to meet a military emergency. These decisions must be made quickly and with imperfect information, and they are then judged by Congress, voters, and posterity. All of these groups tend to be quite forgiving of the president if he triumphs.

. . . .

. . . [Incorporating the lessons of history] has several implications for the War on Terrorism. Most importantly, although President Bush asserted aggressive unilateral executive powers, his response to al Qaeda's September 11, 2001, attacks was fairly mild in comparison with the actions of Lincoln, Roosevelt, and other presidents. Furthermore, like his predecessors, Bush can defend his infringements on civil liberties as necessary to achieve his avowed objective: preventing another terrorist assault. In the past, such success has usually been sufficient for a president to deflect charges that he went overboard.

Indeed, the majority of Americans have always solidly supported antiterrorism efforts. Although the legal and media intelligentsia have been outraged by conditions at Guantanamo Bay, average people do not appear to feel widespread regret that will result in a compensatory increase in civil rights. . . .

. . . .

I. LIMITING CIVIL LIBERTIES TO HELP WIN WARS

Professors have typically argued that presidents like Lincoln, Wilson, Roosevelt, Truman, and Bush have lost their heads in the heat of war and curbed civil liberties to a far greater extent than was needed to ensure victory. They might be right. But they might be wrong. For example, perhaps if Lincoln had been more sensitive to individual constitutional rights, he would have lost the Civil War and the United States would have fractured along North-South lines, and then probably further fragmented into regional nations (or possibly autonomous states). It is intellectually interesting, but pointless, to try to ascertain what might have happened if presidents had taken different courses of action. Put simply, it is impossible to test the libertarian academics' arguments empirically.

More significantly, these critics tend to make two fundamental errors. First, they incorrectly assume that the Constitution supplies fixed legal rules for determining when the president went "too far" in exercising war powers and clearly violated individual rights. Second, they judge federal government officials based on hindsight, rather than on the facts and circumstances that existed at the time those leaders had to make decisions.

A study of the Constitution as written and as actually implemented in wars reveals that the political branches have enormous leeway in exercising military powers to respond to the unique conditions of each armed conflict. Given the complexities of decision-making during a military crisis, it is usually quite difficult to conclude definitively that Congress or the president abused their discretion.

A. The Constitutional Design

The Constitution entrusts the power to make, execute, and evaluate military and foreign policy exclusively to the political departments, which have the democratic legitimacy, institutional competence, and political incentives to defend the nation. In supporting this conferral of plenary authority, Alexander Hamilton declared:

[War] powers ought to exist without limitation: Because it is impossible to foresee or define the extent and variety of national exigencies, or the correspondent extent & variety of the means which may be necessary to satisfy them. The circumstances that endanger the safety of nations are infinite; and for this reason no constitutional shackles can wisely be imposed on the power to which the care of it is committed. This power ought to be co-extensive with all the possible combinations of such circumstances; and ought to be under the direction of the same councils, which are appointed to preside over the common defence [sic].[1]

Specifically, Article I authorizes Congress to provide for the national defense; declare war or otherwise approve it; create, finance, and regulate the armed forces; and suspend the privilege of the writ of habeas corpus "when in Cases of Rebellion or Invasion the public Safety may require it." Article II confers on the president federal "executive power" and enables him to direct the army and navy as "Commander in Chief." Furthermore, the structure of Article II suggests that the president can unilaterally address emergencies because only he, as the sole repository of all executive power and the lone federal official always on duty, can act swiftly and resolutely based on the recommendations of experts who have access to secret military intelligence. By contrast, the other two departments labor in fixed sessions: Congress legislates through a time-consuming process of debate and compromise, while federal courts render judgments only after parties have properly invoked their jurisdiction and lengthy litigation has been completed.

In short, the Constitution grants Congress and the president all conceivable war powers, and gives each branch weapons to check the other. For instance, Congress can investigate the executive branch's conduct of war, halt any armed conflict by cutting off funding, and impeach executive officials for egregious misconduct. Conversely, the president can veto legislation that he believes hampers the military and can exploit the institutional advantages of the unitary executive to maintain a singular focus that often overwhelms the multi-member Congress, especially when it is sharply divided along party lines.

Not surprisingly, Article III gives the judiciary no role in warfare. Thus, claims that a military action violated Articles I or II are political, not judicial, questions. The only time judicial review might be proper would be when the exercise of war powers allegedly violated individual legal rights. Unfortunately, the historical record is silent as to whether such cases should be dismissed as nonjusticiable, treated the same as decisions made in ordinary contexts, or addressed through a compromise approach of asserting jurisdiction but demonstrating extraordinary deference to the political branches. The Court adopted the latter position, which seems to be the best way to balance the Constitution's institution of judicial review with its provisions entrusting national security primarily to Congress and the president.

In implementing the Constitution, all three branches have determined that sometimes individual rights and liberties must yield to the national imperative of winning a war. The primary actor has been the president, who has had to make swift decisions based on a constantly shifting military situation and imperfect intelligence. As long as they acted reasonably under the circumstances, strong presidents who have forcefully and successfully responded to military crises have always enjoyed the support of Congress, the courts, and the American people. Thus, modern laments that these presidents have gone "too far" often smack of Monday-morning quarterbacking. The examples of Lincoln and Roosevelt are especially illuminating.

B. Lincoln's Constitutionalism

. . . .

Perhaps most famously, Lincoln suspended the writ of habeas corpus and jailed thousands of civilians without affording them any judicial process. Initially, Lincoln's main fear was that Maryland would secede, which would hinder and perhaps destroy the war effort by cutting off Washington from the rest of the Union. Accordingly, Lincoln ordered the army to place Confederate sympathizers in Maryland in military prisons. Merryman, one such detainee, filed a habeas petition to the Circuit Court manned by Chief Justice Taney. He ordered the release of Merryman after concluding that Lincoln had broken his oath to faithfully execute the law by usurping (1) Congress's Article I power to suspend habeas corpus, and (2) the judiciary's Article III function of deciding whether citizens had been unconstitutionally detained.

Lincoln refused to comply. Soon thereafter, when Congress had reassembled, Lincoln justified his conduct in a special address. He contended that the president's oath to "preserve, protect and defend the Constitution" as a whole justified taking any actions he deemed necessary to save the Union, even those that temporarily disregarded individual constitutional provisions. In Lincoln's own words: "[M]easures, otherwise unconstitutional, might become lawful, by becoming indispensable to the preservation of the Constitution, through the preservation of the nation." As for habeas specifically, Lincoln rhetorically asked: "[A]re all the laws, but one, to go unexecuted, and the government itself go to pieces, lest that one be violated?"[2]

Yet Lincoln was not the tyrant that some have made him out to be. On the contrary, he had a profound reverence for constitutional democracy. Accordingly, Lincoln recognized that he needed the approval of

Congress, especially because it was the only branch that could constitutionally continue to fund the war. Congress ratified Lincoln's actions (including his suspension of habeas) and supported him for the remainder of the war.

A chastened Court also fell into line. In *The Prize Cases* (1866), a majority of justices upheld the validity of Lincoln's blockade against a challenge by owners of seized vessels who claimed that their property had been taken without due process. The Court concluded that it could not review the president's exercise of political discretion, which Article II confided in him as commander-in-chief, to "determine what degree of force the crisis demands" (such as the blockade).

Likewise, *Ex parte Vallandigham* (1863) rejected a due process challenge to an army tribunal created under Lincoln's orders. The Court disavowed any power to "review or pronounce any opinion upon the proceedings of a military commission" or similar executive wartime decisions.

Finally, Lincoln fulfilled his pre-election promise to decline to adhere to the Court's constitutional holding in *Dred Scott v. Sandford* (1856) that the federal government could not intrude upon state power over slavery. Invoking his authority as commander-in-chief, Lincoln emancipated millions of slaves in rebellious Southern areas, even though such a hugely consequential policy determination seemed to fall squarely within the legislative domain.

The Civil War teaches that a strong president can sweep aside significant constitutional provisions—including both clauses that confer powers on Congress or the courts and those that protect individual rights and liberties—if he determines that this course must be taken to address a military emergency. Modern libertarians who assert that Lincoln went "too far" cannot easily explain the contemporaneous consensus that he did not. The president himself, among the most profound constitutional thinkers America has ever produced, did not consider his actions excessive under the circumstances. Neither did Congress, which approved his conduct. Neither did the Court as an institution (as distinguished from individual justices like Taney), which concluded either that the Constitution left wartime decisions entirely to the president's discretion or upheld them on the merits. Last, but not least, posterity has lionized Lincoln, who is equaled only by George Washington in the presidential pantheon.

Modern presidents absorbed the lesson of the Civil War. For example, Woodrow Wilson had no qualms about sacrificing individual liberties if doing so, in his judgment, would help achieve victory in World War I. Indeed, even after the war had ended, Wilson continued to suppress freedom of expression. Wilson, however, was merely a warm up for Roosevelt, who emulated Lincoln in the sheer audacity and scope of his assertions of war powers.

C. Roosevelt: Lincoln Redux

Even before Congress declared war in December 1941, Roosevelt had independently engaged in negotiations over military and foreign affairs with Great Britain, sent troops to the North Atlantic, ordered Nazi U-boats shot on sight, and declared a state of "unlimited national emergency." After America entered World War II, Roosevelt did whatever he deemed necessary to win it, which included suppressing constitutional liberties.

Roosevelt followed Lincoln in two specific ways. First, FDR successfully seized private property, including over sixty plants where labor disputes and other problems had impeded the war effort. Second, he created military commissions to try enemies charged with war crimes. In *Ex parte Quirin* (1942), the Court sustained a commission's imposition of the death penalty against Nazi spies (including an American citizen) who had stealthily entered the United States, and rejected their claim that the Constitution guaranteed their right to a trial in civilian court with ordinary procedural protections. Roosevelt had used intermediaries to inform the justices that he intended to execute the saboteurs whatever the Court decided, and he had marshaled massive popular support in this matter.

FDR's most novel, and notorious, decision was his executive order (issued on the advice of his generals, and reinforced by an Act of Congress) removing Americans of Japanese descent from the West Coast to prison camps to prevent espionage and sabotage on behalf of Japan. Even though it eventually became apparent that there was no credible evidence of such disloyal activities, the Court in *Korematsu* (1944) concluded that it could not use hindsight to condemn the actions taken in the emergency that followed Pearl Harbor. Therefore, the Court held that military necessity justified the severe infringement of the detainees' rights to liberty and equality.

In his dissent, Justice Jackson sagely noted that the "chief restraint" on the president and his military subordinates was "their responsibility to the political judgments of their contemporaries and to the moral judgments of history."[3] Roosevelt's "contemporaries" obviously approved his conduct. He was the only president elected more than twice, and his convincing reelection to a fourth term in 1944 indicated broad popular support for his handling of World War II. Congress also backed FDR's military decisions. Similarly, the Court rejected every constitutional challenge to his exercise of war powers.

The "moral judgments of history" are mixed. On the one hand, Roosevelt is considered the greatest twentieth-century President, in large part because he led America to victory in a war that mortally threatened not only the United States but all democracies. On the other hand, FDR's internment of Japanese Americans is a stain on his legacy, an overreaction to Pearl Harbor that reflected racism more than military exigencies.

The overall picture, however, is best captured by America's decision to build a monument honoring Roosevelt, as it did for Lincoln. These marble symbols send the clear message that, in a high-stakes war, presidents should err on the side of using too much force (including intrusions on constitutional liberties) to win, rather than risk defeat by showing greater sensitivity for individual rights.

D. Bush and the War on Terrorism

Since September 11, 2001, America has been engaged in a unique conflict. Unlike past wars, America is not fighting a nation-state for a finite time period in a series of battles. Rather, we are confronting shadowy worldwide private terrorist groups like al Qaeda, which strike indiscriminately in a struggle that will probably never end. Accordingly, the Bush administration responded with equally innovative strategies and tactics. The War on Terrorism raises difficult constitutional questions concerning how to strike the optimum balance between national defense and individual rights.

Most legal academics and commentators, however, see the issues as straightforward. They have accused President Bush of unparalleled misconduct. Indeed, many professors ... have argued that he and many of his military and legal officials should be prosecuted for war crimes. I find such rhetoric overheated, particularly when one compares Bush's specific policies to those adopted in previous wars.

1. The Main Features of the Antiterrorism Effort

In this essay, I can merely provide an outline of the relevant law. This summary will focus on the two key statutes passed by overwhelming margins shortly after the 9/11 attacks.

First, Congress authorized the president to use "all necessary and appropriate force" against those who planned, committed, or aided the terrorist attacks. Invoking this "Authorization for Use of Military Force" (AUMF) and his independent Article II powers, Bush deployed troops to Afghanistan (whose government had backed al Qaeda) and beefed up antiterrorism efforts both at home and abroad. Among other things, Bush claimed the power to indefinitely detain "enemy combatants" (a status determined by the executive branch) and, at his discretion, to try them by military commissions appointed by the secretary of defense.

Second, the "Uniting and Strengthening America by Providing Appropriate Tools Required to Intercept and Obstruct Terrorism" (USA PATRIOT) Act increased surveillance of suspected terrorists, especially by reducing restrictions on domestic gathering of foreign intelligence; facilitated the deportation of immigrants suspected of involvement with terrorism; authorized law enforcement officials to search homes and businesses without prior notice to the owners ("sneak and peek"); permitted government searches of telephone, internet, financial, and other records; and enhanced the treasury secretary's power to regulate and monitor financial transactions involving suspected terrorists and their allies. The USA PATRIOT Act's foes have argued that it violates constitutional rights and liberties in many ways, most notably by allowing either the indefinite detention or arbitrary deportation of immigrants and by authorizing federal law enforcement officials to search private homes, business[es], and records without the affected party's knowledge.

The AUMF and the USA PATRIOT Act have generated multiple lawsuits, although to date the Supreme Court has adjudicated only actions taken under the former statute. Before discussing those cases, I want to highlight three aspects of the War on Terrorism that suggest President Bush actually showed more restraint than his predecessors.

First, unlike Lincoln and Wilson, Bush did not censor speech or the press or criminally prosecute his critics, despite their vehement and often vicious verbal attacks on him and his antiterrorism policies. Admittedly, the USA PATRIOT Act has raised legitimate First Amendment concerns, but they are of a far smaller magnitude than those that resulted from previous presidents' flagrant suppression of valid opposition to their wartime actions.

Second, in contrast to FDR's treatment of Japanese Americans, President Bush worked with Congress to specifically prohibit and condemn discrimination against Arab and Muslim Americans and to ensure review of all allegations of civil rights abuses. Such sensitivity was welcome in the emotionally charged aftermath of the September 11 attacks.

Third, Lincoln suspended the writ of habeas corpus unilaterally and broadly, whereas Bush and Congress left it intact. The only exception was for a few hundred foreign suspected terrorists imprisoned at the US naval base in Guantanamo Bay, Cuba, who were given extensive administrative and judicial review as a substitute.

Of course, President Bush made many mistakes. Even though he won the 2000 election by a razor-thin margin and with help from a controversial Supreme Court decision, Bush governed as if he had a mandate. He came into office with no national experience and little knowledge about military affairs, foreign policy, or constitutional law. After 9/11, Bush asserted sweeping unilateral war powers under Article II, thereby unnecessarily antagonizing a Congress that had given him all the authority he could possibly need in fighting terrorism. Despite the potential for interbranch conflict, Bush's handling of this crisis earned him extraordinary popular support.

His downfall began with the March 2003 invasion of Iraq, which rested on several assumptions: that Iraq had supported al Qaeda, that it possessed weapons of mass destruction, that victory would be easy, and that a thriving democracy would sprout up. When these suppositions proved to be false, Bush's popularity began to decline, but then increased just enough in the fall of 2004 to ensure his reelection. Yet the Iraq war dragged on and imposed huge costs, which exacerbated the economic devastation wrought by the September 11 attacks. A weakened economy encouraged the government to dramatically decrease interest rates and to tolerate lax lending (especially for housing), which ultimately led to a financial meltdown.

As these troubles piled up, Bush's popularity hit historic lows. Nonetheless, he continued to assert aggressive executive powers as if the United States were in a continuing military emergency akin to the Civil War or World War II, even though the carnage and destruction were clearly not equivalent. Moreover, Bush never demanded the national mobilization and shared sacrifice that characterized such all-out wars. Another intractable political problem inhered in the peculiar nature of the War on Terrorism, which measured success primarily in negative terms—thwarting attacks, the details of which could not be publicized for national security reasons—rather than positive battlefield victories, such as Gettysburg and D-Day. Symbolically, then, it was far easier for Bush to rally the public in the wake of the tangible 9/11 atrocities than in the vague domain of undisclosed possible assaults that did not occur.

My preliminary assessment, then, is that Bush consistently took strong actions to fight terrorism; that Americans (and their representatives in Congress) always supported these efforts; but that the Iraq War and the economic downturn fatally weakened his presidency. Bush did not, however, adopt many of the liberty-infringing policies of his predecessors, such as censoring the press or imprisoning members of a particular ethnic group.

In one area, though, Bush did follow the lead of every president dating back to Washington: using military commissions to try enemy combatants charged with war crimes. Historically, the Court had rebuffed those few military prisoners who challenged the constitutionality of military tribunals, as in *Vallandigham* and *Quirin*. Recently, however, a majority of justices have become far more receptive to such claims and others relating to habeas corpus.

Editors' Note: The author's discussion, following, of the enemy combatant decisions is included in part 5 of this volume. Sections II and III, which address whether wartime restrictions on civil rights act as catalysts for improving civil rights are not included in the interest of space.

. . . .

CONCLUSION

War is hell. Winning one requires many hard decisions based on constantly changing military circumstances and incomplete information. Presidents in the midst of a national security crisis often conclude that they have to do unspeakably awful things, as when Lincoln ordered that Union Army deserters be shot and Truman chose to drop atomic bombs.

Keeping in mind the emergency conditions that actually existed and the facts the president had available, it is usually difficult to conclude with certitude that his specific infringement of civil liberties was unnecessary for military success. . . .

As with all armed conflicts, reasonable people can disagree about the optimum balance between individual rights and collective security in the War on Terrorism. In evaluating the response of the Bush and Obama administrations to this threat, it is important to recognize the validity of a range of possible responses and to compare presidents to their real-life predecessors, not to some idealized leader.

BROKEN PROMISES OR UNREALISTIC EXPECTATIONS?
Comparing the Bush and Obama Administrations on Counterterrorism
(2011)

Tung Yin

By Election Day 2008, the US detention facility on Guantanamo Bay had already festered for six years in the eyes of the international community as a symbol of the perceived arrogance and lawlessness of the United States under President Bush. Perhaps not surprisingly, both presidential candidates, Senators Barack Obama and John McCain, had pledged to close down Guantanamo.

When it became clear that night that Obama had defeated McCain, critics of the Bush administration's counterterrorism policies no doubt looked forward to an end to waterboarding and other forms of coercive interrogation, detention without criminal charges of captured fighters at Guantanamo Bay, and general defiance of international law and standards. Domestic and international expectations were high; whereas President Bush had been denounced as a war criminal, Obama found himself accepting the Nobel Peace Prize just a few months after his inauguration.

Yet, as of President Obama's first official State of the Union address in 2010, there were still a couple of hundred detainees at Guantanamo Bay; the president had decided to send additional troops to Afghanistan; and US aerial drones were circling the skies of Pakistan's remote regions on hunt-and-destroy missions.

It would be inaccurate and unfair to say that President Obama has simply continued President Bush's counterterrorism policies. Obama immediately issued an executive order banning waterboarding and other forms of coercive interrogation, and suggested that military commissions, if used, would require more procedural protections to defendants. However, on the high-level issues—indefinite detentions, drone-launched missile attacks, and military commissions—the similarities between the past and present dwarf the differences. The high-level similarities lead one to ask whether President Obama broke campaign promises regarding counterterrorism policies, or whether the expectations that Bush administration critics had for Obama were completely unrealistic.

I begin in Part I with discussion of what I call the criminal prosecution-military force divide. This is the fracture point between competing theories of how the United States should respond to the terrorist group al Qaeda, whether through the traditional criminal justice system, armed conflict, or some hybrid of the two.

Part II then considers the consequences of the military force paradigm as applied against al Qaeda and the Taliban following the 9/11 attacks, focusing on the three high-level issues noted earlier (indefinite detentions, drone strikes, and military commissions). For each issue, I note the respective actions and legal positions of the Bush and Obama administrations.

Finally, Part III provides a normative comparison of the Bush and Obama administration counterterrorism policies. I draw three tentative conclusions from the general similarity in both administrations' response to al Qaeda: (1) military force is a necessary, but not sufficient, counterterrorism tool; (2) like domestic law, international law will likely end up adapting to the needs of the present by accepting the legality of the use of military force against non-state actors; and (3) international opinions toward the Bush and Obama administration counterterrorism policies are based less on substance than on perception.

BROKEN PROMISES OR UNREALISTIC EXPECTATIONS?

I. THE CRIMINAL PROSECUTION-MILITARY FORCE DIVIDE

Prior to the 9/11 terrorist attacks, American legal policy reserved the use of military force primarily for campaigns against enemy states. Terrorism, even on an international scale, largely remained a criminal matter to be prosecuted in civilian federal courts.

. . . .

American responses to threats and attacks from foreign sources from 1979 to 2001 follow this consistent use of the criminal justice system to respond to terrorism. Two major terrorist attacks took place on US soil in the mid-1990s. First, a cell led by Ramzi Yousef and inspired by Omar Abdel-Rahman (aka the Blind Sheikh) exploded a truck bomb in the underground parking lot of the World Trade Center in 1993, killing six people and injuring over a thousand. Second, American military veterans Timothy McVeigh and Terry Nichols blew up the Murrah Federal Building in Oklahoma City in 1995, killing 168 and injuring almost 700 people. In both instances, the Clinton Department of Justice investigated the attacks, identified and apprehended the perpetrators, and prosecuted them for federal crimes.

More numerous attacks took place in the 1990s against US interests overseas. . . .

The 9/11 attacks, on the other hand, engendered a much different response. Rhetorically, President Bush promised "to strike back with a 'hammer of vengeance'"[1] against the perpetrators of the attack. That hammer took the form of military airstrikes against the Taliban strongholds and al Qaeda training camps in Afghanistan, not criminal indictments. Not long after, US Special Forces joined with the Taliban's indigenous foes, the Northern Alliance, in ground combat. The military strikes killed a number of suspected militants, including Mohammed Atef, supposedly al Qaeda's military chief. US armed forces also took custody of thousands of suspected Taliban and al Qaeda fighters, sending about a thousand for detention at the US naval base on Guantanamo Bay, and keeping the rest in Afghanistan.

For the purposes of this article, I will refer to these competing positions as the Law Enforcement Paradigm and the Military Force Paradigm. Under the Law Enforcement Paradigm, even international terrorism on the scale of that inflicted by al Qaeda is still a matter for the civilian criminal justice system, supplemented by international cooperation regarding the investigation, location, arrest, and extradition of criminal suspects. Taken to its ultimate conclusion, the Law Enforcement Paradigm has led to declarations that "the indefinite detention of suspects without charges" was an illegal practice.[2]

Under the Military Force Paradigm, on the other hand, the mass scale of human and economic carnage inflicted by the 9/11 attacks, combined with al Qaeda's avowed desire for even more spectacular terrorism, present a level of threat to the United States equal to that posed by enemy nations. Responding to this threat therefore requires equivalent national force. In addition, criminal prosecution comes into play after a crime has been committed; its focus is retrospective, aimed at punishing the perpetrator. Proponents of the Military Force Paradigm argue that future acts of terrorism on the scale of 9/11 must be prevented before they occur, not punished after the fact. Prevention of such terrorist attacks requires the use of military force to disrupt terrorist training camps and to kill terrorists before they can strike. Finally, military force proponents argue that civilian trials, due to their openness, will compromise the security of classified information and sources.

To be clear, these two paradigms do not represent the only possible methods of dealing with the threat posed by al Qaeda. Various commentators have called for some sort of hybrid approach such as limited emergency powers to augment (but not supplant) the regular criminal process. . . .

. . . .

Nor is it the case that American presidents have opted for one approach or the other exclusively. Notwithstanding his invocation of the rhetoric of war to justify the use of military force against al Qaeda, President Bush's Justice Department prosecuted hundreds of persons for terrorism-related crimes since September 11, 2001. And presidents before George W. Bush did not rely solely on the criminal justice system to respond to terrorism. . . .

Theory therefore has not described reality accurately with respect to past or current counterterrorism practices. Actual practice since at least the 1990s has been nuanced, often involving criminal prosecution, but even before 9/11, the United States did not restrict itself to using the military only against other states. In the following part, I discuss and analyze the legal justifications and consequences of the use of military force against combatants, both historically and in the present day.

II. JUSTIFICATIONS AND CONSEQUENCES OF THE MILITARY FORCE PARADIGM

. . . .

A. Indefinite Detention Absent Criminal Charges

The first defining feature of the use of military force against al Qaeda has been the indefinite detention, without criminal charges, of hundreds of persons in Afghanistan or at the US naval base on Guantanamo Bay, Cuba. As the Supreme Court noted, such detention was commonplace in traditional armed conflicts between states; what has been striking about the Bush and Obama administrations' use of military detention has been the fact that many of the detainees have not been members of the armed forces of a state.

1. Detention in Traditional Armed Conflicts

The laws of war have largely resolved these issues with respect to traditional armed conflict between nation-states. Warring nations are lawfully entitled to detain captured enemy soldiers as prisoners of war for preventative incapacitation purposes. Such detention can last the entire conflict. . . .

. . . .

. . . Of course, a key distinction between those past conflicts (World War I, World War II, the Korean War, and the Vietnam War) and the global war on terrorism is that the latter has involved enemy combatants who were neither members of the armed forces of a nation nor irregular fighters who spontaneously took up arms on behalf of their nation.

2. Detention After 9/11

[T]he Bush administration sent hundreds of suspected al Qaeda and Taliban fighters to Guantanamo Bay for indefinite detention, interrogation, and possible military prosecution. They were not designated POWs.

One criticism of the Bush administration went to the implementation of its detention policies. If detention were predicated on the laws of war, then why weren't the Guantanamo detainees accorded POW status? . . . The Bush administration responded that al Qaeda was not a country and therefore could not be a signatory to the Geneva Convention. It conceded that the Taliban were covered by the Geneva Convention as the rulers of Afghanistan, but took the position that the Taliban had forfeited their right to POW status en masse due to their failure to comply with the terms of the Geneva Convention. Even if the detainees weren't entitled to POW status, why were so many kept in conditions that most closely approximated those in supermax prison facilities?

The second criticism leveled at the Bush administration was more severe: it argued that under both domestic and international law, the United States lacked legal authority to detain nonsoldiers absent regular criminal process. In other words, this criticism absolutely embraced the Law Enforcement Paradigm.

Under domestic law, however, the United States' use of military force against suspected al Qaeda and Taliban militants in Afghanistan and Pakistan is arguably justified pursuant to the congressional Authorization to Use Military Force (AUMF), which was a joint resolution enacted by Congress on September 17, 2001. The AUMF directed President Bush to "use all necessary and appropriate force against those nations, organizations, or persons he determines planned, authorized, committed, or aided the terrorist attacks" or "harbored such organizations or persons. . . ."

Such AUMFs are the functional equivalent of a declaration of war. . . .

Because the national war powers are shared between Congress and the president, the president is at his maximum authority to use military force against al Qaeda, because he has not only his inherent commander-in-chief power, but also congressional authorization. The argument that domestic law nonetheless restricts the president from using military force against al Qaeda must therefore rest on unlikely grounds.

. . . .

[A]s a matter of domestic law, Congress and the president have both spoken clearly and unequivocally: the primary target of the AUMF is the al Qaeda terrorist group, not a foreign nation, though Afghanistan has served as the primary geographic location of the military conflict, and its former rulers, the Taliban, were initially a secondary target because they had been harboring al Qaeda. Proponents of the view would therefore need the courts to intervene and impose more restrictive interpretations of the war-making powers of the political branches. However, notwithstanding the Supreme Court's post-9/11 terrorism cases, which were generally seen as rebukes of the Bush administration, federal courts have a long history of deferring to Congress and the president about the legitimacy of declarations of war or equivalent statutory authorizations.

Moreover, the Supreme Court's decision in *Hamdan v. Rumsfeld* (2006) presupposes the legitimacy of use of military force against non-state actors. In a key part of that opinion, the Court rejected the Bush administration's argument that Hamdan—alleged to have been al Qaeda leader Osama bin Laden's personal driver and bodyguard—was not entitled to any privileges under the Geneva Convention. The gravamen of the Bush administration's position was that al Qaeda, as a non-state group, was not a signatory to the Geneva Convention and therefore its members could not claim its protections. This position was widely criticized by international law scholars, who argued that if al Qaeda members were not POWs covered by the Third Geneva Convention, then they had to be treated as civilians covered by the Fourth [Geneva] Convention.

Significantly, *Hamdan* concluded that even al Qaeda fighters were covered by Common Article 3 of the Geneva Convention, which states that "[i]n the case of armed conflict not of an international character occurring in the territory of one of the High Contracting Parties, each Party to the conflict shall be bound to apply, as a minimum," certain minimum standards of humane treatment. . . .

President Obama's campaign pledge to close the detention facility at Guantanamo Bay could have been understood at the time as evincing opposition to the concept of indefinite detention without charges, but it could also have been simply opposition to the perceived abuses at Guantanamo joined with recognition that the detention facility had become a toxic symbol.

By mid-2010, it was apparent that President Obama did not oppose indefinite detention. A task force convened for the purpose of formulating the new administration's detainee policy concluded that some detainees should be prosecuted in civilian courts and some in military courts, and a small group of other detainees could not be prosecuted yet were too dangerous to be released. Furthermore, Camp Delta remained an operational detention facility at Guantanamo Bay. Though President Obama's failure to meet his own stated deadline was largely the product of political obstacles (both domestic and international), those thwarted plans demonstrate an acceptance of the Military Force Paradigm. . . . In late 2009, President Obama had shifted focus primarily to his domestic agenda, particularly healthcare reform, which dominated media headlines into spring 2010. . . . [T]here were no high-profile plans in the first half of 2010 to alter the government's position regarding the legality of military detention.

B. Military Prosecutions After 9/11

Under the Military Force Paradigm, the United States can not only detain captured fighters indefinitely, but also prosecute them in military courts for individual war crimes. This is true because the laws of war extend combatant immunity only as to lawful targets. That is, soldiers cannot be prosecuted for murdering enemy soldiers on the battlefield (unless those enemy soldiers have surrendered or are otherwise helpless). Civilians, however, are never lawful targets, and therefore soldiers who intentionally kill civilians are subject to military prosecution for doing so.

At the outset, it will be useful to distinguish between courts-martial and military tribunals (or commissions). Military prosecutions for war crimes differ from civilian trials in substance and procedure. Both of these are military courts in that their jurisdiction extends over military personnel and combatants, not civilians, and the subject matter of the criminal conduct is of military law; as a result, the jury pool consists of military personnel, not civilians.

As with military detention of enemy combatants, military prosecutions have been part and parcel of American warfare dating back to the Revolutionary War.... During World War II, eight German soldiers who sneaked into the United States with plans to sabotage American industrial plants and other targets were tried in an ad hoc military commission established by an executive order by President Roosevelt.[3]

1. The Bush Administration's Military Commissions

In November 2001, President Bush issued an executive order that called for the use of military commissions to prosecute noncitizen international terrorists. This executive order was far broader in scope than the congressional AUMF, for the former purported to apply to any foreign international terrorist, whereas the latter covered only those who were members of the group that carried out the 9/11 attacks.

It did not take long for the Bush administration to designate a small number of detainees for military prosecution. One of the first was Salim Ahmed Hamdan, allegedly a personal driver and bodyguard for Osama bin Laden. However, Hamdan's prosecution ground to a halt immediately. The Defense Department did not promulgate rules for these military commissions until it was pushed to do so by Lt. Cmdr. Charles Swift, the navy lawyer assigned to represent Hamdan. Swift had begun to represent his client aggressively, challenging the military commissions' lack of rules and regulations through habeas petitions. Further litigation delayed Hamdan's prosecution. Meanwhile, critics charged that the Bush administration's military commissions were going to be unfair because the rules allowed the defendant to be removed too easily from the proceedings, hearsay evidence could be admitted against the defendant, and the defendant was denied meaningful access to classified material.

Then, in *Hamdan v. Rumsfeld*, after ruling on jurisdictional issues, the Supreme Court concluded that the Defense Department military commission procedures conflicted with the Uniform Code of Military Justice. Because *Hamdan* was essentially a decision of statutory interpretation, however, the Court left it open to the president to secure congressional approval for his military commissions. In 2006, Congress enacted the Military Commissions Act, which codified nearly all of the key rules and regulations underlying President Bush's planned military commissions.

Of the initial group of defendants slated for military prosecution, by the time President Bush completed his second term of office, only two—Hamdan and David Hicks—had actually been called before any kind of military commission. Hicks pleaded guilty to providing material support to the Taliban in March 2007, for which he received a sentence of nine months; he was allowed to serve his sentence in his native country of Australia. Hamdan proceeded to trial, was convicted in August 2008, and received a sentence of sixty-six months; with credit for the sixty-one months of detention he had already endured, he faced just five more months of incarceration. In November 2008, the United States repatriated Hamdan to Yemen to serve the rest of his sentence.

Though the Bush administration never clearly explained its decisions to classify enemy fighters as criminal defendants or as enemy combatants, it appears that, with a notable, early exception, American citizens suspected of terrorist links to al Qaeda have been prosecuted in federal court for terrorism-related offenses, regardless of their place of capture. For noncitizens, on the other hand, place of capture has, again with a few exceptions, proven to be the determinative factor in their classification; those captured outside the United States were detained in Afghanistan or at Guantanamo Bay, while those captured within the United States have been prosecuted in federal courts.

2. The Obama Administration's Military Commissions

Upon assuming office, President Obama issued an executive order setting forth his intention to close the detention facility at Guantanamo Bay; as part of this order, Obama suspended all pending military commissions. Less than four months later, however, the Obama administration reversed course and indicated that it might proceed with military prosecution with revised rules and procedures that were more favorable to defendants.

Notwithstanding this apparent change in strategy, the Obama administration did not refer any Guantanamo detainees for prosecution in military commissions in 2009. Instead, on November 13, 2009, it broke sharply with its predecessor when Attorney General Eric Holder announced that Khalid Sheikh Mohammed, Ramzi Binalshibh, and several other so-called high-value detainees would be transferred from Guantanamo Bay to New York, where they would stand trial in a federal court. As might be expected, this decision engendered considerable opposition from the president's critics, who raised the same general criticisms of the Law Enforcement Model described earlier—that classified information would be disclosed during the trial and that military commissions were a more appropriate forum for prosecution—as well as concerns that New York would be at increased risk of further terrorist attacks. The decision to seek a federal indictment of Khalid Sheikh Mohammed and others for prosecution in federal court would necessarily have represented a change in course from the Bush administration's strategy.

. . . At the same time that Attorney General Holder stated his intent to prosecute KSM [Khalid Sheikh Mohammed] in federal court, the Obama administration also made clear that it reserved the right to prosecute other appropriate cases in military commissions. [Editors' Note: In April 2011, Holder announced KSM would be tried in Guantánamo.]

The story has not ended yet. . . . In the face of crumbling support for the federal court prosecutions, Attorney General Holder subsequently seemed open to having KSM tried in a military commission. . . . Furthermore, by summer [2010], the Obama administration had obtained its first conviction of a low-level al Qaeda member via a guilty plea.

C. Lethal Aerial Drone Strikes

More proof that the Obama administration has not abandoned the military force paradigm can be seen in its escalation of the use of armed unmanned aerial drones to target suspected al Qaeda leaders in

Afghanistan and Pakistan. Such drone attacks killed dozens of suspected al Qaeda or Taliban militants during 2009.

It would be hard to justify the use of air-to-ground missile strikes from military-operated aerial drones under the Law Enforcement Paradigm. In fall 2002, for example, the United States used a Predator drone to destroy a vehicle in Yemen that was carrying Qaed Salim Sinan al-Harethi and four other men (one of whom was an American citizen), killing all of them. US officials believed that al-Harethi was a key planner of the bombing of the USS Cole and an active al Qaeda member. Numerous legal commentators voiced outrage over [what] they perceived to have been an extrajudicial assassination. The United Nations special rapporteur wrote a report reaching a similar conclusion and sought an explanation from the United States. Notably, however, there was not similar widespread condemnation from foreign governments.

It is useful to consider the obligations of and restrictions on government officials under domestic law if the Law Enforcement Paradigm dictated how al-Harethi should have been dealt with. Because al-Harethi had not been convicted of any crimes in the United States or Yemen at the time he was targeted for the lethal missile strike, he might therefore be analogized to a fleeing felony suspect.

The Constitution permits the use of lethal force against such a person only when the suspect represents a significant threat of serious injury or death to others (including the law enforcement officers). Whether al-Harethi in fact represented a significant threat of serious injury or death to others, however, was disputed. On the one hand, it appeared that US forces had had al-Harethi under active surveillance, not just at that moment, but for a number of weeks, suggesting that we could have waited for an opportune moment to apprehend him. On the other hand, a previous attempt to capture him resulted in the death of eighteen Yemeni soldiers.

Under the Military Force Paradigm, on the other hand, there is nothing wrong with a targeted strike against a military enemy. During World War II, when American cryptologists intercepted a message containing Japanese Admiral Yamamoto's flight plan for a secret mission in 1943, President Roosevelt ordered the navy to "get Yamamoto." A strike force of American fighter planes intercepted Yamamoto's flight group on April 18 and shot down the two bomber planes carrying Yamamoto and his military staff. If Yamamoto had been a criminal defendant, this aerial ambush could have been condemned in the same terms as the Yemen Predator strike, as "extrajudicial assassination." Yet, the weight of history has never viewed the Yamamoto ambush as an illegitimate assassination.

. . . .

In short, once al-Harethi is assumed to be a legitimate target, the main bases for criticizing the Predator strike collapse into operational arguments: how accurate was the information that al-Harethi was actually in the car, and were there so many other noncombatants in the vehicle so as to render killing everyone too disproportionate to the goal of killing al-Harethi.

III. A NORMATIVE ANALYSIS OF THE SHIFT IN COUNTERTERRORISM STRATEGY FROM BUSH TO OBAMA

The Obama administration's counterterrorism strategy cannot be considered a wholesale rejection of that of its predecessor, not when there are still thousands of suspected fighters detained without criminal charges at Bagram Airbase, when there are Guantanamo detainees slated for prosecution in military courts, and when aerial drones are engaged in seek-and-destroy missions in Afghanistan and Pakistan.

And yet, if there is not a sharp break between the two administrations, it cannot be said that President Obama has simply adopted his predecessor's policies in toto. Both presidents have rejected torture as an interrogation tool, but the Bush administration devoted considerable attention to distinguishing and justifying various forms of coercive and abusive interrogation as not being torture. President Bush's last attorney general, former District Judge Michael Mukasey, refused during his confirmation hearings to testify that waterboarding—simulating drowning —was torture. The controversial "torture memo" did argue in part that the president had inherent authority to order the torture of captured enemy combatants to extract relevant information, but a large portion of the memo attempted to define torture narrowly so that interrogation techniques like waterboarding would not qualify as prohibited conduct.

The Obama administration viewed waterboarding differently. Unlike Mukasey, Obama's nominee for attorney general—Eric Holder—unequivocally stated during his confirmation hearings that he believed waterboarding to be torture. President Obama quickly banned the procedure upon assuming office.

One might therefore describe the Obama administration as having continued in the same direction of counterterrorism strategy as the Bush administration, but as having moderated the more extreme elements of the latter. We can draw some tentative conclusions from this contrast and comparison:

A. "Military force is a necessary (but not sufficient) counterterrorism tool"

As clearly as he repudiated waterboarding and other forms of coercive interrogation, President Obama has equally clearly rejected the Law

Enforcement Paradigm. The use of missile-firing aerial drones alone proves as much, for such attacks would usually constitute unjustified force, if not outright murder, in any civilian context. So too would detention absent charges, a practice that the Obama administration has carried over at our military bases at Guantanamo Bay, Cuba, and Bagram Air Base in Afghanistan. But no one should be surprised at President Obama's use of the military to attack al Qaeda. As a candidate, he declared forcefully that if the United States had "actionable intelligence" and Pakistan refused to act, he was completely willing to order American military forces to take action.

Military force is a necessary tool in the fight against al Qaeda because there are limits to the reach of law enforcement....

. . . .

C. "International opinions toward the Bush and Obama administration counterterrorism policies are based less on substance than on perception."

. . . .

In the immediate aftermath of 9/11, President Bush's domestic popularity soared. Nearly every nation expressed sympathy toward the United States. Not surprisingly, there was broad support for the United States' plan to attack al Qaeda and the Taliban in Afghanistan; the North American Treaty Alliance (NATO) declared that 9/11 represented an attack on all alliance members.

When the world saw the first images from Guantanamo Bay— hooded detainees kneeling in the hot sun—President Bush's secretary of defense, Donald Rumsfeld, sought to reassure viewers that these detainees were the "worst of the worst." Subsequent analysis of public information about the detainees, however, called that assessment into question.

Meanwhile, the Bush administration began to focus on Iraq in 2002, culminating in the 2003 attack based on the articulated belief that Iraqi leader Saddam Hussein was continuing to develop nuclear, chemical, or biological weapons in violation of United Nations Security Council Resolutions 687 and 1441. Despite having failed to obtain a subsequent UN Security Council resolution explicitly authorizing a military attack, the United States and United Kingdom launched an invasion of Iraq in March 2003. The American and British militaries succeeded in capturing Saddam Hussein but failed to locate any banned weaponry or armaments. Whether it was reasonable to believe that Saddam Hussein still had chemical or biological weapons or was secretly reconstituting a nuclear weapons program, there were outcries that the Bush administration had willfully misled the American public (and the world).

In short, objections to President Bush's counterterrorism policies might be seen "as applied" in addition to "on their face." One could accept the legality of the use of military force against a non-state group such as al Qaeda, yet question the Bush administration's actual implementation of armed conflict. . . .

. . . .

CONCLUSION

It may have taken more than a year to reach a general consensus, but it is now readily apparent that the Obama administration is pursuing a counterterrorism strategy [that] is broadly consistent with that of the Bush administration. Differences exist, particularly as to the legality of certain interrogation methods; but the broad strategy remains largely the same despite the change in administration.

Not surprisingly, consensus as to the positive description of what the Obama administration has been doing has not resulted in a consensus of normative opinions about those actions. Some who had hoped that President Obama would completely repudiate his predecessor's policies were predictably outraged. Supporters of the previous administration, on the other hand, took delight in their seeming vindication.

President Obama's supporters may feel legitimate disappointment over his failure to have closed the detention facility at Guantanamo Bay, as he had promised during his campaign. But closing that detention facility or keeping it open was just a tactical-level decision. The use of military force, on the other hand, was a strategic decision with far greater ramifications; and Obama clearly telegraphed his strategic position during his candidacy.

However, assuming that President Obama continues his current counterterrorism approach of prosecuting some suspected terrorists, such as Faisal Shahzad (the so-called Times Square Bomber), in civilian courts, while detaining others, such as the high-level al Qaeda suspects, one can predict that erosion of his credibility will likewise increase domestic and international opposition to military detention without civilian charges and targeted missile strikes.

PART 2

INTERROGATION PRACTICE

From Tortue to *Miranda* Warnings

RELIABILITY, WATERBOARDED CONFESSIONS AND RECLAIMING THE LESSONS OF *BROWN V. MISSISSIPPI* IN THE TERRORISM CASES
(2009)

M. Katherine B. Darmer

INTRODUCTION

Recent debates regarding where Khalid Shaikh Mohammed ("KSM") and other accused terrorists will be tried is certain to revive the debate about the use of "waterboarding" to obtain confessions from him. KSM was subjected to waterboarding 183 times. While some will contend that waterboarding is not torture, I . . . agree with those who have forcefully argued that waterboarding does constitute torture. With that premise on the table, this essay seeks to draw on lessons from our past jurisprudence to illustrate that the results of waterboarded confessions cannot be used in any criminal trial and should not be used in any other proceeding that has as its purpose ascertaining whether a person engaged in terrorism or any other criminal act. It also argues, however, that while "waterboarded" confessions should present relatively easy cases for exclusion (especially in conventional criminal trials), current jurisprudence leaves problematic "protection gaps" that could arguably permit the introduction of tortured confessions in trials and other contexts.

This essay traces the most problematic "protection gap" to a shift away from a concern with reliability in the Supreme Court's post-*Miranda* confessions jurisprudence, particularly in *Colorado v Connelly*, where the Court maintained that a confession's potential unreliability did not make its admission unconstitutional. While that case involved the confession of a person suffering from psychotic delusions, I here develop the argument that *Connelly* has significant implications for the terrorism and national security cases. In order to avoid results that are plainly inconsistent with the Supreme Court's repudiation of the use of a tortured confession almost 75 years ago in the important case of *Brown v. Mississippi*, notions of due process need to be interpreted more broadly, consistent with *Brown*'s recognition of an absolute prohibition on torture in our adversarial system.

Even ten years ago, torture was not really part of our national debate. That has changed since 9/11. Indeed, no longer is torture unthinkable because we know it has occurred. The Abu Ghraib scandal revealed that American soldiers had badly mistreated detainees. American agents have repeatedly waterboarded suspects. Some suspects have died in custody.

Torture is sometimes debated in deontological terms, and sometimes on utilitarian grounds. In the former context, arguments are made about the *wrongness* of torture, even if it "sometimes works." The latter debate instead asks *whether torture works* (by yielding reliable evidence) and *whether using torture is worth it.* . . . My hope is to draw from our collective history to suggest that, from the standpoint of the *law*, at least, the question of *whether torture yields reliable evidence* has been settled. In *Brown v. Mississippi* the Court denounced torture, declaring that confessions wrought through brutality are unreliable. That proposition should remain settled.

Historically, the Court has emphasized that, regarding confessions, reliability is necessary but not sufficient in order for a confession to be admissible into evidence. Because tortured confessions have been considered, under the law, to be unreliable, they are *per se* excluded. Reliance on such evidence undermines the integrity of any system that purports to be fairly adjudicating guilt or innocence, and institutional integrity was of central importance to the *Brown* Court. My hope is to turn away from the particular focus of whether torture may have extracted reliable information in a particular case (e.g., the case of KSM) and instead focus on torture as a practice that has been properly rejected as a matter of institutional integrity.

Following this introduction, I will turn to the Court's pre-*Miranda*, twentieth-century confessions jurisprudence, which until 1966 developed under the Due Process Clause. The year 1966 marked a turning point with the Court's landmark decision in *Miranda v. Arizona*. While intended to be a progressive decision that would further protect defendants' rights, the decision had the unfortunate effect, during the development of a grudging post-*Miranda* jurisprudence, of de-emphasizing reliability. This jurisprudential shift has unfortunate implications in the post-9/11 era. Thus, I will discuss the *Miranda* case and the post-*Miranda* cases in order to illuminate fissures that have left suspects vulnerable to a return to the days when guilt could be determined based on tortured confessions. While the terrorism cases present a myriad of difficult issues, my goal in this essay is relatively modest. My ultimate aim is to demonstrate that reliability is absolutely necessary, though not sufficient, and that the lessons of *Brown* have important implications for a robust understanding of the demands of due process. As the branches of government struggle with how to deal with the terrorism cases, we would be wise to learn from the lessons of our own history.

I. RELIABILITY DURING THE DEVELOPMENT OF CONFESSIONS LAW UNDER THE DUE PROCESS REGIME

Prior to its landmark decision in *Miranda v. Arizona*, the Supreme Court developed a confessions jurisprudence under the due process clauses, which provides that no state may "deprive any person of life, liberty, or property, without due process of law." In determining whether a confession violated the due process clause, the Court focused historically on the question of "voluntariness."

As the Court explained almost fifty years ago, "a complex of values" underlay the Court's prohibition on the use of confessions deemed "involuntary." One key consideration under the voluntariness test was preventing the introduction into evidence of false, or unreliable, confessions, including those obtained through physical coercion.

A. *Brown v. Mississippi* and the Condemnation of Torture

In *Brown v. Mississippi*,[1] the Court unequivocally condemned a state court's reliance on tortured confessions as being inconsistent with the due process clause, overturning a conviction obtained though the use of confessions wrought through brute force. Officials, accompanied by an angry mob, extracted a confession from one suspect after hanging him from a limb of a tree with a rope, tying him to the tree, whipping him, then whipping him again on a separate occasion. Two other suspects were whipped with a leather strap and buckle. The facts relating to the defendants' torture and abuse were undisputed. With regard to the first defendant,

> they hanged him by a rope to the limb of a tree, and, having let him
> down, they hung him again, and when he was let down the second

time, and he still protested his innocence, he was tied to a tree and whipped, and, still declining to accede to the demands that he confess, he was finally released, and he returned with some difficulty to his home, suffering intense pain and agony. The record of the testimony shows that the signs of the rope on his neck were visible during the so-called trial. A day or two thereafter the said deputy, accompanied by another, returned to the home of the said defendant and arrested him, and departed with the prisoner towards the jail in an adjoining county, but went by a route which led into the state of Alabama; and while on the way, in that state, the deputy stopped and again severely whipped the defendant, declaring that he would continue the whipping until he confessed, and the defendant then agreed to confess to such a statement as the deputy would dictate, and he did so, after which he was delivered to jail.

Accounts of "waterboarding" are also horrifying. As a United States aviator subjected to the practice by Japanese captors described it:

I was put on my back on the floor with my arms and legs stretched out, one guard holding each limb. The towel was wrapped around my face and put across my face and water poured on. They poured water on this towel until I was almost unconscious from strangulation, then they would let up until I'd get my breath, then they'd start over again.[2]

As described by a journalist who voluntarily underwent the experience during recent debates about the practice:

[I]nhalation brought the damp cloths tight against my nostrils, as if a huge wet paw had been suddenly and annihilatingly clamped over my face. Unable to determine whether I was breathing in or out, and flooded more with sheer panic than with mere water, I triggered the pre-arranged signal and felt the unbelievable relief of being pulled upright.... [Following a second episode], I was an abject prisoner of my gag reflex. The interrogators would hardly have had time to ask me any questions and I would quite readily have agreed to supply any answer.[3]

In a unanimous decision seventy-three years ago in *Brown*, the Court found a "clear denial of due process" where torture was relied upon, noting further that its decision did not depend upon the application of the self-incrimination clause (which did not yet apply to the states). The Court explained that the self-incrimination clause is directed to "the process . . . by which the accused may be called as a witness and required to testify. Compulsion by torture to extort a confession is a different matter." It is significant that the Court here recognized a due process right to procedures involving confessions, wholly apart from the right against self-incrimination.

. . . .

The Court described a trial as "mere pretense" when state authorities "have contrived a conviction resting solely upon confessions obtained by violence." Applying those principles to the case before it, the Court found that "[i]t would be difficult to conceive of methods more revolting to the sense of justice than those taken to procure the confessions of these petitioners"; the use of such confessions at trial "was a clear denial of due process." The Supreme Court found it significant that the trial court both knew of how the confessions had been obtained and knew that there was no other evidence upon which to base a conviction. The ensuing conviction and sentence were thus "void for the want of the essential elements of due process."

Reliability was a central concern of the *Brown* Court. As Laurie

Magid has noted, "In *Brown* and other early cases, the Court clearly believed that innocent persons had been convicted, and that their confessions were unreliable."[4]

In an important article exploring the difference between the illegal procurement of evidence and the illegal use of evidence, Arnold Loewy notes that *Brown* involved a case in which the confession was unconstitutionally obtained. In his words, "For an extreme example, consider *Brown v. Mississippi*, in which the defendants were severely beaten and were threatened with continuous beatings unless they confessed. Such police conduct is clearly wrong in itself, regardless of whether any confession is used or even obtained. Consequently, defendants like Brown, but unlike Miranda, can sue the police officers for violating their constitutional rights."[5] While Loewy is almost certainly correct that, modernly, officers engaged in the conduct at issue in *Brown* would be subject to suit, that issue was not before the *Brown* Court. Moreover, while the *Brown* Court condemned the actions of the law enforcement officers, its holding also spoke to the wrongful use of the tortured confessions and the complicity of the trial court in knowingly permitting their introduction. *Brown* is not just a case about the wrongful extraction of a confession but a case about the violence done to due process by the later use of those confessions. This fact has implications for current debates about bringing suspected terrorists to justice.

B. Reliability in the Post-*Brown* Era

In terms of the Court's due process confessions jurisprudence, the role of reliability in post-*Brown* cases was less plain. Rather, "[e]ven though reliability was clearly uppermost in the Court's mind when it decided *Brown v. Mississippi*, the Court gave mixed and confusing signals in subsequent cases about the precise rationale for the voluntariness requirement."[6] In *Lisenba v. California* (1941), for example, the Court noted that "[t]he aim of the requirement of due process is not to exclude presumptively false evidence, but to prevent fundamental unfairness in the use of evidence, whether true or false." In *Lisenba* the Court affirmed the conviction, finding that the conduct of law enforcement in obtaining a confession was not "grave" enough to warrant reversal.

In most of the post-*Brown* cases, however, reliability was implicitly considered to be of fundamental importance. In moving beyond *Brown*, the Court made clear that some police methods falling short of the rank brutality of *Brown* were also inconsistent with due process. *Brown* was a floor but not a ceiling. In the same way, even if not explicitly stated, reliability was generally a floor but not a ceiling: a confession could be deemed "involuntary" and thus inadmissible even if there was no real concern with reliability.

. . . .

II. THE PROBLEMATIC SHIFT AWAY FROM THE ESSENTIAL IMPORTANCE OF RELIABILITY

A. The Self-Incrimination Clause and Due Process

With its decision in *Miranda v. Arizona*, the Court made the Fifth Amendment self-incrimination clause the centerpiece of its analysis of future confessions, at least of those in routine interrogation cases. In *Miranda*, of course, the Court held that "custodial interrogation" is inherently coercive and that any confession taken in police custody will be presumed coerced unless the now-famous *Miranda* warnings are given. Because the Fifth Amendment explicitly provides that no one shall be required in "any criminal trial" to be a witness against him/herself, the protections of the Fifth Amendment are triggered, in the custodial inter-rogation context, only when there is a criminal trial. It does not apply in other contexts and does not act as a "check" on abusive police conduct itself, as illustrated in the recent case *Chavez v. Martinez*.[7]

In *Chavez*, the Court held that the Fifth Amendment did not apply in circumstances where a suspect shot by the police was later questioned relentlessly in a hospital. Because the statements were never used against the defendant at a trial, his claims under the Fifth Amendment were unavailing. The Supreme Court left open the possibility, however, that police had violated the suspect's due process rights, and the Ninth Circuit ultimately held that the facts indeed suggested a due process violation:

> The Fourteenth Amendment's Due Process Clause protects individ-uals from state action that either "shocks the conscience," or interferes with rights "implicit in the concept of ordered liberty." Martinez alleges that Chavez brutally and incessantly questioned him, after he had been shot in the face, and back and leg and would go on to suffer blindness and partial paralysis, and interfered with his medical treat-ment while he was "screaming in pain . . . and going in and out of con-sciousness." . . . A clearly established right, fundamental to ordered liberty, is freedom from coercive police interrogation. . . . [U]nder the facts alleged by Martinez, Chavez violated Martinez's clearly estab-lished due process rights.

The difference between the use of a confession at trial in derogation of the Fifth Amendment and the wrongful extraction of a confession that might violate the due process clause but not the self-incrimination clause is usefully illustrated in Justice Marshall's dissenting opinion in *New York v. Quarles*.[8] In that case, police asked a suspect about the loca-tion of a gun without first providing *Miranda* warnings. The Court, in a majority opinion written by Justice Rehnquist, found that *Miranda*'s "doctrinal underpinnings" did not require that it "be applied in all its rigor" to questions reasonably motivated by public safety concerns. The Court created a "public safety" exception to *Miranda*.

Justice Marshall forcefully argued, in dissent, that the creation of such an "exception" was inconstant with the underlying rationale of *Miranda*, which held that custodial interrogation is inherently coercive (and is no less coercive when "emergency questioning" might be justified). If there is a threat to the public safety, Marshall agreed, the police should by all means question a suspect but the results of the questioning cannot be introduced at trial. Questioning is *itself* not constitutionally infirm; rather, it is the *use* of the presumptively coerced confession at a trial that implicates the Fifth Amendment. The due process clause sets limits on police conduct but the Fifth Amendment's self-incrimination clause, standing alone, does not. In Marshall's words:

> If a bomb is about to explode or the public is otherwise imminently imperiled, the police are free to interrogate suspects without advising them of their constitutional rights. . . . If trickery is necessary to protect the public, then the police may trick a suspect into confessing. While the Fourteenth Amendment sets limits on such behavior, nothing in the Fifth Amendment or our decision in *Miranda v. Arizona* proscribes this sort of emergency questioning. All the Fifth Amendment forbids is the introduction of coerced statements at trial.

Marhsall's understanding of the limits of Fifth Amendment protections was precisely at issue in *Chavez*. Regardless of the brutality that may be employed, the Fifth Amendment does not "kick in" unless and until such tortured confessions are used at trial. Rather, due process is the only real limit on law enforcement tactics themselves.

The protections of due process are also complete, however. Indeed, the intersection of the Fifth Amendment and the due process clauses yield problematic "protection gaps" not only regarding possible mistreatment, but even regarding conviction or imprisonment. Specifically, suspects are vulnerable to being subject to convictions or other deprivations of liberty based upon unreliable confessions, including even those extracted by the type of torture that was unanimously condemned by the Court almost seventy-five years ago in *Brown*. That is because the Court's later jurisprudence has de-emphasized reliability.

I have argued elsewhere that, by its terms, the Fifth Amendment should prevent the introduction of any "truly compelled statements" at trial, whether or not those statements are extracted by United States law enforcement officers or by foreign agents in the terrorism context. Under an appropriately robust interpretation of the Fifth Amendment's prohibition on compelled self-incrimination, waterboarded statements would be forbidden in a trial. Other interpretations of the Fifth Amendment's proscription of self-incrimination, however, suggest that that particular constitutional protection is not directed at forbidding the results of brutality. As the *Brown* Court itself stated when deciding that case on due process grounds: the self-incrimination clause is directed to "the process . . . by which the accused may be called as a witness and required to testify. Compulsion by torture to extort a confession is a different matter."

By the time *Miranda* was decided, the Court was more concerned with psychological rather than physical intimidation and was struggling to simplify its confessions jurisprudence, which had become tangled and unclear during the development of the due process voluntariness test, post-*Brown*. Few cases since *Brown* have dealt with instances of police brutality, and where confessions are rejected on that basis, the Court has continued to rely on the due process clause, which serves as a "'backup' test that is increasingly difficult to meet."[9]

B. The Court's Innervated Due Process Jurisprudence After *Colorado v. Connelly*

At first blush, it might not appear that *Colorado v. Connelly*[10] is problematic from the perspective of ensuring that there are limits on what can be done to terrorism suspects. The police in that case were responsible for no harsh treatment of a suspect whatsoever. Rather, a suspect literally approached a police officer on the street and said that he wanted to discuss a murder he had committed. The officer gave the defendant *Miranda* warnings, but the suspect persisted in his stated desire to confess, provided information about a murder, and took the police to the alleged location of the murder. The Court focused on the lack of any misconduct by officers and on the underlying "deterrence" rationale of excluding evidence.

In the course of deciding the case, however, the Court denigrated reliability concerns, narrowing the focus of the earlier *Brown* Court's concern about reliable process. This severing of "reliability" from the considerations of due process is deeply problematic from the perspective of ensuring that trials and trial-like proceedings are not tainted by the use of unreliable evidence.

At a pretrial hearing in *Connelly*, a state psychiatrist testified that Connelly was "suffering from chronic schizophrenia" and had experienced "command hallucinations" and that his confession was motivated by psychosis. The Colorado trial court suppressed the statements as "involuntary" and the Colorado Supreme Court affirmed, finding that the introduction of the statements alone was sufficient "state action" to implicate the due process clause of the Fourteenth Amendment.

The Supreme Court, in a majority opinion written by Chief Justice Rehnquist, disagreed with the state courts, finding that a due process violation depends upon a finding of "coercive police activity," which was not present in *Connelly* because the defendant had walked up to an officer on the street to confess. The Court emphasized that "coercive police misconduct" was the "catalyst" for the Court's decision in *Brown v. Mississippi*, where of course the brutal police conduct contrasted sharply with the benign conduct of officers in *Connelly*.

Implicitly criticizing the Colorado Supreme Court for finding that "the very admission of the evidence in a court of law was sufficient state action to implicate the due process clause," Justice Rehnquist noted that the Court's cases since *Brown* "have focused upon the crucial element of police overreaching. While each confession case has turned on its own set of factors justifying the conclusion that police conduct was oppressive, all have contained a substantial element of coercive police conduct. Absent police conduct causally related to the confession, there is simply no basis for concluding that any state actor has deprived a criminal defendant of due process of law."

Focusing on the deterrence rationale of the exclusionary rule and the lack of any wrongful conduct on the part of police, the Court declined to "require sweeping inquires into the criminal mind of a criminal defendant who has confessed." Conceding that a confession such as Connelly's might prove "quite unreliable," it determined that such issues were matters for the laws of evidence and did not implicate the Constitution. Reducing the purpose of the exclusionary rule simply to deterrence, the Court asserted that the purpose of "excluding evidence seized in violation of the Constitution is to substantially deter future violations of the Constitution." Because there was no misconduct of law enforcement to deter in this case, the Court essentially found that to be the end of the inquiry.

In his dissenting opinion, Justice Brennan emphasized that the voluntariness inquiry regarding confessions has historically been concerned not just with police misconduct but also with a suspect's free will and with reliability.

In that opinion, Brennan tacitly addressed the issue that, prior to *Connelly*, a finding of reliability was necessary but not sufficient in order for a confession to be admitted:

> The instant case starkly highlights the danger of admitting a confession by a person with a severe mental illness. The trial court made no findings concerning the reliability of Mr. Connelly's involuntary confession, since it believed that the confession was excludable on the basis of involuntariness. However, the overwhelming evidence in the record points to the unreliability of Mr. Connelly's delusional mind....

> ....

> Minimum standards of due process should require that the trial court find substantial indicia of reliability, on the basis of evidence extrinsic to the confession itself, before admitting the confession of a mentally ill person into evidence.... To hold otherwise allows the State to imprison and possibly to execute a mentally ill defendant based solely upon an inherently unreliable confession.

As I have argued elsewhere, the majority's almost exclusive focus on deterrable police misconduct leaves suspects vulnerable to having confessions introduced against them if those confessions were extracted by, for example, foreign agents over whom the United States has no control. But, importantly, the seminal decision in *Brown* did not simply turn on the fact that the sheriff and his deputies abominably abused the defendants. Rather, the Court focused on the use of the confession at a trial, finding that it was the use of the confession itself that violated due process. Justice Rehnquist's quote of just a phrase of *Brown*, i.e., that the police action at issue was "revolting to the sense of justice," overlooks that the Court went on to say that it was the confession's "use" that violated due process.

To be sure, the conduct of the police officers in *Connelly* appears to be above reproach and dramatically different than the abusive conduct of the *Brown* law enforcement officers. But it is an overly narrow reading of *Brown* to suggest that that was just a case about "misconduct" by law enforcement officers. It was also a case about trial integrity, and the expectation that trial judges should serve as gatekeepers in preventing the introduction of patently unreliable evidence obtained through torture. Indeed, the eminent confessions law scholar Yale Kamisar has opined that the outcome in *Brown* would have been the same if the confessions in that case had been obtained by "torturous acts of the Ku Klux Klan" rather than through official brutality.[11] A close reading of *Brown* reveals that the Court seemed particularly concerned that a judge would participate in a "pretense of a trial" that relied upon such evidence. As Mark Godsey has pointed out regarding *Connelly*, "In holding that there was no 'state action' in the case, because the officer did nothing to induce Connelly's confession, the Court ignored the admission into evidence of the confession as a possible basis for state action. The admission into evidence of a false confession had been the predicate 'state action' in *Brown v. Mississippi*."[12]

The *Connelly* Court's cramped view of the state's responsibilities with respect to the use of unreliable confessions is particularly problematic in light of later jurisprudence taking a more expansive view of "state action." In *Edmonson v. Leesville Concrete Co.*, for example, the Court held that a private litigant's exercise of racially discriminatory peremptory strikes against jurors amounted to state action because it arose in the context of a trial in which even private litigants act pursuant to state rules and procedures. If a private litigant's acts can implicate the Fourteenth Amendment, surely should also the introduction into trial of an unreliable confession.

Of course, the author of *Connelly*—Chief Justice Rehnquist—joined O'Connor's dissenting opinion in *Edmonson*, which argued that "[n]ot everything that happens in a courtroom is state action."

The *Connelly* case has been much criticized, and most of the focus has been on the case's implication for mentally incompetent defendants. I believe there are troubling implication in the terrorism context, as well, and that the case results in "protection gaps" for terrorism suspects.

III. IMPLICATIONS OF HISTORIC JURISPRUDENCE IN THE TERRORIST CASES

A. Confessions Obtained by US Agents

1. Conventional Criminal Trials

The announcement that KSM and others would be tried in conventional criminal trials was controversial, in part because of the "expansive protections" that are normally accorded to defendants in conventional criminal courts. Under either a Fifth Amendment or due process analysis, "waterboarded" confessions should prevent an easy case for exclusion. In a conventional criminal court, terrorism suspects may even be able to claim *Miranda* rights. I have argued elsewhere that *Miranda* both overprotects and underprotects in the terrorism context, and that terrorism suspects should not have the benefit of *Miranda* warnings. Even leaving aside the Court's *Miranda* jurisprudence, however, a confession obtained by waterboarding at the hands of United States agents fails the due process inquiry. Since *Brown*, it has been well established that confessions obtained through torture should be categorically forbidden.

Upon a closer look, however, the case may not be as easy as it seems.

RELIABILITY, WATERBOARDED CONFESSIONS

When one looks at *Connelly*'s focus on the need for deterrence, the question of exclusion of such confessions gets tangled up in the question of whether agents who administered waterboarding acted illegally. This question, in turn, is complicated by the fact that former administration lawyers wrote lengthy memoranda seeking to justify tactics such as waterboarding for particular detainees. Most notoriously, the Bybee-Yoo Torture and Power Memorandum ("BYTAP") opined that an interrogation method would not constitute "torture" unless the pain inflicted was tantamount to the pain consistent with "a sufficiently serious physical condition or injury such as death, organ failure, or serious impairment of bodily functions." While I agree with those who argue that waterboarding constitutes torture even under this narrow BYTAP definition, that proposition remains unsettled, and it seems plain that agents acting under the authority of BYTAP would argue that they believed in good faith that waterboarding was permitted. Indeed, later administration legal memoranda specifically permitted waterboarding, including that used against KSM. If agents used waterboarding in "good faith" reliance upon legal memoranda, was there "misconduct" to "deter" under the rationale of *Connelly*? *Connelly*'s narrow focus on the lack of "wrongdoing" by law enforcement in that case and its complete deconstitutionalization of issues of reliability, standing alone, suggest that it is not inconceivable that arguments could be made to support the use of waterboarded confessions even in conventional criminal trials.

To be sure, the current attorney general is on record that "waterboarding" constitutes torture, but we have seen this administration retreat from other civil liberties positions relevant to the War on Terror since the election. Moreover, fundamental human rights protections should not be subject to the vagaries of who inhabits the White House. The strong message of *Brown*—that a trial lacks integrity if it relies in any way upon torture—is an enduring lesson that risks being undermined by *Connelly*.

2. Proceedings Outside of the Conventional Court System

Some detainees will be tried before military commissions, rather than in conventional criminal courts. Proceedings before military commissions provide fewer formal rights than do trials. The Military Commissions Act of 2006 ("MCA") provides "vastly more limited protections than do either ordinary criminal trials or traditional military courts martial." While purporting to ban "torture," again, United States agents could plausibly argue that they understood waterboarding *not to constitute torture*. The MCA includes a "good-faith defense" that applies retroactively to cover the period between September 11, 2001, and the passage of the Detainee Treatment Act of 2005 ("DTA"). Moreover, statements can be introduced in military commission proceedings when the amount of "coercion" used is the subject of dispute.

Even more troubling is the fact that detainees can be held indefinitely as "enemy combatants" based merely on flawed Combatant Status Review Tribunals ("CSRTs"). CSRTs specifically permit holding detainees based upon information obtained through torture. While the DTA (also known as the McCain Amendment) purported to deal with the torture problem, its antitorture provision applies only to future CSRTs, not to those held before the passage of the act. The DTA bans interrogation techniques that are not authorized by the Army Field Manual (which prohibits waterboarding) but it does not ban other disputed techniques, such as "forced standing."

The fact that the DTA does not apply retroactively, and provides for a "good faith defense" for those who may have waterboarded before its passage, means that detainees could continue to be held based upon the results of brutality. Yet the lesson of *Brown* is that we can have no confidence, as an institutional matter, if decisions regarding guilt or indefinite detention are based upon tortured confessions.

RELIABILITY, WATERBOARDED CONFESSIONS

A. Confessions Obtained by Foreign Agents

Connelly has even more dire implications for the use of confessions obtained by foreign agents over whom the United States exercises no control. *Connelly*'s focus on deterrence and deconstitutionalization of reliability means that a tortured confession obtained abroad by foreign agents could be introduced into an American court consistent with *Connelly*'s interpretation of due process. Notably, I am not referring here to the practice of "extraordinary rendition," which presents a wholly different problem. In cases where the United States deliberately renders a suspect abroad on the understanding that he will be tortured, there is "deterrable" misconduct if United States officials participated in the rendering, and arguably such conduct could run afoul even of *Connelly*'s narrowed view of due process (although questions of "good faith" outlined above would still adhere). Where confessions are obtained with no involvement by US agents, however, *Connelly* would suggest that confessions could be used despite unreliability. This is deeply problematic.

CONCLUSION

The lesson of *Brown* is that courts should act as gatekeepers to forbid the use of tortured confessions in court. Even beyond conventional criminal courts, any system designed to adjudicate guilt or innocence with integrity cannot rely on tortured confessions. Our own Supreme Court recognized that due process is offended by torture almost seventy-five years ago. And the due process violation it identified was not just the torture inflicted by law enforcement, but the systematic offense to due process wrought by the reliance on torture at the "pretense" of a trial.

After 2001, we are in danger of failing the lessons of *Brown*. A more robust interpretation of due process, with a focus on both reliability of confessions and the integrity of judicial and quasi-judicial proceedings, is truer to our history and values[13] than the notion that exclusion serves no goal other than deterrence and that reliability serves no part of the Constitution.

MEMORANDUM FOR ALBERTO R. GONZALES, COUNSEL TO THE PRESIDENT

US Department of Justice
Office of Legal Counsel

Office of the
Assistant Attorney General

Washington, DC 20530

August 1, 2002

Re: Standards of Conduct for Interrogation
Under 18 U.S.C. §§ 2340–2340A

Y ou have asked for our Office's views regarding the standards of conduct under the Convention against Torture and Other Cruel, Inhuman, and Degrading Treatment or Punishment as implemented by Sections 2340–2340A of title 18 of the United States Code. As we understand it, this question has arisen in the context of the conduct of interrogations outside of the United States. We conclude below that Section 2340A proscribes acts inflicting, and that are specifically intended to inflict, severe pain or suffering, whether mental or physical. Those acts must be of an extreme nature to rise to the level of torture within the meaning of Section 2340A and the Convention. We further conclude that certain acts may be cruel, inhuman, or degrading, but still not produce pain and suffering of the requisite intensity to fall within Section 2340A's proscription against torture. We conclude by examining possible defenses that would negate any claim that certain interrogation methods violate the statute.

In Part I, we examine the criminal statute's text and history. We conclude that for an act to constitute torture as defined in Section 2340, it must inflict pain that is difficult to endure. Physical pain amounting to torture must be equivalent in intensity to the pain accompanying serious physical injury, such as organ failure, impairment of bodily function, or even death. For purely mental pain or suffering to amount to torture under Section 2340, it must result in serious psychological harm of significant duration, for example, lasting for months or even years....

... In Part IV, we examine international decisions regarding the use of sensory deprivation techniques. These cases make clear that while many of these techniques may amount to cruel, inhuman, or degrading treatment, they do not produce pain or suffering of the necessary intensity to meet the definition of torture. From these decisions, we conclude that there is a wide range of such techniques that will not rise to the level of torture.

In Part V, we discuss whether Section 2340A may be unconstitutional if applied to interrogations undertaken of enemy combatants pursuant to the President's Commander in Chief powers. We find that in the circumstances of the current war against al Qaeda and its allies, prosecution under Section 2340A may be barred because enforcement of the statute would represent an unconstitutional infringement of the President's authority to conduct war. In Part VI, we discuss defenses to an allegation that an interrogation method might violate the statute. We conclude that, under the current circumstances, necessity or self-defense may justify interrogation methods that might violate Section 2340A.

MEMORANDUM FOR ALBERTO R. GONZALES, COUNSEL TO THE PRESIDENT

I. 18 U.S.C. §§ 2340–2340A

Section 2340A makes it a criminal offense for any person "outside the United States [to] commit or [attempt] to commit torture." Section 2340 defines the act of torture as an:

> act committed by a person acting under the color of law specifically intended to inflict severe physical or mental pain or suffering (other than pain or suffering incidental to lawful sanctions) upon another person within his custody or physical control.

. . . .

. . . The key statutory phrase in the definition of torture is the statement that acts amount to torture if they cause "severe physical or mental pain or suffering." In examining the meaning of a statute, its text must be the starting point. . . . The statute does not, however, define the term "severe." "In the absence of such a definition, we construe a statutory term in accordance with its ordinary or natural meaning." *FDIC v. Meyer* (1994). The dictionary defines "severe" as "[u]nsparing in exaction, punishment, or censure" or "[I]nflicting discomfort or pain hard to endure; sharp; afflictive; distressing; violent; extreme; as *severe* pain, anguish, torture." *Webster's New International Dictionary* 2295 (2d ed. 1935). . . . Thus, the adjective "severe" conveys that the pain or suffering must be of such a high level of intensity that the pain is difficult for the subject to endure.

Congress's use of the phrase "severe pain" elsewhere in the United States Code can shed more light on its meaning. . . . Significantly, the phrase "severe pain" appears in statutes defining an emergency medical condition for the purpose of providing health benefits. . . . They treat severe pain as an indicator of ailments that are likely to result in permanent and serious physical damage in the absence of immediate medial treatment. Such damage must rise to the level of death, organ failure, or the permanent impairment of a significant body function. These statutes suggest that "severe pain," as used in Section 2340, must rise to a similarly high level—the level that would ordinarily be associated with a sufficiently serious physical condition or injury such as death, organ failure, or serious impairment of body functions—in order to constitute torture. . . .

Section 2340 gives further guidance as to the meaning of "severe mental pain or suffering," as distinguished from severe physical pain and suffering. The statute defines "severe mental pain or suffering" as:

> the prolonged mental harm caused by or resulting from—
>
> (A) the intentional infliction or threatened infliction of severe physical pain or suffering;
>
> (B) the administration or application, or threatened administration or application, of mind-altering substances or other procedures calculated to disrupt profoundly the senses or the personality;
>
> (C) the threat of imminent death; or
>
> (D) the threat that another person will imminently be subjected to death, severe physical pain or suffering, or the administration or application of mind-altering substances or other procedures calculated to disrupt profoundly the senses or personality.

18 U.S.C. § 2340(2). In order to prove "severe mental pain or suffering," the statute requires proof of "prolonged mental harm" that was caused by or resulted from one of four enumerated acts. . . .

. . . .

IV. INTERNATIONAL DECISIONS

International decisions can prove of some value in assessing what conduct might rise to the level of severe mental pain or suffering. Although decisions by foreign or international bodies are in no way binding authority upon the United States, they provide guidance about how other nations will likely react to our interpretation of the CAT [Convention against Torture] and Section 2340. As this part will discuss, other Western nations have generally used a high standard in determining whether interrogation techniques violate the international prohibition on torture. In fact, these decisions have found various aggressive interrogation methods to, at worst, constitute cruel, inhuman, and degrading treatment, but not torture. These decisions only reinforce our view that there is a clear distinction between the two standards and that only extreme conduct, resulting in pain that is of an intensity often accompanying serious physical injury, will violate the latter.

A. European Court of Human Rights

An analogue to CAT's provisions can be found in the European Convention on Human Rights and Fundamental Freedoms (the "European Convention"). This convention prohibits torture, though it offers no definition of it. It also prohibits cruel, inhuman, or degrading treatment or punishment. By barring both types of acts, the European Convention implicitly distinguishes between them and further suggests that torture is a grave act beyond cruel, inhuman, or degrading treatment or punishment. Thus, while neither the European Convention nor the European Court of Human Rights decisions interpreting that convention would be authority for the interpretation of Sections 2340–2340A, the European Convention decisions concerning torture nonetheless provide a useful barometer of the international view of what actions amount to torture.

The leading European Court of Human Rights case explicating the differences between torture and cruel, inhuman, or degrading treatment or punishment is *Ireland v. the United Kingdom* (1978). . . . Careful attention to this case is worthwhile . . . also because the Reagan administration relied on this case in reaching the conclusion that the term torture is reserved in international usage for "extreme, deliberate, and unusually cruel practices." (S. Treaty Doc. 100-20, at 4).

The methods at issue in *Ireland* were:

(1) Wall Standing. The prisoner stands spread eagle against the wall, with fingers high above his head, and feet back so that he is standing on his toes such that all of his weight falls on his fingers.

(2) Hooding. A black or navy hood is placed over the prisoner's head and kept there except during the interrogation.

(3) Subjection to Noise. Pending interrogation, the prisoner is kept in a room with a loud and continuous hissing noise.

(4) Sleep Deprivation. Prisoners are deprived of sleep pending interrogation.

(5) Deprivation of Food and Drink. Prisoners receive a reduced diet during detention and pending interrogation.

The European Court of Human Rights concluded that these techniques used in combination, and applied for hours at a time, were inhuman and degrading but did not amount to torture. In analyzing whether these methods constituted torture, the court treated them as part of a single program. The court found that this program caused "if not actual bodily injury, at least intense physical and mental suffering to the person subjected thereto and also led to acute psychiatric disturbances during the interrogation." Thus, this program "fell into the category of inhuman treatment." The court further found that "[t]he techniques were also degrading since they were such as to arouse in their victims feeling of fear, anguish, and inferiority capable of humiliating and debasing them and possible [*sic*] breaking their physical or moral resistance." Yet, the court ultimately concluded:

> Although the five techniques, as applied in combination, undoubtedly amounted to inhuman and degrading treatment, although their object was the extraction of confession, the naming of others and/or information and although they were used systematically, they did not occasion suffering of the particular *intensity* and *cruelty* implied by the word torture. . . .

Thus, even though the court had concluded that the techniques produce "intense physical and mental suffering" and "acute psychiatric disturbances," they were not sufficient intensity or cruelty to amount to torture.

The court reached this conclusion based on the distinction the European Convention drew between torture and cruel, inhuman, or degrading treatment or punishment. The court reasoned that by expressly distinguishing between these two categories of treatment, the European Convention sought to "attach a special stigma to deliberate inhuman treatment causing very serious and cruel suffering." According to the court, "this distinction derives principally from a difference in the intensity of the suffering inflicted." The court further noted that this distinction paralleled the one drawn in the UN Declaration on the Protection from Torture, which specifically defines torture as "an aggravated and deliberate form of cruel, inhuman, or degrading treatment or punishment."

The court relied on this same "intensity/cruelty" distinction to conclude that some physical maltreatment fails to amount to torture. For example, four detainees were severely beaten and forced to stand spread eagle up against a wall. Other detainees were forced to stand spread eagle while an interrogator kicked them "continuously on the inside of the legs." Those detainees were beaten, some receiving injuries that were "substantial," and others received "massive" injuries. Another detainee was "subjected to . . . 'comparatively trivial' beatings" that resulted in a perforation of the detainee's eardrum and some "minor bruising." The court concluded that none of these situations "attain[ed] the particular level [of severity] inherent in the notion of torture."

. . . .

V. THE PRESIDENT'S COMMANDER IN CHIEF POWER

Even if an interrogation method arguably were to violate Section 2340A, the statute would be unconstitutional if it impermissibly encroached on the President's constitutional power to conduct a military campaign. As Commander in Chief, the President has the constitutional authority to order interrogations of enemy combatants to gain intelligence information concerning the military plans of the enemy. The demands of the Commander in Chief power are especially pronounced in the middle of a war in which the nation has already suffered a direct attack. In such a case, the information gained from interrogations may prevent future attacks by foreign enemies. Any effort to apply Section 2340A in a manner that interferes with the President's direction of such core war matters as the detention and interrogation of enemy combatants thus would be unconstitutional.

MEMORANDUM FOR ALBERTO R. GONZALES, COUNSEL TO THE PRESIDENT

A. The War with al Qaeda

At the outset, we should make clear the nature of the threat presently posed to the nation. While your request for legal advice is not specifically limited to the current circumstances, we think it is useful to discuss this question in the context of the current war against the al Qaeda terrorist network. The situation in which these issues arise is unprecedented in recent American history. Four coordinated terrorist attacks, using hijacked commercial airliners as guided missiles, took place in rapid succession on the morning of September 11, 2001. These attacks were aimed at critical government buildings in the nation's capital and landmark buildings in its financial center. . . . They caused thousands of deaths. . . . Moreover, these attacks are part of a violent campaign against the United States. . . .

In response, the government has engaged in a broad effort at home and abroad to counter terrorism. . . .

Despite these efforts, numerous upper-echelon leaders of al Qaeda and the Taliban, with access to active terrorist cells and other resources, remain at large. . . .

Al Qaeda continues to plan further attacks, such as destroying American civilian airliners and killing American troops, which have fortunately been prevented. It is clear that bin Laden and his organization have conducted several violent attacks on the United States and its nationals, and that they seek to continue to do so. Thus, the capture and interrogation of such individuals is clearly imperative to our national security and defense. Interrogation of captured al Qaeda operatives may provide information concerning the nature of al Qaeda plans and the identities of its personnel, which may prove invaluable in preventing further direct attacks on the United States and its citizens. Given the massive destruction and loss of life caused by the September 11 attacks, it is reasonable to believe that information gained from al Qaeda personnel could prevent attacks of a similar (if not greater) magnitude from occurring in the United States. The case of Jose Padilla, a.k.a. Abdullah al Mujahir, illustrates the importance of such information. Padilla allegedly had journeyed to Afghanistan and Pakistan, met with senior al Qaeda leaders, and hatched a plot to construct and detonate a radioactive dispersal device in the United States. After allegedly receiving training in wiring explosives and with a substantial amount of currency in his [possession], Padilla attempted in May 2002 to enter the United States to further his scheme. Interrogation of captured al Qaeda operatives allegedly allowed US intelligence and law enforcement agencies to track Padilla and to detain him upon his entry into the United States.

B. Interpretation to Avoid Constitutional Problems

. . . .

In order to respect the President's inherent constitutional authority to manage a military campaign against al Qaeda and its allies, Section 2340A must be construed as not applying to interrogations undertaken pursuant to his Commander in Chief authority. As our Office has consistently held during this administration and previous administrations, Congress lacks authority under Article I to set the terms and conditions under which the President may exercise his authority as Commander in Chief to control the conduct of operations during a war. . . .

. . . .

C. The Commander in Chief Power

. . . .

The text, structure, and history of the Constitution establish that the Founders entrusted the President with the primary responsibility, and therefore the power, to ensure the security of the United States in situations of grave and unforeseen emergencies. . . . [T]he structure of the Constitution demonstrates that any power traditionally understood as pertaining to the executive—which includes the conduct of warfare and the defense of the nation—unless expressly assigned in the Constitution to Congress, is vested in the President. Article II, Section 1 makes this clear by stating that the "executive Power shall be vested in a President of the United States of America." That sweeping grant vests in the President an unenumerated "executive power" and contrasts with the specific enumeration of the powers—those "herein"—granted to Congress in Article I. The implications of constitutional text and structure are confirmed by the practical consideration that national security decisions require the unity in purpose and energy in action that characterize the presidency rather than Congress.

. . . .

One of the core functions of the Commander in Chief is that of capturing, detaining, and interrogating members of the enemy. . . . It is well settled that the President may seize and detain enemy combatants, at least for the duration of the conflict, and the laws of war make clear that prisoners may be interrogated for information concerning the enemy, its strength, and its plans. Numerous Presidents have ordered the capture, detention, and questioning of enemy combatants during virtually every major conflict in the nation's history, including recent conflicts such as the Gulf, Vietnam, and Korean wars. Recognizing this authority, Congress has never attempted to restrict or interfere with the President's authority on this score.

Any effort by Congress to regulate the interrogation of battlefield combatants would violate the Constitution's sole vesting of the Commander in Chief authority in the President. There can be little doubt that intelligence operations, such as the detention and interrogation of enemy combatants and leaders, are both necessary and proper for the effective conduct of a military campaign. . . .

VI. DEFENSES

. . . Even if an interrogation method . . . might arguably cross the line drawn in Section 2340, and application of the statute was not held to be an unconstitutional infringement of the President's Commander in Chief authority, we believe that under the current circumstances certain justification defenses might be available that would potentially eliminate criminal liability. Standard criminal law defenses of necessity and self-defense could justify interrogation methods needed to elicit information to prevent a direct and imminent threat to the United States and its citizens.

A. Necessity

We believe that a defense of necessity could be raised, under the current circumstances, to an allegation of a Section 2340A violation. Often referred to as the "choice of evils" defense, necessity has been defined as follows:

Conduct that the actor believes to be necessary to avoid a harm or evil to himself or to another is justifiable, provided that:

(a) the harm or evil sought to be avoided by such conduct is greater than that sought to be prevented by the law defining the offense charged; and

(b) neither the Code nor other law defining the offense provides exceptions or defenses dealing with the specific situation involved; and

(c) a legislative purpose to exclude the justification claimed does not otherwise plainly appear.

Model Penal Code § 3.02.

. . . .

It appears to us that under the current circumstances the necessity defense could be successfully maintained in response to an allegation of a Section 2340A violation. On September 11, 2001, al Qaeda launched a surprise covert attack on civilian targets in the United States that led to the deaths of thousands and losses in the billions of dollars. According to public and governmental reports, al Qaeda has other sleeper cells within the United States that may be planning similar attacks. Indeed, al Qaeda plans apparently include efforts to develop and deploy chemical, biological, and nuclear weapons of mass destruction. Under these circumstances, a detainee may possess information that could enable the United States to prevent attacks that potentially could equal or surpass the September 11 attacks in their magnitude. Clearly, any harm that might occur during an interrogation would pale to insignificance compared to the harm avoided by preventing such an attack, which could take hundreds or thousands of lives.

Under this calculus, two factors will help indicate when the necessity defense could appropriately be invoked. First, the more certain that government officials are that a particular individual has information needed to prevent an attack, the more necessary interrogation will be. Second, the more likely it appears to be that a terrorist attack is likely to occur, and the greater the amount of damage expected from such an attack, the more that an interrogation to get information would become necessary. Of course, the strength of the necessity defense depends on the circumstances that prevail, and the knowledge of the government actors involved, when the interrogation is conducted. While every interrogation that might violate Section 2340A does not trigger a necessity defense, we can say that certain circumstances could support such a defense.

. . . .

B. Self-Defense

Even if a court were to find that a violation of Section 2340A was not justified by necessity, a defendant could still appropriately raise a claim of self-defense. The right to self-defense, even when it involves the use of deadly force, is deeply embedded in our law, both as to individuals and as to the nation as a whole. . . .

. . . .

CONCLUSION

For the foregoing reasons, we conclude that torture as defined in and proscribed by Sections 2340–2340A, covers only extreme acts. Severe pain is generally of the kind difficult for the victim to endure. Where the pain is physical, it must be of an intensity akin to that which accompanies serious physical injury such as death or organ failure. Severe mental pain requires suffering not just at the moment of infliction but it also requires lasting psychological harm, such as seen in mental disorders like posttraumatic stress disorder. Additionally, such severe mental pain can arise only from the predicate acts listed in Section 2340. Because the acts inflicting torture are extreme, there is significant range of acts that though they might constitute cruel, inhuman, or degrading treatment or punishment fail to rise to the level of torture.

Further, we conclude that under the circumstances of the current war against al Qaeda and its allies, application of Section 2340A to interrogations undertaken pursuant to the President's Commander in Chief powers may be unconstitutional. Finally, even if an interrogation method might violate Section 2340A, necessity or self-defense could provide justifications that would eliminate any criminal liability.

Please let us know if we can be of further assistance.
[signed]
Jay S. Bybee
Assistant Attorney General

TORTURE AND POSITIVE LAW
Jurisprudence for the White House
(2005)

Jeremy Waldron

In recently published memoranda, Justice Department lawyers have suggested that it is not in all circumstances wrong or unlawful to inflict pain in the course of interrogating terrorist suspects. Also, at least one legal scholar has suggested that the United States might institute a system of judicial torture warrants, to permit coercive interrogation in cases where it might yield information that will save lives.

The shocking nature of these suggestions forces us to think afresh about the legal prohibition on torture. This article argues that the prohibition on torture is not just one rule among others, but a legal archetype—a provision which is emblematic of our larger commitment to nonbrutality in the legal system. Characterizing it as an archetype affects how we think about the implications of authorizing torture (or interrogation methods that come close to torture). It affects how we think about issues of definition in regard to torture. And it affects how we think about the absolute character of the legal and moral prohibitions on torture.

On this basis, the article concludes not only that the absolute prohibition on torture should remain in force, but also that any attempt to loosen it (either explicitly or by narrowing the definition of "torture") would deal a traumatic blow to our legal system and affect our ability to sustain the law's commitment to human dignity and nonbrutality even in areas where torture as such is not involved.

INTRODUCTION

My starting point is the dishonor that descended upon the United States early in 2004 as a result of revelations about what was happening under American control in Abu Ghraib prison in Iraq. That dishonor involved more than the Abu Ghraib nightmare itself—the photographs of sexual humiliation, the dogs, the hoods, the wires, the beatings. It has become apparent that what took place there was not just a result of the depravity of a few poorly trained reservists, but the upshot of a policy determined by intelligence officials to have military police at the prison "set favorable conditions" (that was the euphemism) for the interrogation of detainees.

The concern and the dishonor intensified when it was revealed that abuses were not isolated in this one prison, but that brutal interrogations were also being conducted by American officials elsewhere. We know now that a number of captured officers in Iraq and Afghanistan, including general officers, were severely beaten during interrogation by their American captors, and in one case killed by suffocation. We know too that terrorist suspects, enemy combatants, and others associated with the Taliban and al Qaeda held by the United States in the camps at Guantánamo Bay were interrogated using physical and psychological techniques that had been outlawed by the European Court of Human Rights after their use by British forces against terrorist suspects in Northern Ireland in the early 1970s, and outlawed by the Israeli Supreme Court after their use by security forces in Israel against terrorist suspects in the 1990s.

Above all, my starting point is the realization that these abuses have taken place not just in the fog of war, but against a legal and political background set by discussions among lawyers and other officials in the White House, the Justice Department, and the Department of Defense about how to narrow the meaning and application of domestic and international legal prohibitions relating to torture.

It is dispiriting as well as shameful to have to turn our attention to this issue. In 1911, the author of the article on "Torture" in the *Encyclopaedia Britannica* wrote that "[t]he whole subject is now one of only historical interest as far as Europe is concerned." But it has come to life again. . . .

Perhaps what is remarkable is not that torture is used, but that it (or something very close to it) is being defended, and by well-known American jurists and law professors. Here are three examples:

(i)   Professor John Yoo now teaches law at the University of California at Berkeley. While on leave from Boalt Hall as a deputy assistant attorney general in the Justice Department, Professor Yoo was the lead author of a January 2002 memorandum persuading the Bush administration to withdraw its recognition of the rules imposed by the Geneva Conventions so far as the treatment of prisoners belonging to al Qaeda and the Taliban was concerned. This pertained particularly to the issue of interrogation and torture. Professor Yoo argued that captured members of al Qaeda and the Taliban were not protected by any prohibition on torture or cruel interrogation arising out of the Geneva Conventions because the particular category of armed conflict in which they were involved was not explicitly mentioned in any of the conventions under a description that the Bush administration would accept. . . .

(ii)   Alan Dershowitz is a professor at Harvard Law School who, in two well-publicized books, has argued that torture may be a morally and constitutionally acceptable method for United States officials to use to extract information from terrorists when the information may lead to the immediate saving of lives. He has in mind forms of nonlethal torture, such as "a sterilized needle inserted under the fingernails to produce unbearable pain without any threat to health or life. . . ."[1] Professor Dershowitz wants us to consider the possibility that it might be appropriate for torture of this kind to receive explicit authorization in the form of judicial torture warrants.

(iii) Jay Bybee is a judge on the Ninth Circuit and former law professor at Louisiana State University and the University of Nevada. Between 2001 and 2003, Bybee was head of the Office of Legal Counsel in the Department of Justice, and in that capacity he put his name on a memorandum sent to the White House purporting to narrow the definition (or the administration's understanding of the definition) of "torture" so that it did not cover all cases of the deliberate infliction of pain in the course of an interrogation. The word "torture" and the prohibition on torture should be reserved, Bybee argued, only for the infliction of the sort of extreme pain that would be associated with death or organ failure. He also argued that legislation restricting the use of torture by US forces under any definition might be unconstitutional as a restriction on the president's power as Commander-in-Chief. [Editors' Note: The memorandum described here is the one referred to as BYTAP in chapter 11, "Waterboarding and the Legacy of the Bybee-Yoo 'Torture and Power' Memorandum: Reflections from a Temporary Yoo Colleague and Erstwhile Bush Administration Apologist."]

These proposals have not arisen in a vacuum. The United States suffered a catastrophic series of terrorist attacks on September 11, 2001, and since then the Bush administration has committed itself to a "war on terror" and an active doctrine of preemptive self-defense. In al Qaeda it faces a resourceful enemy that obeys no legal restraints on armed conflict and may attack without warning at any time. The issue of torture arises because of the importance of intelligence in this conflict: Success in protecting a country from terrorist attack depends on intelligence more than brute force; good intelligence is also necessary for protecting our armed forces from insurgent attack in countries like Iraq (whose occupation by the United States is connected with the War on Terror).

I have heard colleagues say that what the Bush administration is trying to do in regard to torture should be understood sympathetically in light of these circumstances, and that we should be less reproachful of the administration's efforts to manipulate the definition of "torture" than we might be in peacetime. I disagree; I do not believe that "everything is different" after September 11. The various municipal and international law prohibitions on torture are set up precisely to address the circumstances where torture is likely to be most tempting. If the prohibitions do not hold fast in those circumstances, then they are of little use in any circumstance. . . .

. . . .

In what follows, I want to do several things. In part 1 of this article, I shall explore the idea that there is something wrong with trying to pin down the prohibition on torture with a precise legal definition. Insisting on exact definitions may sound very lawyerly, but there is something disturbing about it when the quest for precision is put to work in the service of a mentality that says, "Give us a definition so we have something to work around, something to game, a determinate envelope to push."

Part 2 of this article will consider whether the rule against torture can be regarded as an absolute. This is often treated as a moral question, but I also want to consider the idea of a legal absolute. . . . I want to consider the persuasiveness of claims made by Professor Dershowitz and others that we should be willing to recognize legal exceptions to this rule.

Part 3 of this article continues the exploration of the idea that the rule against torture may have extraordinary legal force. . . . I shall argue that the rule against torture operates in our law as an archetype—that is, as a rule which has significance not just in and of itself, but also as the embodiment of a pervasive principle. As the notion of a legal archetype is new and unfamiliar, I shall spend some time outlining and illustrating the jurisprudence that is necessary to make sense of this idea.

. . . .

I. LEGAL DEFINITIONS

A. The Texts and the Prohibitions

The law relating to torture comprises a variety of national, regional, and international norms. The basic provision of human rights law is found in the International Covenant on Civil and Political Rights (which I shall refer to hereinafter as "the Covenant"):

> Article 7. No one shall be subjected to torture or to cruel, inhuman or degrading treatment or punishment.

Article 4 of the Covenant provides that "[i]n time of public emergency which threatens the life of the nation and the existence of which is officially proclaimed, the States Parties to the present Covenant may take measures derogating from their obligations under the present Covenant to the extent strictly required by the exigencies of the situation," but article 4 also insists that no derogation from article 7 may be made under that provision. The United States ratified the Covenant in 1994, though with the following reservation:

> [T]he United States considers itself bound by Article 7 to the extent that "cruel, inhuman or degrading treatment or punishment" means the cruel and unusual treatment or punishment prohibited by the Fifth, Eighth, and/or Fourteenth Amendments to the Constitution of the United States.

This is part of a pattern of reservations from human rights conventions in which the United States asserts its right to rely on its own constitutional law in any case of overlap with international human rights law where the international standards might prove more demanding.

Besides the Covenant, we also have to consider a more specific document—the international Convention Against Torture (which I shall refer to hereinafter as "the Convention"). This instrument requires states to "take effective legislative, administrative, judicial or other measures to prevent acts of torture in any territory under its jurisdiction," and to "ensure that all acts of torture are offences under its criminal law." . . . In addition, the Convention goes beyond the Covenant (not to mention other regional human rights instruments such as the European Convention on Human Rights [ECHR]), in that it attempts to give a definition of torture:

> For the purposes of this Convention, the term "torture" means any act by which severe pain or suffering, whether physical or mental, is intentionally inflicted on a person for such purposes as obtaining from him or a third person information or a confession, punishing him for an

act he or a third person has committed or is suspected of having committed, or intimidating or coercing him or a third person, or for any reason based on discrimination of any kind, when such pain or suffering is inflicted by or at the instigation of or with the consent or acquiescence of a public official or other person acting in an official capacity. It does not include pain or suffering arising only from, inherent in or incidental to lawful sanctions.

This definition, particularly in its reference to the intentional infliction of severe pain, was the starting point of the recent American discussion by Jay Bybee and others.

In pursuance of its obligations under the Convention, the United States has enacted legislation forbidding torture outside the United States by persons subject to US jurisdiction....

. . . .

Finally, there are the Geneva Conventions, which deal with the treatment of various categories of vulnerable individuals in circumstances of armed conflict. The best-known provision is article 17 of the Third Geneva Convention, which provides that "[n]o physical or mental torture, nor any other form of coercion, may be inflicted on prisoners of war to secure from them information of any kind whatever." In addition, the four Geneva Conventions share a common article 3, which provides as follows:

Persons taking no active part in the hostilities, including members of armed forces who have laid down their arms . . . shall in all circumstances be treated humanely. . . .

. . . [T]he following acts are and shall remain prohibited at any time and in any place whatsoever with respect to the above-mentioned persons:

(a) violence to life and person, in particular murder of all kinds, mutilation, cruel treatment and torture; . . .

(c) outrages upon personal dignity, in particular[,] humiliating and degrading treatment. . . .

Common article 3 applies to all the persons the Geneva Conventions protect, which include not just prisoners of war, but wounded soldiers, shipwrecked sailors, detained members of irregular forces, and so on.

These provisions, together with the protections that law routinely provides against serious assault and abuse, add up to an interlocking set of prohibitions on torture. They are what I have in mind when I refer to "the prohibition on torture" (or "the rule against torture"). . . .

B. Rules and Backgrounds

What is the effect of these provisions? How should we approach them as lawyers? Should we use the same strategies of interpretation as we use elsewhere in the law? Or is there something special about the prohibitions on torture that requires us to treat them more carefully or considerately? . . .

I want to begin this discussion by considering the scope and application of the prohibitions on torture. John Yoo has suggested that the Geneva Conventions, read literally, apply to some captives or detainees but not others, and that they do not apply to al Qaeda and Taliban detainees in the war on terror. What sort of reading, what sort of interpretive approach is necessary to reach a conclusion like that? To answer this question, it is helpful to invoke the old distinction between *malum prohibitum* and *malum in se*—two ways in which a legal prohibition may be regarded.

On the malum prohibitum approach, we may think about the text of a given legal provision as introducing a prohibition into what was previously a realm of liberty. Consider the introduction of parking regulations as an analogy. . . .

The other approach is a malum in se approach. Some things are just wrong, and would be wrong whether positive law prohibited them or not. . . .

The distinction between malum prohibitum and malum in se might seem to depend on a natural law theory, in which some of law's functions are related to the administration of natural law prohibitions while other functions are related to positive law's capacity to generate new forms of regulation. But that need not be so. All we need in order to make sense of *malum in se* and distinguish it from malum prohibitum is to discern some preexisting normative background to the prohibition that is legally recognizable. That normative background may be a shared moral sense or it may be some sort of higher or background law: natural law, perhaps, or international law. We should note, however, that the distinction between malum in se and malum prohibitum is not clear cut. Even in our parking example, there will have been some background reasons governing the way it was appropriate to park even before the regulations were introduced: Do not park unsafely or inconsiderately, do not block access, and so on. These reasons do not evaporate when the explicit regulations are introduced.

Now let us apply these distinctions to the rule against torture. I think it is obvious that the US antitorture statute cannot plausibly be construed according to the malum prohibitum model. It does not represent the first introduction of a prohibition into an area that was previously unregulated and in which everyone was previously at liberty to do what they liked. On the contrary, the statute fulfilled a treaty obligation that the United States already had under the Convention, and it also applied and extended the spirit of existing criminal law. . . .

It might be thought that the Geneva Conventions are a special case because they are designed to limit armed conflict, and there the background or default position is indeed that anything goes. That is, one might think that armed forces are normally at liberty to do anything they like to enemy soldiers in time of war—bombard, shoot, kill, wound, maim, and terrify them—and that the function of the Geneva Conventions is precisely to introduce a degree of unprecedented regulation into what would otherwise be a horrifying realm of freedom. Under this reasoning, the malum prohibitum approach is appropriate, and therefore we have no choice but to consult the strict letter of the texts of the Conventions to see exactly what is prohibited and what has been left as a matter of military freedom. John Yoo's memorandum approaches the Geneva Conventions in that spirit. He implies that absent the Conventions we would be entitled to do anything we like to enemy detainees; grudgingly, however, we must accept some limits (which we ourselves have negotiated and signed up for). But we have signed up for no more than the actual texts stipulate. When we run out of text, we revert to the default position, which is that we can do anything we like. Now—this line of reasoning continues—it so happens that as a result of military action in Afghanistan and Iraq, certain individuals have fallen into our hands as captives who do not have the precise attributes that the Geneva Conventions stipulate for persons protected by its prohibitions. So—the conclusion runs—the textual prohibitions on maltreatment do not apply to these detainees, and we are back in the military default position: We can do with them whatever we like.

Yoo's approach is wrong in three ways. First, its narrow textualism embodies a bewildering refusal to infer anything along *ejusdem generis* lines from the existing array of categories of detainees that are covered. . . .

In any case, it is simply not true that the texts of the Geneva Conventions represent the first introduction of prohibitions into a previously unregulated area. The Geneva Conventions, like the Convention Against Torture and the International Covenant, respond to a strongly felt and well-established sense that certain abuses are beyond the pale, whether one is dealing with criminal suspects, political dissidents, or military detainees, and that they remain beyond the pale even in emergency situations or situations of armed conflict. . . .

Third, Yoo's analysis lacks a sense of the historic context in which the conventions governing captives and detainees were negotiated and reformulated in 1949. . . .

. . . .

D. The Bybee Memorandum

I now want to focus more specifically on the August 2002 memorandum written for the CIA and the White House by Jay Bybee, chief of the Office of Legal Counsel in the Department of Justice. The fifty pages of the Bybee memorandum give what some have described as the most lenient interpretation conceivable to the Convention and other antitorture provisions. Although the memorandum was subsequently officially repudiated, large sections of the Bybee memorandum were incorporated more or less verbatim into what is now known as the Haynes memorandum, produced by a working group set up in the Pentagon in January 2003 to reconsider interrogation methods.

According to Bybee, the relevant legal provisions prohibit as torture "only extreme acts" and penalize as torture "only the most egregious conduct." He notes that the American ratification of the Convention Against Torture was accompanied by an express understanding that "in order to constitute torture, an act must be a deliberate and calculated act of an extremely cruel and inhuman nature, specifically intended to inflict excruciating and agonizing physical or mental pain or suffering." In discussions at the time, it was suggested that the word "torture" should be reserved for practices like "sustained systematic beatings, application of electric currents to sensitive parts of the body and tying up or hanging in positions that cause extreme pain." Administration officials added that such "rough treatment as generally falls into the category of 'police brutality,' while deplorable, does not amount to 'torture.'" Although he conceded that this sort of brutality might amount to "inhuman treatment," Bybee noted that the United States made a reservation to that part of the Convention Against Torture as well, to the effect that the prohibition on inhuman treatment would not apply to the extent that it purported to prohibit anything permitted by the US Constitution as currently interpreted. From all this, Bybee concluded that "certain acts may be cruel, inhuman, or degrading, but still not produce pain and suffering of the requisite intensity to fall within [the] proscription against torture."

It is clear, then, what sort of continuum Bybee thinks interrogators should be on, in the interest of knowing the precise location of a torture threshold. It is not a continuum of pressure, nor is it a continuum of unwelcome penalties, nor is it a continuum of discomfort. Interrogators, in Bybee's opinion, are permitted to work somewhere along the continuum of the deliberate infliction of pain, and the question is: Where is the bright line along that continuum where the specific prohibition on torture kicks in? If we cannot answer this, Bybee fears, our interrogators may be chilled from any sort of deliberate infliction of pain on detainees. . . .

. . . .

All of this goes to the general character of Bybee's analysis. Let us turn now to its detail. How, exactly, does Bybee propose to pin down a meaning for "severe pain or suffering"? It is all very well to talk about "requisite intensity," but how are we to determine the appropriate measure of severity? With a dictionary in hand, Bybee essays a proliferation of adjectives—"grievous," "extreme," and the like. But they all seem to defy operationalization in the same way: The intensity, the severity, and the agonizing or excruciating character of pain are all subjective and, to a certain extent, inscrutable phenomena. One thing Bybee said, in an attempt to give the definition of torture a somewhat less phenomenological basis, was that "the adjective 'severe' conveys that the pain or suffering must be of such a high level of intensity that the pain is difficult for the subject to endure." But that is not going to give him the distinction he wants. Presumably that is the whole point of any pain imposed deliberately in cruel and inhuman interrogation, not just the extreme cases Bybee wants to isolate.

A more promising approach involves drawing on statutes governing medical administration, where Bybee said that attempts to define the phrase "severe pain" had already been made. He wrote this:

> Congress's use of the phrase "severe pain" elsewhere in the United States Code can shed more light on its meaning. Significantly, the phrase "severe pain" appears in statutes defining an emergency medical condition for the purpose of providing health benefits. See, e.g., 8 U.S.C. § 1369 (2000); 42 U.S.C. § 1395w-22 (2000); id. § 1395x (2000); id. § 1395dd (2000); id. § 1396b (2000); id. § 1396u-2 (2000). These statutes define an emergency condition as one "manifesting itself by acute symptoms of sufficient severity (including *severe pain*) such that a prudent lay person, who possesses an average knowledge of health and medicine, could reasonably expect the absence of immediate medical attention to result in—[(i)] placing the health of

the individual . . . [ ] in serious jeopardy, (ii) serious impairment to bodily functions, or (iii) serious dysfunction of any bodily organ or part." Id. § 1395w-22(d)(3)(B) (emphasis added). Although these statutes address a substantially different subject from Section 2340, they are nonetheless helpful for understanding what constitutes severe physical pain.

From this, Bybee concluded that severe pain amounting to torture must be equivalent in intensity to the pain accompanying serious physical injury, such as organ failure, impairment of body function, or even death.

It is hard to know where to start in criticizing this analysis. One could comment on the strange assumption that a term like "severe pain" takes no color from its context or from the particular purpose of the provision in which it is found, but that it unproblematically means the same in a medical administration statute (with the purposes characteristically associated with statutes of this kind) as it does in an antitorture statute (with the purposes characteristically associated with statutes of that kind). Never mind that the latter provision is intended to fulfil our international obligations under the Convention, while the former addresses the resource problems of our quite peculiar healthcare regime. Bybee argues that the medical administration statute can still cast some light on the definition of torture.

Even that glimmer of light flickers out when we consider a couple of glaring defects of basic logic in the detail of the analysis itself. First, the healthcare provision that Bybee refers to uses certain conditions—(i) to (iii) in the excerpt above—to define the phrase "emergency condition," not to define "severe pain." The medical administration statute says that severe symptoms (including severe pain) add up to an emergency condition if any of the three conditions are satisfied. These conditions provided Bybee with his formulations about organ failure and death, but since the antitorture statute does not use the term "emergency condition," the logic of their use in the healthcare statute makes them utterly irrelevant to the definition of severe pain, there or anywhere else. Second, Bybee's analysis reverses the causality implicit in the medical administration statute: That statute refers to the likelihood that a severe condition will lead to organic impairment or dysfunction if left untreated, whereas what Bybee infers from the healthcare statute is that pain counts as severe only if it is associated with (naturally read as "caused by") organic impairment or dysfunction. To sum up: Bybee takes a definition of "emergency condition" (in which severe pain happens to be mentioned), reverses the causal relationship required between the emergency condition and organ failure, and concludes—on a matter as important as the proper definition of torture—that the law does not prohibit anything as torture unless it causes the same sort of pain as organ failure.

The quality of Bybee's legal work here is a disgrace when one considers the service to which this analysis is being put. Bybee is an intelligent man, these are obvious errors, and the Department of Justice—as the executive department charged with special responsibility for the integrity of the legal system—had a duty to take special care with this most important of issues. Bybee's mistakes distort the character of the legal prohibition on torture and create an impression that there is more room for the lawful infliction of pain in interrogation than a casual acquaintance with the antitorture statute might suggest. Fortunately, someone in the administration felt that he had gone too far: This part of Bybee's memorandum was not incorporated into the Haynes memorandum (although most of the rest of it was), and much of the Bybee approach to the definition of torture appears to have been rejected by the administration in its most recent deliverances on the subject.

II. LEGAL ABSOLUTES

. . . .

B. The Dershowitz Strategy

. . . Law school and moral philosophy classes thrive on hypotheticals that involve grotesque disproportion between the pain that a torturer might inflict on an informant and the pain that might be averted by timely use of the information extracted from him: a little bit of pain from the needles for him versus a hundred thousand people saved from nuclear incineration. Of course after September 11, 2001, the hypotheticals are beginning to look a little less fantastic. Professor Dershowitz asks: What if on September 11 law enforcement officials had arrested terrorists boarding one of the planes and learned that other planes, then airborne, were heading towards unknown occupied buildings? Would they not have been justified in torturing the terrorists in their custody—just enough to get the information that would allow the target buildings to be evacuated? How could anyone object to the use of torture if it were dedicated specifically to saving thousands of lives in a case like this? That is the question that Dershowitz and others regard as a useful starting point in our thinking about torture. The answer it is supposed to elicit is that torture can never be entirely out of the question, if the facts are clear and the stakes are high enough.

Should it worry us that once one goes down this road, the justification of torture—indeed, the justification of anything—is a matter of simple arithmetic coupled with the professor's ingenuity in concocting the appropriate fact situation? As Seth Kreimer observes, "a sufficiently large fear of catastrophe could conceivably authorize almost any plausibly efficacious government action."[2] The tactics used to discredit absolute prohibitions on torture are tactics that can show in the end, "to borrow the formula of Dostoevsky's Ivan Karamazov, ... [that] everything is permitted."[3] Dershowitz concedes the point, acknowledging that there is something disingenuous about his own suggestion that judicial torture warrants would be issued to authorize nothing but nonlethal torture. If the number of lives that can be saved is twice the number necessary to justify nonlethal torture, why not justify lethal torture or torture with unsterilized needles? Indeed, why just torture? Why not judicial rape warrants? Why not terrorism itself? The same kind of hypotheticals will take care of these inhibitions as well.

Still, this concern alone does not dispose of Dershowitz's question. Might we be willing to allow the authorization of torture at least in a "ticking bomb" case—make it a ticking nuclear bomb in your hometown, if you like—where we are sure that the detainee we are proposing to torture has information that will save thousands of lives and will give it up only if subjected to excruciating pain?

For what it is worth, my own answer to this question is a simple "No." I draw the line at torture. I suspect that almost all of my readers will draw the line somewhere, to prohibit some actions even under the most extreme circumstances. ... But in any case, one's answer is less important than one's estimation of the question. An affirmative answer is meant to make us feel patriotic and tough-minded. But the question that is supposed to elicit this response is at best silly and at worst deeply corrupt. It is silly because torture is seldom used in the real world to elicit startling facts about particular ticking bombs; it is used by American interrogators and others to accumulate lots of small pieces of relatively insignificant information which may become important only when accumulated with other pieces of similar information elicited by this or other means. And it is corrupt because it attempts to use a far-fetched scenario, more at home in a television thriller than in the real world, deliberately to undermine the integrity of certain moral positions.

Some replies to Dershowitz's question—and to my mind, they are quite convincing—say that even if the basic fact situation he posits is no longer so fantastic in light of the bizarre horrors of September 11, nevertheless the framing of the hypothetical is still farfetched, inasmuch as it asks us to assume that torture warrants will work exactly as Professor Dershowitz says they should work. The hypothetical asks us to assume that the power to authorize torture will not be abused, that intelligence officials will not lie about what is at stake or about the availability of the information, that the readiness to issue torture warrants in one case (where they may be justified by the sort of circumstances Dershowitz stipulates) will not lead to their extension to other cases (where the circumstances are somewhat less compelling), that a professional corps of torturers will not emerge who stand around looking for work, that the existence of a law allowing torture in some cases will not change the office politics of police and security agencies to undermine and disempower those who argue against torture in other cases, and so on.

. . . .

The important point is that the use of torture is not an area in which human motives are trustworthy. Sadism, sexual sadism, the pleasure of indulging brutality, the love of power, and the enjoyment of the humiliation of others—these all-too-human characteristics need to be kept very tightly under control, especially in the context of war and terror, where many of the usual restraints on human action are already loosened. . . . Remember too that we are not asking whether these motives can be judicially regulated in the abstract. We are asking whether they can be regulated in the kind of circumstances of fear, anger, stress, danger, panic, and terror in which, realistically, the hypothetical case must be posed.

. . . .

Considerations like these might furnish a pragmatic case for upholding the rule against torture as a legal absolute, even if we cannot make a case in purely philosophical terms for a moral absolute. However, I do not want to stop there. Though I think the pragmatic case for a legal absolute is exactly right, in the rest of this article I want to explore an additional idea. This is the idea that certain things might just be repugnant to the spirit of our law, and that torture may be one of them. Specifically, I want to make and explore the claim that the rule against torture plays an important emblematic role so far as the spirit of our law is concerned.

III. LEGAL ARCHETYPES

A. Repugnance to Law

. . . .

. . . American judges have always been anxious to distance themselves from what Justice Stevens has referred to as "the kind of custodial interrogation that was once employed by the Star Chamber [and] by 'the Germans of the 1930's and early 1940's.'" . . .

Justice Black saw torture as characteristic of tyrannical, not free, governments:

... The rack, the thumbscrew, the wheel, solitary confinement, pro-tracted questioning and cross questioning, and other ingenious forms of entrapment of the helpless or unpopular had left their wake of mutilated bodies and shattered minds along the way to the cross, the guillotine, the stake and the hangman's noose.

Torture may be something that happens elsewhere in the world, but not in a free country.... Our constitutional arrangements are spurred precisely by the desire to set the face of our law against such "ancient evils." ...

B. Positivism and Legal Archetypes

One of the things that people have consistently found wrong with the jurisprudence of legal positivism is that it views law simply as a heap or accumulation of rules, each of which might be amended, repealed, or reinterpreted with little or no effect on any of the others....

. . . .

When I use the term "archetype," I mean a particular provision in a system of norms which has a significance going beyond its immediate normative content, a significance stemming from the fact that it sums up or makes vivid to us the point, purpose, principle, or policy of a whole area of law.... They work in the foreground as rules or precedents, but in doing so, they sum up the spirit of a whole body of law that goes beyond what they might be thought to require on their own terms. The idea of an archetype, then, is the idea of a rule or positive law provision that operates not just on its own account, and does not just stand simply in a cumulative relation to other provisions, but operates also in a way that expresses or epitomizes the spirit of a whole structured area of doctrine, and does so vividly, effectively, and publicly, establishing the significance of that area for the entire legal enterprise.

. . . .

The best example, I think, is given by the habeas corpus statutes. The importance of "the Great Writ" is not exhausted by what it does in itself, overwhelmingly important though that is. Habeas corpus is also archetypal of our legal tradition's emphasis on liberty and freedom from physical confinement. It is also archetypal of the law's opposition to arbitrariness in regard to actions that have an impact on that right. . . .

C. What Is the Rule Against Torture Archetypal Of?

. . . .

The rule against torture is archetypal of a certain policy having to do with the relation between law and force, and the force with which law rules. The prohibition on torture is expressive of an important underlying policy of the law, which we might try to capture in the following way: Law is not brutal in its operation. Law is not savage. Law does not rule through abject fear and terror, or by breaking the will of those whom it confronts. . . . People may fear and be deterred by legal sanctions; they may dread lawsuits; they may even on occasion be forced by legal means or legally empowered officials to do things or go places against their will. But even when this happens, they will not be herded like cattle or broken like horses; they will not be beaten like dumb animals or treated as bodies to be manipulated. Instead, there will be an enduring connection between the spirit of law and respect for human dignity—respect for human dignity even in extremis, where law is at its most forceful and its subjects at their most vulnerable. I think the rule against torture functions as an archetype of this very general policy. It is vividly emblematic of our determination to sever the link between law and brutality, between law and terror, and between law and the enterprise of breaking a person's will.

E. Undermining an Archetype

. . . .

. . . [T]he archetype idea is the reverse of a slippery slope argument. It is sometimes argued that if we relax some lesser constitutional inhibition, we will be on the downward slide towards an abomination like torture. But I am arguing in the other direction: Starting at the bottom of the so-called slippery slope, I am arguing that if we mess with the prohibition on torture, we may find it harder to defend some arguably less important requirements that—in the conventional mode of argument—are perched above torture on the slippery slope. The idea is that our confidence that what lies at the bottom of the slope (torture) is wrong informs and supports our confidence that the lesser evils that lie above torture are wrong too. Our beliefs—that flogging in prisons is wrong, that coerced confessions are wrong, that pumping a person's stomach for narcotics evidence is wrong, that police brutality is wrong—may each be uncertain and a little shaky, but the confidence we have in them depends partly on analogies we have constructed between them and torture or on a sense that what is wrong with torture gives us some insight into what is wrong with these other evils. If we undermine the sense that torture is absolutely out of the question, then we lose a crucial point of reference for sustaining these other less confident beliefs.

. . . .

The damage done to our system of law by undermining the prohibition on torture is, I think, just like this. If we were to permit the torture of al Qaeda and Taliban detainees, or if we were to define what most of us regard as torture as not really "torture" at all to enable our officials to inflict pain on them during questioning, or if we were to set up a Dershowitz regime of judicial torture warrants, maybe only a few score detainees would be affected in the first instance. But the character of our legal system would be corrupted. We would be moving from a situation in which our law had a certain character—a general virtue of nonbrutality—to a situation in which that character would be compromised or corrupted by the permitting of this most brutal of practices. We would have given up the linchpin of the modern doctrine that law will not operate savagely or countenance brutality. We would no longer be able to state that doctrine in any categorical form. Instead we would have to say, more cautiously and with greater reservation: "In *most* cases the law will not permit or countenance brutality, but since torture is now permitted in a (hopefully) small and carefully cabined class of cases, we cannot rule out the possibility that in other cases the use of brutal tactics will also be permitted to agents of the law." In other words, the repudiation of brutality would become a *technical* matter—"Sometimes it is repudiated, sometimes not"—rather than a shining issue of principle.

. . . .

As we have seen, the prohibition on torture is a point of reference to which we return over and over again in articulating legally what is wrong with cruel punishment or distinguishing a punishment that is cruel from one that is not: We do not equate cruelty with torture, but we use torture to illuminate our rejection of cruelty. And the same is true of procedural due process constraints, certain liberty-based constraints of substantive due process, and our general repudiation of brutality in law enforcement. So, in order to see what might go wrong as a result of undermining the prohibition on torture, we have to imagine Eighth Amendment jurisprudence without this point of reference—arguing about cruelty without the assumption that torture, at any rate, is wholly out of the question. Or we have to imagine Fifth Amendment jurisprudence without this point of reference, where arguments about coerced confessions and self-incrimination must be made against the background of an assumption that torture is sometimes legally permissible. The halting and hesitant character of such argumentation would itself be a blight on our law, in addition to the actual abuses that would result. Or rather, the two would not be separated: Because law is an argumentative practice, the empirical consequences for our law would be bound up with the corruption of our ability to make arguments of a certain kind, or to assert principles which put torture unequivocally beyond the pale and used that to provide a vivid and convincing basis for the elaboration of a general principle of nonbrutality.

. . . .

CONCLUSION

Let me end with a few cautionary remarks about the concept of legal archetype that I have been using.

. . . .

. . . There are all sorts of reasons to be concerned about torture, and I am under no illusion that I have focused on the most important. The most important issue about torture remains the moral issue of the deliberate infliction of pain, the suffering that results, the insult to dignity, and the demoralization and depravity that is almost always associated with this enterprise whether it is legalized or not. The issue of the relation between the prohibition on torture and the rest of the law, the issue of archetypes, is a second-tier issue. By that I mean it does not confront the primary wrongness of torture; it is a second-tier issue like the issue of our proven inability to keep torture under control, or the fatuousness of the suggestion made by Professor Dershowitz and others that we can confine its application to exactly the cases in which it might be thought justified. Given that we are sometimes tongue-tied about what is really wrong with an evil like torture, work at this second tier is surely worth doing. Or it is surely worth doing anyway, as part of the general division of labor, even if others are managing to produce a first-tier account of the evil.

I have found this second-tier thinking about archetypes helpful in my general thinking about law. I have found it helpful as a way of thinking about what it is for law to structure itself and present itself in a certain light. I have found it helpful to think about archetypes as a general topic in legal philosophy, as a corrective to some of the simplicities of legal positivism, and as an interesting elaboration of Dworkin's jurisprudence. Most of all, I have found this exploration helpful in understanding what the prohibition on torture symbolizes. By thinking about the prohibition as an archetype, I have been able to reach a clearer and more substantive sense of what we aspire to in our jurisprudence: a body of law and a rule of law that renounces savagery and a state that pursues its purposes (even its most urgent purposes) and secures its citizens (even its most endangered citizens) honorably and without recourse to brutality and terror.

INTERROGATING SUSPECTED TERRORISTS
Should Torture Be an Option?
(2002)

John T. Parry and Welsh S. White

In the wake of the September 11 terrorist attacks on the United States, voices in and out of the government have called for allowing interrogators to use torture to obtain information from suspected terrorists. The magnitude and shock of the attacks, the difficulties of the investigation, and the need to prevent future attacks place immense pressure on law enforcement officials. When suspects refuse to talk, investigators will understandably consider using extreme methods to obtain desperately needed information.

Federal investigators' experience with suspects believed to be involved in the attacks provides one example of interrogators' frustration. Shortly after the attacks, FBI agents and Justice Department investigators detained suspects who were believed to be connected to the attacks either because they were traveling with "false passports" and were carrying "box cutters, hair dye, and $5,000 in cash," or because they had "links to al Qaeda."[1] In seeking information from these suspects, FBI agents not only employed traditional interrogation tactics but also offered the suspects unusual incentives such as "a new identity and life in the United States for them and their family members."[2] When all such efforts proved unsuccessful, one agent stated, "We are known for humanitarian treatment, so basically we are stuck. . . . Usually there is some incentive, some angle to play, what you can do for them. But it could get to that spot where we could go to pressure . . . where we won't have a choice and we are probably getting there."[3]

When confronted with these difficult situations, what kinds of pressures should interrogators be permitted to use? Experts have suggested various strategies, including using drugs and extraditing suspects to allied countries where less humane interrogation tactics are employed. In extreme situations, moreover, even traditionally liberal commentators have advocated that US interrogators should be permitted to use physical force or other abusive interrogation methods in order to force the disclosure of vital information.

One prominent civil libertarian, Harvard law professor Alan Dershowitz, has argued that when lives are at stake interrogators should sometimes be allowed to torture suspects to obtain information.[4] As one example, Professor Dershowitz cites a case "in which . . . [t]he kidnapper refuse[s] to disclose" the location of "a kidnapped child [who has] been buried in a box with two hours of oxygen."[5] In this and related situations, Dershowitz suggests that judges should issue "torture warrants" so that interrogators will be permitted to employ torture in extraordinary cases within our legal system rather than "outside of the law."[6] Other commentators have made similar arguments or have admitted that torture cannot be ruled out categorically.

The United Nations Convention against Torture and Other Cruel, Inhuman, or Degrading Treatment or Punishment erects an absolute ban on torture, which it defines as: any act by which severe pain or suffering, whether physical or mental, is intentionally inflicted on a person for such purposes as obtaining from him or a third person information or a confession, punishing him for an act he or a third person has committed or is suspected of having committed, or intimidating or coercing him or a third person, or for any reason based on discrimination of any kind, when such pain or suffering is inflicted by or at the instigation of or with the consent or acquiescence of a public official or other person acting in an official capacity. It does not include pain or suffering arising only from, inherent in, or incidental to lawful sanctions.

The United States has adopted a more restrictive definition of torture that requires specific intent and narrows the definition of mental harm but nonetheless covers most of the same territory. International law also distinguishes between torture and other less precisely defined yet nonetheless illegal forms of "cruel, unhuman, or degrading" treatment. Although the meaning of the latter phrase is unclear, the United States interprets it as equivalent to "the cruel, unusual, and inhumane treatment or punishment prohibited by the Fifth, Eighth, and Fourteenth Amendments to the Constitution of the United States." In this article, we use "torture" in a more general sense to refer to any coercive interrogation practice that involves the infliction of pain or extreme discomfort.

As Professor Dershowitz admits, the notion that interrogators will be permitted to torture or otherwise mistreat suspects to obtain information in any situation is "very troubling." In deciding when, if ever, interrogators should be allowed to employ such extreme techniques, several questions relating to interrogation law and practice seem relevant. First, from a legal standpoint, what guidance do the Supreme Court's interrogation cases provide for determining the circumstances under which police interrogators should be permitted to employ torture? Second, from a pragmatic standpoint, will police interrogating suspected terrorists be more likely to obtain useful information through employing torture rather than interrogation techniques employed by the police in other serious cases? Third, assuming there are situations in which torture would be more effective than other interrogation techniques, when, if ever, should the police be permitted to employ it? . . .

. . . We admit that torture may be understandable in extreme situations. Nonetheless, we argue torture should remain illegal under all circumstances and victims of torture should have a full array of available remedies. At the same time, however, a government official accused of using torture should be able to raise the necessity defense in a subsequent criminal prosecution to the extent the defense would otherwise be available.

I. THE LAW OF TORTURE IN THE UNITED STATES

A. The Supreme Court's Prohibition on Interrogators' Use of Torture

In the early twentieth century, some police interrogators routinely employed torture to obtain information from criminal suspects. They subjected suspects to physical brutality with the aid of various instruments, including boxing gloves, rubber hoses, placing a rope around the suspect's neck, or using the "water cure," which involved slowly pouring water into the nostrils of a suspect who was held down on his back. In addition, they employed other abusive practices, such as stripping the suspect of clothing, placing him in an airless, overcrowded unsanitary room, and subjecting him to protracted questioning without sleep.

When practices of this type came under attack, police defended them on the ground that confessions induced by such practices were often the only means through which they could solve serious crimes. They maintained that the truthfulness of the resulting confessions could be verified by requiring the suspect to provide details that would be known only to the perpetrator. The end—obtaining reliable evidence necessary to solve serious crimes—justified the means of using abusive interrogation practices.

In 1931, however, the Wickersham Commission issued a report that unequivocally condemned police use of abusive interrogation practices. The report disputed the claim that such practices promoted effective law enforcement, observing that the practices often produced false confessions, which sometimes led to wrongful convictions. In addition, the report condemned interrogators' abusive practices not only because they violated suspects' rights but also because they degraded law enforcement officers, reducing them to the level of the criminals they were seeking to apprehend.

The Wickersham Report significantly influenced the development of the law imposing constitutional restrictions on interrogators. Prior to the commission's report, the Supreme Court had not considered any state cases in which the admissibility of a defendant's confession was at issue. In a line of cases beginning in 1936, however, the Supreme Court decided that the admission of a confession obtained as a result of abusive interrogation practices violated the due process clause of the Fourteenth Amendment. In three of these cases, the Court not only cited the Wickersham Report, but made it clear that it fully endorsed the report's position: law enforcement's practice of obtaining confessions through torture or other abusive interrogation practices should be eliminated.

Although the Court's due process confession cases ostensibly decided only whether confessions obtained by police interrogators were properly admitted against criminal defendants, the Court nevertheless indicated that certain interrogations were unequivocally impermissible. In *Brown v. Mississippi*, the first in this line of cases, a white deputy sheriff obtained confessions from three black suspects by whipping them until they confessed. The Court stated that "[i]t would be difficult to conceive of methods more revolting to the sense of justice than those taken to procure the confessions." In *Ashcraft v. Tennessee*, decided six years later, Justice Jackson, while dissenting from the Court's holding that the admission of a confession obtained after thirty-six hours of virtually continuous interrogation violated due process, sought to distinguish between permissible and impermissible interrogation techniques by stating, "[i]nterrogation per se is not, while violence per se is, an outlaw." In other words, in deciding whether a confession obtained by prolonged police questioning would be inadmissible, courts would have to examine the questioning's effect on the suspect. When the police employed violence to produce a confession, however, no such inquiry would be necessary. The confession would be excluded because police interrogators are absolutely prohibited from using violence to obtain statements. . . .

. . . .

At least two lessons can be drawn from the Court's due process confession cases. First, police interrogation practices that severely infringe on a suspect's mental or physical autonomy violate the due process clause regardless of whether they produce statements that are admitted against the suspect. An interrogator's torture of a suspect would thus ordinarily result in a violation of the suspect's constitutional rights—an issue we discuss again in the next section. Second, law enforcement officers' right to employ extreme interrogation practices apparently does not vary depending on law enforcement's need for information. Rather, interrogation practices that are prohibited because they impose too severe infringements on individual autonomy will be impermissible regardless of the law enforcement interest at stake.

B. Torture beyond Confessions

As we suggested in the previous section, the legal consequences of a coercive interrogation go beyond an inadmissible confession. The use of coercion in interrogation violates the victim's due process rights whether or not the government ever seeks to use the confession. Thus, the victims of coercive interrogation—whether or not it rises to the level of torture—may bring a Bivens or § 1983 action for damages against their interrogators.

. . . .

In addition, state and federal law criminalizes all conduct that fits within the definition of torture, as well as most conduct that would fall under the more ambiguous category of "cruel, inhuman, and degrading treatment or punishment." . . .

In sum, a variety of laws and constitutional provisions indicate that torture is illegal and unconstitutional in any context. As the State Department recently summarized the law:

> Torture is prohibited by law throughout the United States. It is categorically denounced as a matter of policy and as a tool of state authority. Every act constituting torture under the [Convention against Torture] constitutes a criminal offense under the law of the United States. No official of the government, federal, state, or local, civilian or military, is authorized to commit or to instruct anyone else to commit torture. Nor may any official condone or tolerate torture in any form. No exceptional circumstances may be invoked as a justification for torture. US law contains no provision permitting otherwise prohibited acts of torture or other cruel, inhuman or degrading treatment of punishment to be employed on grounds of exigent circumstances (for example, during a "state of public emergency") or on orders from a superior officer or public authority, and the protective mechanisms of an independent judiciary are not subject to suspension.

The relevance of these statements and the case law should not be overestimated, however. US law on torture has developed in situations in which the individual interests at stake are to be weighed against law enforcement's general interest in solving or punishing a crime; it has not been tested against the more extreme circumstances presented by terrorism.

When government officials are seeking information from a suspected terrorist, they may be seeking to protect national security or even to prevent the imminent loss of life. When interests of this magnitude are involved, arguably the balance struck in cases like Chambers—where the government's only interest is in solving a completed crime—should be recalibrated. Nevertheless, the evolution of the Court's due process confession cases, as well as other discussions of torture, provide a clear warning that allowing police interrogators to employ torture in any situation would be contrary to safeguards that have become a part of our constitutional heritage.

II. MODERN INTERROGATION PRACTICES

In the wake of the Court's prohibition of abusive interrogation practices, interrogators developed sophisticated psychologically oriented interrogation techniques that were designed to convince suspects it was in their own best interest to make truthful statements to interrogators. As they refined these techniques, interrogators discovered that the new techniques were more effective than the old. Interrogators who skillfully employed psychologically oriented techniques were generally able to convince suspects that it was in their best interest to talk to the police. In contrast to the abusive tactics employed in the past, moreover, interrogators' proper use of the new techniques was generally likely to elicit truthful statements from suspects.

. . . .

Even with the addition of the protections afforded by the *Miranda* warnings, modern interrogators have been remarkably successful at convincing suspects that it is in their own best interest to make a statement to the police. Studies indicate that, in most jurisdictions, police interrogators are able to persuade suspects to waive their *Miranda* rights and to make a statement to the police in more than 80 percent of all cases. Even when the police are not able to obtain a *Miranda* waiver, moreover, they are sometimes able to persuade suspects to make a statement that will assist the police in solving a crime, even if it cannot be introduced into evidence.

In some cases, of course, interrogators' use of standard interrogation techniques will not produce a statement. There is a small group of suspects—including professional criminals—who operate on the assumption that they will "say nothing" to the police. If law enforcement officials wish to obtain statements from suspects in this category, they will have to employ more extreme interrogation tactics than those permitted in ordinary criminal cases. If suspected terrorists are likely to fit within this category, then it may be necessary to consider what types of interrogation tactics have the best chance of securing information from individuals who are determined not to disclose it.

Are suspected terrorists likely to be hard-core suspects in the sense that they will refuse to disclose information? Obviously, suspected terrorists cannot all be placed in a single category. Even aside from the fact that many of those suspected of terrorism may be innocent, some suspects who are connected with terrorist activity will be so naive and vulnerable that they may easily be induced to speak through psychologically oriented interrogation tactics. On the other hand, some individuals are undoubtedly so committed to terrorist objectives that they would be adamant in their refusal to disclose useful information to the police.

When dealing with the latter category of suspects, what interrogation methods are most likely to lead to the disclosure of useful information? Even with suspects who refuse to cooperate, practices short of torture would sometimes be likely to produce useful information. When interrogators believe it is critical to determine whether a suspect has knowledge of specific facts, using cutting-edge technology to evaluate suspects' brain waves may soon be effective. Moreover, although there is considerable debate regarding the efficacy of so-called truth serums, some experts believe that interrogators' use of sodium pentothal or other compounds will sometimes lead suspects to reveal secret information. And as in ordinary cases, when interrogators have sufficient time to employ the full range of psychologically oriented interrogation methods, their patient efforts to extract information through gaining the suspect's trust and establishing a rapport may be surprisingly likely to produce positive results.

In some cases, however, interrogators may reasonably believe that the only way in which they can obtain vital information from suspects is through the use of torture or other abusive interrogation practices. When cases of this type arise, what approach should courts take in regulating the conduct of interrogators?

III. TORTURE AND NECESSITY

. . . .

A. The Israeli Experience

Editors' Note: In this section, omitted due to space constraints, the authors address the Israeli Supreme Court's ban on torture but also its willingness to accept a "necessity defense."

B. Applying the Necessity Defense to the Torture of Terrorists

Consider the following hypothetical. Federal law enforcement officials receive credible information that a specific, known terrorist group has planted a nuclear device in a major US city, and the device will detonate in a few hours. Time is so short that only a relatively small number of those in the city could be evacuated to safety. Soon thereafter, officials apprehend in the vicinity of the targeted city an individual known to be among the leadership of the terrorist group. After an interrogation employing as many standard techniques as possible in the limited time available, the terrorist refuses to admit or deny that a nuclear device has been planted and refuses to provide any other information. With time running out, should torture be an option?

We believe the answer in that situation is yes, regardless of the legal status of torture. That is, under extreme "ticking time bomb" circumstances, torture may be the least worse choice. But this hypothetical proves little. Anyone can devise a fact pattern that would convince nearly everyone to permit torture under the specific circumstances. The normal case—if there is such a thing—in which officials will be tempted to torture is likely to depart significantly from our hypothetical. For example, law enforcement rarely will have specific information about the nature, location, and timing of the attack, the group carrying it out, or the identities of those who have knowledge of the attack. In fact, officials may not even know whether there is a specific attack planned at all.

The more likely case is the one currently facing the federal government with some of those captured in the aftermath of September 11: law enforcement officials have captured someone whom they have reason to believe is a member of a terrorist group, and they seek information from that person about past attacks and possible future attacks. Put differently, officials may interrogate for the purpose of solving past crimes, getting additional information about past crimes whether or not they have already been solved, and obtaining information that would help foil future attacks whether or not any particular attacks are on the drawing board. Officials may have reason to believe that the person they have captured knows something about past attacks or future plans, but they cannot be sure. If the suspect refuses to provide any information (or worse, mocks their efforts), they may become frustrated and angry. In such cases, should torture be an option?

In rough terms, we believe the Israeli approach provides the best answer. Torture is categorically illegal under international law, the federal Constitution and statutes, and state law. Regardless of the claimed purpose or need, it should remain so. No court, legislature, or executive official should encourage or condone torture in any way. In addition, victims of torture should have the full array of available remedies: criminal prosecutions, damages actions, and injunctive relief where appropriate.

Our rationales are both moral and pragmatic. We believe torture is wrong in nearly every circumstance. Moreover, legalizing torture would create administrative difficulties that would raise further moral issues. For example, if some form of torture were legal, Congress would have to craft legislative standards for when and how to torture (e.g., how long can interrogators hold someone's head under water?), delegate that task to the executive, or entrust the torture decision to executive branch discretion. If the executive branch drafted regulations, the courts would engage in Chevron review to make sure the executive's interpretations were reasonable and within the range of permitted activity, and would preside over any subsequent cases. All three branches would thus play a role in creating the framework for torture, and all three branches would become complicit in it. Finally, no matter how carefully the respective branches performed their appointed tasks, the resulting standards would inevitably be overinclusive, resulting in unnecessary torture.

Authorizing law enforcement officials to use torture even in extremely limited circumstances would also send a variety of undesirable messages. Once torture is available for terrorists in extreme circumstances, someone inevitably will demand it in less extreme circumstances, and then for suspected serial rapists or murderers, or even for those accused of lesser crimes. The slippery slope problem with torture and the related risk of abuse is real, and the harms that would inevitably result from a loosening of standards are significant. Authorizing torture would also betray well-established constitutional values and teach citizens that principles are among the first things to be jettisoned in an emergency.

A claim by the United States that it may torture in extreme circumstances would have serious international consequences as well. Such a claim would undermine the "painfully won and still fragile consensus" against torture. Absent an absolute ban on torture, other countries or even terrorist groups could claim they were simply following the example of the United States. The frequency of torture in many countries could increase, which would also increase the chance that a US national would be tortured if kidnapped or captured by terrorists or the military forces of another country.

For these reasons, the government should not have the authority to torture even in the extreme-circumstances scenario discussed above, in which we conceded that torture could be permitted. Rather, the best approach is to place the decision squarely on the shoulders of the individuals who order or carry out torture. Government agents should use torture only when it provides the last remaining chance to save lives that are in imminent peril. If interrogators know that they act at their peril, because the law provides no authority for torture under any circumstances, then they are likely to be deterred from acting except when the choice—however distasteful—seems obvious.

When a government agent uses torture to gain information that would avert a future terrorist act, the necessity defense should be available in any resulting criminal prosecution. A successful necessity claim requires proof that the defendant reasonably believed his harmful actions were necessary to avert a greater, imminent harm. A better—though less popular—description of the defense is that necessity claims turn on whether the defendant's conduct, however harmful, was "right and proper . . . under the circumstances."[7] Under either formulation, a government agent who tortures to save lives has a fair chance of mounting a successful defense.

Allowing the necessity defense in torture cases is consistent with providing strong deterrence against torture. Most officials probably believe that torture is prohibited, but they are less likely to know that the necessity defense could be available despite that prohibition. Ignorance of the exception to the rule would promote deterrence. Even if interrogators know that the necessity defense is available, they will not be able to predict with certainty before they act whether the defense would be successful, and the resulting uncertainty would also foster deterrence. The primary obstacle to deterrence is prosecutorial discretion. An interrogator might assume that the government will not prosecute if torture reveals critical information. For that reason, the Department of Justice should have a clear and public policy of prosecuting without exception any law enforcement official who uses torture.

. . . .

IV. CONCLUSION

To paraphrase Justice Jackson, torture is an "outlaw." Our experience with abusive police interrogation practices during the past century taught us that police use of torture to obtain confessions is not the best way to obtain reliable evidence. More importantly, torture violates fundamental human rights protected by the Constitution and international law and degrades law enforcement by reducing it to the level of the criminals it seeks to apprehend. During the pre-*Miranda* era, Supreme Court decisions regulating police interrogation thus held that the government is absolutely prohibited from using torture to obtain incriminating statements. Over the past decade, this principle has been confirmed and expanded. Under our current law, torture is absolutely prohibited. Moreover, state-sponsored torture cannot be justified by any exceptional circumstances.

These principles were formulated before the attacks of September 11 precipitated our present concern with protecting innocent people from imminent terrorist attacks. Nevertheless, we believe these principles provide the framework within which government officials interrogating suspected terrorists should be required to operate. There will, of course, be "ticking bomb" hypotheticals in which an officer's decision to use torture to obtain vital information would be viewed by everyone as the best choice under the circumstances. But such situations will rarely, if ever, arise in practice. In the great majority of cases, an officer will not plausibly be able to claim that he believed that torturing a suspected terrorist was the only means through which he could avert an imminent loss of life.

Accordingly, whenever a government officer employs torture, he should be subjected to criminal prosecution. If the officer claims that he reasonably believed his criminal behavior was immediately necessary to avert a greater harm (such as the loss of innocent lives), he should be allowed to raise a necessity defense which can be evaluated by a judge or jury. Through this means, officers who torture in true "ticking bomb" situations may be relieved of criminal liability, a result that seems consistent with normative standards of fairness. At the same time, however, through maintaining the principle that torture is prohibited, we will provide maximum deterrence against government use of torture and thereby, to the extent possible, prevent the government from degrading itself by engaging in behavior that is inconsistent with our constitutional heritage and condemned by civilized nations.

WATERBOARDING AND THE LEGACY OF THE BYBEE-YOO "TORTURE AND POWER" MEMORANDUM

Reflections from a Temporary Yoo Colleague and Erstwhile Bush Administration Apologist
(2009)

M. Katherine B. Darmer

INTRODUCTION

It is commonly said that we are a nation of laws, not men. And we are. But beyond the laws, we are also a nation of men and women with a common ethic. Some things are not American. Torture, for damned sure, is one of them.[1]

This essay argues that waterboarding is torture and that torture is illegal and wrong. It strikes me as unfortunate that these are really debatable propositions [today], but we know all too well that our country has engaged in waterboarding and that prominent academics and lawyers continue to defend such tactics today.

When I first read the August 1, 2002, Department of Justice Memorandum by Jay Bybee and John Yoo regarding torture, my reaction was one that occurs "[t]oo often in the academy." We "talk in muted voices, hushed, pseudo-intellectual whispers, unsure whether we should take a stand. . . ."[2] Despite my initial reticence, the memorandum was roundly, almost uniformly condemned in the academic community. While I did join the choir of condemners, my voice was not among the early, courageous voices of criticism.

Perhaps I was overawed by the credentials of those who produced the memorandum and felt enduring ties of loyalty to a Justice Department I had only recently left. Perhaps I noted that, beyond the memorandum's authors, there were other serious lawyers and academics who defended the administration as taking prudent, defensive measures. Having lived and worked in Manhattan, I was deeply affected by the tragedy of September 11 and was reluctant, even within the academy and far removed from real-world decision making, to be "on record" opposing any legitimate tactic that might make us safer. I failed to appreciate that what the memo was defending were tactics like waterboarding. I was not yet willing to believe that the Justice Department—in which I had substantial faith—was actually defending torture. Rather, I noted the administration's disavowal of the memo, assumed the memo was not broadly representative of administration views, and accepted the explanation that Abu Ghraib was perpetrated by a "few bad apples." I was unwilling to accept the notion that the memo reflected and sought to justify a "torture culture." The term "waterboarding" was not yet in the popular lexicon.

In the immediate aftermath of the attacks, moreover, I was fully supportive of what appeared to be appropriate law enforcement responses. I was impressed with President Bush's declaration that hate crimes against Muslims would not be tolerated and by his administration's swift move against the perpetrators of hate crimes. Aggressive use of material witness warrants and other temporary detentions struck me as prudent.

As time went on, however, unease set in, and then alarm. Those of Middle Eastern descent were targeted for questioning. Detentions at Guantanamo continued, with minimal process for detainees. Even more troubling, it became plain that tactics such as waterboarding had been used by our country in interrogating suspects. Those who had read the August 1, 2002, memo with a more jaundiced view than I had were already on record with dire warnings regarding the memo's implications. Their concerns were realized.

This short essay, thus, is largely simply an acknowledgment of the important role played in this debate by voices more forceful and pre-scient than my own. Because the August 1, 2002, memo and related memoranda have been so thoroughly and effectively addressed by others, I will draw heavily on that work to address the question whether waterboarding is torture and then turn to a January 29, 2009, *Wall Street Journal* op-ed published by Professor John Yoo. . . .

Professor Yoo himself has defended waterboarding quite recently. In his January 29, 2009, op-ed, for example, Yoo decried the Obama administration's decision to terminate the CIA's "special authority to interrogate terrorists" and suggested that "coercive interrogation methods," including waterboarding, were appropriately used in the prior administration.[3] In light of this continued debate, I believe it is impor-tant to acknowledge the extensive and thorough extant criticism of Yoo's role in developing a "torture culture" during the War on Terror.

This paper is an outgrowth of [a] Symposium presentation on a panel entitled "Civil Liberties for Civil Rights: Justifying Wartime Decline of Civil Liberties by a Gain of Civil Rights,"[4] a title that reflects some ambi-guity. . . . [I]t strikes me that those who framed this discussion had in mind that we have given up certain freedoms in order to gain more safety. Indeed, Yoo himself subscribes to this view, rejecting as "naïve" and "high-flying rhetoric" President Obama's inaugural speech statement "that we can 'reject as false the choice between our safety and our ideals.'"[5] This essay subscribes to [the view], . . . however, that holding certain ideals as sacrosanct can be done consistent with making us safer, particularly in the long run. While some minor inconveniences such as longer lines at airports and greater scrutiny of luggage may have made us marginally safer, the fundamental transgressions of civil liberties that are the topic of this particular paper have not, I submit, made us more secure. Instead, they have resulted in a "plunge from the moral heights"[6] with no demonstrable increase in our safety. Indeed, torture arguably makes us less safe because it makes it more likely that our own troops will be tortured in return and also inflames anti-American sentiment. Perhaps more important, even if waterboarding has made us safer, it is an abandonment of core principles to engage in it and thus we should reject it categorically, Yoo's past and current arguments notwithstanding.

I. THE BYBEE-YOO TORTURE AND POWER MEMORANDUM

The August 1, 2002, memorandum, prepared for Alberto R. Gonzalez, counsel to the president, was prepared by the United States Department of Justice Office of Legal Counsel ("OLC") and signed by Jay S. Bybee, then Assistant Attorney General and now a Ninth Circuit judge. John Yoo, a professor of law at Berkeley who served in the OLC when the memorandum was prepared, drafted and defended the memo, which is sometimes referred to as the "Yoo Memorandum," sometimes as the "Bybee Memorandum," and sometimes as the "Torture Memorandum." Because Yoo is widely acknowledged as the primary author but Bybee, who was Yoo's superior, actually signed the memo and bears ultimate responsibility for its contents, I believe it more appropriate to refer to the memorandum as the "Bybee-Yoo Memorandum." Moreover, the memorandum is as astonishing for its arrogation of virtually unlimited executive powers as it is for its narrowly circumscribed definition of "torture," and so I will refer to the memorandum as the "Bybee-Yoo Torture and Power Memorandum," or BYTAP Memo.[7]

Two provisions of the BYTAP Memo have come under the most sustained attack: (1) the narrow definition of "torture," which evidence suggests was solicited in order to justify waterboarding tactics the administration was already using when the memo was written; and (2) the claim of unlimited executive power to engage in any tactic, including torture.

With regard to the narrow definition, the BYTAP Memo starts with the statutory prohibition on torture, which forbids the infliction of "severe physical or mental pain or suffering." The full definition of "torture" is as follows:

> "torture" means an act committed by a person acting under the color of law specifically intended to inflict severe physical or mental pain or suffering (other than pain or suffering incidental to lawful sanctions) upon another person within his custody or physical control;

> "severe mental pain or suffering" means the prolonged mental harm caused by or resulting from—

> the intentional infliction or threatened infliction of severe physical pain or suffering;

> the administration or application, or threatened administration or application, of mind-altering substances or other procedures calculated to disrupt profoundly the senses or the personality;

> the threat of imminent death; or

> the threat that another person will imminently be subjected to death, severe physical pain or suffering, or the administration or

application of mind-altering substances or other procedures calculated to disrupt profoundly the senses or personality. . . .

The BYTAP Memo then borrows from language contained in a
statute addressing medical care and concludes that those statutes suggest
that "severe pain" as used in the antitorture statute "must rise to a similarly
high level—the level that would ordinarily be associated with a sufficiently
serious physical condition or injury such as death, organ failure, or serious
impairment of bodily functions—in order to constitute torture."

But even this narrowed definition would not limit the president,
according to the BYTAP Memo. Rather, "[i]n order to respect the President's inherent constitutional authority to manage a military campaign
against al Qaeda and its allies, Section 2340A must be construed as not
applying to interrogations undertaken pursuant to his Commander in
Chief authority." In other words, despite the constitutional command
that the executive branch execute the laws (including those categorically
forbidding torture), the BYTAP Memo concludes that, simply by
invoking the term "Commander in Chief," the president could authorize
any interrogation technique, including torture. In short, the BYTAP
Memo permitted the conclusion that waterboarding isn't torture, but
even if it is, the president can do it. He can do anything.

The BYTAP Memo has been harshly criticized for, among other
things, failing to construe the torture ban in a way that would avoid conflict with international law, using an unrelated medical statute in order
to reach a narrow definition of "severe pain," failing to recognize that the
statutory ban on torture does not admit of exceptions, and asserting the
view that the president has a "blank check," despite the fact that such a
position "is against the great weight of precedent."[8] The BYTAP Memo
has also been criticized for starting from the premise that international
and domestic laws wrongly frustrate the ability of United States officials

to act with flexibility, while ignoring long-term consequences of acting unilaterally. The BYTAP Memo is premised on "the epic assertions of executive power proclaimed by Yoo."

The conservative Jack Goldsmith, who succeeded Yoo at OLC, found that Yoo's memoranda were not only one-sided but contrary to law. "The idea that Congress could not oversee the interrogation of detainees ... 'has no foundation in prior OLC opinions, judicial decisions, or in any other source of law.'"9 The BYTAP Memo does not acknowledge the president's constitutional obligation to take care that the laws are "faithfully executed," nor does it acknowledge Congress's delegated powers to make rules and regulations for the conduct of the armed forces and for "captures."

Dean Harold H. Koh of the Yale Law School has described the August 1, 2002, BYTAP Memo as "perhaps the most clearly erroneous legal opinion I have ever read."10 Yet the BYTAP Memo has "proved to be enormously influential." Although the Justice Department formally withdrew the BYTAP memo shortly after it was leaked, the administration adhered to many of its premises even while issuing a new memorandum (the "Levin Memo") that embraced the unequivocal rhetoric that "torture is abhorrent." As Professor Margulies points out, "Levin deserves substantial credit for clear and resonant language that accurately represented the consensus on this issue. If one reads the [Levin] memo more carefully, however, loopholes appear, justifying what the Administration had already done."11 One of the tactics the administration sought to justify was waterboarding.

II. WATERBOARDING AND TORTURE

The United States admits to having "waterboarded" suspects under the auspices of the CIA and continued to claim the authority to use the technique as recently as 2005. The BYTAP memo's narrow definition of torture may well have been designed to allow for this particular procedure.

. . . .

The history of water torture has been thoroughly laid out in a recent article by Evan Wallach, a judge on the United States Court of International Trade. Judge Wallach traces the use of the technique throughout history, including by the Japanese against Allied prisoners of war in World War II, by the United States during its occupation of the Philippines, and in one instance, domestically, by a sheriff in Texas. "In all cases, whether the water treatment was applied by Americans or to Americans, or simply reviewed by American courts, it has uniformly been rejected as illegal, often with severely punitive results for the perpetrators."[12]

. . . .

... [I]n the Texas case, law enforcement officers were charged with "handcuffing prisoners to chairs, placing towels over their faces, and pouring water on the cloth until they gave what the officers considered to be confessions."[13] The sheriff was convicted and received a ten-year prison sentence; other defendants also received significant prison sentences. At sentencing, the judge noted that the Texas law enforcement operation would embarrass even a "dictator."[14]

Wallach noted that the "water torture" or "water boarding" technique has long been prized as an interrogation method because it imposes "severe mental trauma and physical pain but no traces of physical trauma that would be discoverable without an autopsy."[15]

During the height of the debate about waterboarding as used by the

United States against terrorist suspects, the journalist Christopher Hitchens chose to voluntarily undergo the experience.[16] ...

. . . .

... Even after the ordeal, Hitchens has experienced feelings of panic upon awakening or in circumstances where he is short of breath. He concludes that "if waterboarding does not constitute torture, then there is no such thing as torture."[17]

A majority of Americans share Hitchens' view that waterboarding constitutes torture. Judge Wallach, too, concludes that waterboarding is torture even under the narrow BYTAP Memo definition. However, the fact that the BYTAP Memo seems to have been designed to exclude tactics such as waterboarding from the definition of torture illustrates BYTAP's biggest problem. Surely waterboarding, under any reasonable definition of torture, is torture.

Torture is illegal, and given our country's (historic) moral stature, we have a "special responsibility" to enforce the prohibition, as noted by the journalist Eyal Press.[18] We lead by example, and, without condemning torture ourselves, we cannot expect others to do so. That condemnation must be more than rhetorical. Insisting that the United States does not torture is empty rhetoric if we make the claim while inflicting waterboarding on suspects.

Equivocating on torture not only causes us to lose moral standing on the international stage but also places our own soldiers at risk. As Professor Philip B. Heymann points out, if we approve torture in particular circumstances, other countries will do the same. It was that concern that led us to accept Geneva Convention prohibitions on torture, despite the cost of obtaining information that "might save dozens of American lives."[19]

III. YOO'S RECENT OP-ED

Yoo continues to view the Geneva Convention restrictions and other limits on the president's use of coercive techniques as wrong-headed and dangerous. In his recent op-ed, Yoo laments that President Obama will likely "declare terrorists to be prisoners of war under the Geneva Convention," whereas the Bush administration classified terrorists "like pirates, illegal combatants who do not fight on behalf of a nation and refuse to obey the laws of war."[20]

Alan Clarke argues that the demonization of an enemy, and the claim that some people are just "outside of the law," are elements of the creation of a torture culture. "We inhabit a world of 'us' against 'the evil doers' which permits a torture culture to take hold. Al-Qaeda becomes equated with pirates and slave traders to be dealt with or extirpated at will."[21] And as Eyal Press argues, torture is "a function not of brute sadism but of the willingness to view one's enemies as something less than human."[22]

Moreover, while some of those classified as "enemy combatants" have in fact been terrorists, others have not been. In demonizing the enemy and acting as though we are justified in treating such a class of persons as "outside the law," we run the grave risk that innocents will be victims, as they have been in the past. As Clarke points out, "[e]xperts estimate that eighty percent of people tortured by our forces and our South Vietnamese allies during the Vietnam War were wholly innocent people who were in the wrong place at the wrong time."[23]

Clarke illustrates in his recent article, "Creating a Torture Culture," that the use of torture is not easily cabined. Rather:

Once started, torture and other abusive practices spread. Their logic cannot be easily contained. If it is right to torture in the extreme situation, what about a slightly less extreme case? . . . In every case, harsh practices can be justified on the ground that the person being questioned may harbor information that could save innocent lives.[24]

Relying on history and behavioral science studies, Clarke also points out that torture is a "true slippery slope." Most of us are capable of torture and, "in the absence of enforced prevention rules, systemic abuses become prevalent."[25]

Even after Abu Ghraib and revelations about the extent to which waterboarding was used, Yoo acknowledges no such risk of systemic abuse, focusing instead only on the risk attendant to foregoing harsh interrogation tactics. With regard to waterboarding specifically, Professor Yoo adheres steadfastly to the view that it is a legitimate practice, acknowledging that President Bush authorized the practice three times and suggesting that President Obama acted precipitously and foolishly in terminating the CIA's "special authority to interrogate terrorists."[26] Yet even before Obama's inauguration, the Department of Justice OLC had "conceded that waterboarding [was] no longer legal" after the passage of the Detainee Treatment Act of 2005 and the Military Commissions Act of 2006, albeit still claiming that the president could authorize waterboarding and other such techniques "in special circumstances."[27] In eschewing any authority for such practices, the new president is doing nothing more than agreeing to follow the law.

President Obama is also reclaiming some of the moral high ground lost when it was revealed that the United States had engaged in torture. While Yoo predicts that "Mr. Obama may have opened the door to further terrorist acts on U.S. soil by shattering some of the nation's most critical defenses,"[28] we can hope that he has instead begun the laborious process of reclaiming the country's moral standing on the international stage. . . .

WATERBOARDING AND THE LEGACY

It is notable that Yoo's opinion piece adhering to the view that water-boarding is an indispensable tool in the War on Terror was written more than eight years after the tragic events of 9/11; it was not written under the same pressures that Yoo and others faced when they first advocated a narrow definition of "torture" when advising the administration. In other words, even after considerable reflection and presumably after considering the virtual cottage industry that has developed to criticize Yoo's wartime memos, Yoo remains strident in defense of his first instincts.

CONCLUSION

Fortunately, the majority of academics and lawyers acted quickly and decisively to illustrate the dangers of instincts that would act to grab power and inflict torture in the name of making us safer. Not only was the BYTAP Memo formally withdrawn by the Justice Department, but it has been thoroughly deconstructed and criticized by an army of academics.

In the opening quote of his piece, "In Torture We Trust?", Eyal Press quotes from John-Paul Sartre: "If patriotism has to precipitate us into dishonour, if there is no precipice of inhumanity over which nations and men will not throw themselves, then, why in fact do we go to so much trouble to become, or to remain, human?"[29] Indeed.

TORTURE

Editorial, New York Times, *April 1, 2010*

The Web site of the United Nations High Commissioner for Human Rights contains a four-page document listing various definitions of the term "torture." Most center on two points: that torture is any act that intentionally inflicts "severe pain or suffering, whether physical or mental," in the words of a 1975 UN declaration, to serve a state purpose like gathering information or intimidating dissenters; and that pain or suffering that arises from lawful punishment does not count.

The debate over how to define torture has taken on new meaning since the Sept. 11 attacks lent a new urgency to counterterrorism efforts. In 2002, officials in the Justice Department's Office of Legal Counsel issued a memo that argued that coercive interrogations constitute torture only if they intentionally caused suffering "equivalent in intensity to the pain accompanying serious physical injury, such as organ failure, impairment of bodily function, or even death." That memo was rescinded in 2004, and since then members of the Bush administration have insisted that torture is "abhorrent" and prohibited by existing regulations.

But the actual limits of permissible techniques during interrogation remain unclear. In October 2007, an article in The *New York Times* revealed that in February 2005, shortly after Alberto R. Gonzales became attorney general, the Justice Department issued a secret memorandum on the subject. The new opinion, according to officials who had seen the document, for the first time provided explicit authorization to barrage terror suspects with a combination of painful physical and psychological tactics, including head-slapping, simulated drowning and frigid temperatures.

Officials in the Bush administration said that harsh interrogation techniques had prevented terrorist attacks. But critics argued that torturing detainees would prevent them from being brought to trial. In January 2009 a senior Pentagon official in the Bush administration, Susan J. Crawford, said that interrogators had tortured a Guantánamo detainee, which led her to decide against prosecuting him.

Days after becoming president, Barack Obama signed a series of executive orders reversing the most disputed counterterrorism policies of the Bush administration. Among Mr. Obama's actions was to require that all interrogations follow the noncoercive methods of the Army Field Manual. He also directed his cabinet to formulate new policies on detaining and interrogating terror suspects. The immediate practical impact of the orders was limited, in part because military interrogators have been required by law to abide by the Army Field Manual since 2005.

In September 2010, a federal appeals court ruled that former prisoners of the CIA could not sue over their alleged torture in overseas prisons because such a lawsuit might expose secret government information.

Public officials and human rights advocates have called for a criminal investigation or an independent panel to look into allegations of torture.

Mr. Obama has played down, while not ruling out, the possibility of such actions, because questions about where such investigations would lead are legally daunting and politically complex. But legal experts across the political spectrum said statements made by Attorney General Eric H. Holder Jr. describing waterboarding as torture would make it difficult to avoid a criminal investigation, even as most also say a successful prosecution might well be impossible.

NATIONAL SECURITY, CIVIL LIBERTIES, AND THE WAR ON TERROR

On Aug. 24, the Justice Department's ethics office has recommended reversing the Bush administration and reopening nearly a dozen prisoner-abuse cases, potentially exposing agency employees and contractors to prosecution for brutal treatment of terrorism suspects, according to a person officially briefed on the matter.

BEYOND *BIN LADEN* AND *LINDH*
Confessions Law in an Age of Terrorism
(2003)

M. K. B. Darmer

INTRODUCTION

In *United States v. Bin Laden*,[1] a federal district court suppressed statements made abroad during the investigation of the 1998 bombings of US embassies in Kenya and Tanzania, holding, in essence, that the suspect should have been given *Miranda* warnings. In 2002, lawyers for the "American Taliban," John Walker Lindh, moved to suppress statements made by their client after his capture in Afghanistan, alleging violations of both his *Miranda* and due process rights. Both cases arose shortly after the Supreme Court's decision in *Dickerson v. United States* (2000), which reaffirmed the continuing validity of *Miranda v. Arizona* (1966). In *Dickerson*, the Court held unconstitutional Congress's efforts to overrule the controversial *Miranda* decision through legislation [contained at 18 U.S.C. § 3501], passed shortly after *Miranda* was decided, that used a "totality of the circumstances" test to determine a confession's admissibility.

Obtaining confessions from suspected terrorists will play an integral role in this country's current "war on terror." Yet [we know that suspects sometimes falsely confess, as was the case with confessions] made by young men convicted in the notorious "Central Park Jogger" case. Similarly, in a case involving an Egyptian national detained as a material witness after the terrorist attacks on September 11, 2001, the witness falsely confessed to owning a suspicious radio device that was discovered in a hotel across the street from the former World Trade Center. This article examines the current state of confessions law in light of society's need for confessions and proposes specific approaches designed to serve the legitimate needs of law enforcement while remaining true to the Constitution.

. . . .

While there are inherent difficulties in balancing the rights of criminal suspects with the legitimate goals of law enforcement, these difficulties are magnified in cases involving terrorism and national security. Confessions may be critical to such cases, and obtaining justice in cases involving terrorism is of critical importance.

Part I of this article traces the development of confessions law in the United States. . . . It discusses the Supreme Court's . . . return to the Fifth Amendment as the anchor for its landmark decision in *Miranda v. Arizona.* . . .

Part II then turns to the special issues raised by interrogation that occurs outside the territorial limits of the United States. It takes a close look at a district court's recent decision in *United States v. Bin Laden,* which held that the privilege against self-incrimination applied even to nonresident aliens whose only connection to the United States was their prosecution in this country for the bombing of the US embassies in Kenya and Tanzania. While I agree that the self-incrimination clause applies to aliens tried in United States courts, I do not agree that the clause is implicated by a technical violation of *Miranda* when the confession is voluntary, and I propose a "foreign interrogation" exception to *Miranda.*

Part III . . . argues that truly compelled statements should never be admitted into evidence. It is those statements—rather than statements taken in technical violation of *Miranda*—that violate the self-incrimination clause.

I. THE EVOLUTION OF CONFESSIONS LAW
IN THE UNITED STATES

A. The Fifth Amendment and Bram

The Fifth Amendment provides that "No person . . . shall be compelled in any criminal case to be a witness against himself." . . . Since the Supreme Court's 1966 *Miranda* decision, the Fifth Amendment has been associated with the right to refuse to answer police questions. . . .

. . . .

D. The Court's Post-*Miranda* Jurisprudence

Ultimately . . . *Miranda* changed the landscape of confessions law less than might have been predicted. . . . Since *Miranda* was decided, the Court has held that statements taken without providing warnings can be used to impeach a defendant, has recognized a "public safety exception" to the provision of warnings, and has [limited the scope of the decision in other ways].

Despite strong language in *Miranda* itself about the constitutional nature of that decision and its relationship to the Fifth Amendment, the Court later undermined the holdings of *Miranda* by describing the *Miranda* rules as merely "prophylactic." In *New York v. Quarles* (1984), for example, the Court declined to suppress the defendant's answer to a question about the location of a gun, despite the fact that the question was not preceded by warnings. In an opinion authored by Justice Rehnquist, the Supreme Court found that "this case presents a situation where concern for public safety must be paramount to adherence to the literal language of the prophylactic rules enunciated in *Miranda*."

The Court emphasized that there was no suggestion that the statements at issue were "actually compelled by police conduct which overcame [the defendant's] will to resist." Accordingly, the Court framed the issue as whether the officer had been "justified in failing to make available to respondent the procedural safeguards associated with the privilege against compulsory self-incrimination since *Miranda*." The Court held that the officer was justified and that "the doctrinal underpinnings of *Miranda*" do not require that it "be applied in all its rigor to a situation" in which questions are "reasonably prompted by a concern for the public safety."

The Rehnquist opinion drew a sharp dissent from three other justices. Justice Marshall asserted that, in crafting a "public safety" exception:

> [T]he majority makes no attempt to deal with the constitutional presumption established by [*Miranda*]. . . . Without establishing that interrogations concerning the public's safety are less likely to be coercive than other interrogations, the majority cannot endorse the "public-safety" exception and remain faithful to the logic of *Miranda v. Arizona*.

In the dissent's view, authorities faced with a genuine emergency that demands immediate answers are not confronted with a dilemma. Rather:

> If a bomb is about to explode or the public is otherwise imminently imperiled, the police are free to interrogate suspects without advising them of their constitutional rights. . . . If trickery is necessary to pro-

tect the public, then the police may trick a suspect into confessing. While the Fourteenth Amendment sets limits on such behavior, nothing in the Fifth Amendment or our decision in *Miranda v. Arizona* proscribes this sort of emergency questioning. All the Fifth Amendment forbids is the introduction of coerced statements at trial.

Justice Marshall was quite right in insisting that the Court's decision betrayed the logic of *Miranda*. By emphasizing that Quarles's statements were not "actually compelled," the Court drew a line between real compulsion and the presumption of compulsion that inheres in every situation involving custodial interrogation, according to *Miranda*. Yet the irrebuttable presumption established by *Miranda* is itself problematic.

Given the Court's repeated reference to *Miranda* as a "prophylactic" decision that "sweeps more broadly than the Fifth Amendment itself," many expected the Court to overrule *Miranda* outright when it was given the chance in *Dickerson v. United States*. In that case, however, the Court rejected a statute designed to replace *Miranda* that prescribed a totality-of-the-circumstances test to determine whether a confession was coerced. The Court referred to *Miranda* as a "constitutional decision" that Congress cannot overrule. Acknowledging that cases such as *Quarles* had carved out exceptions to its rule, Chief Justice Rehnquist, writing for the Court, noted that those decisions:

> illustrate the principle—not that *Miranda* is not a constitutional rule—but that no constitutional rule is immutable. No court laying down a general rule can possibly foresee the various circumstances in which counsel will seek to apply it, and the sort of modifications represented by these cases are as much a normal part of constitutional law as the original decision.

II. THE APPLICATION OF *MIRANDA*
TO SUSPECTS QUESTIONED ABROAD

A. The *Bin Laden* Case

One set of circumstances that the *Miranda* Court perhaps did not foresee was the application of the rules to nonresident aliens captured abroad. In *United States v. Bin Laden*, a district court confronted this issue when dealing with the admissibility of confessions made by two suspected bin Laden confederates in connection with the bombing of US embassies in Kenya and Tanzania.

In addressing the issue as "a matter of first impression," Judge Leonard B. Sand asked whether a nonresident alien defendant's non-Mirandized statements were admissible at trial in the United States when the statements were the result of interrogations conducted abroad by US law enforcement officials. The court concluded that the Fifth Amendment's right against self-incrimination applies to the extent that the alien suspect is on trial in the United States. In addition, US law enforcement agents conducting investigations abroad should still use the familiar *Miranda* warnings framework, "even if [the] interrogation by US agents occur[s] wholly abroad . . . while [the defendant is] in the physical custody of foreign authorities."

The court refused to define the issue as one of extraterritorial application of the Fifth Amendment, despite the government's argument that it should. The government's definition of the issue as whether Fifth Amendment rights "reach out to protect individuals . . . outside the United States" failed to convince the court because "any violation of the privilege against self-incrimination occurs, not at the moment law enforcement officials coerce statements through custodial interrogation, but when a defendant's involuntary statements are actually used against him at an American criminal proceeding." Therefore, according to this court, the admissibility of custodial confessions hinges upon the scope of the privilege as it applies to a nonresident alien defendant currently subject to American domestic criminal proceedings.

The court noted that the "expansive language" of the Fifth Amendment "neither denotes nor connotes any limitation in scope." The use of "no person" instead of the familiar phrase "the people" suggests that the right against self-incrimination applies "without apparent regard to citizenship or community connection." The Supreme Court has already determined that the Fifth and Fourteenth amendments' due process protections apply without limitation to "every one." Judge Sand determined that even without an explicit Supreme Court ruling granting the privilege against self-incrimination in this context, the circumstances exemplified the widely accepted notion that these protections apply "universally to any criminal prosecution brought by the United States within its own borders." Notably, the US Supreme Court has defined the right against self-incrimination as a "fundamental trial right of criminal defendants." Finally, Judge Sand believed that the underlying policies of the Fifth Amendment "are no less relevant when the criminal defendant at issue is an unconnected, non-resident alien."

Judge Sand further held that "a principled, but realistic application of *Miranda*'s familiar warning/waiver framework . . . is both necessary and appropriate under the Fifth Amendment." *Miranda* is required because "the inherent coerciveness of [police interrogation] is clearly no less troubling when carried out beyond our borders and under the aegis of a foreign stationhouse." . . .

Judge Sand acknowledged that the specific *Miranda* warnings related to the right to counsel and the ability to have counsel appointed are subject to modification in the context of foreign interrogation, where counsel may be unavailable. He held, however, that "the specific admonitions recited should conform to the local circumstances regarding access to counsel." As Mark Godsey has recently argued, Judge Sand imposed upon US agents conducting investigations abroad an extraordinary and unrealistic duty to discern relevant foreign law, and Godsey proposed an alternative modification to the *Miranda* warnings abroad.

I would go even further than Godsey by carving out a "foreign interrogation" exception to *Miranda* in situations such as those present in *Bin Laden*.

B. The Implication of Interpreting *Miranda* as Only a Trial Right

Before analyzing the justification of Judge Sand's holding that *Miranda* warnings are required abroad, however, it is important to scrutinize the theoretical underpinnings of that holding. Central to Judge Sand's analysis was the notion that a *Miranda*-based violation of the Fifth Amendment does not occur until the trial itself. This view is exemplified in *Kastigar v. United States* and the rest of the immunity line of cases, in which witnesses have been granted immunity from prosecution in exchange for their testimony. In those cases, "the Supreme Court made clear that the 'sole concern' of the privilege was not the forcible extraction of statements; rather, the privilege only prohibits the introduction into evidence of such statements at trial or similar proceeding to inflict criminal penalties upon the person who has been 'compelled' to speak."[2]

Applying this interpretation of the privilege to the context of custodial questioning of suspects, the interrogation process itself works no Fifth Amendment violation; an interrogator could ask questions without providing warnings—and could even brutalize or torture a suspect—without violating the self-incrimination clause. Justice Marshall espoused just this view of the Fifth Amendment in his dissenting opinion in *Quarles*, and the implications of that view are once again relevant, particularly in the terrorism context:

> If a bomb is about to explode or the public is otherwise imminently imperiled, the police are free to interrogate suspects without advising them of their constitutional rights. . . . If trickery is necessary to protect the public, then the police may trick a suspect into confessing. While the Fourteenth Amendment sets limits on such behavior, nothing in the Fifth Amendment or our decision in *Miranda* proscribes this sort of emergency questioning. All the Fifth Amendment forbids is the introduction of coerced statements at trial.

Judge Sand, echoing the views of Justice Marshall, similarly suggested that American intelligence efforts abroad would not be unduly impeded by applying the *Miranda* rules abroad: "To the extent that a suspect's *Miranda* rights allegedly impede foreign intelligence collection, we note that *Miranda* only prevents an unwarned or involuntary statement from being used as evidence in a domestic criminal trial; it does not mean that such statements are never to be elicited in the first place."

Similarly, in *United States v. Verdugo-Urquidez* (1990), upon which Judge Sand explicitly relied, the Supreme Court described the privilege against self-incrimination as a "fundamental trial right of criminal defendants." Accordingly, "[a]lthough conduct by law enforcement officials prior to trial may ultimately impair that right, a constitutional violation occurs only at trial." [Editors' Note: The Supreme Court reaffirmed this principle in *Chavez v. Martinez* (2003)]. The question remains: Does it violate the Fifth Amendment to introduce into evidence at trial a statement, taken by American agents abroad, that was not preceded by *Miranda* warnings?

C. Creating a Foreign Interrogation Exception to *Miranda*

The Fifth Amendment provides that "No person ... shall be compelled in any criminal case to be a witness against himself." *Miranda* ... presumes that any statement given without the benefit of the warnings is compelled. That presumption ... often breaks down in practice. As discussed above, for example, the Court has created a "public safety" exception to *Miranda*. In addition, lower courts have admitted into evidence statements made to foreign police that were not preceded by the warnings, so long as the statements were actually voluntary (as opposed to being simply "presumptively compelled" under *Miranda*). The rationale for admitting such statements into evidence in American courts, despite the lack of warnings, is that "the *Miranda* requirements were primarily designed to prevent United States police officers from relying on improper interrogation techniques" and have "little, if any, deterrent effect upon foreign police officers."[3]

Although the Supreme Court has not yet addressed the question of the admissibility of a statement taken by foreign authorities that was not preceded by American-style *Miranda* warnings, it would almost certainly approve the lower courts' reasoning on this point. Those cases are consistent with other Supreme Court cases holding that the presumption of compulsion does not always apply. As George C. Thomas III has put it: "The Court chooses sometimes not to apply the *Miranda* presumption of compulsion even though 'actual' compulsion would produce an outcome in favor of the defendant."[4]

If statements taken without *Miranda* warnings truly amounted to "compulsion" forbidden by the Fifth Amendment, then the question whether exclusion would "deter" misconduct should be irrelevant, and unwarned statements taken by either American or foreign police should be excluded. Unlike the exclusionary sanction in connection with the

Fourth Amendment, which does not by its terms require that evidence seized in an illegal search be excluded, the Fifth Amendment by its terms forbids the introduction into evidence of "compelled" testimony. *Miranda* presumes compulsion where it does not necessarily exist, however. As Justice O'Connor recently wrote in a powerful dissenting opinion in *Withrow v. Williams* (1993):

> Because *Miranda* "sweeps more broadly than the Fifth Amendment itself," it excludes some confessions even though the Constitution would not.... *Miranda*'s overbreadth, of course, is not without justification.... But, like the exclusionary rule for illegally seized evidence, *Miranda*'s prophylactic rule does so at a substantial cost. Unlike involuntary or compelled statements, which are of dubious reliability and are therefore inadmissible for any purpose, confessions obtained in violation of *Miranda* are not necessarily untrustworthy. In fact, because voluntary statements are "trustworthy" even when obtained without proper warnings, their suppression actually impairs the pursuit of truth by concealing probative information from the trier of fact.

The juxtaposition of the Court's recent *Miranda* and due process jurisprudence might lead to the bizarre result that unreliable confessions extracted by foreign agents using brute force would be admissible as evidence in American courts, whereas reliable and voluntary confessions taken by US agents who failed to give *Miranda* warnings would be inadmissible. Whether *Miranda* warnings were given should not be the *sine qua non* for the admissibility of statements made in response to foreign interrogation, however. Rather, the Court should focus on the historic concern for reliability and have a healthy regard for the demands of national security in this context.

While the *Miranda* decision was recently reaffirmed, the Court explicitly acknowledged its mutability. Cases involving foreign interrogation of terrorism suspects present a situation ripe for another *Miranda* exception. The need for information in such cases is even more pressing than was the need for information in *Quarles*. In *Quarles* the police needed to locate a gun that they believed the suspect had discarded in a grocery store; in cases in which US agents travel overseas to interrogate terrorism suspects, the stakes are potentially much higher. Agents should be able to question suspects freely in such circumstances, without the constraints of *Miranda* and without having to establish that, before questioning began, there was an immediate safety concern that justified dispensing with *Miranda* under *Quarles*. In cases involving foreign interrogation of suspected terrorists, the courts should not require agents to advise suspects of *Miranda* rights, regardless of the citizenship of the suspect.

This new exception could be squared with the Court's *Miranda-Quarles-Dickerson* jurisprudence. While the *Dickerson* Court noted that *Miranda* "concluded that the coercion inherent in custodial interrogation blurs the line between voluntary and involuntary statements," *Dickerson* did not reiterate *Miranda*'s claim that all unwarned statements will be presumed compelled. Indeed, it could not have done so; *Quarles* is squarely to the contrary. Rather, the Court's primary rationale for reaffirming *Miranda* was stare decisis. *Miranda*, however, dealt only with domestic questioning in routine criminal cases; foreign interrogation was not at issue, much less foreign interrogation of terrorism suspects. Accordingly, Supreme Court doctrine in no way requires extending the "warnings requirement" beyond those circumstances in which it has already been applied.

Without a foreign interrogation exception, American agents investigating terrorism may be forced to choose between intelligence gathering in the broad interests of preventing future attacks and evidence gathering for the purpose of bringing criminals to justice. This is an untenable dilemma. In the name of upholding purported constitutional rights,

American agents may have a perverse incentive to turn suspected terror-ists over to foreign agents, who may be under no constraints regarding the use of physical force or brutality, rather than risk the exclusion of non-Mirandized statements taken by American law enforcement repre-sentatives. In such a case, the prophylactic goals of *Miranda* backfire, although the Fifth Amendment itself poses no such dilemma.

The Fifth Amendment prohibits compelled statements, of course, and if statements are truly involuntary, they should be excluded on that basis. Unwarned statements are of a different order. George C. Thomas III has argued compellingly that the requirement for *Miranda* warnings is better understood as a requirement for due process notice than as a Fifth Amendment self-incrimination clause requirement. I would argue, moreover, that the Court's post-*Miranda* "involuntary confession" cases should have been analyzed under the auspices of the self-incrimination clause because that clause specifically forbids "compelled" testimony. Instead, even after *Miranda*, the Court has deemed "truly compelled" statements a violation of due process, relegating the self-incrimination clause to a mere backdrop to the resolution of *Miranda* claims.

. . . .

Editors' Note: The discussion of the Court's due process jurisprudence and the case of John Walker Lindh in part III of the article has been eliminated because of space constraints.

CONCLUSION

Cases involving foreign interrogation inevitably will recur. Such interro-gation is limited by both the self-incrimination clause and the due process clause, the goals of which are closely related. The *Miranda* decision presents a flawed analysis of Fifth Amendment "compulsion," but the Court's recent *Dickerson* decision means that courts must continue to reckon with *Miranda*. Consistent with the Constitution, however, the courts can carve out a "foreign interrogation" exception to *Miranda* analogous to the "public safety" exception in *Quarles*. Specifically, the courts should permit into evidence un-Mirandized statements made during investigations of terrorism conducted abroad, so long as such statements were not forcibly extracted. It would be inconsistent with the Constitution, however, to permit into evidence a confession extracted by force, regardless of whether compulsion was applied by foreign or domestic agents.

. . . .

HOLDER'S PROMISING INTERROGATION PLAN

Suspects are more likely to shut up after a courtroom appearance than after a quickly recited *Miranda* warning.
(May 22, 2010)

Stuart Taylor Jr.

In 1966, the Supreme Court instructed police, in *Miranda v. Arizona*, to tell arrested suspects that "you have the right to remain silent." But, in fact, you don't.

Rather, police—or more to the point of current debate, federal agents interrogating suspected terrorists—can skip the famous *Miranda* warnings and even use some degree of coercion to extract a confession, all quite legally. Indeed, you can even be jailed for refusing to answer questions after being granted immunity from any prosecution.

The problem for law enforcement—especially in the terrorism context—is that any statements obtained from an arrested suspect without *Miranda* warnings, or by directly coercing an involuntary confession, ordinarily cannot be used against the person in a criminal case.

A less familiar but perhaps more important problem is that current federal law also bars the use of most statements made more than six hours after a suspect's arrest without first taking him to a magistrate judge for a "presentment" hearing. In a terrorism incident, such an interruption could derail a promising effort to get information about coconspirators and planned attacks.

The combined effect is to force officials to make an unnecessarily difficult choice: They can put terrorism suspects through the kind of prolonged, uninterrupted interrogation that is their best hope of preventing future attacks. Or they can maximize the chance of a successful prosecution. But they can't count on doing both, unless they get lucky.

This dilemma creates unhealthy incentives either to shun aggressive interrogation—which the Obama administration has sometimes seemed all too ready to do—or to subject suspects to the indefinite military detention, interrogation, and trial that the Bush administration favored.

The need to alleviate this problem—and to parry Republican political attacks in the process—is why Attorney General Eric Holder has announced plans to propose legislation making it easier for the feds to extract as much information as possible from captured terrorism suspects and prosecute them, too. Civil-libertarian doves attack the incipient Holder proposal, which has not been publicly detailed, as a threat to constitutional freedoms. But any such threat is quite modest compared with the danger that the status quo poses to innocent lives.

Meanwhile, conservative hawks clamor for Holder and President Obama to hand suspected terrorists over to the military as enemy combatants. But they ignore the damage that this approach does to America's image abroad; the large risk that any convictions by military commissions will crash on appeal; the dangers of subjecting possibly innocent people to decades of detention; and judicial decisions requiring that "enemy combatants" be given lawyers and other rights.

A *Miranda* primer: The decision was a very broad reading of the Fifth Amendment's guarantee that "no person . . . shall be compelled in any criminal case to be a witness against himself." The Court found interrogations of arrested suspects to be inherently coercive. From this premise, it held that any confessions should be deemed "compelled"—

and inadmissible in any criminal case—unless the authorities first dispel the coercive atmosphere.

The Court's prescribed method for doing this was to tell suspects that they have a right to remain silent and to have a lawyer present during any interrogation, and that anything they say can be used against them in court.

But *Miranda*'s holding that it is illegal to use a suspect's un-Mirandized statements to prosecute him did not make it illegal to extract such statements in the first place. The reason that most people have long assumed the opposite is that the primary purpose of interrogating a suspect has almost always been to obtain evidence to prosecute that person. So the ban on using un-Mirandized statements in court has, in practice, been treated as a ban on interrogating a suspect without *Miranda* warnings.

But what if the arrested suspect—such as the US citizens accused of seeking to blow up an airliner over Detroit on Christmas Day and to set off a car bomb in Times Square on May 1—may have information that could save lives by thwarting planned attacks or leading authorities to confederates?

In such a case, the primary goal should be to extract as much information as possible as fast as possible to protect public safety. And as long as this information is not used to prosecute the suspect, there is no violation of either the Fifth Amendment self-incrimination clause or *Miranda*, because there is no compulsion "to be a witness against himself." The Court made this clear in a 2003 case, *Chavez v. Martinez*.

Other decisions suggest that it would also be legal for federal agents to seek potentially lifesaving information by grilling suspects for hours using such coercive methods as yelling, bright lights, sleep deprivation, and death-penalty threats.

Such coercion would, like *Miranda*, make the information obtained inadmissible in court. But under the logic of a 1998 decision, *County of Sacramento v. Lewis*, the coercion itself would violate the Fifth Amendment's due process clause (not the self-incrimination clause) only if it were so extreme as to "shock the conscience" or "intended to injure in some way unjustifiable by any government interest."

The bottom line is that the justices might well uphold the constitutionality of a few hours or days of un-Mirandized interrogation of a suspect deemed by the government to have information that could save lives. But *Miranda*, or the presentment rules, or both would probably bar use of some statements from such a suspect to prosecute him.

To be sure, a 1984 decision called *New York v. Quarles* created a "public safety" exception to *Miranda* to admit into evidence a gun that police had found after spontaneously asking a suspect who was wearing an empty holster when he was arrested after a chase through a supermarket where he had hidden his weapon.

Officials invoked this public safety exception to avoid immediately Mirandizing Faisal Shahzad, who is accused of bringing the car bomb to Times Square, and Umar Farouk Abdulmutallab, who was caught trying to blow up the airliner over Detroit. But officials proceeded to give *Miranda* warnings relatively quickly, apparently out of concern that courts might refuse to extend the public safety exception to interrogations lasting for hours or days.

Holder wants Congress to expand the exception to include lengthy interrogation of suspected terrorists who may have actionable intelligence, without Mirandizing them. Some experts predict that the justices will balk. I think that they might defer, as they should, to the elected branches' judgment that national security calls for some stretching of the public safety exception.

Holder's second goal is to modify federal laws that bar use of evidence obtained without bringing the suspect before a magistrate within six hours of arrest, and perhaps to also create an exception to a Fourth Amendment precedent that sets a presumptive outer limit of forty-eight hours after warrantless arrests.

The need to relax these hearing requirements may be even more pressing than the necessity to expand the public safety exception to *Miranda*.

Many talkative suspects, including Shahzad, just keep talking even after agents quickly recite *Miranda* warnings, experts say. Suspects are more likely to shut up after a courtroom presentment appearance, which includes *Miranda*-like warnings, a defense lawyer, and other formalities. The especially chatty Shahzad repeatedly waived his right to a presentment hearing until two weeks after his arrest. But others may not.

The main purpose of presentment hearings is to prove to the courts that suspects arrested without warrants (the usual situation) are not being arbitrarily detained. Holder's proposed legislation may seek to provide a similar assurance without interrupting the interrogation by bringing the suspect into court. One approach, suggested by Brookings Institution scholar Benjamin Wittes, might be a high-level certification that there is probable cause of a terrorist crime and strong evidence that the suspect may have potentially lifesaving intelligence in a national security emergency.

Such a certification might also overcome a more formidable obstacle to prolonged, uninterrupted interrogation: the 1991 ruling in *County of Riverside v. McLaughlin* that the Fourth Amendment requires another type of preliminary hearing—to determine whether there is probable cause that the suspect committed a crime—within forty-eight hours of any warrantless arrest.

I'd be surprised, however, if Holder proposes to delay a terrorism suspect's first appearance before a judge by more than a week or two, except perhaps in extremely rare circumstances. The actionable-intelligence benefit of any information extracted from a captured terrorist by incommunicado interrogation shrinks, and the civil-liberties cost grows, with each passing day.

By striking a judicious balance in this precarious area, a new law just might help avert attacks so numerous or catastrophic as to drive the government to measures far more drastic and dangerous to liberty than anything we have seen so far.

15

MIRANDA AND "ENHANCED INTERROGATIONS"
May 10, 2010

Wendy Kaminer

Merely two months ago, Attorney General Eric Holder strongly defended the issuance of *Miranda* warnings to terror suspects and reminded his Republican critics that, since 9/11, the criminal justice system has generally proved quite effective in prosecuting failed terror attacks, like the aborted Christmas Day bombing of a Northwest airlines flight. Holder's defense of liberty, justice, and reason—like the administration's determination to close Guantanamo and try the 9/11 defendants in federal court—was nice while it lasted. Now the attorney general is asking Congress to enact legislation codifying an exception to the *Miranda* rule in cases of suspected terrorism.

Why the change in policy? Current (and longstanding) rules governing interrogations are too inflexible and insufficiently "consistent with the threat we now face," Holder explained. It's not clear that the threat of terrorism has substantially changed since he extolled the current rules, although the perceived political threat of resisting Republican criticisms may have increased. Nor is the need for additional flexibility immediately apparent: the administration has acknowledged delaying the issuance of *Miranda* warnings in the interrogations of would-be Christmas Day bomber Umar Farouk Abdulmutallab and Times Square suspect Faisal Shahzad. But, as the *New York Times* observed, interrogators have been "stretching the traditional limits" of a public safety exception to the *Miranda* rule, and Congressional approval of these ad hoc interrogation practices would make them much less vulnerable to judicial challenges. Or maybe *Miranda v. Arizona* is an example of liberal judicial activism recently lamented by the president. In any case, legislation loosening if not entirely repealing *Miranda* rules (perhaps over the opposition of a few civil libertarians in Congress) seems inevitable.

This may not enhance the prosecution of terror suspects or the administration's reputation among Republicans for protecting national security. Will it enhance interrogations? Will it effectively legalize torture? Is legalizing torture an underlying purpose of the drive to deny terror suspects (and the operative word is "suspects") their *Miranda* rights (among others)? *Miranda* warnings are mechanisms for enforcing the constitutional privilege against self-incrimination, which is, in part, a safeguard against (unreliable) coerced confessions. The Supreme Court generally focused on deterring psychological coercion when it issued the *Miranda* rule in 1966. But, as Justice Rehnquist (not known for his liberal activism) observed in *Dickerson v. US*, a 2000 decision declining to repeal *Miranda*, rules against coerced confessions are rooted in English common law and partly reflect a reaction to the use of torture.

Miranda was a controversial decision, accompanied by "stinging dissents," The *New York Times* reported at the time, and some law-and-order conservatives have never accepted it. But law enforcement adapted to it long ago; it has "become embedded in routine police practice," Justice Rehnquist concluded in *Dickerson*. The Rehnquist Court's refusal to overrule *Miranda* quelled (or depressed) opposition to it for a time, and Republicans did not denounce the Bush administration's adherence to it in criminally prosecuting terror suspects (notably aborted shoe bomber Richard Reid), as Holder stressed, in vain, two months ago.

But if rational, fact-based arguments are irrelevant in these battles, concessions may be politically futile. A policy of appeasement will only encourage, not deter, partisan attacks. Administration critics will still clamor to submit terror suspects to "enhanced interrogations," designate them as enemy combatants, and formally strip them of their citizenship (supposedly moderate Massachusetts Senator Scott Brown is cosponsoring a citizenship-stripping bill targeting people who allegedly support terrorism). Even if it endorsed these draconian, unconstitutional proposals, the administration would still be portrayed as weak on national security; in addition, it would have to plead guilty to being weak on the rule of law.

16

SHAHZAD AND *MIRANDA* RIGHTS
May 5, 2010

Orin Kerr

The *New York Times* reports about the interrogation of Faisal Shahzad, who was arrested for trying to explode a bomb in Times Square:

> The suspect, Faisal Shahzad, was interrogated without initially being read his Miranda rights under a public safety exception, and provided what the F.B.I. called "valuable intelligence and evidence."
>
> After investigators determined there was no imminent threat to be headed off, Mr. Shahzad was later read his rights to remain silent, but he waived them and continued talking, the F.B.I. said. Authorities charged him as a civilian on Tuesday, but postponed plans to bring him to court.

Based on what we know, it sounds like the FBI made a good judgment call here. Shahzad is a US citizen who has been living in the United States and was caught in the United States for a crime committed in the United States: Surely this is a case for federal court.

Plus, the FBI's strategy was a smart one if you recognize the detailed maze of *Miranda* doctrine. It's a reasonably safe bet that a court would allow an initial pre-*Miranda* inquiry to be admissible under the public safety exception of *New York v. Quarles* (1984). Then, after Shahzad made clear that he's a talker, the FBI could insert the *Miranda* warnings and get the waiver and then get Shahzad to repeat what he just said pre-waiver. Because the two-stage interview was not an intentional two-step interrogation technique designed to violate *Miranda*, a court would allow the post-*Miranda* statement under Justice Kennedy's controlling opinion in *Missouri v. Seibert* (2004). So from a legal standpoint, this was pretty cleverly done.

The countervailing concern is that perhaps Shahzad would invoke his *Miranda* rights and then stop giving the FBI the information they need. Perhaps obtaining the information was more important than getting a statement that would be admissible in court. But even if that's true, that's a call that the FBI could make on the ground. Consider the facts. The FBI had taken Shahzad into custody and started to question him initially without *Miranda* warnings under the public safety exception. Let's imagine that Shahzad's demeanor left the impression that he might speak to the FBI without *Miranda* warnings but that he might clam up if read the warnings. If that were the case, the FBI could lawfully make the decision of whether to continue to question Shahzad without *Miranda* warnings or whether to give him the warnings and obtain a waiver. In other words, the FBI could make the call on the ground based on his conduct.

Importantly, though, it would *not* have violated Shahzad's constitutional rights to not read him his *Miranda* rights. A lot of people assume that the police are required to read a suspect his rights when he is arrested. That is, they assume that one of a person's rights is the right to be read their rights. It often happens that way on *Law & Order*, but that's not what the law actually requires. Under *Chavez v. Martinez* (2003), it is lawful for the police to not read a suspect his *Miranda* rights, interrogate him, and then obtain a statement that would be inadmissible in court. *Chavez* holds that a person's constitutional rights are violated only if the prosecution tries to have the statement admitted in court. Indeed, the prosecution is even allowed to admit any physical evidence discovered as a fruit of the statement obtained in violation of *Miranda*—only the actual statement is excluded. See *United States v. Patane* (2004). So while it may sound weird, it turns out that obtaining a statement outside *Miranda* but not admitting it in court is lawful.

As a result, the FBI would have acted entirely lawfully in making a choice on the ground as to whether to read Shahzad his *Miranda* rights. The choice would have been between the odds of getting a statement that they could not use in court without the warnings versus the odds of getting a statement that they *could* use in court with the warnings. Shahzad turned out to be a talker, so the FBI gave him the warnings, got his waiver, and then continued to get more statements from him—all of which will be admissible in federal court.

PART 3

IMMIGRATION AND RACIAL PROFILING

UNSECURED BORDERS
Immigration Restrictions, Crime Control, and National Security
(2007)

Jennifer M. Chacón

I. INTRODUCTION

. . . .

One notable feature of the recent immigration debate is the degree to which the rhetoric of security has served as the touchstone of calls for immigration reform.

At times, the term signifies traditional national security issues, including antiterrorism efforts. Immigration enforcement at the various points of entry and the surveillance of noncitizens in the interior are presented as a means to defend the nation's security. In this context, discussing immigration measures as a part of national security policy is both meaningful and necessary. This was clear to the members of the National Commission on Terrorist Attacks Upon the United States. The 9/11 Commission Report identified several immigration administration functions as important national security priorities. For example, the report proposed the use of biometric identifiers on entry documents to be used at all ports of entry, including points of entry along the land border. That proposal was combined with a recommendation for an effective database to track the entering and exit of noncitizens holding various kinds of US visas. These issues fall into the areas where immigration and core national security interests converge.

At other times, however, the language of national security has been invoked in discussions concerning more general immigration control and crime control measures, particularly those measures aimed at immigrants who have committed crimes. The borders between crime control, immigration control, and national security measures have never been secure, but these borders have become much more permeable in the period following the terrorist attacks of September 11, 2001. Indeed, in the area of immigration law more than any other, these boundaries are melting away at a startling pace. While the US government and populace are eager to police the borders of the United States, they are less interested in mapping out exactly where the "border" ends. The consequence is a general failure to acknowledge the distinct, and sometimes competing, goals of immigration policy, crime control initiatives, and national security measures. Policy makers and pundits increasingly portray "border security" initiatives—characterized by border militarization, increasingly expansive grounds for deportation, and relaxed procedural standards for immigration investigation—as effective means to secure ill-defined national security goals. Irregular migration, crime committed by noncitizens (or those perceived as noncitizens), and terrorist threats are all subsumed under the broad rubric of national security threats. The expanded and accelerated removal of noncitizens is presented, incorrectly, as an answer to all of these problems, even while core security initiatives languish.

In this article, I explore the origins and consequences of the blurred boundaries between immigration control, crime control, and national security specifically as related to the removal of noncitizens. Part II of this article focuses on the question of how immigration control and crime control issues have come to be subsumed by national security rhetoric. Discussions about the removal of noncitizens have been treated as "national security" issues, when in fact the driving motivation is basic criminal law enforcement. Part III of this article disentangles the use of removal for criminal and immigration law enforcement ends from national security removals. Noncitizens are seldom removed on national security grounds. At the same time, the government has relied upon "national security" justifications to explain the removals of thousands of noncitizens who pose no demonstrated security risk. This strategy does little to enhance national security, and undermines the important national security objective of protecting civil liberties. Part IV of this article explains that the vast majority of removals effectuated each year are carried out on the basis of a noncitizen's violation of the immigration law or criminal law, but unfortunately, there is little reason to believe that this expansion in the removal of noncitizens will serve as an effective or efficient means of decreasing domestic crime or preventing undocumented migration. The insistence on formulating immigration policy while gazing through a distorting lens of "national security" perversely ensures that the law is ill-suited to achieve either national security or other immigration policy goals.

II. THE RHETORIC OF REMOVAL: OR HOW THE ALIEN BECAME A NATIONAL SECURITY THREAT

The rhetoric of national security has long been used by the courts to mask the most virulent aspects of US immigration policy. A classic example can be found in the *Chinese Exclusion Case*. The Supreme Court upheld the application of the Chinese Exclusion Act of 1882 to a long-term resident of the United States, Chae Chan Ping. Chae Chan Ping left the United States to visit China, and in accordance with the legal requirements of the time, obtained documentation that would permit him to return to the United States. He was denied entry upon his return because an October 1, 1888, amendment to the Chinese Exclusion Act revoked his outstanding authorization for re-entry. In enacting the Chinese Exclusion Act and subsequent amendments, Congress had been motivated by racism against the Chinese—racism that had been brought into sharp focus in a time of economic uncertainty. But in rejecting Chae Chan Ping's challenge to the law, the Supreme Court did not justify the exclusions expressly on economic grounds or on the basis of perceived racial superiority, although those factors clearly motivated the law and lurk behind the Court's decision. Instead, the Court disguised its rationale, upholding the law on grounds of national security:

> That the government of the United States, through the action of the legislative department, can exclude aliens from its territory is a proposition which we do not think open to controversy. Jurisdiction over its own territory to that extent is an incident of every independent nation. It is a part of its independence. If it could not exclude aliens it would be to that extent subject to the control of another power.

The influx of "vast hordes" of Chinese citizens into the United States was, in the Court's view, a form of "aggression and encroachment" that justified congressional regulation of Chinese immigration, even in the absence of actual hostilities between the United States and China. In this analysis, the Court relies upon the very racial stereotyping that makes the law so troubling in order to explain the link between Chinese exclusion and security. The Court reasoned that:

> If, therefore, the government of the United States, through its legislative department, considers the presence of foreigners of a different race in this country, who will not assimilate with us, to be dangerous to its peace and security, their exclusion is not to be stayed because at the time there are no actual hostilities with the nation of which the foreigners are subjects.

238

As this statement reveals, the refusal of the Chinese to assimilate is both presumed and presumed dangerous.

Almost 120 years have passed since the Supreme Court decided the *Chinese Exclusion Case*, but the underlying rationale of the decision still undergirds contemporary immigration law. Throughout the past century, courts and lawmakers have used the rhetoric of security to justify US immigration restrictions and harsh US removal policies. Such rhetoric is most common in times of crisis, when racialized assumptions about dangerousness prompt crisis responses aimed at certain groups of noncitizens and their communities.

One such crisis moment undoubtedly began on September 11, 2001, when hijackers took control of four large passenger jets and used them as weapons to destroy the two towers of the World Trade Center in New York and to damage the Pentagon in Washington, DC. Since the attacks of September 11, the language of security has once again come to dominate discussions of immigration policy. There is no doubt that the attacks of September 11 exposed vulnerabilities in US intelligence, but the immigration debate soon took center stage. As in the past, the rhetoric of national security in these immigration discussions conceals complex assumptions about immigration, race, assimilability, and criminality. In contemporary discussions of policies aimed at removing "undesirable" noncitizens, distinctions between undocumented migrants, "criminal aliens," and individuals who pose threats to national security are often blurred. . . .

A. Conflating Immigration Control With Crime Control

The notion of the outsider as a threat is as old as human history and it transcends national boundaries. The trope has played itself out in US law and politics throughout the history of the nation. Thus, it is hardly surprising that the immigrant outsider often emerges as the criminal in national lore. But in the United States, the law itself has played a central role in constructing the image of the immigrant as a criminal threat.

1. The Construction of the "Illegal Alien"

For much of its early history, the United States was a land of relatively open borders—that is to say, the federal government did little to regulate migration into the United States. No federal mechanism of deportation existed until Congress enacted the Immigration Act of 1891, which permitted the deportation of people who entered the United States without authorization and created the Office of Immigration within the Department of Treasury. These first-time efforts to regulate immigration on the national level went hand-in-hand with an effort to exclude a particular group of immigrants—the Chinese. . . .

The Immigration Act of May 26, 1924, however, fundamentally altered the landscape of US immigration law and policy. The act mandated the creation of a quota system, completed in 1929, to parcel out the limited number of slots available to lawful immigrants each year. The resulting system was clearly designed to favor the migration of northern Europeans, to disfavor southern Europeans, and to preclude Asian migration entirely. Although no express racial quotas were imposed on the Western Hemisphere, immigration from Latin America, including Mexico, was increasingly restricted through new, vigorous enforcement of grounds for exclusion and deportation. The act also distinguished the "white" race from "colored" races, so that no matter what the country of origin, the "colored" races "lay outside the concept of nationality and, therefore, citizenship." Colored races were not "even bona fide immigrants."[1]

As immigration law became a tool for controlling the racial makeup of the country, the government put new mechanisms into place to enforce the new policy. A 1929 law criminalized the act of illegal entry for the first time, providing a means to criminally punish the growing class of aliens present without authorization. Congress enacted a law making it a misdemeanor to enter at a point not designated by the US government, or by means of fraud or misrepresentation. Reentry of a previously deported alien became a felony. In other words, in 1929 the act of immigration itself, when performed outside of legal channels, became a violation of the criminal law for the fist time. . . .

Popular characterizations of "irregular migrants" followed these changes in law. Until the 1930s, immigrants were categorized in the national discourse as either "legitimate" immigrants on the one hand, or "illegitimate" or "ineligible" immigrants on the other. Congress's criminalization of unauthorized migration created the "illegal alien." By the 1950s, the phrases "illegal immigrant" and "illegal alien" had become a staple of the popular lexicon. Today, the press, politicians, and individuals and organizations promoting restrictionist immigration laws commonly use the phrases "illegal alien" and "illegal immigrant" when describing unauthorized migrants in the United States. Thus, in law and language, there is a clear link between irregular status and illegality. Care is not always used in how the "illegal immigrant" label is applied. With their entry and their labor criminalized, certain groups of migrants—most commonly Mexicans—increasingly bear the label "illegal aliens," whether or not that label applies to them. In other words, the term "illegal alien" (which has no clear legal meaning) is not only used to signify irregular migrants, but also often applied to those perceived as irregular migrants, regardless of actual immigration status. These perceptions of undocumented status are heavily influenced by racial stereotypes. The linkage between perceived alien status and illegal status is thus cemented in the public mind in racialized terms.

2. The "Illegal Alien" as a Criminal Threat

While law and the language that the law has engendered partially account for the attributed linkage between unauthorized migration and criminality, it does not explain the prevalent belief that noncitizens are generally more likely to commit crimes. Yet, the notion that immigrants have a propensity toward general criminality has a surprising degree of currency in public discussion and policy debates, even though there is virtually no empirical data to support this conclusion. . . .

Certain vocal proponents of restrictionist immigration policies have been instrumental in cultivating this notion. In the 1990s, relying largely on unsupported assertions, advocates of restrictionist immigration policies touted the alleged link between unauthorized migrants—or "illegal aliens"—and criminality. In particular, efforts aimed at limiting the distribution of benefits to noncitizens present in the United States without legal authorization relied, at least in part, upon generating mental linkages between crime and immigration.

. . . On April 24, 1996, President Clinton signed the Antiterrorism and Effective Death Penalty Act (AEDPA). This was followed by the enactment of the Illegal Immigration Reform and Immigrant Responsibility Act of 1996 (IIRIRA), signed by President Clinton on September 30, 1996. These two laws represented some of the most significant procedural and substantive changes in US immigration law since the early 1920s. These laws, and the discussions surrounding their enactment, played a major role in linking migrants with crime in the national discourse.

The debate over IIRIRA centered in part on . . . resource questions. . . . IIRIRA contained a provision designed to limit the distribution of public benefits to unauthorized noncitizens. The 1996 welfare reform act—the Personal Responsibility and Work Opportunity Reconciliation Act—also contained provisions designed to limit such benefits. As a consequence of these laws, with limited exceptions, undocumented migrants became ineligible for all federal public benefits, including loans, licenses, food and housing assistance, and postsecondary education. IIRIRA also authorized states to restrict or prohibit cash public assistance to noncitizens to the extent allowed for comparable federal provisions. "Much of the public anger toward immigrants center[ed] on a perception that they receive more in Government benefits than they pay in taxes."[2]

Although the articulated concerns were economic . . . images of migrant criminality became an important justification for the legislation. . . . [M]embers of Congress made unsubstantiated statements about migrant criminality. For example, Representative Orrin Hatch (R-UT) stated, "We can no longer afford to allow our borders to be just overrun by illegal aliens. . . . Frankly, a lot of our criminality in this country today happens to be coming from criminal, illegal aliens who are ripping our country apart. A lot of the drugs are coming from these people."[3] The unsubstantiated linkage between migrants and criminality thus served as an important ingredient in the passage of major national immigration legislation in 1996. Unfortunately, just as positive law constructed the "illegal alien" in the twentieth century, positive law has increasingly operated to construct the "criminal alien"—or as Representative Hatch might say, "criminal, illegal aliens"—in the twenty-first century.

3. The Ever-Widening Category of "Criminal Aliens"

The 1996 immigration laws were not only the product of a worldview that conflated "illegal immigrants" with crime—the laws also operated to reify the links between all immigrants and criminality. The 1996 laws altered prior national policies by increasing penalties for violations of immigration laws, expanding the class of noncitizens subject to removal for the commission of crimes, and imposing a system of tough penalties that favor removal even in cases involving relatively minor infractions or very old crimes. . . .

Trends in federal immigration prosecutions further buttress the popular conflation of the "illegal immigrant" and the "criminal alien." One of the most important developments fueling the growth in the class of removable "aliens" is the increasing prosecution of immigration crimes. In 2004, federal prosecutors filed charges in 37,854 cases on the basis of criminal immigration law violations. This is a 125 percent increase since 2000, and it means that immigration violations that year made up the single largest category of federal crimes, surpassing even drug prosecutions. Most people convicted of criminal immigration violations are noncitizens whose convictions render them removable. Thus, increased criminal prosecution of immigration violations creates a new category of removable noncitizens, some of whom are formally categorized by law as "criminal aliens."

This, in turn, has given rise to new enforcement actions that again feed and fuel the notion of dangerous classes of aliens—in this case, the "fugitive alien." Unauthorized reentry after removal actually made up 59 percent of the immigration prosecutions in federal district courts in 2004, and the prosecutions of illegal reentry after removal continued to be the largest category of federal immigration prosecutions in 2006. . . .

In short, the 1996 laws have expanded the category of criminal aliens in a way that sweeps in many noncitizens formerly ineligible for removal or at least eligible for relief from removal. At the same time, the increased prosecution of immigration offenses has created a whole new class of immigrants legally constructed as criminals. Noncitizens whose only legal violation is unauthorized presence are increasingly caught in the web of immigration enforcement initiatives styled as anticrime measures.

It is hardly surprising that these changes in the law have shored up the popular construction of immigrants as criminal threats. Over the past decade, images of migrant criminality have persisted and proliferated.

4. The Modern Myth of Migrant Criminality

. . . .

This implicit acceptance of the link between criminality and alien status has only become more pronounced in recent years. In his address to the nation on May 15, 2006, President George W. Bush reasserted the link, with the claim that "[i]llegal immigration puts pressure on public schools and hospitals, it strains state and local budgets, *and brings crime to our communities*."[4] Comments by local law enforcement officers reinforce the linkage between crime and migration.

This conflation of migrants and criminality is rampant in the media. . . .

. . . This view logically presents immigration control as a means of controlling crime. But the underlying premise of migrant criminality is flawed, and efforts to control crime through accelerating deportations are unlikely to succeed in controlling either crime or undocumented migration.

B. The Alien as National Security Threat

Like the conflation of migrant status and criminality, the linkages between immigration status and national security threats have deep historical roots that have been reinforced through law. In wartime and other times of national security crises, whether real or perceived, the nation's leaders have used the rhetoric of security to justify heightened immigration restrictions. . . .

The groundwork for the post-September 11 rhetorical shift was laid in the 1990s. In 1994, President William Jefferson Clinton made comments epitomizing the deliberate lack of precision that has come to characterize immigration "security" issues. He explained that the militarization of the southern border was an effort to stop the "terrorization" of American citizens by foreigners stating, "The simple fact is that we must not and we will not surrender our borders to those who wish to exploit our history of compassion and justice. We cannot . . . allow our people to be endangered by those who would enter our country to terrorize Americans. . . ."[5] President Clinton's remarks prefigured two trends that have taken firm hold in the period following September 11, 2001. First, his comments equate border control with the anticrime agenda, thus implicitly relying upon the link between migrant status and criminality. . . . Second, his comments depict migrant criminality as a "terrorist" threat. In so doing, he demonstrated political prescience; statements like these have become the norm in the contemporary immigration debate. Such statements were less common, however, in the mid-1990s. This is evident in the debates surrounding the enactment of AEDPA and IIRIRA, two bills that significantly altered the legal terrain of immigration law.

AEDPA was passed on April 24, 1996, in response to a terrorist act: the Oklahoma City bombings. That act was, ironically, carried out entirely by citizens. Some of the legislation had been intended as a response to the 1992 World Trade Center bombings, but it was the horror of the Oklahoma City bombings that spurred the bill to passage. Consequently, the focus of the legislation was upon curbing future threats of terrorism. . . . In discussing the AEDPA legislation, enacted in April of 1996, lawmakers in Congress invoked the "terrorist" threats posed by noncitizens as a justification for the special removal provisions and expanded definitions of "terrorist aliens" contained in the legislation. Speedier deportations thus figured as an antiterrorism initiative.

In spite of the focus on terrorism, more general notions of the criminality of migrants did infect the AEDPA discussions. Abrogated removal procedures would apply not just to "terrorist aliens" but to "criminal aliens" more generally. Members of Congress used crime and terrorism interchangeably in explaining the need for the expedite removal provisions. Nevertheless . . . broader immigration issues were not subsumed in the security legislation, but instead were debated and implemented under the rubric of separate legislation, primarily IIRIRA.

. . . .

Since September 11, 2001, the bulk of the immigration debate has centered itself around the term "national security." The term is deployed in a nebulous manner that blurs the boundary between freedom from crime—or personal "security"—and national security. As a consequence, the removals of noncitizens on the grounds of criminal violations can be, and frequently are, depicted as national security policy. With regard to border enforcement efforts, the phrase "border security" has become a ubiquitous descriptive term for immigration reform in 2006. This is evidenced by the one piece of immigration legislation that Congress managed to pass in 2006: the Secure Fence Act. In the 1996 debates, the notion of "border control" is not linked to discussions of national security, but of crime and immigration control. Retrospective descriptions of IIRIRA refer to the bill as "border security" legislation, using the term that has been the hallmark of the current immigration debate. Such descriptions are anachronistic; IIRIRA was an immigration and crime control measure, not a "border security" measure as that

term has come to be understood. But these retrospective characterizations highlight the degree to which the separation between migration,
crime, and national security issues has completely broken down over the
past few years.

. . . .

III. RHETORIC V. REALITY: THE TRUTH ABOUT REMOVAL AND NATIONAL SECURITY

In 2004, ICE [US Immigration and Customs Enforcement] completed
202,842 removals of noncitizens from the United States. Of those
removed, 88,897 were classified as "criminal aliens." A total of 1,241,089
foreign nationals were detained by the Department of Homeland Security
(DHS) during the year 2004, although many of them "voluntarily
departed" without further proceedings. The year 2004 is not anomalous; it
simply continues a significant upward trend in the detention and removal
of noncitizens, which began in the mid-1990s and accelerated after 2001.
The removal of noncitizens has been the focus of a great deal of national
attention and spending in post-September 11 efforts at achieving national
security through immigration policy. In reality, however, current removal
policies have almost nothing to do with national security.

A. Removal is Seldom a Security Tool

. . . .

Of the 208,521 people removed in 2005, only ten were removed on
security grounds. This is consistent with the pattern of the past five

years. In spite of the fact that security-based removals have decreased since September 11, 2001, ICE persists in presenting ever-widening deportation initiatives as directly related to national security. As a factual matter, in cases where the government actually has evidence that noncitizens—including undocumented noncitizens—pose a genuine security risk to the United States, the government generally prosecutes these noncitizens in criminal proceedings rather than remove them on the grounds of their immigration violations. Removal, on the other hand, is primarily used by the government in cases involving noncitizens who have committed immigration violations or removable criminal offenses. In other words, removal is a tool reserved for those who do *not* pose serious national security risks. Consequently, there is little alignment between the government rhetoric surrounding removal and the government's actual policies. The remainder of this section explores some of the consequences of the misalignment of rhetoric and reality.

B. Security as Pretext for Removals: Some Examples

. . . .

... In the weeks that followed the September 11 attacks, the government initiated a broad investigation that led to the arrest and detention of more than 760 people, mostly of Middle Eastern and South Asian origin. Rather than initiating criminal prosecutions against these individuals— painted as potential terrorists—the government held the detainees (and ultimately expelled several hundred of them) on immigration violations. The government took advantage of expansive powers to detain noncitizens. Many decried the use of massive preventative detention in these cases, where there was apparently no evidence that the vast majority of detainees had anything to do with the events of September 11.

Some government officials rejected the term "preventative detention" in describing these cases, characterizing them instead as "preventative prosecutions." In other words, government officials suggested that they were actively "prosecuting" these immigrants, at least on immigration violations. Their incarceration was not "preventative detention," the government argued, it was a valid, nonpunitive, and administrative component of their removal proceedings. . . .

To the extent that "charges" were ever brought in any of these "prosecutions," they were charges of immigration violations—lapsed visas, failure to take the proper number of classes while on a student visa, or even failure to register a change of address—but not terrorism and not security threats. The supposed wrongdoing used to publicly justify their detentions never translated into charges of terrorism. Many individuals "voluntarily" departed simply to get out of detention. And "[a]lthough DOJ explicitly used removal proceedings as a proxy for terrorism prosecutions, the detainees, typically in closed proceedings, had no right to counsel."[6]

C. The Costs of the Security Pretext

One might attempt to justify these "preventative prosecutions" in much the way that Robert F. Kennedy justified the use of tax violations to prosecute criminal syndicates who could not be caught in any other way. But the situations are not comparable for several reasons. First, in the case of criminal syndicates, the government had identified potential suspects based on apparent patterns of criminal activity prior to initiating investigation and prosecution of tax violations. In the case of many individuals removed in the aftermath of September 11, the primary means of identifying the targets of immigration investigation and detention were country of origin, race, ethnicity, and religion. Thus, post-9/11 investigations presented a more invidious and wide-ranging exercise of prosecutorial discretion. Second, in tax evasion prosecutions, all of the standard criminal procedural protections applied. In the case of the "immigration violator," the individual is effectively accused of constituting a security threat, and is treated as such, but is subject to the much less protective standards of administrative removal. Finally, in the case of criminal syndicates, the ultimate sanction—incarceration—achieved the same incapacitation effects as would have been achieved through prosecutions for other crimes. The same cannot be said in the case of those removed by the US government or those who voluntarily depart because of immigration violations. Those individuals who pose security threats prior to removal are not prevented from future acts that pose a threat to security—their sphere of activity simply shifts.

1. Race, Religion, and National Origin: Proxies for Danger

In the wake of the September 11 attacks, Attorney General John Ashcroft used the power of his office to strengthen the ability of the government to rely on the crudest forms of criminal profiling. He issued Justice Department guidelines on racial profiling expressly authorizing ICE officials to engage in racial and ethnic profiling, which is formally prohibited in other federal law enforcement endeavors. Even before those regulatory changes, racial profiling had become an important component of the law enforcement response to September 11. However, in June 2003, with the passage of new guidelines on racial profiling, the Justice Department formally sanctioned the use of race in the context of "national security" investigations.

As a legal matter, race-based immigration enforcement is sanctioned in a way that would never be permissible in the criminal context. The Supreme Court has often ratified the use of suspect classifications in the drafting and enforcement of immigration law. Similarly, courts have long declined to examine the reasons that the government chooses to charge certain immigration violators and not others. This trend has been reaffirmed in the post-September 11, 2001, era. Consequently, noncitizens have had little recourse when race and ethnicity came to be treated as a proxy for danger.

2. The Procedural Price of Pretextual Removal

In spite of the breadth of power consigned to Congress to regulate immigration matters, courts have recognized that certain protections of the United States Constitution do apply to noncitizens in the United States. . . .

. . . .

While recognizing certain constitutional protections for noncitizens in criminal proceedings, the Court has also imposed significant limitations upon these protections. . . . Nevertheless, until recently, when state and federal government officials have subjected a noncitizen to the criminal law, they have provided those noncitizens with many of the same protections due to citizens, in spite of their citizenship status.

The increasing reliance on immigration enforcement to achieve security objectives undercuts these protections. The due process rights available to noncitizens in criminal proceedings do not extend to removal proceedings. It is true that some form of due process is required in removal proceedings, but the process is not as protective as the process guaranteed by the US Constitution to those in criminal proceedings. This is true despite the apparently punitive nature of certain removal proceedings because the courts have long maintained a legal distinction between removal and criminal punishment.

Under immigration law, the federal government's power to remove carries with it broad administrative discretion to investigate noncitizens and to detain them during removal proceedings. . . .

In response to the events of September 11, government officials modified immigration laws and implemented regulations in ways that further diminish procedural protections in immigration-related detentions when compared to criminal punishment. Title IV of the USA PATRIOT Act permits the detention of a noncitizen if there are "reasonable grounds to believe" that the individual may be a threat to national security—in other words, it countenances arrest on the basis of reasonable suspicion. Such individuals can be held for seven days prior to the commencement of criminal or removal proceedings, in contrast to the usual requirement that a person be charged within forty-eight hours of arrest. Significantly, these procedural shortcuts are not limited to those noncitizens who are under suspicion of posing a security threat, because arrests can be effectuated by ICE based solely on reasonable suspicion that an individual is present in violation of the immigration laws. . . .

The combination of expansive removal authority and diminished procedural protections for noncitizens in immigration detention and removal applies only to noncitizens. However, the effects of these provisions extend to citizens as well. Immigration law, after all, has played a fundamental role in how race is defined in the United States. One consequence is that certain groups are viewed as perpetual outsiders. For some, race ensures their vulnerability to "reasonable suspicions" about their immigration status, no matter what their actual citizenship status might be. Historically contingent notions of who is really a "citizen" and who is an "alien" ensure that many Latinos, Asian Americans, Arabs and Muslims—citizens as well as lawful permanent residents, other authorized noncitizens, and the undocumented—have been and will continue to be subjected to the racial profiling that is legally sanctioned in the border control context.

The asymmetric protections applied in the criminal and immigration settings, combined with the increasing reliance on immigration law to enforce the government's purported security goals, have resulted in the evolution of a two-tier justice system. One set of criminal investigatory and procedural methods are governed by strict laws and regulations; another is subject to looser constraints. While we have seen this two-tiered mechanism in place before during crisis moments, the contemporary manifestation of the bifurcated system of justice is distinct by virtue of its increasing institutionalization as reliance on deportation expands.

3. The Absence of Incapacitation

There is at least one additional reason we should worry about the characterization of the ongoing, mass deportations from the United States as a "security" measure: there is no reason to believe that removal will be an effective security tool. In their 1930 assessment of British transportation policy, George Rusche and Otto Kircheimer concluded that, as a penological matter, transportation policy had been a failure.[7] In particular, they noted that criminals who were transported merely shifted the locus of their criminal activity. To the extent that any noncitizen deported is actually prone to commit future harms, there is no reason to believe that removal will alter her willingness to do so. Removal shifts the locus of the activity, but does nothing to remedy it.

When a person who poses a "national security" risk to the United States shifts the locus of their criminal activity, this does not necessarily increase US security. Such a person can also engage in acts outside of the United States that threaten US interests. Removing people who pose security threats to the United States ensures that the government has no further control over them, but it does not ensure that they are disabled from harming US interests overseas or domestically.

History has illustrated that serious domestic attacks can be carried out by people who are lawfully present in the United States. These attacks can also be carried out by citizens. Moreover, attacks can be carried out on US citizens and facilities outside of the territory of the United States. . . .

The best way to prevent acts of terrorism against the United States by people present on US soil is through criminal investigations and detentions of both citizens and noncitizens alike. Such investigations and detentions are necessarily governed by constitutional criminal procedural constraints. Of course, such investigations require resources, and many of those resources are currently allocated to fund the investigation, detention, and removal of noncitizens who have run afoul of the immigration laws in any one of dozens of ways.

D. The Security Question

The changes in law and law enforcement strategies in favor of the rapid detention and removal of noncitizens arguably provide a disincentive for charging someone with removability on security grounds. It has become so easy to detain and remove noncitizens by other means that there is no need in most cases for the government to demonstrate that a noncitizen is removable on terrorism grounds or other security grounds. Unfortunately, it does little to improve security and much to undermine procedural protections for the citizen and the noncitizen alike. Moreover, it does little to achieve other purported goals of immigration policy: crime and immigration control.

IV. REMOVAL POLICIES ALSO FAIL AS
CRIME AND IMMIGRATION CONTROL

Even if deportation is not a commonly used or effective mechanism for addressing genuine national security concerns such as terrorism, it is still worth asking whether it serves as a tool for promoting immigration control and crime control. After all, the government officials responsible for overseeing the rapidly increasing use of deportation have defined "national security in such a way that it encompasses not just terrorist threats, but also street crime and simple immigration violations."

. . . .

A. The Wave of Removals Does Not Improve Personal Security

In the period leading up to the 1996 legislation, most of the discussions of "security" in the immigration context involved not national security, but the personal security of citizens in the form of freedom from crime. In the period since September 11, 2001, the rhetoric of national security has been deployed even when the substance of the discussion rotates around personal security concerns. It is therefore important to ask whether the massive increase in the removal of noncitizens serves legitimate criminal law enforcement goals, regardless of its efficacy (or lack thereof) as a national security strategy.

Unfortunately, it seems unlikely that the present strategy of broadening the categories of "criminal aliens" and increasing law enforcement and immigration enforcement measures aimed at detaining and removing these "criminal aliens" has had much of an impact on crime. It is important to point out as an initial matter that no empirical studies have been done to substantiate the links between the increasing criminalization of immigration and decreasing crime. Interestingly, as deportation is on the rise, violent crime is increasing, not decreasing. . . .

I. Migrant Criminality is Overstated

In spite of the persistent belief that immigrant groups are more likely to commit crime than the native born, the available evidence suggests that the belief is unfounded. Using data from the 2000 census, a team of sociologists at U.C. Irvine recently compiled statistics that demonstrate the significant degree to which reality fails to square with the myth of migrant criminality. The study found that the incarceration rate of the US-born was 3.51 percent, while the incarceration rate of the foreign born was a mere quarter of that, at a rate of 0.86 percent. Non-Hispanic, white, native-born US citizens are twice as likely as the foreign born to be incarcerated, with an incarceration rate of 1.71 percent. These facts are particularly striking when one takes into account the upsurge in criminal prosecutions for immigration violations, which almost always involve the prosecutions of noncitizens. Another striking finding of the study was that "the lowest incarceration rates among Latin American immigrants are seen for the least educated groups: Salvadorans and Guatemalans (0.52%) and Mexicans (0.70%)." "These are precisely the groups most stigmatized as 'illegals' in the public perception and outcry about immigration."[8] The study highlights the dangerous gaps between public perception and reality, and it is not an outlier. . . .

An irony revealed in the study is that incarceration rates increase for US-born coethnics in every ethnic group studied. In other words, "while incarceration rates are found to be extraordinarily low among immigrants, they are also seen to rise rapidly by the second generation."[9] Even so, at least some data suggests that "second-generation immigrants are doing better, on the whole, than [other] native born" when it comes to having lower crime rates.[10] This data suggests that the focus of anticrime strategies really ought to be on citizens, not noncitizens.

2. Removal Policy is Overbroad

Vast resources are now expended on removing noncitizens, whether they are security threats, "criminal aliens," or immigration violators. From fiscal year 1993 to fiscal year 2005, the Border Patrol budget quadrupled from $362 million to $1.4 billion, with the largest annual increase taking place after the events of September 11, 2001. . . .

The expansive efforts to remove certain noncitizens do not necessarily mean that the government is now prudently choosing to target the most serious criminal offenders for removal. A close look at the categories of noncitizens who have been removed raise questions about the degree to which the enforcement of these laws are actually improving personal security. First, the massive increase in the category of removable aliens, and the decreased discretion that judges can exercise in these cases, ensures that governmental resources are expended on expelling noncitizens who almost certainly do not pose any kind of a threat to the United States. . . .

. . . .

V. CONCLUSIONS

Like the effort to tackle crime through the so-called "war on drugs," current immigration policy relies upon a military metaphor—that of "border security." And like the effort to tackle crime through the "war on drugs," waging a security war within our borders poses challenges to traditional criminal procedural protections. But security metaphors have more potency in the context of immigration than in the context of the war on drugs precisely because the courts long have analogized congressional and executive power over immigration with foreign policy and war powers, rather than with domestic social control. The conflation of immigration enforcement, crime control initiatives, and security measures thus pose an even greater threat to our constitutional order and to human rights.

Few measured benefits have come in exchange for these costs. More troublingly, policy makers and the general citizenry seem to be content to guess, rather than assess, the costs and benefits of our immigration policies. In this article, I have tried to raise some questions that deserve to be answered before immigration "reform" takes us further down a very questionable path.

THE SKIES WON'T BE SAFE UNTIL WE USE COMMONSENSE PROFILING
(2002)

Stuart Taylor Jr.

The government's effort to upgrade airport security [in the months after 9/11] has been massive and expensive: federalizing airport security forces; confiscating toenail clippers; frisking randomly chosen grandmothers, members of Congress, former CIA directors, and decorated military officers; stationing National Guard troops in airports; putting sky marshals on planes. Has it been effective? Not effective enough. The main reason is that civil libertarians, Arab American activists, editorial writers, and most of polite society have virtuously eschewed the one measure—profiling based in part on national origin—that holds out the best hope of thwarting any skillful al Qaeda terrorists who may try to smuggle bombs aboard airliners. . . .

. . . .

It's easy to understand the reluctance . . . to target passengers for individual searches based solely on how they look and sound. History gives us ample reasons to fear the slippery slope to which such profiling could lead. But the next Mohamed Atta may give us no other clue that would trigger an individual search. It's an agonizing dilemma.

I fear that a policy of ignoring apparent national origin and ethnicity may court disaster. And the social taboo against any approach that could be characterized (unfairly) as racial profiling has muzzled honest discussion of profiling, in the media and among politicians. Fewer than 10 percent of all checked bags go through any kind of bomb-detection machine, because we now have fewer than two hundred of the more than twenty-two hundred high-tech, minivan-sized bomb-detection machines that it would take to screen all bags. Only a small fraction of passengers and bags can be searched by hand without intolerable delays. The stopgap bag-matching system instituted earlier this year does not match bags to passengers on connecting flights and would have no effect on suicidal terrorists.

In short, as the *New York Times* reports, the "soothing veneer of security . . . may be far thinner than many passengers imagine," and "no real progress has been made on bomb detection." What the *Times* won't tell you, lest it break the taboo, is that we might be able to make flying far safer almost overnight by using profiles that take account not only of suspicious behaviors, gender, and age, but also of the outwardly apparent traits shared by most militant Muslims from those regions where al Qaeda finds most of its recruits—the very traits that the government's published rules tell security screeners to ignore. A well-designed profile that included such traits would properly be called "national-origin profiling," not "racial profiling." The main difference is that millions of Americans of Middle Eastern ethnicity would not fit the profile, because their speech patterns and travel documents would clearly indicate that they are long-standing residents of this country.

To be sure, a profile that takes account of apparent national origin (as well as one that does not) might miss a John Walker Lindh or a Timothy McVeigh. No profile is foolproof. But that doesn't justify being foolish. A well-designed profiling system would have singled out all nineteen of the September 11 hijackers for special attention. And even though box cutters were not then prohibited on planes, security screeners might have wondered why groups of four and five Middle

Eastern men were all carrying such potential weapons onto airliners the same morning.

The odds that any Middle Eastern passenger is a terrorist are, of course, tiny. But if you make the plausible assumptions that al Qaeda terrorists are at least one hundred times as likely to be from the Middle East as to be native-born Americans, and that fewer than 5 percent of all passengers on domestic flights are Middle Eastern men, it would follow that a randomly chosen Middle Eastern male passenger is roughly two thousand times as likely to be an al Qaeda terrorist as a randomly chosen native-born American. It is crazy to ignore such odds.

While the politically correct approach to profiling still seems to be an article of faith in many quarters, some liberals (along with many conservatives) are talking sense. One is Rep. Barney Frank (D-MA), perhaps the smartest civil libertarian in Congress. During a March 6 [2002] debate at Georgetown University Law Center, Frank forthrightly asserted that airline security profiles should take account of national origin. He cautioned that a well-designed profile would also include "a bunch of factors" that may warrant suspicion; that "if only . . . young men from the Middle East were being profiled, it would be a problem"; and that the ideal system would be to search all passengers and their luggage thoroughly for bombs and other weapons. But Frank also stressed: "I do think that at this point, [national] origin would be part of it. . . . In certain countries, people are angrier at us than elsewhere."

Frank distinguished such airport profiling from the discredited police practice of "pulling over some black kid because he's driving," to search for drugs, which he called "a terrible intrusion." In airport screening, Frank said, the stakes are much higher—with many lives at risk if a bomb or weapon slips through—and the "incremental" intrusion on those profiled is minimal. "If no harm is being done, and you're not being in any way disadvantaged, I am reluctant to think that there's any great problem," he said.

THE SKIES WON'T BE SAFE UNTIL WE USE COMMONSENSE PROFILING

The vacuousness of the arguments that have been made against politically incorrect profiling is typified by a . . . *Newsweek* column by Anna Quindlen asserting that the case for "selective screening" based on ethnicity "collapsed amid reports that nine of the September 11 hijackers were indeed specially screened." That's about 180 degrees off. Those nine were apparently chosen based on their reservation-buying patterns, not ethnicity or national origin. And the screening appears to have been limited largely to searching checked bags: Arab American activists and civil libertarians had prevailed on the government, not only to bar any profiling based on ethnicity, religion, or national origin in its Computer-Assisted Passenger Prescreening System, but also to avoid intrusive searches of the persons or carry-on bags of even those passengers who did fit the CAPPS profile.

Similar lobbying also succeeded in denying security screeners any access to law enforcement databases. That may help explain why the two hijackers who were on the CIA-FBI "watch list" of suspected terrorists were nonetheless able to board airliners with such ease on September 11. The new profiling system will include sharing of such intelligence. Good. But most al Qaeda terrorists—including seventeen of the September 11 hijackers—appear in no intelligence database.

"The most offensive profiles are those that are based on characteristics a person cannot change," including "race, religion, national origin, [and] gender," Katie Corrigan of the American Civil Liberties Union said in congressional testimony on February 27. But offensive or no, the only profiles likely to be effective against a well-trained terrorist are those triggered by traits that he cannot change or easily conceal. Corrigan added that profiling is a cheap, imperfect alternative to expensive security devices. She's right. But those security devices are not and will not be in place for many months, perhaps years. For now, intelligent profiling is indispensable.

The blessed absence of terrorist attacks on airliners since September 11 (excepting would-be shoe-bomber Richard Reid) appears to be fostering the complacent assumption that our security system works. The assumption is dubious. The politically correct approach to profiling amounts to a bet that al Qaeda is no longer interested in airline terrorism. The bet is irrational.

Editors' Note: This opinion piece was written shortly after 9/11. Issues related to the legitimacy of profiling at airports continue to be debated. In 2010, President Obama announced that citizens of fourteen countries (including Pakistan, Saudi Arabia, and Yemen) would be subject to "intensive screening when flying to the United States" (*New York Times*, January 5, 2010).

THE LAST MINSTREL SHOW?
Racial Profiling, the War on Terrorism, and the Mass Media (2009)

John Tehranian

I. INTRODUCTION

In New York City, more than 3,250 intersections offer push button boxes. The boxes help pedestrians halt traffic when they approach a busy street, allowing them to cross safely—in theory, that is. In fact, a 2004 investigation revealed that the vast majority of the push button boxes actually do not work at all. Even more surprisingly, the lack of function comes by design. Over the years, city officials have deactivated the push button boxes because they interfered with the coordination of the computer programming of lights that the city uses to better regulate traffic flow. Removal is more expensive than simply leaving the boxes. But the boxes provide a surprising secondary effect. New Yorkers, despite knowing better, continue to use them. In the words of Michael Zuo, the boxes offer "harried walkers a rare promise of control over their pedestrian lives."[1] Even if that promise is illusive, the masses continue to push the button in full cognizance of their state of disrepair. The illusion of control, it seems, is sometimes just as powerful as control itself.

Without belittling the consequences at stake, the war on terrorism shares at least this one commonality with the war on traffic. One of the most terrifying results of globalization is our increased vulnerability to terrorism. In truth, there is only so much that a government can realistically do to protect its citizenry from extremists hell-bent on senselessly sacrificing innocent lives along with their own. Unfortunately, racial profiling has taken its place alongside the screening of all shoes through x-ray scanners as an effort that at least makes us feel that the government is doing something to respond to the threat. Unlike the relatively harmless, impotent push button boxes, however, racial profiling has profoundly negative consequences. In promulgating policies targeting individuals on the basis of their race, we are sacrificing, among other things, fealty to our most precious democratic principles. As David Cole reminds us, "The argument that we cannot afford to rely on something other than racial or ethnic proxies for suspicion after all, is precisely the rationale used to intern 110,000 persons of Japanese ancestry during World War II."[2]

But, of course, racial profiling in the war on terrorism has its supporters. And the most prominent defense by its advocates, both enthusiastic and even reluctant, comes from one seemingly irrefutable fact: each one of the 9/11 perpetrators was a man of Middle Eastern descent. Yet this ostensibly unimpeachable summation of 9/11 is, in fact, a product of a biased lens. In an alternative world, using the same set of facts, the interpretive narrative could have been constructed quite differently. The attacks could have been anthologized as the work of a group of anti-Americans, of frustrated young men, of the disenfranchised and socioeconomically disadvantaged, of Saudi Arabians, or of Islamic radicals (with no specific racialized elements). Thus, our collective epistemological summation of the perpetrators could have reduced them to any number of other identity signifiers, including shared ideology, age, socioeconomic status, gender, religion, or nationality. But it did not. The terrorists were, above all, racialized. Such a bent not only compromises the protection of basic civil liberties and risks making the war on terrorism a war on a race; its misguided reductionism is also bad public policy.

THE LAST MINSTREL SHOW?

Support for racial profiling in the war on terrorism continues unabated, despite its underlying irrationality, because of fear—an emotion that has animated ill-conceived and discriminatory government projects since time immemorial. The specter of another 9/11 causes otherwise sound policy makers to support antiterrorism policies that target individuals of Middle Eastern descent. The average American has little direct contact with the Middle East or even with Middle Easterners. Instead, popular perceptions are driven by indirect contact through the mediating force of mass communications. In news and entertainment programming, fear is reflected, cultivated, and magnified to devastating effect.

This article traces racial profiling's problematic discourse of legitimation, deracinating its unsound roots. It then analyzes the particular role of the mass media in fueling support for such policies by both ossifying and perpetuating stereotypes about the Middle East. In particular, the article highlights the grave and underappreciated toll of such representations on the Middle Eastern American community. . . .

II. RACIAL PROFILING AND ITS DISCOURSE OF LEGITIMATION

A. The Myth of Colorblindness

In the war on terrorism, Middle Eastern Americans and our constitutional values have paid a high price. Powerful forces on both the political left and right have been complicit. Some liberals, anxious to capture the national security vote and prove their antiterrorism bona fides, have singled out entities with Middle Eastern ties for special treatment. . . .

Meanwhile, many groups have shown little compunction about targeting individuals of Middle Eastern descent in the war on terrorism despite their steadfast assertion that we have a color-blind Constitution that virtually dictates race-blindness. Vociferously opposing the use of race in any government policy, Chief Justice Roberts recently posited that "[t]he way to stop discrimination on the basis of race is to stop discriminating on the basis of race."[3] But Roberts' tautological edict against discrimination apparently gave a federal appellate court no pause when it declared in 2008 that race or ethnic origin of a passenger may, depending on context, be relevant information in the total mix of information raising concerns that transport of a passenger might be inimical to safety. On this basis, the First Circuit took the remarkable step of reversing the jury verdict for a plaintiff who, because of his Middle Eastern appearance, had been forcibly deplaned despite clearing all security checks.

Despite the conservative trope of colorblindness, courts have been similarly unsympathetic to many recent efforts by Middle Easterners to vindicate their civil rights, virtually immunizing certain discrimination from adequate legal remedies. For example, in 2005, a federal jury held that Abdul Azimi, a Muslim immigrant from Afghanistan, had suffered years of vicious racial invective and physical abuse at his workplace. The evidence established that coworkers had regularly taunted Azimi with the "N-word," linked him, by blood, to Osama bin Laden and Saddam Hussein, and left him notes with swastikas and profanity-laced vituperations against his faith. They even assaulted him, forcing pork into his mouth and pockets as they denounced his religion in the crudest terms imaginable. Shortly after finally filing a complaint against this hateful and abusive treatment, and just a few weeks after the attacks of 9/11, Azimi was summarily fired.

Despite wholeheartedly agreeing that Azimi had suffered discrimination, the jury found that the unlawful harassment had not caused Azimi "to be damaged by emotional distress, pain, suffering, emotional anguish, loss of enjoyment of life[,] and/or inconvenience." Azimi did not receive a single penny in damages. On appeal, the unfathomable verdict was affirmed, making it fair to wonder whether the courthouse door is effectively shut for Middle Easterners seeking redress for brazen civil rights violations. The ruling therefore threatens to provide a virtual carte blanche for the targeting of Middle Easterners in the workplace.

Shockingly, as far as civil rights suits involving Middle Easterners go, Azimi was a relative success for the plaintiff. In 2007, the year of the Azimi decision, courts reported decisions on sixty-nine employment discrimination cases involving claims by Muslims, many of Middle Eastern descent. Azimi, with at least its acknowledgement of discrimination, was the only "victory"—in the words of Adam Liptak—"if you can call it that."[4]

B. The Epistemology of Fear: Narrating the Middle Eastern Threat

All the while, racial profiling policies, especially after 9/11, continue unabated. Supporters of policies targeting Middle Eastern individuals have defended the practices as rational responses to a legitimate threat to the United States. A mass e-mail that has floated about cyberspace over the past several years captures this prevalent mindset. Encapsulating the prevailing zeitgeist and providing a power testament, through its repeated forwarding, to its resonance with the public, the e-mail purports to represent a transcript of a speech, entitled "AMERICA, WAKE UP!," given by Navy Captain Dan Ouimette before the Pensacola Civitan Club, a service organization in Florida.[5] The speech views the events of 9/11 as part of a continuing chain of events that began with the American Hostage Crisis in November 1979. "Most Americans think [9/11] was the first attack against US soil or in America. How wrong they are. America has been under a constant attack since 1979 and we chose to hit the snooze alarm and roll over and go back to sleep." Billed with the subject line "When WWIII Started—1979," the email specifically posits that events during the past quarter century form a systematic campaign of Middle Eastern terrorism against the United States. Understood in a vacuum and as a purely factual and unbiased history lesson, the analysis appears eminently well-reasoned, making it virtually impossible for any rational reader not to conclude that there is a monumental race war at hand, pitting two distinct civilizations against each other. However, analyzed more carefully and in a fuller context, the pedantic chronology exemplifies the sophomoric reductionism that has unfortunately framed perceptions of the Middle East. Indeed, the selective list of events highlighted—the Iranian hostage crisis in 1979, the attacks on American embassies in Beirut and Kuwait in 1983, the bombings of TWA Flight 840 over Argos, Greece, in 1986 and Pan Am Flight 103 over Lockerbie, Scotland, in 1988, the World Trade Center bombing in 1993, the attacks on American embassies in Kenya and Tanzania in 1998, the bombing of the USS Cole in 2000 in Aden, Yemen, and the horrific attacks of September 11, 2001—is but one oversimplified narrative of a history of recent mass violence involving much more than Middle Eastern terrorism. As uniformly tragic and inexcusable as each of these vicious and barbarous acts was, they were not alone. Indeed, one could construct a similar narrative involving incidents on American soil—the Oklahoma City bombings, the Columbine massacre, the Waco conflagration, the standoffs with militiamen in Idaho, and various abortion clinic bombings—and conclude that we are facing a systematic threat to our basic freedoms and way of life from Anglo-Saxon conservative Christian evangelicals. Such racist reductionism, however, is unwarranted. Unfortunately for the purveyors of the "AMERICA, WAKE UP!" vision, reality is much more nuanced and complex than the myth of the Middle Eastern peril would allow.

It is instructive to compare our collective response to the "AMERICA, WAKE UP!" trope to a possible narrative involving the terrorist threat from Anglo-Saxon conservative Christian evangelicals. Take our national reaction to the largest terrorist attack on American soil prior to 9/11: the Oklahoma City bombing. Although the mainstream media and the American public initially speculated that the attack was the product of Middle Eastern terrorism, investigations proved otherwise. Some observers have noted that law enforcement's focus on Middle Eastern suspects in the wake of the attacks may have even allowed Timothy McVeigh to initially evade the authorities. As we now know, the perpetrators of the Oklahoma City bombing were a cell of crew-cut sporting, blue-eyed American sons of European descent. Interestingly, the response to the Oklahoma City bombing, and the problem of "domestic" terrorism, never took on a racialist bent. "Timothy McVeigh did not produce a discourse about good whites and bad whites, because we think of him as an individual deviant, a bad actor," notes Leti Volpp. "We do not think of his actions as representative of an entire racial group. This is part and parcel of how racial subordination functions, to understand nonwhites as directed by group-based determinism but whites as individuals."[6] For example, antiabortion bombers are not identified on the basis of their race (often white) or their religion (often evangelical Christian), and they are certainly not billed as terrorists. When a Christian individual of European descent commits a barbaric act against civilians, he is simply an outlier, a crazed lone gunman. By contrast, when a Muslim of Middle Eastern descent commits a barbaric act against civilians, his acts of terrorism are imputed to all members of his race and religion.

. . . .

Of course, many individuals continue to insist that the only rational response to the terror threat is the continued targeting of Middle

Eastern Americans. In this regard, Middle Eastern Americans are asked—or, more accurately, told—that they need to take one for the team. Take a recent incident at the University of California at Los Angeles in November 2006, when an Iranian American student, Mostafa Tabatabainejad, was repeatedly tasered after failing to show identification to campus police at the library. The brutal episode, captured on film by an eyewitness, presents a scene almost as disturbing and difficult to watch as the Rodney King beating some fifteen years earlier. After the first round of tasering, Tabatabainejad lay incapacitated on the ground, yet the police repeatedly commanded him to get up. When he was unable to do so, the police callously tasered him again and again as he screamed in pain. They continued to taser him even as he was handcuffed and, as the police dragged him through the room, he wailed "I'm not fighting you" and "I said I would leave." Yet, unlike the Rodney King beating (which was, admittedly, more brutal), the event did not make national headlines or even receive widespread condemnation, and it certainly did not trigger a debate about law enforcement's treatment of Middle Easterners.

. . . [A] simple examination of the most realized terrorist threats against the United States since 9/11 [reveal that] . . . the face of terrorism does not even reflect the prevailing Middle Eastern racial profile.

Richard Reid was the notorious shoe bomber convicted on charges of terrorism for attempting to blow up an American Airlines flight on December 22, 2001. While en route from Paris to Miami, he attempted to light [a] match to detonate plastic explosives hidden in his shoes. Reid is a British citizen of English and Jamaican descent. Jose Padilla, the American citizen detained since 2002 as an enemy combatant by the Bush administration for his alleged role in a dirty bomb plot, was born in Brooklyn and is of Puerto Rican descent. More recently, on June 22, 2006, the FBI arrested seven individuals in connection with their alleged terrorist plot against such buildings as Chicago's Sears Tower and sites in Miami. Of the seven, five were American citizens and the other two were Haitian nationals. Moreover, the group had no apparent ties to al Qaeda or other foreign terrorist organizations. Similarly, on May 7, 2007, the federal government arrested six individuals with a domestic plot to attack Fort Dix. While two of the individuals were from Jordan and Turkey, the remaining four, including a group of three brothers, were born in Yugoslavia and were of Yugoslavian descent. On June 2, 2007, the government arrested four individuals involved in planning a deadly terrorist attack at JFK airport. None of the four individuals hailed from the Middle East.

Most recent terrorist acts on American soil also have no Middle Eastern connection. The deadliest shooting in American history took place on the morning of April 16, 2007, at Virginia Tech and resulted in the death of thirty-three people, including the perpetrator, Seung-Hui Cho who was an American of Korean descent. The second deadliest shooting on American soil occurred at the University of Texas some four decades earlier. On August 1, 1966, Charles Whitman, a blonde-haired, blue-eyed ex-Marine and former altar boy, an American citizen of European descent, went on a killing spree at the university's clock tower, killing fourteen people and wounding an additional thirty-one. Finally, the third deadliest massacre—and perhaps most vivid in the minds of Americans—took place at Columbine High School in Colorado. On April 20, 1999, Eric Harris and Dylan Klebold took their own lives as well as those of thirteen of their classmates and teachers. Harris, a native Kansan of European descent, was raised as a Catholic and Klebold, a native Coloradan also of European descent, was raised as a Lutheran. Indeed, recent years have witnessed an alarming increase in acts of domestic terrorism. In a span of little more than a month, dating from August 24 through October 2, 2006, four separate deadly acts of terrorism took place in our nation's schools: a fatal shooting of a teacher followed by the suicide of the perpetrator, Christopher Williams, an African American, on August 24 at Essex Elementary School in Vermont; the fatal shooting of a hostage following the sexual assault of six school girls by Duane Roger Morrisson, a fifty-three year old American of European descent, at Platte Canyon High School in Bailey, Colorado, on September 27; the fatal shooting of a school principal by Eric Hainstock, a fifteen-year-old student of European descent, at Weston High School in Cazenovia, Wisconsin, on September 29; and finally, the deadly shooting of five Amish girls at a schoolhouse in Nickel Mines, Pennsylvania, on October 2 by Charles Carl Roberts IV, an American milk truck driver of European descent.

. . . .

Profiling has also threatened to relegate Americans of Middle Eastern descent to the status of second-class citizens and cement their position as perpetual foreigners who can never quite become American. In short, the practice betrays our most basic and cherished values of inclusiveness and equality. . . .

C. The Problem with Profiling

The effectiveness of racial profiling is also problematic, even if one wishes to target on the basis of apparent Arab ancestry. Criminologist Albert Alschuler has noted that the defensibility of racial profiling rests on the ability of law enforcement to distinguish members of different racial groups. Courts have already questioned the ability to identify Latinos by their appearance, and one can critique efforts to profile Arabs on similar grounds. As Susan Akram and Maritza Karmely posit, "Arabs are even less racially or ethnically homogeneous than Mexicans or Hispanics—those fitting stereotypical 'Arab-appearance' will most likely be profiled and stopped, while many Arabs will not be."[7] Thus, even if there is a meaningful correlation between Arab or Muslim background and terror risk, the policy is both wildly over- and underinclusive—a fact with which I am intimately familiar. I am frequently perceived as an Arab Muslim. I am neither Arab nor a Muslim.

Our racial profiling practices are not only bad policy, however. They also fail to pass muster under the Constitution, which requires any government policy implicating race to be narrowly tailored to further a compelling government interest. While our national security undoubtedly constitutes a compelling government interest, the racial profiling of Middle Easterners as a part of the war on terrorism is not a narrowly tailored policy under existing Supreme Court jurisprudence.

In *Craig v. Boren* (1976), the Supreme Court addressed an equal protection challenge to a government policy based on gender classifications—a type of discrimination traditionally subject to lesser scrutiny by the courts than racial categorizations. Law enforcement statistics have long confirmed that young men, especially those between the ages of eighteen and twenty-one, are far more likely than young women of the same age to engage in drunk driving. Drawing on this fact, the state of Oklahoma set two different minimum ages for the purchase of alcohol: eighteen for females, twenty-one for males. When the policy was challenged by an underage man and a female beer vendor, the Supreme Court struck down the law on the grounds that it violated the Constitution's Equal Protection Clause. As the Court readily admitted, the fact that only 0.18 percent of females but 2 percent of males between the ages of 18 and 20 had engaged in drunk driving represented a "disparity [that] is not trivial in a statistical sense." Yet, as the Court concluded, such a disparity "hardly can form the basis for employment of a gender line as a classifying device. Certainly if maleness is to serve as a proxy for drinking and driving, a correlation of 2 percent must be considered an unduly tenuous 'fit.'" As legal scholar David Cole reminds us, "[T]he vast majority of persons who appear Arab and Muslim—probably well over 99.9 percent—have no involvement with terrorism."[8] As such, the percentage of drunk drivers among college-age men is undoubtedly far greater than the percentage of terrorists among men of Middle Eastern appearance. If a classification based on gender is impermissible under the former fact, then surely classification based on race is manifestly unconstitutional under the latter fact.

As the facts reveal, terrorism knows no creed or color. By thinking otherwise, we not only sacrifice our true national security, but we threaten to make the war on terrorism a race war. By abandoning the rule of law, we betray the principles of equality and nondiscrimination that form the bedrocks of our democracy. The tale of John Walker Lindh, the American Taliban, is revealing on several levels. First, Lindh demonstrates that the terror threat can come from socioeconomically advantaged American men of European descent. More importantly, it reveals the impending danger that the war on terrorism will indeed degenerate into a war on a particular race.

After his capture while fighting for al Qaeda in the hills of Afghanistan, Lindh was tried for his treasonous actions in a federal court where, among other things, he enjoyed full due process protection, the requirement of a unanimous jury for conviction, strict admissibility rules for evidence used against him, and, perhaps most significantly, a top-notch legal defense team composed of attorneys from one of the most reputable law firms in the country. At the same time, 158 nonwhites captured for their alleged activities against the United States (including some individuals who were fighting alongside Lindh) were held in cages at a United States military base in Guantanamo Bay, Cuba, conveniently located outside of the United States proper to avoid complications with constitutional protections. These individuals were held indefinitely without charges and the government refused to accord them basic protections under the Geneva Conventions. The government also denied them individualized hearings to determine the lawfulness of their detainment. When asked why Lindh enjoyed the benefits of civil justice while others were relegated to a regime of military justice with substantially fewer protections for the accused, the Bush administration claimed Lindh was an American, while the others were foreign nationals. But that distinction held no weight. Not long after proffering this rationalization, the administration discovered that Yasser Hamdi, one of the individuals held at Guantanamo Bay, had been born in Louisiana and was, therefore, an American citizen. Yet Hamdi did not receive the rights enjoyed by Lindh. Although our government eventually transferred Hamdi from Guantanamo Bay to the continental United States, it "continued to assert authority to hold him under the same conditions as the foreign nationals held in Guantanamo Bay: indefinitely, without charges, without trial, without access to a lawyer, and, for all practical purposes, incommunicado."[9] Ultimately, the Supreme Court rejected the constitutionality of the administration's treatment of Hamdi. In a 6-3 decision, the Court sustained the government's right to hold American citizens as enemy combatants without criminal charges if they were engaged in hostilities against the United States. But, in a repudiation of the Bush administration's position, the Court found that Hamdi had a right to petition civil courts with the assistance of effective counsel to challenge his status as an enemy combatant.

One further note on Hamdi bears mentioning. Instead of pushing forward with the proceedings following the Supreme Court's ruling, the government released and deported Hamdi to Saudi Arabia in October 2004. In return, Hamdi simply agreed to renounce his American citizenship and comply with strict travel restrictions going forward. Hamdi's release represents a shocking turn of events involving a supposedly grave threat to our national security. If Hamdi were really as dangerous as the government repeatedly asserted, his release is a stunning abdication of the government's duty to protect us from terrorism. If he is not as dangerous as claimed, his treatment deserves scrutiny and demands, at the very least, a compelling justification.

Whether right or wrong, our constitutional jurisprudence draws a sharp divide between the rights to which citizens are entitled and the rights afforded to noncitizens. But the stark contrast in treatment between Lindh and Hamdi suggests that the civil right entitlements are even more fractured than that. Specifically, we appear to have two distinct classes of citizenship: the White and the Other. The prevalent discourse surrounding the Lindh affair epitomized this double standard. Lindh was repeatedly portrayed as just a lost, confused teenager experimenting with alternative ways of life. Indeed, no less than George H. W. Bush referred to Lindh as merely "some misguided Marin County hottubber."[10] Our former president's word choice is emblematic of our problematic approach to the war on terrorism. The white American of European descent who fights for al Qaeda is just "misguided." The darker skinned man who fights for al Qaeda is a terrorist and an embodiment of the anti-American hostility ubiquitous throughout the Middle East.

III. CINEMA AND STEREOTYPE

[Editors' Note: The author here discussed the problem of stereotyping of Middle Easterners, including in such popular movies as *Rules of Engagement*].

....

Stereotypical depictions reinforce clichéd perceptions, which, in turn, produce discriminatory conduct. Middle Easterners are portrayed as the perpetual foreigner, the enemy, the Other, the terrorists, the uncivilized heathens who threaten the American way of life with their inhumane thirst for violence. The impact of such prevalent prejudice is grave, and is reflected on a daily basis in government antiterrorism policies that respond to our most irrational and stereotype-driven fears by specifically targeting individuals of Middle Eastern descent.

Historically, no country has ever been more open and welcoming to immigrants than the United States, and no country has ever demonstrated a greater respect for civil rights and the protection of minorities. With respect to Middle Eastern Americans, however, we have work to do. And an important first step involves addressing their persistent demonization in news and entertainment programming....

PART 4

SECRECY AND SURVEILLANCE

LITIGATING SECRETS
Comparative Perspectives on the State Secrets Privilege (2009)

Sudha Setty

INTRODUCTION

The state secrets privilege is a common law evidentiary privilege, which enables the government to prevent disclosure of sensitive state secrets in the course of litigation. The claim of privilege by the government, if upheld by a court, can result in consequences ranging from the denial of a discovery request for a particular document to the outright dismissal of a suit. Some describe the state secrets privilege as the "most powerful secrecy privilege available to the president"[1] and the executive branch. Its scope is coextensive with any kind of information classified as "secret" or a higher level of secrecy, and applies to both criminal and civil lawsuits.

The privilege has been invoked by every administration since the Supreme Court acknowledged its existence in the 1953 case of *United States v. Reynolds*, which was based in large part on English precedent. . . .

Congress reintroduced reform legislation in February 2009 after the Obama administration appeared to adopt the Bush administration's stance in favor of a broad and sweeping invocation and application of the state secrets privilege. The proposed legislation is pending even as the Obama administration released a new policy for the Department of Justice, mandating a more rigorous internal review prior to invoking the state secrets privilege.

As with many other initiatives related to the prosecution of the War on Terror, the question of the appropriate application of the privilege turns on the balance between national security and the need to preserve the rule of law, individual rights, liberty interests, and government accountability. Congress's reform efforts continue to be necessary to restore the long-term appropriate balance among these competing interests.

. . . .

I. WHY REFORM THE STATE SECRETS PRIVILEGE?

In January 2008, a bipartisan group of senators introduced the State Secrets Protection Act, calling for the passage of a "safe, fair, and responsible state secrets privilege Act."[2] In March 2008, members of the House of Representatives introduced their own State Secret Protection Act of 2008, seeking to establish "safe, fair, and responsible procedures and standards for resolving claims of state secret privilege."[3] Representative Jerrold Nadler, chairman of the House Judiciary Subcommittee on the Constitution, Civil Rights, and Civil Liberties, described the need to reform the privilege as follows:

> If you have an administration that is abusing civil liberties, improperly arrests someone, improperly tortures that person, one presumes that that administration will not prosecute itself [or] its own agents for those terrible acts.
>
> The normal remedy in American law—the only remedy I know of—is for that person, once recovered from the torture, to sue for various kinds of damages and in court elucidate the facts and get some

justice and perhaps bring out to light what happened so that that administration would not do it again or the next one wouldn't.

If, however, that lawsuit can be dismissed right at the pleadings stage by the assertion of state secrets, and if the court doesn't look behind the assertion and simply takes it at face value the government says state secrets would be revealed and it would harm the national security if this case went forward, therefore case dismissed, which seems to be the current state of the law—if that continues and we don't change that, what remedy is there ever to enforce any of our constitutional rights?[4]

Although the impetus for legislative reform appeared to weaken with the election of President Obama, recent invocations of the privilege by the Obama administration and pressure applied by the Obama administration to foreign governments making their own state secrets determinations prompted Congress to reintroduce similar legislation in February 2009.

By reassessing the privilege, Congress is taking an important first step toward providing additional rule-of-law protections against executive branch overreaching, maintaining the judicial role in executive oversight, and strengthening the protections for individual litigants bringing suit against the government. In doing so, Congress appropriately took into account the changing national security landscape in the years since the recognition by the Supreme Court of the US [states secrets] privilege in *United States v. Reynolds*.

A. *United States v. Reynolds*: The Domestic Standard Is Established

The formal acknowledgement of the state secrets privilege in the United States is, perhaps surprisingly, rather recent. The 1953 case of *United States v. Reynolds* stands as the seminal case in which the US approach to invocations of the state secrets privilege was established.

In *Reynolds*, the family members of three civilians killed in the crash of a military plane sought compensation from the government for wrongful death. The government asserted the state secrets privilege in response to a document request by plaintiffs for the flight accident report. The trial court directed the government to produce the report to the court for a determination of privilege. When the government refused, the judge made an adverse inference and ordered a $250,000 judgment for the plaintiffs. The Third Circuit affirmed the decision, noting that a court should diligently refuse to accept blindly all claims of privilege; instead, a court should conduct an ex parte examination of the evidence to make an individualized privilege determination.

The Supreme Court reversed, although it agreed with part of the Third Circuit's reasoning in noting that the greater the necessity for the allegedly privileged information in presenting the case, the greater the need for the court to "probe in satisfying itself that the occasion for invoking the privilege is appropriate." The Court further reasoned that "[j]udicial control over the evidence in a case cannot be abdicated to the caprice of executive officers." However, the Court acknowledged the strength of the evidentiary privilege of the executive, and noted in passing that some commentators believed the privilege to be constitutionally grounded as well.

The Court ultimately upheld the right of the government to refuse to provide evidence and laid out a more deferential analytical framework by which future courts should evaluate a claim of privilege: (1) the claim must be asserted by the head of the department which has the responsibility for the information and evidence in question; (2) the court has the responsibility to determine whether the disclosure in question would pose a "reasonable danger [to] national security"; (3) the court should take into account the plaintiff's need for information to litigate its case; (4) the court should, if necessary, undertake an ex parte, in camera review of the information at issue to determine whether a reasonable danger exists; and (5) if the court determines that the "reasonable danger" standard is met, the privilege is absolute—it cannot be overcome by the plaintiff's showing of a need for the information, whether the case involves issues of human rights or any other countervailing considerations.

Given the ease with which the government could satisfy the low "reasonable danger" standard, the *Reynolds* court decided that the trial court did not need to examine the flight accident report over which the government was claiming the privilege, noting that "this is a time of vigorous preparation for national defense." If it had ordered disclosure for the court's review, it may have discovered what was revealed only when the report was declassified in the 1990s: there were no military secrets in the report, as claimed by the government, but there was evidence that the plane lacked standard safeguards that might have prevented its crash—the very negligence on which the family members in *Reynolds* based their lawsuit. The decision by the *Reynolds* Court to decline to at least ascertain whether the document in question contained the information claimed to be privileged was a fundamental and determinative flaw—one that has been replicated by many courts in the intervening years.

Reynolds is the only instance in which the Supreme Court has articulated a standard for the state secrets privilege; given the dearth of US precedent, the Court based its reasoning on numerous other sources, including the English case of *Duncan v. Cammel, Laird, & Co.*, decided in 1942. *Cammel, Laird*'s acknowledgement of a robust evidentiary privilege available to the executive was not, however, the only basis on which the *Reynolds* court made its decision; the Court also considered other sources, such as earlier US cases involving various privileges and Wigmore's treatise on evidence. Wigmore noted the need for a state secrets privilege, but cautioned—even then, in 1940—that the privilege "has been so often improperly invoked and so loosely misapplied that a strict definition of its legitimate limits must be made,"[5] and that courts, not the executive branch itself, were the appropriate decision-makers regarding the privilege.

In *Reynolds*, the Supreme Court established a standardized doctrine by which to evaluate claims of a state secrets privilege; this doctrine balanced national security matters with adherence to the rule of law and attention to rights of individual litigants. However, the balancing test set forth in Reynolds has often been subsumed by a judicial tendency to uphold claims of privilege without engaging in a meaningful analysis of the underlying evidence or the government's claimed need for nondisclosure. In recent years, that tendency has come under scrutiny as the current War on Terror has led to numerous lawsuits in which national security programs have been implicated.

B. Impetus for Reform

Congress took up the question of the privilege in 2008 for several reasons. First, the "war on terror" has led to highly controversial actions such as the National Security Agency's warrantless wiretapping program as well as the extraordinary rendition of individuals by the Central Intelligence Agency. Second, the unprecedented level of secrecy within the George W. Bush administration led to suspicions that the government was not necessarily acting in good faith in invoking the privilege, and that such trends would persist in future administrations. Further, a "mosaic theory" of terrorist activity would create a broad protection over large swaths of relevant information that may not, at least regarding individual documents, satisfy the *Reynolds* standard. Third, many critics see the state secrets privilege as a broad and expansive means for executive branch overreaching in which the bad actions of the administration are withheld from private litigants and the judicial system, and concealed from Congress and the public.

The administration's warrantless wiretapping program was challenged numerous times in court, but the government's frequent invocation of the state secrets privilege meant that plaintiffs met with little success in pursuing lawsuits against the government regarding the program. Specifically, the government has invoked the state secrets privilege on several occasions to protect records that would have allowed the plaintiffs to prove that they were subject to wiretapping and thus had standing to challenge the program.

An emblematic case is that of the al-Haramain Islamic Foundation, an Islamic charity based in Saudi Arabia and operating worldwide, including in the United States, which filed suit against the US government for being subject to allegedly unconstitutional warrantless wiretapping of telephone conversations by the National Security Agency (NSA). Al-Haramain was in the unique position of being able to offer documented proof that it was subject to NSA wiretapping, since the government had accidentally turned over transcripts and records of the wiretapping activity to an Al-Haramain lawyer. The Bush administration sought to recover most copies of the report in the possession of Al-Haramain's counsel and others, but did not try to recover those copies that had been sent outside of the United States.

The government moved to dismiss Al-Haramain's case based on the state secrets privilege; the motion was denied, although the presiding judge agreed to exclude the wiretapping report from the evidence available to plaintiffs. The Ninth Circuit reversed and remanded the case from an interlocutory appeal, holding that because the privilege surrounding the wiretapping records was "absolute," the district court's decision to use affidavits was unacceptable. Because the district court should not have considered the document in any respect, the Ninth Circuit reasoned that plaintiffs could not establish an injury in fact, and, therefore, lacked standing. On remand, the district court was tasked to determine whether Foreign Intelligence Surveillance Act ("FISA") pre-empts the state secrets privilege such that the lawsuit could survive. The court concluded that FISA trumped the state secrets privilege, noting that "[t]he enactment of FISA was the fruition of a period of intense public and Congressional interest in the problem of unchecked domestic surveillance by the executive branch."

The court reasoned that section 1806(f) of FISA governed how sensitive government information resulting from surveillance ought to be handled by the courts, and that 1806(f) trumped the *Reynolds* framework for analyzing state secrets claims. The court went further still, holding that 1806(f) was "in effect a codification of the state secrets privilege for purposes of relevant cases under FISA, as modified to reflect Congress's precise directive to the federal courts for the handling of materials and information with purported national security implications. [T]he *Reynolds* protocol has no role where section 1806(f) applies." The district court's holding kept the plaintiff's claim alive, with Al-Haramain bearing the burden of proving surveillance apart from the wiretapping records that were inadvertently produced by the government. In April 2009, the district court indicated that the government would not have carte blanche to assert the privilege by instructing both parties to work together to draft a protective order to delineate how classified and sensitive information will be treated. The court also admonished Obama administration lawyers for their continued attempts to garner a stay and delay the disclosure of information relevant to the plaintiff's case.

A second motivating factor for the current push of state secrets reform is growing evidence of extreme cases of detainee mistreatment that have shocked the public: emblematic is the case of Khaled El-Masri, a German citizen who was subjected to extraordinary rendition by the US government in what was later acknowledged as a case of mistaken identity.

In December 2003, El-Masri was taking a holiday from his hometown of Ulm, Germany, to Skopje, Macedonia. He was taken into custody by Macedonian authorities while on a bus crossing the border from Serbia. According to El-Masri, in January 2004, he was transported to an airport where he was beaten, stripped naked, photographed, and then sodomized. He was then subject to "extraordinary rendition" by the CIA, who transported him to a prison in Kabul, Afghanistan.

El-Masri was finally released on May 28, 2004, after having been in captivity for approximately five months, during which he was allegedly subject to numerous harsh interrogations by the CIA, which included "threats, insults, pushing, and shoving," as well as force-feeding through a nasal tube.[6] Upon his release, El-Masri sought out German officials, who launched an investigation regarding his allegations of abduction, detention, and abuse.

In 2005, El-Masri sued George Tenet, the former director of the Central Intelligence Agency, the airlines complicit in his rendition, and various other individuals. The government argued for dismissal of the suit based on the state secrets privilege, claiming that national security interests would be compromised if the litigation were to continue, and that state secrets were central to El-Masri making his case against the government. This privilege claim was made despite the United States' admission of the existence and operation of a rendition program, as well as the support for El-Masri's factual account by German investigators and prosecutors. The federal district court agreed with the government's claim and dismissed El-Masri's suit at the motion-to-dismiss stage of the litigation, prior to the government's filing an answer to El-Masri's complaint. The federal appeals court sustained the dismissal, and the Supreme Court denied certiorari in 2007.

In denying certiorari, the Supreme Court essentially chose to let stand the lack of clarity surrounding the standard for determining what procedures a court should use to evaluate potentially privileged evidence, whether a court should dismiss a suit in response to a valid privilege claim, and whether dismissal can occur prior to evidentiary discovery or even the filing of an answer to the complaint.

[Likewise], the Ninth Circuit [en banc] decision in *Mohamed v. Jeppesen Dataplan, Inc.*, [follows] the Fourth Circuit's reasoning in *El-Masri* [but] articulates a narrower standard for upholding an invocation of the state secrets privilege. In *Mohamed*, the district court dismissed a suit brought by five detainees against a Boeing subsidiary allegedly involved in the transportation of the detainees for government-directed rendition and torture. The district court cited many of the same reasons that the courts in *El-Masri* relied on, including the need to dismiss the suit because the subject matter at issue was itself a state secret that, if revealed, could jeopardize national security interests. [A] Ninth Circuit [panel] reversed [in 2009], adhering closely to the standard as articulated by the Court in *Reynolds* and rejecting the government's claims that the suit needed to be dismissed outright based on its subject matter. [Editors' Note: In September 2010, the Ninth Circuit sitting en banc dismissed the plaintiffs' suit but expressed concerns about the lack of remedy available to plaintiffs, going so far as to suggest the possibility of compensation from the administration or a congressionally fashioned remedy for the plaintiffs.]

The dismissal of *El-Masri*, which was affirmed by the Fourth Circuit and was subsequently denied certiorari, the recent Ninth Circuit decision in *Mohamed*, [and recent developments, such as the invocation in September 2010 of the state secrets privilege in litigation over the targeted extraterritorial killings of US citizens by the US government,] make clear that Congress should step in and clarify the state secrets privilege. The current application of the state secrets privilege raises numerous questions that require clarification: when the government can invoke the privilege, and what can be protected from disclosure;

whether it is appropriate to grant a motion to dismiss based on a state secrets claim at the initial pleadings stage; the appropriate relief for a valid claim of the privilege; and how deeply the court must examine the government's claim.

More fundamentally, the petition for certiorari by *El-Masri* reflects broader concerns that the *Reynolds* framework should be reevaluated in light of serious constitutional issues—including allegations of gross violations of the right to privacy and the right to due process—raised in current cases that were not present in *Reynolds*. Additionally, critics have noted that the nature of national security concerns has changed significantly in recent decades, and the courts' ability to adjudicate cases while protecting sensitive information has improved dramatically in the decades since *Reynolds*.

The *El-Masri* certiorari petition asserted that it was time for the Court to revisit the *Reynolds* standard and the state secrets privilege generally, arguing that since *Reynolds* was decided, the privilege has been broadened inappropriately and "has become unmoored from its evidentiary origins" and now provides a type of blanket immunity for bad actions by the government.

Indeed, the Bush administration invoked the state secrets privilege with far greater frequency, in cases of greater national significance, and sought broader immunity for alleged bad acts by the government than did previous administrations. It also extended the ability to classify documents as "secret" to additional administrative agencies. These claims of state secrets, as *El-Masri* noted, have been raised frequently at the initial pleadings stage, allowing the government to seek dismissal prior to discovery. Further, courts often have not examined the documents over which the privilege has been claimed, relying solely on government affidavits to determine that the privilege applies and that the suit must be dismissed prior to the commencement of discovery. Given the likelihood of continued litigation raising issues of national security for the foreseeable future, reassessing *Reynolds* in light of modern standards is necessary.

C. Proposed Reforms

The 2008 and 2009 proposed reforms mark the first sustained attempt by Congress to address the concerns of lawmakers, scholars, and activists to allow courts greater flexibility in their evaluation and application of the privilege while protecting sensitive government information.

Both the 2009 Senate and House bills offer a uniform set of procedures for federal judges to employ when the government asserts the privilege, modeled in large part after the Classified Information Procedures Act (CIPA) of 1980, which established procedures for the use of classified information in criminal trials.

Under the proposed legislation, courts would have the ability to conduct hearings on the documents claimed to be privileged in camera, ex parte, or through the participation of attorneys and legal experts with "appropriate security clearances" to review the materials. The bills also require the government to produce each piece of evidence it claims is protected for in camera review, along with a signed affidavit from the head of the agency in possession of the evidence. The Senate bill also requires the government to attempt to produce a nonprivileged substitute—such as a redaction or summary—for any piece of evidence for which the privilege is upheld by the court.

These proposed reforms mark a stark contrast to the current situation in which the government's common practice is to rely solely on affidavits to assert the privilege and move for dismissal of a suit. Judges would be prevented from dismissing cases based on the privilege before plaintiffs have had a chance to engage in evidentiary discovery, and the level of deference to be accorded to the executive branch would change from the current standard of giving the "utmost deference" to administration claims to one in which judges give only "substantial weight" to such claims.

D. Critiques and Concerns Over Reforming the Privilege

The 2008 proposed reforms were met with immediate and strong opposition from the Bush administration. In a March 31, 2008, letter to the Senate Judiciary Committee, then-Attorney General Michael Mukasey offered numerous critiques, including that the state secrets privilege is constitutionally rooted, and not solely a common law evidentiary privilege; that the courts are not the appropriate decision-makers regarding national security matters; that other aspects of S. 2533, including reporting requirements to Congress, are constitutionally suspect; and that the proposed reforms would compromise the state secrets privilege to the detriment of national security.

First, the Bush administration offered the article II-based argument that congressional regulation of the privilege is overreaching because the state secrets privilege is not a purely evidentiary privilege for which the parameters can be set by Congress. Instead, the Bush administration and other critics argued that the state secrets privilege is grounded in the president's inherent executive power, a position articulated by the Supreme Court in the dicta of *United States v. Nixon*, and mentioned in passing in a footnote in *Reynolds*.

Since *Reynolds*, most courts have construed the state secrets privilege simply as a common law evidentiary privilege, created and enforced to protect information when "disclosure would be inimical to the national security [interests]."[7] In 2005, the Court decided *Tenet v. Doe* and made clear the distinction between applying the state secrets privilege and deciding the threshold question of justiciability. In *Tenet*, two foreign nationals who allegedly worked on behalf of the Central Intelligence

Agency (CIA) in return for the promise of financial support and residency in the United States brought claims against the CIA. The Supreme Court dismissed the claims of the alleged agents based squarely on the justiciability doctrine announced in *Totten v. United States* rather than looking to the state secrets privilege for guidance. In the course of its reasoning in *Tenet*, the Court clarified that the state secrets privilege addressed in *Reynolds* ought to be viewed as purely evidentiary in nature.

. . . .

The Bush administration wanted to see a continuation of the status quo, and believed that the deferential *Reynolds* standard was preferable to creating a stronger judicial oversight mechanism. To date, the common application of *Reynolds* is what still governs, and it is unclear whether the Obama administration and . . . Congress will pass legislation to address the process and rule-of-law problems that *Reynolds* has engendered. To evaluate whether *Reynolds* and its progeny offer the appropriate standard to apply, however, it is useful to look back at how the US state secrets privilege evolved to its current state.

II. THE HISTORY AND EVOLUTION OF THE US STATE SECRETS PRIVILEGE

. . . .

A. The UK Origins of the US State Secrets Privilege

Although precedent from England was not the only legal basis for the *Reynolds* decision, it played an instrumental role for the Supreme Court, which had little domestic doctrine to rely upon. However, what the *Reynolds* court viewed as simply English precedent actually represented two distinct and, to some extent, contrary legal precedents from England and Scotland.

. . . .

B. History of the US State Secrets Privilege

Prior to *Reynolds*, US jurisprudence on the state secrets privilege was limited and vague, and failed to set forth a standardized doctrine by which privilege claims ought to be evaluated. Some scholars argue that the state secrets privilege simply did not exist in US jurisprudence prior to *Reynolds*, but some evidence does exist that courts accepted the general notion of executive privilege, albeit in the specific context of an informer's privilege and deliberative privilege, not a state secrets privilege. As early as *Marbury v. Madison*, the Court mentions the existence of presidential prerogatives not delineated in the Constitution, but does not clarify the nature or extent of those prerogatives. In accepting a presidential prerogative as a natural derivation of the Crown privilege, the Court did not acknowledge the significantly different nature of the Crown or the judiciary in England; unlike US judges, English judges were not independent from Parliament after being appointed. Ironically, *Marbury* is best known for formalizing the US doctrine of judicial review, but the decision operated under the assumption that there were certain executive privileges that may be beyond the purview of the judiciary.

. . . .

The nature of a state secrets privilege remained relatively static until the 1875 Supreme Court decision of *Totten v. United States*. The plaintiff in *Totten* brought suit to enforce an alleged government contract for espionage during the Civil War; the Supreme Court held that it was inappropriate for the lower court to hear the case in the first place, since "public policy forbids the maintenance of any suit in a court of justice, the trial of which would inevitably lead to the disclosure of matters which the law itself regards as confidential, and respecting which it will not allow the confidence to be violated." *Totten* embodied the idea that some claims against the government are simply not justiciable based on the nature of the claim being made and the need for government secrecy.

However, the relevance of *Totten* to the state secrets privilege is open to debate. Although the *Reynolds* Court cited to *Totten* as evidence that an evidentiary privilege against revealing state secrets existed, the Supreme Court stated unequivocally in 2005 that *Totten* does not involve the state secrets privilege. The Court in *Tenet* found that *Totten* dealt with baseline questions of justiciability, and the state secrets privilege as articulated in *Reynolds* required a balancing test for the admissibility of evidence, which may or may not necessitate dismissal of a case.

Even setting *Totten* aside as distinct from the state secrets privilege, the application of a national security-related privilege is found in several cases in the early twentieth century. Other national-security cases involved the invocation of a state secrets privilege in the criminal context. For example, in *United States v. Haugen*, a district court acquitted a defendant charged with forgery while working under a military contract, based largely on the fact that the contract in question could not be compelled for production by the government. Although each of these cases dealt with the question of how to handle state secrets in the litigation context, they did so without a judicial or legislative standard or unifying doctrine in place.

After World War II, the number of lawsuits involving questions of state secrets increased significantly, largely due to the enactment of the Federal Tort Claims Act, which permitted individuals to sue the government for allegedly tortious conduct. This development set the stage for the Supreme Court to establish a standard for the state secrets privilege in the seminal case of *United States v. Reynolds*.

The early 1970s saw an increase in the number of lawsuits in which the government invoked the state secrets privilege. This trend was fueled by several factors. In 1971 the Supreme Court held in *Bivens v. Six Unknown Named Agents of Federal Bureau of Narcotics* that private litigants could seek compensation for the government's constitutional violations, which opened the door for numerous types of lawsuits against the government. Further, the Watergate scandal broke and propelled a massive push for government accountability, including the fortification of the Freedom of Information Act, the establishment of additional congressional oversight mechanisms, and the passage of the Foreign Intelligence Surveillance Act [FISA].

As oversight and lawsuits increased, the state secrets privilege offered a mechanism for the executive branch to both protect sensitive national security information and avoid higher levels of transparency and accountability. The problem faced by courts has been determining which of these two administrative motivations was at play in a given situation, and to navigate the interbranch tension inherent in a confrontation with an executive branch assertion of power. The result has often been that courts decline to get involved in the process of weighing evidence altogether: in fact, since 1990, judges have conducted an in camera review of documents over which the privilege has been claimed in only about twenty percent of state secrets privilege cases.

In the post-September 11, 2001, era, the question of proper invocation of the state secrets privilege resurfaced, particularly in light of controversial programs such as warrantless surveillance and extraordinary rendition. Some of the state secrets cases in the post-September 11 era have involved government attempts to prevent the disclosure of technical information related to military issues, somewhat akin to the situation in *Reynolds*. Other cases involved government contracting and business management issues, or internal policies and procedures arguably related to national security. Finally, in cases like *El-Masri* and *Al-Haramain*, the privilege was invoked to terminate litigation that involved allegations of gross violations of individual civil and human rights.

III. COMPARATIVE PERSPECTIVES ON THE STATE SECRETS PRIVILEGE

. . . .

IV. VIEWING US REFORM EFFORTS WITHIN A COMPARATIVE CONTEXT

Although the current US use and application of the state secrets privilege is roughly analogous to that of England . . . , England's current application of the privilege may be more narrow than that of the United States. . . . [T]he English court [recently] . . . considered expanding the scope of its own public interest immunity under threat of national security repercussions from the United States. The transnational implications of US pressure regarding the state secrets privilege may be that even if other nations' courts use a narrower standard for the privilege, those standards may be undermined if the US government uses its considerable clout to pressure governments to claim state secrets in cases where US government actions are implicated.

US courts are also less deferential to the executive branch than India, but much more so than Scotland and Israel. The proposed congressional reforms offer some positive steps to establish procedural safeguards that strike an appropriate balance between national security interests and the rule of law, government accountability, and individual liberty. However, Congress should consider going further in addressing the need for litigation to compensate those who have suffered gross constitutional and human rights violations at the hands of the government.

A. Future Reform Efforts Should Consider Explicitly Accounting for Alleged Human Rights Abuses

If the legislative reforms are adopted, the United States' application of the state secrets privilege would align with the Scottish courts' treatment of public interest immunity. However, the reforms proffered in the United States fall short of the Israeli standard of justiciability in national security matters—the Israeli standard explicitly requires consideration of allegations of human rights abuses, whereas the proposed safeguards in the United States do not.

Of course, the Israeli test for justiciability is not directly analogous to the United States doctrine regarding the state secrets privilege. However, reforms in the United States should require courts to consider potential human rights abuses in determining whether a lawsuit should go forward, particularly with regard to whether a case ought to be ultimately dismissed. Although the nature of the allegations should not be determinative as to whether litigation should proceed, it would be appropriate for US judges—like their Israeli counterparts—to undertake a balancing test which accounts for the nature of the claim when deciding whether a case ought to go forward at the discovery stage. After all, the cases of *El-Masri*, *Al-Haramain*, and *Mohamed*, and the violations of human rights and constitutional safeguards that they represent, are at the heart of the impetus for reforming the privilege.

B. Congressional Reforms Should Encompass Both the State Secrets Privilege and Justiciability

Congress should consider proposing reforms that encompass both the evidentiary issues of the state secrets privilege and the justiciability questions surrounding *Totten* and its progeny. Although the Supreme Court clarified in *Tenet v. Doe* that questions of justiciability should be considered independently of the state secrets privilege, courts have struggled with this distinction. It would be appropriate and useful for Congress to assist in the clarification between the state secrets privilege and *Totten*'s standard of dismissal based on the subject matter of the litigation.

Such clarification should be undertaken simultaneously with state secrets reform because it would close a potential avenue for the executive branch to avoid disclosure of evidence. The post-Watergate era saw a spike in invocations of the state secret privilege precisely because reform efforts had opened avenues for individual litigants to seek redress and information from the government. A partial reform effort which addresses the state secrets privilege but not the question of justiciability may inadvertently provide an incentive to the executive branch to attempt to dismiss cases based on *Totten*'s nonjusticiability standard. Congressional reform efforts should include a justiciability assessment by which courts dismiss cases that fall squarely within the ambit of *Totten* (involving secret deals related to national security and espionage), but should make clear that all other cases should be evaluated under the state secrets privilege, with an additional criterion of accounting for allegations of human rights abuses. Such a measure would preclude subsequent abuse of the *Totten* doctrine as an alternative means for the executive branch to avoid liability or disclosure of allegedly sensitive information.

C. Reforming the Privilege Should Remain a Priority

The national security programs created or enhanced since 2001 as part of the "war on terror" have come under a great deal of scrutiny, but very few concrete oversight measures have taken hold for a number of reasons.

Legislative inertia and a high level of deference to executive branch decision-making have hobbled many avenues for genuine legislative oversight or any kind of substantial reform efforts with regard to national security and the rule of law. This legislative inertia and deference was particularly pronounced from 2001 through 2006, when both houses of Congress and the presidency were controlled by Republicans.

Reform and oversight efforts began to increase when Democrats gained control of Congress in 2006 and initiated investigations and attempted to pass meaningful oversight measures. However, the Democratically-controlled Congress continued to defer to the Bush administration on most national security matters. For example, in July 2008 Congress passed amendments to the Foreign Intelligence Surveillance Act, which stripped jurisdiction over allegations of illegal wiretapping from Article III courts, extended executive branch authority to conduct warrantless surveillance, and immunized telecommunications companies from liability regarding their assistance to the government in conducting warrantless wiretapping of US citizens.

. . . Congress should consider the long-term effects of not reforming the privilege and act to restore the rule of law and appropriate balance of power among the branches of government.

. . . [A]lthough public outcry regarding the administration of national security programs has been muted at times, the cases which serve as the impetus for the proposed 2008 reforms are specific, public, and graphic—El-Masri's case of mistaken identity resulted in a horrific experience of alleged abduction and torture, which was reported widely in great detail.

. . . [W]hereas various oversight measures attempted by Congress have been met with constitutional avoidance by the executive branch (where it has refused to enforce portions of legislation as written), reform of the state secrets privilege would avoid the same fate, since the power to apply the reforms would fall to the courts instead of the executive branch. If the government fails to comply with a court's request to provide documents for in camera review, the government could be held in contempt or a court could decide to enter a default judgment in favor of the plaintiffs, as the lower court in *Reynolds* did.

CONCLUSION

Invocations of the state secrets privilege have occurred in every administration since *Reynolds* was decided and, given the current national security landscape, litigation which involves sensitive government information is likely to continue for the foreseeable future.

The extensive and expansive use of the state secrets privilege by the Bush administration illustrates the need for process changes to be implemented in order to deal with the most extraordinary situations, when national security concerns are heightened and the temptation to abuse power and maximize secrecy is at its highest. The Bush administration set a precedent that allows President Obama and any future president to continue on a path of exerting a tremendous amount of political power with very little oversight.

The Obama administration['s] decision to embrace the Bush administration's expansive view of the state secrets privilege underscores the need for reform as a part of a long-term commitment to the rule of law even in the national security arena. The administration's pressure on the British government [in the *Mohamed* case] reflects the transnational impact of US policies: the broad US interpretation of the privilege almost trumped the domestic analysis of the privilege by UK courts. The long-term effects of such pressure are yet to be seen, but the decisions in the *Mohamed* case reflect the possibility that the US application of the privilege could be exported more widely under threat to other countries of national security repercussions from the United States.

The Obama administration's new policy to determine whether to invoke the state secrets privilege is demonstrably better than the previous policy: the new structure mandates layers of review within the Justice Department, including an initial determination by a Justice Department official, a recommendation by a newly established State Secrets Review Committee, and approval of the attorney general before invoking the state secrets privilege in court. As promising as this new policy seems, congressional reform is still needed to ensure an external, long-term check on executive branch overreaching that would exist independent of what internal policy is adopted by an administration. Passage of a strong state secrets reform measure can ensure a fair standard in the courts and an opportunity for redress for those alleging grave violations of civil rights and civil liberties.

THE NATIONAL SECURITY AGENCY'S DOMESTIC SPYING PROGRAM
Framing the Debate
(2006)

David Cole and Martin S. Lederman

On Friday, December 16, 2005, the *New York Times* reported that President George W. Bush had secretly authorized the National Security Agency (NSA) to conduct warrantless surveillance of Americans' telephone and e-mail communications as part of an effort to obtain intelligence about future terrorist activity. The *Times* report was based on leaks of classified information, presumably by NSA officials concerned about the legality of the program. The *Times* reported that at the president's request it had delayed publication of the story for more than a year.

Once its existence was disclosed, the NSA program caused a firestorm of controversy because the program appeared to violate specific statutory limits on electronic surveillance contained in the Foreign Intelligence Surveillance Act (FISA). FISA is a landmark statute enacted with the approval of the president in 1978 and amended numerous times since. The president's authorization of the NSA program appeared to contravene both FISA's criminal prohibition on statutorily unauthorized electronic surveillance, and another statutory provision specifying that FISA's procedures are to be the "exclusive means" by which such surveillance can be lawfully performed for foreign intelligence purposes. Senator Arlen Specter, chair of the Senate Committee on the Judiciary, immediately questioned the legality of the program, and announced that his committee would hold hearings on the issue early in the new year. The Bush administration responded with an aggressive public relations campaign, in which the vice president, the attorney general, General Michael Hayden (the principal deputy director for national intelligence), and the president himself defended the program in multiple fora.

[F]our [key] documents, . . . taken together, set forth the basic arguments concerning the lawfulness of the secret NSA surveillance program. The debate outlined by the four documents raises important issues about statutory interpretation in the face of claims of constitutional conflict, executive power during times of war, fundamental privacy rights of Americans, and ultimately, the rule of law in the War on Terror.

It is important to clarify, as well, what the debate is *not* about— namely, whether the president should be able to intercept phone calls made between al Qaeda members abroad and persons within the United States. There is broad consensus that federal authorities should monitor calls involving al Qaeda. Indeed, FISA does not prohibit such surveillance. For one thing, the statute has no application at all to surveillance targeted at persons abroad and collected overseas.[1] And it authorizes domestic surveillance targeted at US persons in the United States, as long as a court finds probable cause to believe that the target of the surveillance is an agent of a foreign power and that the facilities or places at which the electronic surveillance is directed are being used by such an agent of a foreign power.[2] Moreover, FISA permits surveillance to be initiated before court approval so long as approval is sought within seventy-two hours, and it also permits surveillance without court approval during the first fifteen days of a war, during which time Congress can consider proposals for wartime statutory amendments.

Notwithstanding these broad statutory authorizations, the president has authorized the NSA both to circumvent FISA's court-approval process with respect to electronic surveillance that would be authorized by FISA,[3] and, almost certainly, to engage in forms of surveillance that FISA prohibits.[4]

In December 2005, the administration set forth its legal defense of the NSA program in a letter from the Department of Justice (DOJ) addressed to the leaders of the Senate and House Intelligence Committees. That letter outlined a three-part defense of the program: Most prominently, DOJ argued that Congress had implicitly authorized the NSA's warrantless surveillance program when it authorized the use of military force against al Qaeda in September 2001. More obliquely, the DOJ suggested that to interpret the 2001 force authorization statute as *not* authorizing the NSA program would raise a serious constitutional question, because in that case FISA's prohibition of the surveillance would interfere with the president's authority as commander in chief to execute the war against al Qaeda in the manner he thought most effective. Finally, the letter argued that the wiretapping program does not violate the Fourth Amendment.

In response to the administration's letter, we worked with a group of constitutional scholars and former government officials to draft a letter in response. . . . In our letter, dated January 9, 2006, we argued: (1) that the authorization to use military force against al Qaeda cannot be read to authorize warrantless electronic surveillance in the face of clear and specific statutory prohibitions on that conduct—including the provision specifying that FISA shall be the "exclusive means" of performing electronic surveillance and another provision of FISA specifically addressing the president's surveillance authority in wartime; (2) that the canon of constitutional avoidance—that ambiguous statutes should be construed to avoid serious constitutional questions—is inapposite here, where Congress had extensively grappled with the constitutional question in the legislative process and had crafted the statute specifically in order to preclude the president from invoking a constitutional authority to engage in electronic surveillance outside the "exclusive means" that FISA prescribes; (3) that interpreting FISA to prohibit such wiretapping does *not* unconstitutionally interfere with the president's role as commander in chief; and (4) that based on the publicly available information, the NSA wiretapping program appears to raise serious constitutional questions under the Fourth Amendment.

The Bush administration subsequently submitted a much more extensive "white paper" to Congress further developing its legal position. . . . In that white paper, the administration again argued that the 2001 military force authorization resolution provided statutory authority to engage in electronic surveillance outside the "exclusive means" prescribed by FISA. In addition, the DOJ white paper argued more explicitly, and at much greater length, that "serious constitutional questions" are raised whenever Congress enacts statutes that "interfere . . . at all" with what the administration calls "a core exercise of Commander in Chief control over the Armed Forces during armed conflict"—in particular, "the Commander-in-Chief's control of the means and methods of engaging the enemy." On that theory, serious constitutional doubt would arise whenever Congress regulates not only the wiretapping of domestic communications performed as part of the war effort, but also the detention of those suspected of being enemy combatants (including US citizens), the interrogation of those who might provide information relevant to the war (including by torture or other forms of cruel, inhuman, and degrading treatment), or when a statute determines the scope of a war, such as by prescribing or regulating the theatre of war, the use of certain weapons (e.g., land mines), and the identity of the enemy.

In February [2006], our same group of scholars and former government officials drafted a reply to the Bush administration's white paper. . . . This letter further addresses the DOJ's statutory arguments. We also argue in greater detail that the administration's constitutional theory of the commander in chief clause is fundamentally flawed. Each time the

Supreme Court has addressed the issue directly—most recently in cases involving the detention of alleged enemy combatants in the conflict against al Qaeda—the Court has rejected the notion that the commander in chief may disregard statutory constraints enacted pursuant to Congress's enumerated powers.

The question that these documents raise is not whether suspected al Qaeda members' phone calls should be monitored, but whether wiretapping of Americans in pursuit of that objective should be done pursuant to law, or pursuant to secret orders issued by the president in contravention of law. Our view is that if the president finds federal law inadequate in some measure, the proper course is to ask Congress to change it. What the president cannot do in our democracy is order that the law be violated in secret.

IN RE NATIONAL SECURITY AGENCY TELECOMMUNICATIONS RECORDS LITIGATION

United States District Court, Northern District of California

This order pertains to:

Al-Haramain Islamic Foundation, Inc, an Oregon Nonprofit Corporation; Wendell Belew, a United States Citizen and Attorney at Law; Asim Ghafoor, a Unites States Citizen and Attorney at Law, Plaintiffs,

v.

Barack H. Obama, President of the United States; National Security Agency and Keith B. Alexander, its Director; Office of Foreign Assets Control, an office of the United States Treasury, and Adam J. Szubin, its Director; Federal Bureau of Investigation and Robert S. Mueller III, its Director, in his official and personal capacities, Defendants.

March 31, 2010.

MEMORANDUM OF DECISION AND ORDER

VAUGHN R. WALKER, Chief Judge.

. . . .

DECISION

. . . .

I

Plaintiffs filed their lawsuit in the United States District Court for the District of Oregon on February 28, 2006. Their complaint alleged that plaintiffs had been subject to warrantless electronic surveillance and sought civil damages under section 1810 of the Foreign Intelligence Surveillance Act ("FISA"). Plaintiffs also alleged violations of the separation of powers principle, the First, Fourth and Sixth Amendments of the United States Constitution and the International Covenant on Civil and Political Rights. Along with their complaint, plaintiffs filed under seal a copy of what has been referred to throughout this litigation as the "Sealed Document," a classified document that had inadvertently been disclosed by defendant Office of Foreign Assets Control ("OFAC") to counsel for Al-Haramain as part of a production of unclassified documents relating to Al-Haramain's designation as a "Specially Designated Global Terrorist" ("SDGT") organization. The previous phases of this litigation largely focused on whether plaintiffs could use the Sealed Document.

Defendants filed their first motion for dismissal or for summary judgment, arguing that the Sealed Document could not be used in the litigation and that the common-law state secrets privilege ("SSP") required dismissal of the case. The Oregon district court (King, J[udge]) denied the motion, explaining that "plaintiffs should have an opportunity to establish standing and make a prima facie case, even if they must do so in camera." The court noted that "plaintiffs need some information in the Sealed Document to establish their standing and a prima facie case, and they have no other available source for this information," and that given defendants' many public acknowledgments of the warrantless electronic surveillance program beginning in 2005, the program itself was not a secret. Nonetheless, the court determined that the Sealed

Document remained highly classified, ordered plaintiffs to hand over all copies of the Sealed Document to the court, refused media requests to unseal records, and plainly contemplated maintaining the secrecy of the Sealed Document while proceeding with the litigation.

. . . .

The court of appeals considered three issues on interlocutory review: (1) whether the very subject matter of the litigation is a state secret; (2) whether Al-Haramain can establish standing to bring suit, absent the Sealed Document; and (3) whether Al-Haramain can establish a prima facie case, and the government can defend against Al-Haramain's assertions, without resorting to state secrets.

. . . .

As to the first issue, the court of appeals held that while Al-Haramain's case involved privileged information, "that fact alone does not render the very subject matter of the action a state secret" and affirmed the district court's denial of dismissal on that basis.

. . . .

The court of appeals [also] . . . determined that plaintiffs could not establish standing to proceed with their lawsuit without the Sealed Document because they could not establish a "concrete and particularized" injury-in-fact . . . , unless the courts determined that FISA, rather than the SSP, governed this case: "Al-Haramain cannot establish that it has standing, and its claims must be dismissed, unless FISA preempts the [SSP]. . . ."

On the basis of the rule set forth in [the Supreme Court case] *Singleton v. Wulff* (1976), that a court of appeals should not ordinarily consider an issue not ruled on in the district court, the court of appeals declined to decide whether FISA preempts the SSP. Instead, writing that "the FISA issue remains central to Al-Haramain's ability to proceed with this lawsuit," it remanded the case to this court to consider that question "and for any proceedings collateral to that determination." . . .

. . . .

By order dated July 2, 2008, the court held that FISA's legislative history unequivocally established Congress's intent that FISA preempt or displace the SSP in cases within the reach of its provisions.

. . . .

. . . The court dismissed plaintiffs' complaint with leave to amend, explaining: "[t]o proceed with their FISA claim, plaintiffs must present to the court enough specifics based on non-classified evidence to establish their 'aggrieved person' status under FISA."

Plaintiffs timely filed an amended pleading, the First Amended Complaint ("FAC"). The FAC retained the same six causes of action as the original complaint, including, as relevant here, one cause of action under FISA encompassing both a request under for suppression of evidence obtained through warrantless electronic surveillance and a claim for damages under section 1810.

The most noteworthy change in the FAC was the ten-fold expansion of plaintiffs' factual recitation, which newly detailed a number of public pronouncements by government officials and publicly-available press reports disclosing post-9/11 warrantless electronic surveillance activities, as well as events publicly known about these activities, such as a much-publicized hospital room confrontation between former Attorney General John Ashcroft and then-White House counsel (later Attorney General) Alberto Gonzales. The FAC also recited a sequence of events pertaining directly to the government's investigations of Al-Haramain, a *sine qua non,* in the court's view, to establishing their "aggrieved person" status.

The FAC may be briefly summarized in the following two paragraphs:

Various government officials admitted the existence of a program of warrantless surveillance under which the NSA was authorized by the president to intercept certain international communications in which one party was outside the United States and one party was reasonably believed to be a member or agent of international terrorist network al Qaeda or an affiliated terrorist organization. Al-Haramain's assets were blocked by the Treasury Department in February 2004 pending an investigation of "possible crimes relating to currency reporting and tax laws," but neither OFAC's press release nor March 2004 congressional testimony of a[n] FBI official about the investigation suggested that Al-Haramain had links to al Qaeda. In June 2004, an OFAC official testified in Congress that in investigating terrorist financing, OFAC used classified information sources.

Between March and June 2004, several phone conversations took place between plaintiffs Belew and Ghafoor in the United States on the one hand and Soliman al-Buthi, a director of Al-Haramain located in Saudi Arabia, on the other; in these conversations, the participants made reference to various individuals associated with Osama bin Laden, the founder of al Qaeda. In September 2004, OFAC formally designated Al-Haramain as a[n] SDGT organization and, in a press release, specifically cited "direct links between the U.S. branch [of Al-Haramain]" and Osama bin Laden; this was the first "public claim of purported links between [ ] Al-Haramain and [ ] bin-Laden." The FBI and the Treasury Department have stated publicly that they relied on classified information, including "surveillance" information, to designate Al-Haramain as a terrorist organization associated with al Qaeda and bin Laden. In testimony before Congress in 2006 and 2007, top intelligence officials including defendant Keith B. Alexander stated that a FISA warrant is required before certain wire communications in the United States can be intercepted. In a separate criminal proceeding against Ali al-Timimi in 2005, the government disclosed that it had intercepted communications between al-Timimi and Al-Haramain's director al-Buthi.

. . . .

On September 30, 2008, the parties filed cross-motions. Plaintiffs moved under FISA's section 1806(f) for discovery of evidence pertaining to the lawfulness of the alleged surveillance. Defendants brought their third motion to dismiss or, in the alternative, for summary judgment.

. . . .

In its order of January 5, 2009, the court ruled that plaintiffs had made out a *prima facie* case that they are "aggrieved persons" who had been subjected to "electronic surveillance" within the meaning of section 1810. In doing so, the court employed the analysis and standard for establishing a *prima facie* case of electronic surveillance used by the Ninth Circuit in *United States v. Alter* (1973), and more recently by the DC Circuit in *In re Sealed Case* (*Horn v. Huddle*) (2007), a case in which, as in *Al-Haramain*, the plaintiff sought damages under FISA's section 1810.

The court explained that the approach employed in *Alter* was appropriate in this case arising under FISA's section 1810 given the lack of precedent in the Ninth Circuit because the *Alter* test's "stringency makes it appropriate in cases arising in the somewhat more restrictive environment where national security dimensions are present."

The court rejected defendants' contention that only when the government has openly acknowledged conducting warrantless electronic surveillance of an individual can that individual establish standing to sue:

> The court declines to entertain further challenges to plaintiffs' standing; the July 2 order gave plaintiffs the opportunity to "amend their claim to establish that they are 'aggrieved persons' within the meaning of 50 USC § 1801(k)." Plaintiffs have alleged sufficient facts to withstand the government's motion to dismiss. To quote the Ninth Circuit in *Alter*, "[t]he [plaintiff] does not have to plead and prove his entire case to establish standing and to trigger the government's responsibility to affirm or deny." Contrary to defendants' assertions, proof of plaintiffs' claims is not necessary at this stage. The court has determined that the allegations "are sufficiently definite, specific, detailed, and nonconjectural, to enable the court to conclude that a substantial claim is presented."

The court concluded: "[w]ithout a doubt, plaintiffs have alleged enough to plead 'aggrieved person' status so as to proceed to the next step in the proceedings under FISA's sections 1806(f) and 1810."

The January 5 order announced several next steps in the litigation that were designed to prioritize two interests: "protecting classified evidence from disclosure and enabling plaintiffs to prosecute their action."

The court announced its intention to review the Sealed Document ex parte and in camera, then to issue an order stating whether plaintiffs could proceed—specifically, whether the Sealed Document established that plaintiffs were subject to electronic surveillance not authorized by FISA. The court explained:

> As the court understands its obligation with regard to classified materials, only by placing and maintaining some or all of its future orders in this case under seal may the court avoid indirectly disclosing some aspect of the Sealed Document's contents. Unless counsel for plaintiffs are granted access to the court's rulings and, possibly, to at least some of defendants' classified filings, however, the entire remaining course of this litigation will be *ex parte*. This outcome would deprive plaintiffs of due process to an extent inconsistent with Congress's purpose in enacting FISA's sections 1806(f) and 1810.

The order directed the government to begin processing security clearances for members of plaintiffs' litigation team so that they would be able to read and respond to sealed portions of the court's future orders and, if necessary, some portion of defendants' classified filings.

The court also directed defendants to review their classified submissions to date and to determine whether the Sealed Document and/or any of defendants' classified submissions could be declassified. Upon completion of this review, defendants informed the court that nothing they had filed under seal during the three years in which the case had by then been pending could be declassified.

What followed were several months of which the defining feature was defendants' refusal to cooperate with the court's orders punctuated by their unsuccessful attempts to obtain untimely appellate review. . . .

. . . .

The court ordered defendants to show cause why, as a sanction for failing to obey the court's orders: (1) defendants should not be prohib-.

ited from opposing the liability component of plaintiffs' claim—that is, from denying that plaintiffs are "aggrieved persons" who had been subjected to electronic surveillance; and (2) the court should not deem liability under 50 USC § 1810 established and proceed to determine the amount of damages to be awarded to plaintiffs. The court also ordered plaintiffs to submit a memorandum addressing whether it would be appropriate for them to file a motion for summary judgment on their FISA claim.

After hearing argument on the order to show cause, the court directed plaintiffs to move for summary judgment on their FISA claim relying only on nonclassified evidence. It further ordered that if and only if defendants were to rely upon the Sealed Document or other classified evidence in response, the court would enter a protective order and produce such classified evidence to plaintiffs' counsel who have obtained security clearances.

The instant cross-motions ensued.

II

Turning first to defendants' motion to dismiss, defendants move under Rule 12(b)(1) for dismissal of plaintiffs' FAC arguing that: (1) plaintiffs lack standing to obtain prospective declaratory or injunctive relief with respect to alleged warrantless surveillance under the Terrorist Surveillance Program ("TSP") because the TSP lapsed or was terminated in January 2007 and (2) the court lacks jurisdiction to review plaintiffs' claim for retrospective damages against the United States under section 1810 of FISA, because section 1810 assertedly does not expressly waive the sovereign immunity of the United States.

[1] Defendants' first argument for dismissal attacks plaintiffs' non-

FISA claims, arguing that these claims seek only "prospective declaratory and injunctive relief against alleged TSP surveillance" and that such relief is not available because the TSP ended in January 2007. This mootness argument is essentially a retread of standing arguments made in March 2008 that were also based on the TSP's purported January 2007 termination. Defendants further assert: "declaratory and injunctive relief are equitable and should for similar reasons be denied as a prudential matter." But defendants' argument rests on a mistaken premise; plaintiffs' prayer for relief seeks various items of equitable relief, but most are not predicated on the continued existence of the TSP or other wiretapping activities.

Plaintiffs seek, for example, a declaration that defendants' warrantless surveillance of plaintiffs "is" unlawful, which may be construed to encompass past surveillance; and orders requiring defendants to turn over to plaintiffs, purge and/or destroy files and records containing information obtained by means of unlawful electronic surveillance. Defendants do not explain what prudential considerations would prohibit such equitable relief, and the court is aware of none.

[2] Defendants' second argument for dismissal is a familiar one; indeed, defendants admit that they have made it before, noting that "the Government respectfully and briefly preserves its position that Section 1810 of the FISA does not waive the sovereign immunity of the United States." The court considered and ruled on this issue in its order of July 2, 2008:

> It is, of course, true that section 1810 does not contain a waiver of sovereign immunity analogous to that in 18 USC section 2712(a) which expressly provides that aggrieved persons may sue the United States for unlawful surveillance in violation of Title III. But FISA directs its prohibitions to "Federal officers and employees" and it is only such

officers and employees acting in their official capacities that would engage in surveillance of the type contemplated by FISA. The remedial provision of FISA in section 1810 would afford scant, if any, relief if it did not lie against such "Federal officers and employees" carrying out their official functions. Implicit in the remedy that section 1810 provides is a waiver of sovereign immunity.

The court's view of this issue has not changed.

Accordingly, the motion to dismiss for lack of jurisdiction is DENIED.

III

The parties' cross-motions for summary judgment present more substantial questions. Rule 56(a) of the Federal Rules of Civil Procedure provides: "A party claiming relief may move, with or without supporting affidavits, for summary judgment on all or part of the claim." Rule 56(d)(2) provides: "An interlocutory summary judgment may be rendered on liability alone, even if there is a genuine issue on the amount of damages." Rule 56(d)(1), moreover, provides that "the court should, to the extent practicable, determine what material facts are not genuinely at issue."

Plaintiffs' motion seeks summary adjudication of two issues: (1) plaintiffs' Article III standing and (2) defendants' liability under FISA's civil liability provision, 50 USC § 1810. Defendants cross-move for summary judgment on plaintiffs' FISA claim and "any remaining claim," arguing that: (1) the Ninth Circuit's mandate in this case "forecloses" plaintiffs' motion; (2) plaintiffs' evidence is too conjectural or circumstantial to establish that plaintiffs are "aggrieved persons" for FISA purposes; and (3) all other potentially relevant evidence—including whether the government possessed a FISA warrant authorizing surveillance of plaintiffs—is barred from disclosure by operation of the SSP.

. . . .

A

. . . .

The court has already determined, based on the body of evidence submitted with plaintiffs' motion under section 1806(f), that plaintiffs have made out a prima facie case of electronic surveillance under the standard set forth in *United States v. Alter*. Under *Alter*, "the burden was then on the government to squarely affirm or deny those charges ... [with an affidavit that is] factual, unambiguous and unequivocal." In FISA proceedings, 50 USC § 1806(f) provides a procedure by which the government may do this in camera, thus avoiding the disclosure of sensitive national security information. Defendants declined to avail themselves of section 1806(f)'s in camera review procedures and have otherwise declined to submit anything to the court squarely addressing plaintiffs' prima facie case of electronic surveillance.

Instead, defendants have interposed three arguments intended to undermine plaintiffs' claim for relief. All three arguments lack merit.

/

First, defendants contend that "the mandate of the Court of Appeals in this case forecloses plaintiffs' motion. The Ninth Circuit expressly held that the information necessary for plaintiffs to establish their standing has been excluded from this case pursuant to the [SSP]," citing *Al-Haramain Islamic Foundation, Inc. v. Bush* (2007).

. . . .

... [T]he court does not agree that plaintiffs are now "foreclosed" from attempting to establish standing without the Sealed Document. It is apparent from the opinion that the court of appeals, having asked plaintiffs' counsel whether the Sealed Document was necessary for plaintiffs to establish standing, simply did not contemplate plaintiffs' later attempt, in light of newly available public evidence, to build a nonclassified evidentiary basis for their suit.

During oral argument on the instant cross-motions, the court asked plaintiffs' attorney about the apparent discrepancy between his representation to the court of appeals in August 2007 that plaintiffs required the Sealed Document to establish standing and his contention in the district court in 2009 that plaintiffs could establish standing without classified evidence of any kind.

. . . .

Plaintiffs' counsel responded that he had not attempted to marshal public evidence because the Oregon district court had ruled that plaintiffs could use the Sealed Document. Counsel went on to explain that there were two crucial pieces of public evidence that he had not discovered as of the August 2007 oral argument: (1) a speech given on October 22, 2007, by FBI Deputy Director John S. Pistole to the American Banker's Association stating that, in developing OFAC's case against Al-Haramain, "we used other investigative tools—like records checks, surveillance, and interviews of various subjects" and (2) "the testimony by members of the Bush administration before Congress that told us how they intercept communications, which is they do it on a wire from routing stations within the United States, which makes it electronic surveillance within the meaning of FISA. . . ." Counsel further expressed doubt that the court of appeals could have anticipated that the FBI would "post on the FBI's website an admission like that."

Simply put, to deem plaintiffs "foreclosed" by part IV of the court of appeals' 2007 opinion from building their case with later-disclosed, publicly available evidence—especially in light of defendants' intransigence following the court's January 5, 2009, order and the limited progress made to date along the normal arc of civil litigation—would violate basic concepts of due process in our system of justice. Defendants' reading of part IV of the court of appeals' opinion fails to account for these circumstances and would lead to a crabbed result the court of appeals could not have contemplated or intended.

2

Defendants' second major contention in opposition to plaintiffs' motion is that defendants cannot—and therefore should not be required to—respond to plaintiffs' prima facie case by showing that "plaintiffs' alleged electronic surveillance was authorized by a FISA warrant, or . . . plaintiffs were not in fact electronically surveilled." "[T]his," defendants argue, "is precisely what was precluded by the Ninth Circuit when it squarely held that 'information as to whether the government surveilled [plaintiffs]' is protected by the [SSP] and is categorically barred from use in this litigation." Defendants' reading of the court of appeals' opinion would require the court to impose a result contrary to the intent of Congress in enacting FISA and, indeed, contrary to the court of appeals' interpretation of FISA in *Al-Haramain*.

Under defendants' theory, executive branch officials may treat FISA as optional and freely employ the SSP to evade FISA, a statute enacted specifically to rein in and create a judicial check for executive-branch abuses of surveillance authority. For example, the House Report on FISA noted: "In the past several years, abuses of domestic national security surveillances have been disclosed. This evidence alone should demonstrate the inappropriateness of relying solely on [E]xecutive branch discretion to safeguard civil liberties."

Perhaps sensitive to the obvious potential for governmental abuse and overreaching inherent in defendants' theory of unfettered executive-branch discretion, defendants protest that "the Government does not rely on an assertion of the [SSP] to cover-up alleged unlawful conduct." Rather, they assert, it does so because "[d]isclosure of whether or not communications related to al-Qaeda have been intercepted, when, how, of who [*sic*], and under what authority would reveal methods by which the government has or has not monitored certain communications related to that organization." By "under what authority," presumably, defendants mean "whether or not pursuant to a FISA warrant"—the very heart of the cause of action under 50 USC § 1810. This fact—the presence or absence of a FISA warrant—is something defendants assert may be cloaked by the SSP, notwithstanding this court's July 2008 determination, pursuant to the court of appeals' remand instructions, that FISA displaces the SSP in cases within the reach of its provisions and that "this is such a case."

In an impressive display of argumentative acrobatics, defendants contend, in essence, that the court's orders of June 3 and June 5, 2009, setting the rules for these cross-motions, make FISA inapplicable, and that "the Ninth Circuit's rulings on the privilege assertion therefore control the summary judgment motions now before the Court." In other words, defendants contend, this is not a FISA case and defendants are therefore free to hide behind the SSP all facts that could help plaintiffs' case. In so contending, defendants take a flying leap and miss by a wide margin. Defendants forewent the opportunity to invoke the section 1806(f) procedures Congress created in order for executive branch agencies to establish "the legality of the surveillance," including whether a FISA warrant for the surveillance existed. Rather, in response to plaintiffs' motion under section 1806(f), defendants declined to make the submissions provided for by that section and instead asserted:

> The discretion to invoke Section 1806(f) belongs to the Attorney General, and under the present circumstances—where there has been no final determination that those procedures apply in this case to overcome the Government's successful assertion of privilege and where serious harm to national security is at stake—the Attorney General has not done so.

Similarly, defendants could readily have availed themselves of the court's processes to present a single, case-dispositive item of evidence at one of a number of stages of this multiyear litigation: a FISA warrant. They never did so, and now illogically assert that the existence of a FISA warrant is a fact within the province of the SSP, not FISA.

But the court of appeals' opinion contemplated that the case would move forward under FISA if FISA were deemed to displace the SSP. The court of appeals did not contemplate that the judicial process should be intentionally stymied by defendants' tactical avoidance of FISA:

> Under FISA, 50 USC §§ 1801 et seq, if an "aggrieved person" requests discovery of materials relating to electronic surveillance, and the Attorney General files an affidavit stating that the disclosure of such information would harm the national security of the United States, a district court may review in camera and ex parte the materials "as may

be necessary to determine whether the surveillance of the aggrieved person was lawfully authorized and conducted." The statute further provides that the court may disclose to the aggrieved person, using protective orders, portions of the materials "where such disclosure is necessary to make an accurate determination of the legality of the surveillance." Id. The statute, unlike the common law [SSP], provides a detailed regime to determine whether surveillance "was lawfully authorized and conducted."

. . . .

[T]he FISA issue remains central to Al-Haramain's ability to proceed with this lawsuit.

At oral argument, plaintiffs' counsel argued that the burden was on defendants to show that they had a warrant because, given that the TSP was in place "in order to evade FISA. . . . why on earth would [defendants] get a FISA warrant to perform surveillance that they believed they had no need to get a FISA warrant for?" and because knowledge of the existence or nonexistence of a FISA warrant was "within [defendants'] exclusive knowledge." The court finds merit in these arguments.

In summary, because FISA displaces the SSP in cases within its purview, the existence of a FISA warrant is a fact that cannot be concealed through the device of the SSP in FISA litigation for the reasons stated in the court's July 8, 2008, order. Plaintiffs have made out a prima facie case and defendants have foregone multiple opportunities to show that a warrant existed, including specifically rejecting the method created by Congress for this very purpose.

Defendants' possession of the exclusive knowledge whether or not a FISA warrant was obtained, moreover, creates such grave equitable concerns that defendants must be deemed estopped from arguing that a warrant might have existed or, conversely, must be deemed to have admitted that no warrant existed. The court now determines, in light of all the aforementioned points and the procedural history of this case, that there is no genuine issue of material fact whether a warrant was obtained for the electronic surveillance of plaintiffs. For purposes of this litigation, there was no such warrant for the electronic surveillance of any of plaintiffs.

3

Defendants' third argument is essentially to quarrel with the court's finding that plaintiffs have made out a prima facie case of electronic surveillance, asserting that plaintiffs' "evidence falls far short of establishing that the Government conducted warrantless electronic surveillance under the TSP of plaintiffs' conversations in March and April 2004."

Because defendants' argument rests on a faulty understanding of the parties' burdens as discussed in the preceding section, a lengthy discussion of these points is not warranted. The following discussion of defendants' handling of certain items of evidence is included for the sake of completeness and is intended to be illustrative. Plaintiffs must—and have—put forward enough evidence to establish a prima facie case that they were subjected to warrantless electronic surveillance.

Among plaintiffs' exhibits is a memorandum from Howard Mendelsohn, Deputy Assistant Secretary at the Department of the Treasury to defendant Adam J. Szubin, Director of OFAC, dated February 6, 2008. This lengthy, redacted document bearing the words "Top Secret" at the top has a stated subject of "redesignation of Al-Haramain Islamic Foundation locations in the United States (AHF-OREGON) and AHF official Soliman AL-BUTHE pursuant to [Executive Order] 13224." In it, Soliman al-Buthe (referred elsewhere in the record as "Al-Buthi") is described as "the Treasurer of AHF-OREGON." The document states that "AL-BUTHE was intercepted in some four conversations with Al-Timimi" on February 1, 2003. Al-Buthi, meanwhile, is alleged in the FAC to be a director of Al-Haramain and the individual whose conversations with Ghafoor and Belew plaintiffs allege were intercepted by means of electronic surveillance in March and April 2004. These documents buttress each other, as does the published speech by John Pistole to the American Bankers' Association admitting "surveillance" of Al-Haramain Oregon.

Defendants attack as insufficient each item of evidence individually, ignoring the cumulative impact of the various documents. . . .

. . . .

Defendants' nit-picking of each item of plaintiffs' evidence, their remarkable insinuation (unsupported by any evidence of their own) that [particular] intercepts might have been pursuant to a FISA warrant and their insistence that they need proffer nothing in response to plaintiffs' prima facie case do not amount to an effective opposition to plaintiffs' motion for summary judgment.

B

[7] The parties' submissions establish that there is no genuine issue as to the . . . material facts, most of which are summarized from plaintiffs' pleadings in the FAC. . . .

. . . .

Because defendants have failed to establish the existence of a genuine issue of material fact warranting denial of plaintiffs' motion for summary judgment on the issue of defendants' liability under FISA, plaintiffs' motion must be, and hereby is, GRANTED. Defendants' motion for summary judgment is DENIED.

. . . .

IT IS SO ORDERED.

FOREIGN INTELLIGENCE SURVEILLANCE ACT (FISA)

Editorial, New York Times, *April 1, 2010*

The Foreign Intelligence Surveillance Act was enacted in 1978, passed in response to revelations by the Church Committee showing widespread abuse of government wiretaps, and to growing concerns on the part of the Supreme Court over eavesdropping practices. The law governs the surveillance of people in the United States for the purpose of collecting intelligence related to foreign powers. A special, secret court, known as the Foreign Intelligence Surveillance, or FISA, court was created to hear requests for such warrants. Safeguards were put in place to ensure that investigators pursuing criminal matters did not obtain warrants under FISA that they could not get from an ordinary judge.

After the September 11 attacks, members of the Bush administration were highly critical of the FISA restrictions. Portions of the Patriot Act expanded the law's reach to cover terrorism suspects as well as agents of foreign countries. But when President Bush ordered an expanded program of surveillance by the National Security Agency, he decided to bypass the FISA process entirely. When news of these warrantless wiretaps was revealed by The *New York Times* in 2005, administration officials argued that working within FISA would have been too cumbersome.

The 2005 disclosure of the existence of the program set off a national debate over the limits of executive power and the balance between national security and civil liberties. The arguments continued over the next three years, as Congress sought to forge a new legal framework for domestic surveillance.

In the midst of the presidential campaign in 2008, Congress overhauled the Foreign Intelligence Surveillance Act to bring federal statutes into closer alignment with what the Bush administration had been secretly doing. The legislation essentially legalized certain aspects of the program. As a senator then, Barack Obama voted in favor of the new law, despite objections from many of his supporters. President Obama's administration now relies heavily on such surveillance in its fight against al Qaeda.

On March 31, 2010, a federal judge ruled that the National Security Agency's program of surveillance without warrants was illegal, rejecting the Obama administration's effort to keep shrouded in secrecy one of the most disputed counterterrorism policies of former President George W. Bush.

In a 45-page opinion, Judge Vaughn R. Walker, the chief judge of the Federal District Court in San Francisco, ruled that the government had violated a 1978 federal statute requiring court approval for domestic surveillance when it intercepted phone calls of Al Haramain, a now-defunct Islamic charity in Oregon, and of two lawyers representing it in 2004. Declaring that the plaintiffs had been "subjected to unlawful surveillance," the judge said the government was liable to pay them damages.

The Justice Department had argued that the charity's lawsuit should be dismissed without a ruling on the merits because allowing it to go forward could reveal state secrets. The judge characterized that expansive use of the so-called state secrets privilege as amounting to "unfettered executive-branch discretion" that had "obvious potential for governmental abuse and overreaching." That position, he said, would enable government officials to flout the warrant law, even though Congress had enacted it "specifically to rein in and create a judicial check for executive-branch abuses of surveillance authority."

The ruling was the second time a federal judge has declared the program of wiretapping without warrants to be illegal. But a 2006 decision by a federal judge in Detroit, Anna Diggs Taylor, was reversed on the grounds that those plaintiffs could not prove that they had been wiretapped and so lacked legal standing to sue.

Several other lawsuits filed over the program have faltered because of similar concerns over standing or because of immunity granted by Congress to telecommunications companies that participated in the NSA program. By contrast, the Haramain case was closely watched because the government inadvertently disclosed a classified document that made clear that the charity had been subjected to surveillance without warrants.

In earlier court rulings, in January 2009, the federal intelligence court itself issued a rare public ruling upholding the 2007 law, validating the power of the president and Congress to wiretap international phone calls and intercept e-mail messages without a specific court order, even when Americans' private communications may be involved. The decision by the Foreign Intelligence Surveillance Court of Review, actually reached the previous August, upheld a secret 2008 ruling issued by the intelligence court that it oversees, the FISA court.

In April 2009, officials revealed that a Justice Department review found that since the passage of the Protecting America Act the NSA intercepted private e-mail messages and phone calls of Americans on a scale that went beyond the broad legal limits established by Congress.

The overcollection problems appear to have been uncovered as part of a twice-annual certification that the Justice Department and the director of national intelligence are required to give to the Foreign Intelligence Surveillance Court on the protocols that the NSA is using in wiretapping. New details also emerged about earlier domestic-surveillance activities, including the agency's attempt to wiretap a member of Congress, without court approval, on an overseas trip.

In July 2009, a report produced by five inspectors general questioned the program's value, saying that its revelations played a limited role in the FBI's counterintelligence work and that other methods had produced more timely information. The report also hinted at political pressure in preparing the so-called threat assessments that helped form the legal basis for continuing the classified program.

24

WRONG IN ALL ASPECTS
(September 15, 2010)

Erwin Chemerinsky

Long ago, in *Marbury v. Madison* (1803), the Supreme Court declared that "[t]he very essence of civil liberty certainly consists in the right of every individual to claim the protection of the laws, whenever he receives an injury." Unfortunately, this was obviously forgotten by the judges in the majority of the Ninth US Circuit Court of Appeals' recent decision that victims of torture could not bring a suit against a company that allegedly actively participated in illegal abductions and inhumane treatment (*Mohamed v. Jepesen Dataplan Inc.*, Ninth Circuit September 8, 2010). In a 6–5 *en banc* decision, the Ninth Circuit reversed a panel's decision and held that the lawsuit had to be dismissed because of the state secrets doctrine.

The case involved several plaintiffs who claimed that they were victims of the CIA's extraordinary rendition program and were illegally abducted, taken in secret to foreign countries, detained in horrible conditions for long periods of time, and tortured. The torture described violated every protocol of human rights laws and included beatings which broke bones, electrodes attached to and administering electric shocks to genitals, and deprivation of food for long periods of time. The psychological torture included threats of harm to family members, extreme degradation, and sleep deprivation.

The plaintiffs sued Jeppesen Dataplan Inc., on the grounds that it "played an integral role in the forced" abductions and detentions. The complaint alleged that Jeppesen had actual or constructive "knowledge of the objectives of the rendition program" including knowledge that the plaintiffs "would be subjected to forced disappearance, detention, and torture" by US and foreign government officials.

Not surprisingly, the Bush administration intervened in the lawsuit and sought to have it dismissed based on the state secrets doctrine. Far more surprising and terribly disappointing, the Obama administration took the same approach in this case. If the allegations of the plaintiffs' complaint are true, the illegal activities by the CIA and others should be public and not hidden, the plaintiffs should receive whatever remedies the law can provide, and all involved should held accountable. It is deeply offensive and simply wrong that the government can violate the most essential norms of human rights and then hide behind secrecy.

Moreover, the central flaw in the Ninth Circuit's opinion was its assumption that state secrets inevitably would be revealed by the litigation. Countless details of the CIA's rendition program already have been made public. The dissenting judges attached a twenty-three-page appendix that lists publicly available information documenting this. At the very least, the plaintiffs should have had the chance to prove their case based on the publicly available material. The defendant's claim that it could not advance a defense without using "state secrets" was premature at the pleading stage of the lawsuit. Besides, surely there are other ways to protect sensitive classified information short of dismissing the plaintiffs' entire complaint.

Indeed, the Ninth Circuit's decision was not justified even under the law of the state secrets doctrine. As the court correctly described, there are two distinct parts of the state secrets doctrine. One, called the "*Totten* bar," requires dismissal of claims which inevitably would reveal disclosure of state secrets. This is based on the Supreme Court's declaration in *Totten v. United States* (1876) that "as a general principle . . . public policy forbids the maintenance of any suit in a court of justice, the trial of which would inevitably lead to the disclosure of matters which the law regards as confidential." As the Ninth Circuit explained, "[t]he *Totten* bar applies only when the 'very subject matter' of the action is a state secret." The Ninth Circuit did not use the *Totten* bar to dismiss the plaintiff's claim.

Rather, the Ninth Circuit relied on the second aspect of the state secrets doctrine, which is an evidentiary privilege that excludes state secrets from being used as evidence. This is based on the Supreme Court's decision in *United States v. Reynolds* (1953). The Ninth Circuit declared: "[W]e hold that dismissal is nonetheless required under Reynolds because there is no feasible way to litigate Jeppesen's alleged liability without creating an unjustifiable risk of divulging state secrets." The court said that "further litigation presents an unacceptable risk of disclosure of state secrets no matter what legal or factual theories Jeppesen would choose to advance during a defense."

The court expressly relied upon a very disturbing decision of the Fourth US Circuit of Appeals [*El-Masri v. United States* (2007)], which ordered dismissal of a suit brought by a man who was allegedly apprehended by the CIA by mistake, brutally tortured, and then released by being dumped on the streets of Albania. Jane Mayer, in her book, *The Dark Side* (2008), describes in detail how Khaled El-Masri was apprehended in Europe because of confusion with someone else of the same name, held for a lengthy period of time, and subjected to truly inhumane treatment, only to be dumped on the streets of a foreign country when the mistake was discovered by the CIA. The Fourth Circuit ordered the case dismissed because there was an unacceptable risk of the disclosure of state secrets.

But both the Fourth and Ninth Circuits were wrong in using the *Reynolds* evidentiary privilege to dismiss a lawsuit at the pleading stage based on a motion to dismiss for failure to state a claim. An evidentiary privilege must be invoked in response to attempts to introduce specific pieces of evidence. It is premature to apply it before any evidence has been proffered. As the five dissenting judges in *Jeppesen* noted: "The state secrets privilege, as an evidentiary privilege, is relevant not to the sufficiency of the complaint, but only to the sufficiency of evidence available to later substantiate the compliant."

Put another way, an evidentiary privilege should not bar the plaintiff's from being able to prove their complaint through other, not privileged evidence. Especially in a situation like this one, where so much information already is public about extraordinary renditions, it is impossible to say at the pleading stage that the plaintiff could not prove its case or that the defendant could not defend itself without use of privileged information. Dismissal, if ever appropriate, was premature at the pleading stage.

Perhaps the case truly could not have been litigated without revealing state secrets and ultimately would have had to be dismissed. Such a conclusion would have been enormously distressing because it would have meant that the government and defendants could violate the law and avoid accountability by hiding behind secrecy. But it is even worse to dismiss at the pleading stage based on an assumption that the case might later require dismissal.

There must be a strong presumption that the legal system should be available to provide a remedy for those who allege that the government and businesses working with them engaged in illegal abductions and torture. The Ninth Circuit was simply wrong in saying that the case should be dismissed because privileged state secrets might later be crucial evidence for the plaintiffs or defendants.

Hopefully, the powerful dissent of five Ninth Circuit judges will persuade the Supreme Court to take the case and reverse this awful decision. The Ninth Circuit's decision just can't be reconciled with *Marbury*'s command that the "very essence of civil liberty" demands that remedies be provided to those whose basic rights have been violated.

PART 5

DETENTIONS AND THE CONSTITUTIONAL BALANCE OF POWER

25

HAMDI V. RUMSFELD

US Supreme Court

Yaser Esam HAMDI and Esam Fouad Hamdi, as next friend of
Yaser Esam Hamdi, Petitioners,

v.

Donald H. RUMSFELD, Secretary of Defense, et al.
Argued April 28, 2004.
Decided June 28, 2004.

Justice O'Connor announced the judgment of the Court and delivered an opinion, in which the Chief Justice, Justice Kennedy, and
Justice Breyer join.

At this difficult time in our nation's history, we are called upon to consider the legality of the Government's detention of a United States citizen
on United States soil as an "enemy combatant" and to address the process
that is constitutionally owed to one who seeks to challenge his classification as such. The United States Court of Appeals for the Fourth Circuit
held that petitioner's detention was legally authorized and that he was
entitled to no further opportunity to challenge his enemy-combatant
label. We now vacate and remand. We hold that although Congress authorized the detention of combatants in the narrow circumstances alleged
here, due process demands that a citizen held in the United States as an
enemy combatant be given a meaningful opportunity to contest the factual basis for that detention before a neutral decisionmaker.

I

On September 11, 2001, the al Qaeda terrorist network used hijacked commercial airliners to attack prominent targets in the United States. Approximately three thousand people were killed in those attacks. One week later, in response to these "acts of treacherous violence," Congress passed a resolution authorizing the President to "use all necessary and appropriate force against those nations, organizations, or persons he determines planned, authorized, committed, or aided the terrorist attacks" or "harbored such organizations or persons, in order to prevent any future acts of international terrorism against the United States by such nations, organizations, or persons." Authorization for Use of Military Force ("the AUMF"). Soon thereafter, the President ordered United States Armed Forces to Afghanistan, with a mission to subdue al Qaeda and quell the Taliban regime that was known to support it.

This case arises out of the detention of a man whom the Government alleges took up arms with the Taliban during this conflict. His name is Yaser Esam Hamdi. Born an American citizen in Louisiana in 1980, Hamdi moved with his family to Saudi Arabia as a child. By 2001, the parties agree, he resided in Afghanistan. At some point that year, he was seized by members of the Northern Alliance, a coalition of military groups opposed to the Taliban government, and eventually was turned over to the United States military. The Government asserts that it initially detained and interrogated Hamdi in Afghanistan before transferring him to the United States Naval Base in Guantanamo Bay in January 2002. In April 2002, upon learning that Hamdi is an American citizen, authorities transferred him to a naval brig in Norfolk, Virginia, where he remained until a recent transfer to a brig in Charleston, South Carolina. The Government contends that Hamdi is an "enemy combatant," and that this status justifies holding him in the United States indefinitely—

without formal charges or proceedings—unless and until it makes the determination that access to counsel or further process is warranted.

In June 2002, Hamdi's father, Esam Fouad Hamdi, filed the present petition for a writ of habeas corpus under 28 U.S.C. § 2241 in the Eastern District of Virginia, naming as petitioners his son and himself as next friend. The elder Hamdi alleges in the petition that he has had no contact with his son since the Government took custody of him in 2001, and that the Government has held his son "without access to legal counsel or notice of any charges pending against him." The petition contends that Hamdi's detention was not legally authorized. It argues that "[a]s an American citizen, . . . Hamdi enjoys the full protections of the Constitution," and that Hamdi's detention in the United States without charges, access to an impartial tribunal, or assistance of counsel "violated and continue[s] to violate the Fifth and Fourteenth Amendments to the United States Constitution." The habeas petition asks that the Court, among other things, (1) appoint counsel for Hamdi; (2) order respondents to cease interrogating him; (3) declare that he is being held in violation of the Fifth and Fourteenth Amendments; (4) "[t]o the extent Respondents contest any material factual allegations in this Petition, schedule an evidentiary hearing, at which Petitioners may adduce proof in support of their allegations"; and (5) order that Hamdi be released from his "unlawful custody." Although his habeas petition provides no details with regard to the factual circumstances surrounding his son's capture and detention, Hamdi's father has asserted in documents found elsewhere in the record that his son went to Afghanistan to do "relief work," and that he had been in that country less than two months before September 11, 2001, and could not have received military training. The twenty-year-old was traveling on his own for the first time, his father says, and "[b]ecause of his lack of experience, he was trapped in Afghanistan once that military campaign began."

. . . .

II

The threshold question before us is whether the Executive has the authority to detain citizens who qualify as "enemy combatants." There is some debate as to the proper scope of this term, and the Government has never provided any court with the full criteria that it uses in classifying individuals as such. It has made clear, however, that, for purposes of this case, the "enemy combatant" that it is seeking to detain is an individual who, it alleges, was "'part of or supporting forces hostile to the United States or coalition partners'" in Afghanistan and who "'engaged in an armed conflict against the United States'" there. We therefore answer only the narrow question before us: whether the detention of citizens falling within that definition is authorized.

The Government maintains that no explicit congressional authorization is required, because the Executive possesses plenary authority to detain pursuant to Article II of the Constitution. We do not reach the question whether Article II provides such authority, however, because we agree with the Government's alternative position, that Congress has in fact authorized Hamdi's detention, through the AUMF.

. . . .

The AUMF authorizes the President to use "all necessary and appropriate force" against "nations, organizations, or persons" associated with the September 11, 2001, terrorist attacks. There can be no doubt that individuals who fought against the United States in Afghanistan as part of the Taliban, an organization known to have supported the al Qaeda terrorist network responsible for those attacks, are individuals Congress sought to target in passing the AUMF. We conclude that detention of individuals falling into the limited category we are considering, for the duration of the particular conflict in which they were captured, is so fundamental and accepted an incident to war as to be an exercise of the "necessary and appropriate force" Congress has authorized the President to use.

The capture and detention of lawful combatants and the capture, detention, and trial of unlawful combatants, by "universal agreement and practice," are "important incident[s] of war." *Ex parte Quirin* (1942). The purpose of detention is to prevent captured individuals from returning to the field of battle and taking up arms once again. . . .

There is no bar to this nation's holding one of its own citizens as an enemy combatant. In *Quirin*, one of the detainees, Haupt, alleged that he was a naturalized United States citizen. . . . While Haupt was tried for violations of the law of war, nothing in *Quirin* suggests that his citizenship would have precluded his mere detention for the duration of the relevant hostilities. . . . Nor can we see any reason for drawing such a line here. . . .

In light of these principles, it is of no moment that the AUMF does not use specific language of detention. Because detention to prevent a combatant's return to the battlefield is a fundamental incident of waging war, in permitting the use of "necessary and appropriate force," Congress has clearly and unmistakably authorized detention in the narrow circumstances considered here.

Hamdi objects, nevertheless, that Congress has not authorized the *indefinite* detention to which he is now subject. The Government responds that "the detention of enemy combatants during World War II was just as 'indefinite' while that war was being fought." We take Hamdi's objection to be not to the lack of certainty regarding the date on which the conflict will end, but to the substantial prospect of perpetual detention. We recognize that the national security underpinnings of the "war on terror," although crucially important, are broad and malleable. As the Government concedes, "given its unconventional nature, the current conflict is unlikely to end with a formal cease-fire agreement." The prospect Hamdi raises is therefore not far-fetched. If the Government does not consider this unconventional war won for two generations, and if it maintains during that time that Hamdi might, if released, rejoin forces fighting against the United States, then the position it has taken throughout the litigation of this case suggests that Hamdi's detention could last for the rest of his life.

It is a clearly established principle of the law of war that detention may last no longer than active hostilities. See Article 118 of the Geneva Convention (III) Relative to the Treatment of Prisoners of War, August 12, 1949 ("Prisoners of war shall be released and repatriated without delay after the cessation of active hostilities"). . . .

Hamdi contends that the AUMF does not authorize indefinite or perpetual detention. Certainly, we agree that indefinite detention for the purpose of interrogation is not authorized. Further, we understand Congress's grant of authority for the use of "necessary and appropriate force" to include the authority to detain for the duration of the relevant conflict, and our understanding is based on longstanding law-of-war principles. If the practical circumstances of a given conflict are entirely unlike those of the conflicts that informed the development of the law of war, that understanding may unravel. But that is not the situation we face as of this date. Active combat operations against Taliban fighters apparently are ongoing in Afghanistan. . . . The United States may detain, for the duration of these hostilities, individuals legitimately determined to be Taliban combatants who "engaged in an armed conflict against the United States." If the record establishes that United States troops are still involved in active combat in Afghanistan, those detentions are part of the exercise of "necessary and appropriate force," and therefore are authorized by the AUMF. . . .

III

Even in cases in which the detention of enemy combatants is legally authorized, there remains the question of what process is constitutionally due to a citizen who disputes his enemy-combatant status. Hamdi argues that he is owed a meaningful and timely hearing and that "extra-judicial detention [that] begins and ends with the submission of an affidavit based on third-hand hearsay" does not comport with the Fifth and Fourteenth Amendments. The Government counters that any more process than was provided below would be both unworkable and "constitutionally intolerable." Our resolution of this dispute requires a careful examination both of the writ of habeas corpus, which Hamdi now seeks to employ as a mechanism of judicial review, and of the Due Process Clause, which informs the procedural contours of that mechanism in this instance.

A

Though they reach radically different conclusions on the process that ought to attend the present proceeding, the parties begin on common ground. All agree that, absent suspension, the writ of habeas corpus remains available to every individual detained within the United States. US Const., Art. I, § 9, cl. 2 ("The Privilege of the Writ of Habeas Corpus shall not be suspended, unless when in Cases of Rebellion or Invasion the public Safety may require it"). Only in the rarest of circumstances has Congress seen fit to suspend the writ. At all other times, it has remained a critical check on the Executive, ensuring that it does not detain individuals except in accordance with law. All agree suspension of the writ has not occurred here. Thus, it is undisputed that Hamdi was properly before an Article III court to challenge his detention under 28 U.S.C. § 2241. Further, all agree that § 2241 and its companion provisions provide at least a skeletal outline of the procedures to be afforded a petitioner in federal habeas review. Most notably, § 2243 provides that "the person detained may, under oath, deny any of the facts set forth in the return or allege any other material facts," and § 2246 allows the taking of evidence in habeas proceedings by deposition, affidavit, or interrogatories.

The simple outline of § 2241 makes clear both that Congress envisioned that habeas petitioners would have some opportunity to present and rebut facts and that courts in cases like this retain some ability to vary the ways in which they do so as mandated by due process. The Government recognizes the basic procedural protections required by the habeas statute, but asks us to hold that, given both the flexibility of the habeas mechanism and the circumstances presented in this case, the presentation of the Mobbs Declaration to the habeas court completed the required factual development. It suggests two separate reasons for its position that no further process is due.

B

First, the Government urges the adoption of the Fourth Circuit's holding below—that because it is "undisputed" that Hamdi's seizure took place in a combat zone, the habeas determination can be made purely as a matter of law, with no further hearing or factfinding necessary. This argument is easily rejected. As the dissenters from the denial of rehearing en banc noted, the circumstances surrounding Hamdi's seizure cannot in any way be characterized as "undisputed," as "those circumstances are neither conceded in fact, nor susceptible to concession in law, because Hamdi has not been permitted to speak for himself or even through counsel as to those circumstances." (Luttig, J., dissenting from denial of rehearing en banc).... Further, the "facts" that constitute the alleged concession are insufficient to support Hamdi's detention. Under the definition of enemy combatant that we accept today as falling within the scope of

Congress's authorization, Hamdi would need to be "part of or supporting forces hostile to the United States or coalition partners" and "engaged in an armed conflict against the United States" to justify his detention in the United States for the duration of the relevant conflict (Brief for Respondents 3). The habeas petition states only that "[w]hen seized by the United States Government, Mr. Hamdi resided in Afghanistan." An assertion that one *resided* in a country in which combat operations are taking place is not a concession that one was "*captured* in a zone of active combat operations in a foreign theater of war," and certainly is not a concession that one was "part of or supporting forces hostile to the United States or coalition partners" and "engaged in an armed conflict against the United States." Accordingly, we reject any argument that Hamdi has made concessions that eliminate any right to further process.

C

The Government's second argument requires closer consideration. This is the argument that further factual exploration is unwarranted and inappropriate in light of the extraordinary constitutional interests at stake. Under the Government's most extreme rendition of this argument, "[r]espect for separation of powers and the limited institutional capabilities of courts in matters of military decision making in connection with an ongoing conflict" ought to eliminate entirely any individual process, restricting the courts to investigating only whether legal authorization exists for the broader detention scheme. At most, the Government argues, courts should review its determination that a citizen is an enemy combatant under a very deferential "some evidence" standard. . . . Under this review, a court would assume the accuracy of the Government's articulated basis for Hamdi's detention, as set forth in the Mobbs Declaration, and assess only whether that articulated basis was a legitimate one. . . .

In response, Hamdi emphasizes that this Court consistently has recognized that an individual challenging his detention may not be held at the will of the Executive without recourse to some proceeding before a neutral tribunal to determine whether the Executive's asserted justifications for that detention have basis in fact and warrant in law. He argues that the Fourth Circuit inappropriately "ceded power to the Executive during wartime to define the conduct for which a citizen may be detained, judge whether that citizen has engaged in the proscribed conduct, and imprison that citizen indefinitely," and that due process demands that he receive a hearing in which he may challenge the Mobbs Declaration and adduce his own counter evidence. The District Court, agreeing with Hamdi, apparently believed that the appropriate process would approach the process that accompanies a criminal trial. It therefore disapproved of the hearsay nature of the Mobbs Declaration and anticipated quite extensive discovery of various military affairs. Anything less, it concluded, would not be "meaningful judicial review."

Both of these positions highlight legitimate concerns. And both emphasize the tension that often exists between the autonomy that the Government asserts is necessary in order to pursue effectively a particular goal and the process that a citizen contends he is due before he is deprived of a constitutional right. The ordinary mechanism that we use for balancing such serious competing interests, and for determining the procedures that are necessary to ensure that a citizen is not "deprived of life, liberty, or property, without due process of law," US Const., Amdt. 5, is the test that we articulated in *Mathews v. Eldridge* (1976). *Mathews* dictates that the process due in any given instance is determined by weighing "the private interest that will be affected by the official action" against the Government's asserted interest, "including the function involved" and the burdens the Government would face in providing greater process. The *Mathews* calculus then contemplates a judicious balancing of these concerns, through an analysis of "the risk of an erroneous deprivation" of the private interest if the process were reduced and the "probable value, if any, of additional or substitute safeguards." We take each of these steps in turn.

I

It is beyond question that substantial interests lie on both sides of the scale in this case. Hamdi's "private interest . . . affected by the official action," is the most elemental of liberty interests—the interest in being free from physical detention by one's own government.

Nor is the weight on this side of the *Mathews* scale offset by the circumstances of war or the accusation of treasonous behavior, for "[i]t is clear that commitment for *any* purpose constitutes a significant deprivation of liberty that requires due process protection," *Jones v. United States* (1983), and at this stage in the *Mathews* calculus, we consider the interest of the *erroneously* detained individual. Indeed, as amicus briefs from media and relief organizations emphasize, the risk of erroneous deprivation of a citizen's liberty in the absence of sufficient process here is very real. See Brief for Ameri-Cares et al. as *Amici Curiae* 13–22 (noting ways in which "[t]he nature of humanitarian relief work and journalism present a significant risk of mistaken military detentions"). Moreover, as critical as the Government's interest may be in detaining those who actually pose an immediate threat to the national security of the United States during ongoing international conflict, history and common sense teach us that an unchecked system of detention carries the potential to become a means for oppression and abuse of others who do not present that sort of threat. See *Ex parte Milligan* (1866) ("[The Founders] knew—the history of the world told them—the nation they were founding, be its existence short or long, would be involved in war; how often or how long continued, human foresight could not tell; and that unlimited power, wherever lodged at such a time, was especially hazardous to freemen"). Because we live in a society in which "[m]ere public intolerance or animosity cannot constitutionally justify the deprivation of a person's physical liberty," *O'Connor v. Donaldson* (1975), our starting point for the *Mathews v. Eldridge* analysis is unaltered by the allegations surrounding the particular detainee or the organizations with which he is alleged to have associated. We reaffirm today the fundamental nature of a citizen's right to be free from involuntary confinement by his own government without due process of law, and we weigh the opposing governmental interests against the curtailment of liberty that such confinement entails.

2

On the other side of the scale are the weighty and sensitive governmental interests in ensuring that those who have in fact fought with the enemy during a war do not return to battle against the United States. As discussed above, the law of war and the realities of combat may render such detentions both necessary and appropriate, and our due process analysis need not blink at those realities. Without doubt, our Constitution recognizes that core strategic matters of warmaking belong in the hands of those who are best positioned and most politically accountable for making them. *Department of Navy v. Egan* (1988) (noting the reluctance of the courts "to intrude upon the authority of the Executive in military and national security affairs"); *Youngstown Sheet & Tube Co. v. Sawyer* (1952) (acknowledging "broad powers in military commanders engaged in day-to-day fighting in a theater of war").

The Government also argues at some length that its interests in reducing the process available to alleged enemy combatants are heightened by the practical difficulties that would accompany a system of trial-like process. In its view, military officers who are engaged in the serious work of waging battle would be unnecessarily and dangerously distracted by litigation half a world away, and discovery into military operations would both intrude on the sensitive secrets of national defense and result in a futile search for evidence buried under the rubble of war. To the extent that these burdens are triggered by heightened procedures, they are properly taken into account in our due process analysis.

3

Striking the proper constitutional balance here is of great importance to the nation during this period of ongoing combat. But it is equally vital that our calculus not give short shrift to the values that this country holds dear or to the privilege that is American citizenship.

It is during our most challenging and uncertain moments that our nation's commitment to due process is most severely tested; and it is in those times that we must preserve our commitment at home to the principles for which we fight abroad.

With due recognition of these competing concerns, we believe that neither the process proposed by the Government nor the process apparently envisioned by the District Court below strikes the proper constitutional balance when a United States citizen is detained in the United States as an enemy combatant. That is, "the risk of erroneous deprivation" of a detainee's liberty interest is unacceptably high under the Government's proposed rule, while some of the "additional or substitute procedural safeguards" suggested by the District Court are unwarranted in light of their limited "probable value" and the burdens they may impose on the military in such cases (*Mathews*).

We therefore hold that a citizen-detainee seeking to challenge his classification as an enemy combatant must receive notice of the factual basis for his classification, and a fair opportunity to rebut the Government's factual assertions before a neutral decision maker. These essential constitutional promises may not be eroded.

At the same time, the exigencies of the circumstances may demand that, aside from these core elements, enemy combatant proceedings may be tailored to alleviate their uncommon potential to burden the Executive at a time of ongoing military conflict. Hearsay, for example, may need to be accepted as the most reliable available evidence from the Government in such a proceeding. Likewise, the Constitution would not be offended by a presumption in favor of the Government's evidence, so long as that presumption remained a rebuttable one and fair opportunity for rebuttal were provided. Thus, once the Government puts forth credible evidence that the habeas petitioner meets the enemy-combatant criteria, the onus could shift to the petitioner to rebut that evidence with more persuasive evidence that he falls outside the criteria. A burden-shifting scheme of this sort would meet the goal of ensuring that the errant tourist, embedded journalist, or local aid worker has a chance to prove military error while giving due regard to the Executive once it has put forth meaningful support for its conclusion that the detainee is in fact an enemy combatant. In the words of *Mathews,* process of this sort would sufficiently address the "risk of erroneous deprivation" of a detainee's liberty interest while eliminating certain procedures that have questionable additional value in light of the burden on the Government.

We think it unlikely that this basic process will have the dire impact on the central functions of warmaking that the Government forecasts. The parties agree that initial captures on the battlefield need not receive the process we have discussed here; that process is due only when the determination is made to *continue* to hold those who have been seized. The Government has made clear in its briefing that documentation regarding battlefield detainees already is kept in the ordinary course of military affairs. Any factfinding imposition created by requiring a knowledgeable affiant to summarize these records to an independent tribunal is a minimal one. Likewise, arguments that military officers ought not have to wage war under the threat of litigation lose much of their steam when factual disputes at enemy-combatant hearings are limited to the alleged combatant's acts. This focus meddles little, if at all, in the strategy or conduct of war, inquiring only into the appropriateness of continuing to detain an individual claimed to have taken up arms against the United States. While we accord the greatest respect and consideration to the judgments of military authorities in matters relating to the actual prosecution of a war, and recognize that the scope of that discretion necessarily is wide, it does not infringe on the core role of the military for the courts to exercise their own time-honored and constitutionally mandated roles of reviewing and resolving claims like those presented here.

In sum, while the full protections that accompany challenges to detentions in other settings may prove unworkable and inappropriate in the enemy-combatant setting, the threats to military operations posed by a basic system of independent review are not so weighty as to trump a citizen's core rights to challenge meaningfully the Government's case and to be heard by an impartial adjudicator.

D

In so holding, we necessarily reject the Government's assertion that separation of powers principles mandate a heavily circumscribed role for the courts in such circumstances. Indeed, the position that the courts must forgo any examination of the individual case and focus exclusively on the legality of the broader detention scheme cannot be mandated by any reasonable view of separation of powers, as this approach serves only to *condense* power into a single branch of government. We have long since made clear that a state of war is not a blank check for the President when it comes to the rights of the nation's citizens. Whatever power the United States Constitution envisions for the Executive in its exchanges with other nations or with enemy organizations in times of conflict, it most assuredly envisions a role for all three branches when individual liberties are at stake. Likewise, we have made clear that, unless Congress acts to suspend it, the Great Writ of habeas corpus allows the Judicial Branch to play a necessary role in maintaining this delicate balance of governance, serving as an important judicial check on the Executive's discretion in the realm of detentions. Thus, while we do not question that our due process assessment must pay keen attention to the particular burdens faced by the Executive in the context of military action, it would turn our system of checks and balances on its head to suggest that a citizen could not make his way to court with a challenge to the factual basis for his detention by his government, simply because the Executive opposes making available such a challenge. Absent suspension of the writ by Congress, a citizen detained as an enemy combatant is entitled to this process.

Because we conclude that due process demands some system for a citizen detainee to refute his classification, the proposed "some evidence" standard is inadequate. Any process in which the Executive's factual assertions go wholly unchallenged or are simply presumed correct without any opportunity for the alleged combatant to demonstrate otherwise falls constitutionally short. . . . Plainly, the "process" Hamdi has received is not that to which he is entitled under the Due Process Clause.

There remains the possibility that the standards we have articulated could be met by an appropriately authorized and properly constituted military tribunal. Indeed, it is notable that military regulations already provide for such process in related instances, dictating that tribunals be made available to determine the status of enemy detainees who assert prisoner-of-war status under the Geneva Convention. In the absence of such process, however, a court that receives a petition for a writ of habeas corpus from an alleged enemy combatant must itself ensure that the minimum requirements of due process are achieved. Both courts below recognized as much, focusing their energies on the question of whether Hamdi was due an opportunity to rebut the Government's case against him. The Government, too, proceeded on this assumption, presenting its affidavit and then seeking that it be evaluated under a deferential standard of review based on burdens that it alleged would accompany any greater process. As we have discussed, a habeas court in a case such as this may accept affidavit evidence like that contained in the Mobbs Declaration, so long as it also permits the alleged combatant to present his own factual case to rebut the Government's return. We anticipate that a District Court would proceed with the caution that we have indicated is necessary in this setting, engaging in a factfinding process that is both prudent and incremental. We have no reason to doubt that courts faced with these sensitive matters will pay proper heed both to the matters of national security that might arise in an individual case and to the constitutional limitations safeguarding essential liberties that remain vibrant even in times of security concerns.

IV

... The judgment of the United States Court of Appeals for the Fourth Circuit is vacated, and the case is remanded for further proceedings.

It is so ordered.

[Editors' Note: Concurring and dissenting opinions are excluded in the interest of space.]

TRADING CIVIL LIBERTIES FOR APPARENT SECURITY IS A BAD DEAL, CONT.
(2009)

Marjorie Cohn

Editors' Note: Other portions of this article are included in part one.

VII. THE SUPREME COURT CHECKS THE EXECUTIVE

During the Bush administration, Congress did little to check the president's usurpation of governmental power. The USA PATRIOT Act, the authorization for Operation Iraqi Freedom, and the Military Commissions Act received very little pushback from the legislative branch. It was the judicial branch that fulfilled its constitutional role to check and balance the executive.

In *Hamdi v. Rumsfeld* (2004), the Supreme Court ruled that due process demands a US citizen held in the United States as an enemy combatant is entitled to a meaningful opportunity to contest the factual basis for his detention before a neutral decision maker.

Hamdi's father, who filed the lawsuit on his son's behalf, said his twenty-year-old son was traveling on his own for the first time, and because of his lack of experience, he became trapped in Afghanistan once the US military campaign began. Hamdi, who, according to his father, went to Afghanistan to do relief work, was there less than two months before September 11, 2001. The government filed a document filled with vague generalities to support Bush's designation of Hamdi as an enemy combatant.

Justice O'Connor wrote for the *Hamdi* Court: "We have long since made clear that a state of war is not a blank check for the President when it comes to the rights of the Nation's citizens." O'Connor noted, "even the war power [of the President] does not remove constitutional limitations safeguarding essential liberties." O'Connor echoed a theme she has raised in prior Court decisions, which is particularly relevant today: "It is during our most challenging and uncertain moments that our Nation's commitment to due process is most severely tested; and it is in those times that we must preserve our commitment at home to the principles for which we fight abroad."

Instead of holding that a president cannot detain an American citizen indefinitely, the Court set forth a balancing test for determining whether a president's designation as an enemy combatant will be upheld. Henceforth, a court reviewing a claim will weigh the private interest of the detained citizen against the governmental interest in determining whether to sustain an enemy combatant designation.

O'Connor made clear that detentions of US citizens must be limited to the Afghanistan context; they are not authorized for the broader "war on terrorism." She acknowledged that "history and common sense teach us that an unchecked system of detention carries the potential to become a means for oppression and abuse of others who do not present that sort of threat."

Justice Souter wrote a concurring opinion, noting that the USA PATRIOT Act authorizes the detention of alien terrorists for no more than seven days in the absence of criminal charges or deportation proceedings. Congress, therefore, would require the government to clearly justify its detention of an American citizen held on home soil incommunicado.

Interestingly, Justice Scalia, in his dissenting opinion joined by Justice Stevens, would not permit the indefinite detention of an American citizen in Hamdi's situation. They would require the government to press criminal charges or release the individual, unless Congress were to suspend the writ of habeas corpus. "The proposition that the Executive lacks indefinite wartime detention authority over citizens is consistent with the Founders' general mistrust of military power permanently at the Executive's disposal," according to Scalia.

Only Justice Thomas held out for blind deference to the president: "This detention falls squarely within the Federal Government's war powers, and we lack the expertise and capacity to second-guess that decision."

In *Hamdan v. Rumsfeld* (2006), the Supreme Court struck down the military commissions that Bush and Rumsfeld had established because they violated the Uniform Code of Military Justice and the Geneva Conventions. The Court affirmed that there are no gaps in the Geneva Conventions—everyone must be given due process and treated humanely.

In 2008, the Supreme Court decided *Boumediene v. Bush*, upholding habeas corpus rights for the Guantánamo detainees. In a 5-4 ruling, the Court held that they have a constitutional right to habeas corpus, and that the scheme for reviewing "enemy combatant" designations under the Combatant Status Review Tribunals is an inadequate substitute for habeas corpus.

Article 1, section 9, clause 2 of the Constitution is known as the suspension clause. It reads, "The Privilege of the Writ of Habeas Corpus shall not be suspended, unless when in Cases of Rebellion or Invasion the public Safety may require it." In section 7(a) of the Military Commissions Act of 2006, Congress purported to strip habeas rights from the Guantánamo detainees by amending the habeas corpus statute. In *Boumediene*, the Court held that section of the act to be unconstitutional, declaring that the detainees still retained the constitutional right to habeas corpus.

Justice Kennedy, writing for the majority, reiterated the Court's finding in *Rasul v. Bush*, that although Cuba retains technical sovereignty over Guantánamo, the United States exercises complete jurisdiction and control over its naval base and thus the Constitution protects the detainees there. Kennedy rejected "the necessary implication" of Bush's position that the political branches could "govern without legal constraint" by locating a US military base in a country that retained formal sovereignty over the area. In his dissent, Chief Justice Roberts flippantly characterized Guantánamo as a "jurisdictionally quirky outpost."

Kennedy worried that the political branches could "have the power to switch the Constitution on or off at will" which would "lead to a regime in which Congress and the President, not this Court, say 'what the law is.'" "Even when the United States acts outside its borders," Kennedy wrote, "its powers are not 'absolute and unlimited' but are subject 'to such restrictions as are expressed in the Constitution.'"

Thus, Kennedy observed, "the writ of habeas corpus is itself an indispensable mechanism for monitoring the separation of powers." Indeed, habeas corpus was one of the few individual rights the Founding Fathers wrote into the original Constitution, years before they enacted the Bill of Rights.

"The test for determining the scope of [the habeas corpus] provision," Kennedy wrote, "must not be subject to manipulation by those whose power it is designed to restrain." It was a Republican-controlled Congress, working hand-in-glove with Bush, that tried to strip habeas corpus rights from the Guantánamo detainees in the Military Commissions Act. The Supreme Court has determined that effort to be unconstitutional. Fulfilling its constitutional duty to check and balance the other two branches, the Court has carried out its mandate to interpret the Constitution and say "what the law is."

Finding that the Guantánamo detainees retained the constitutional right to habeas corpus, the Court turned to the issue of whether there was an adequate substitute for habeas review. The Department of

Defense established Combatant Status Review Tribunals ("CSRTs") to determine whether a detainee is an "enemy combatant." These kangaroo courts provide no right to counsel, only a "personal representative," who owes no duty of confidentiality to his client and often does not even advocate on behalf of the detainee. Some personal representatives have even argued the government's case. The detainee does not have the right to see much of the evidence against him and is very limited in the evidence he can present.

The CSRTs have been criticized by military participants in the process. Lt. Col. Stephen Abraham, a veteran of US intelligence, said they often relied on "generic" evidence and were set up to rubber-stamp the "enemy combatant" designation. When he sat as a judge in one of the tribunals, Abraham and the other two judges—a colonel and a major in the air force—"found the information presented to lack substance" and noted that statements presented as factual "lacked even the most fundamental earmarks of objectively credible evidence." After they determined there was "no factual basis" to conclude the detainee was an enemy combatant, the government pressured them to change their conclusion but they refused.[1] Abraham was never assigned to another CSRT panel. Many believe that Abraham's testimony regarding the shortcomings of the CSRTs in *Boumediene*'s companion case prompted the Supreme Court to issue a rare reversal of its denial of certiorari and agree to review *Boumediene*.

While the Court declined to decide whether the CSRTs satisfied due process standards, it concluded that "even when all the parties involved in this process act with diligence and in good faith, there is considerable risk of error in the tribunal's findings of fact." The Court then had to determine whether the procedure for judicial review of the CSRTs' "enemy combatant" designations constituted an adequate substitute for habeas corpus review. Kennedy wrote:

For the writ of habeas corpus, or its substitute, to function as an effective and proper remedy in this context, the court that conducts the habeas proceeding must have the means to correct errors that occurred during the CSRT proceedings. This includes some authority to assess the sufficiency of the Government's evidence against the detainee. It also must have the authority to admit and consider relevant exculpatory evidence that was not introduced during the earlier proceeding.

But in the Detainee Treatment Act of 2005 ("DTA"), Congress limited appellate review of the CSRT determinations to whether the CSRT complied with its own procedures. The United States Court of Appeals for the District of Columbia Circuit had no authority to hear newly discovered evidence or make a finding that the detainee was improperly designated as an enemy combatant.

The *Boumediene* Court noted that "when the judicial power to issue habeas corpus properly is invoked the judicial officer must have adequate authority to make a determination in light of the relevant law and facts and to formulate and issue appropriate orders for relief, including, if necessary, an order directing the prisoner's release." Since the DTA's scheme for reviewing determinations of the CSRTs did not afford this authority, the Court held that the review of CSRTs was not an adequate substitute for habeas corpus and thus section 7 of the Military Commissions Act functioned as "an unconstitutional suspension of the writ."

In his dissent, Justice Scalia sounded the alarm that the *Boumediene* decision "will almost certainly cause more Americans to be killed." Likewise, the *Wall Street Journal* editorialized, "We can say with confident horror that more Americans are likely to die as a result." Their predictions, however, are not based in fact.

Lakhdar Boumediene and five other Algerian detainees from Bosnia were accused of threatening to blow up an American embassy in Bosnia. The Supreme Court of Bosnia and Herzegovina concluded there was no evidence to continue to detain them and ordered them released. The Bosnian officials turned them over to the United States and they were transported to Guantánamo, where they languished for six years until the Supreme Court decided their case.

Many of the men and boys at Guantánamo were sold as bounty to the US military by the Northern Alliance or warlords for $5,000 a head. Indeed, Brig. Gen. Jay Hood, the former commander at Guantánamo, admitted to the *Wall Street Journal*, "Sometimes we just didn't get the right folks," but innocent men remain detained there because "[n]obody wants to be the one to sign the release papers . . . [t]here is no muscle in the system."

In *Boumediene*, Kennedy quoted Alexander Hamilton, who wrote in Federalist No. 84 that "arbitrary imprisonments, have been, in all ages, the favorite and most formidable instruments of tyranny."

"The laws and Constitution are designed to survive, and remain in force, in extraordinary times," Kennedy wrote; "Liberty and security can be reconciled; and in our system they are reconciled within the framework of the law. The Framers decided that habeas corpus, a right of first importance, must be a part of that framework, a part of that law." Kennedy further elaborated:

Security subsists, too, in fidelity to freedom's first principles. Chief among these are freedom from arbitrary and unlawful restraint and the personal liberty that is secured by adherence to the separation of powers. . . . Within the Constitution's separation-of-powers structure, few exercises of judicial power are as legitimate or as necessary as the responsibility to hear challenges to the authority of the Executive to imprison a person.

TRADING CIVIL LIBERTIES FOR APPARENT SECURITY IS A BAD DEAL

The Supreme Court acted as a check on the some of the worst excesses of the executive branch during the Bush administration. President Obama has begun to reverse some of the most egregious policies of his predecessor. But he will be tested by the hysteria of those like Berkeley law professor John Yoo, who wrote in the January 29, 2009, *Wall Street Journal* that Obama should keep Guantánamo open, continue to hold prisoners, and even authorize waterboarding.[2]

27

JUSTIFYING WARTIME LIMITS ON CIVIL RIGHTS AND LIBERTIES, CONT.
(2009)

Robert J. Pushaw Jr.

Editors' Note: Other excerpted sections of this article appear in part one, chapter 5.

... **B**ush ... follow[ed] the lead of every president dating back to Washington [by] using military commissions to try enemy combatants charged with war crimes. Historically, the Court ha[s] rebuffed those few military prisoners who challenged the constitutionality of military tribunals. ... Recently, however, a majority of justices have become far more receptive to such claims and others relating to habeas corpus.

THE "ENEMY COMBATANT" DECISIONS

This new approach began with two 2004 cases. First, in *Hamdi v. Rumsfeld*, the Court held that "enemy combatants" who were American citizens could not be detained indefinitely, but rather had due process rights to notice and a hearing before an impartial decision-maker (which might include a military commission). Second, *Rasul v. Bush* involved Bush's order detaining noncitizen "enemy combatants" in Guantanamo, which he had made in light of longstanding Supreme Court case law interpreting the federal habeas corpus statute as not applicable to foreigners seized and imprisoned outside of the United States. A majority of justices weakly distinguished this precedent and ruled that this statute permitted these Guantanamo detainees to file habeas petitions.

Congress quickly made clear that, contrary to *Rasul*, its habeas statute did not give any federal court (including the Supreme Court) jurisdiction over aliens at Guantanamo. Instead, Congress worked with the executive branch to craft for these prisoners an elaborate set of procedures, which included several levels of military justice followed by review in the District of Columbia Circuit and Supreme Court. In *Hamdan v. Rumsfeld* (2006), five justices reached the startling conclusion that Congress had not stripped the Court of appellate jurisdiction over the foreign Guantanamo inmates or authorized their trial by military commissions (even though the AUMF [Authorization of Use of Military Force] plainly contemplated such tribunals). Again, Congress had to clarify that it meant what it said: No federal court had jurisdiction to entertain habeas petitions from these detainees, and the president could try them by military commissions.

In response, the same five justices in *Boumediene v. Bush* (2008), disregarded centuries of practice and precedent in holding that the Constitution's writ of habeas corpus extends to alien "enemy combatants" who have been captured and detained outside of the United States' sovereign territory. Accordingly, the Court invalidated Congress's alternative procedures for such detainees as an effective suspension of the constitutional habeas writ and as insufficient to satisfy the due process clause.

Hamdi, *Rasul*, *Hamdan*, and *Boumediene* depart from the Court's usual approach of deferring to the president's exercise of war powers. Instead, they fall within a minority of cases in which the Court has checked a politically weak and unpopular president who persisted in exercising war powers aggressively and in disregard of individual constitutional rights, even though such tough medicine struck the justices as unnecessary because the military emergency had passed.

MILLIGAN AND YOUNGSTOWN

The classic [historical] example is *Ex parte Milligan* (1866), which came down a year after the Civil War had ended. The Court granted the habeas petition of an Indiana citizen who had been given the death penalty by a military tribunal, which violated his constitutional right to an ordinary jury trial because he had never served in the army and the Indiana courts had always remained open. The Court conceded that both this holding and its assertion that "[t]he Constitution . . . [applies] equally in war and in peace" could not be squared with its decisions during the Civil War. The Court apologized for succumbing to the passionate "feelings and interests" caused by the grave threat to "public safety," but vowed in the future to render wholly "legal judgment."

The justices knew, but did not say, that they could successfully thwart Andrew Johnson because of his precarious political situation. The Republican Lincoln had selected the Democrat Johnson, the only Southern senator who remained loyal to the United States, as vice president primarily as an olive branch to the South. After Lincoln's assassination, the politically inept and stubborn Johnson engaged in an acrimonious fight over Reconstruction with the Radical Republicans who controlled Congress, and they eventually impeached him. The last thing Johnson needed was a clash with the Court, which saw little point in allowing a president who did not enjoy congressional support to continue to abridge constitutional liberties.

Unfortunately, the Court quickly broke its promise in *Milligan* to uphold the Constitution "at all times, and under all circumstances" by repeatedly caving in to many acts of Congress during Reconstruction that appeared to violate the Constitution. The justices apparently recognized that they could not risk defying the mighty Congress, just as they had backed down from confrontations with Lincoln. Indeed, the Court resumed its posture of deference until after World War II, when the ghost of *Milligan* reappeared.

In *Youngstown Sheet & Tube Co. v. Sawyer* (1952), six justices rejected President Truman's assertion of independent Article II power to seize and run American steel mills, which faced a labor shutdown, in order to secure steel for the Korean War effort. In the majority's view, Truman had failed to show that military necessity justified his decision to take private property domestically without due process, especially since Congress had not explicitly authorized this action. In his famous concurrence, Justice Jackson argued that Truman had disregarded Congress's will, that in such circumstances the president bore the heavy burden of demonstrating that the Constitution gave him alone the power to act, and that Truman had not met this difficult test. Conversely, Jackson presumed the constitutional validity of congressionally authorized presidential actions, absent an extremely unlikely scenario in which the federal government as a whole lacked power. As Chief Justice Vinson and two other dissenters stressed, however, many federal statutes and Article II allowed the president to do whatever he considered necessary to win wars (including seizing property), and the Court had often sustained such executive actions.

Because the dissent correctly applied the relevant law, the conclusion seems inescapable that practical factors drove the majority's decision. By 1952, Americans were war-weary, Truman's popularity had hit historic lows, and he did not have the political capital or incentives to challenge the Court. Moreover, the majority apparently believed that the president's interference with Fifth Amendment rights could not be excused by his claimed need to vigorously prosecute the Korean War, which did not pose the same life-or-death threat to the United States as World War II or the Civil War.

Libertarians who hail *Youngstown* do not appreciate that the case was about politics, not law. The same holds true for the Court's recent decisions involving "enemy combatants."

THE GUANTANAMO DETAINEE CASES
IN HISTORICAL PERSPECTIVE

Hamdi, *Rasul*, *Hamdan*, and *Boumediene* bear an uncanny resemblance to *Milligan* and *Youngstown*. Once again, a majority of pragmatic justices capitalized on a rare opportunity to uphold individual constitutional rights against an unpopular and politically compromised president, George Bush, who continued to boldly assert war powers long after the crisis of 9/11 had passed.

I seriously doubt that the Court would have rendered the same rulings in late 2001 or 2002, when Americans supported President Bush by huge margins. Moreover, the justices would surely have deferred to him if the War on Terrorism had metastasized into an epic conflict on the scale of the Civil War or the two World Wars, with attendant national mobilization and massive sacrifices. Finally, I predict that when the next Fort Sumter, Pearl Harbor, or September 11 occurs, the president will take whatever military response he deems necessary, and the Court will yield to him.

. . . .

28

BOUMEDIENE V. BUSH

US Supreme Court

LAKHDAR BOUMEDIENE, et al., PETITIONERS

v.

GEORGE W. BUSH, PRESIDENT OF THE UNITEDSTATES, et al.

KHALED A. F. AL ODAH, next friend of FAWZIKHALID
    ABDULLAH FAHAD AL ODAH, et al., PETITIONERS

v.

UNITED STATES et al.

on writs of certiorari to the United States court of appeals for the District of Columbia circuit

[June 12, 2008]

Justice Kennedy delivered the opinion of the Court, in an opinion joined by Justices Stevens, Souter, Ginsburg and Breyer.

Petitioners are aliens designated as enemy combatants and detained at the United States Naval Station at Guantanamo Bay, Cuba. There are others detained there, also aliens, who are not parties to this suit.

Petitioners present a question not resolved by our earlier cases relating to the detention of aliens at Guantanamo: whether they have the constitutional privilege of habeas corpus, a privilege not to be withdrawn except in conformance with the Suspension Clause, Art. I, §9, cl.

2. We hold these petitioners do have the habeas corpus privilege. Congress has enacted a statute, the Detainee Treatment Act of 2005 (DTA), that provides certain procedures for review of the detainees' status. We hold that those procedures are not an adequate and effective substitute for habeas corpus. Therefore §7 of the Military Commissions Act of 2006 (MCA) operates as an unconstitutional suspension of the writ. We do not address whether the President has authority to detain these petitioners nor do we hold that the writ must issue. These and other questions regarding the legality of the detention are to be resolved in the first instance by the District Court.

I

Under the Authorization for Use of Military Force (AUMF), the President is authorized "to use all necessary and appropriate force against those nations, organizations, or persons he determines planned, authorized, committed, or aided the terrorist attacks that occurred on September 11, 2001, or harbored such organizations or persons, in order to prevent any future acts of international terrorism against the United States by such nations, organizations or persons."

In *Hamdi v. Rumsfeld* (2004), five Members of the Court recognized that detention of individuals who fought against the United States in Afghanistan "for the duration of the particular conflict in which they were captured, is so fundamental and accepted an incident to war as to be an exercise of the 'necessary and appropriate force' Congress has authorized the President to use." After *Hamdi*, the Deputy Secretary of Defense established Combatant Status Review Tribunals (CSRTs) to determine whether individuals detained at Guantanamo were "enemy combatants," as the Department defines that term....

Interpreting the AUMF, the Department of Defense ordered the detention of these petitioners, and they were transferred to Guantanamo. Some of these individuals were apprehended on the battlefield in Afghanistan, others in places as far away from there as Bosnia and Gambia. All are foreign nationals, but none is a citizen of a nation now at war with the United States. Each denies he is a member of the al Qaeda terrorist network that carried out the September 11 attacks or of the Taliban regime that provided sanctuary for al Qaeda. Each petitioner appeared before a separate CSRT; was determined to be an enemy combatant; and has sought a writ of habeas corpus in the United States District Court for the District of Columbia.

The first actions commenced in February 2002. The District Court ordered the cases dismissed for lack of jurisdiction because the naval station is outside the sovereign territory of the United States. The Court of Appeals for the District of Columbia Circuit affirmed. We granted certiorari and reversed, holding that 28 U. S. C. §2241 extended statutory habeas corpus jurisdiction to Guantanamo. See *Rasul v. Bush* (2004). The constitutional issue presented in the instant cases was not reached in *Rasul*.

After *Rasul*, petitioners' cases were consolidated and entertained in two separate proceedings. . . .

While appeals were pending from the District Court decisions, Congress passed the DTA. Subsection (e) of §1005 of the DTA amended 28 U. S. C. §2241 to provide that "no court, justice, or judge shall have jurisdiction to hear or consider . . . an application for a writ of habeas corpus filed by or on behalf of an alien detained by the Department of Defense at Guantanamo Bay, Cuba." Section 1005 further provides that the Court of Appeals for the District of Columbia Circuit shall have "exclusive" jurisdiction to review decisions of the CSRTs.

In *Hamdan v. Rumsfeld* (2006), the Court held this provision did not apply to cases (like petitioners') pending when the DTA was enacted. Congress responded by passing the MCA, which again amended §2241. The text of the statutory amendment is discussed below. See Part II, infra. (Four Members of the *Hamdan* majority noted that "[n]othing prevent[ed] the President from returning to Congress to seek the authority he believes necessary." The authority to which [that] concurring opinion referred was the authority to "create military commissions of the kind at issue" in the case. Nothing in that opinion can be construed as an invitation for Congress to suspend the writ.)

Petitioners' cases were consolidated on appeal. . . . The Court of Appeals' ruling is the subject of our present review and today's decision.

The Court of Appeals concluded that MCA §7 must be read to strip from it, and all federal courts, jurisdiction to consider petitioners' habeas corpus applications, that petitioners are not entitled to the privilege of the writ or the protections of the Suspension Clause, and, as a result, that it was unnecessary to consider whether Congress provided an adequate and effective substitute for habeas corpus in the DTA.

We granted certiorari.

II

As a threshold matter, we must decide whether MCA §7 denies the federal courts jurisdiction to hear habeas corpus actions pending at the time of its enactment. We hold the statute does deny that jurisdiction, so that, if the statute is valid, petitioners' cases must be dismissed.

As amended by the terms of the MCA, 28 U. S. C. A. §2241(e) now provides:

> (1) No court, justice, or judge shall have jurisdiction to hear or consider an application for a writ of habeas corpus filed by or on

behalf of an alien detained by the United States who has been determined by the United States to have been properly detained as an enemy combatant or is awaiting such determination.

(2) Except as provided in §§1005(e)(2) and (e)(3) of the DTA no court, justice, or judge shall have jurisdiction to hear or consider any other action against the United States or its agents relating to any aspect of the detention, transfer, treatment, trial, or conditions of confinement of an alien who is or was detained by the United States and has been determined by the United States to have been properly detained as an enemy combatant or is awaiting such determination.

. . . .

We acknowledge . . . the litigation history that prompted Congress to enact the MCA. . . .

If this ongoing dialogue between and among the branches of Government is to be respected, we cannot ignore that the MCA was a direct response to *Hamdan*'s holding that the DTA's jurisdiction-stripping provision had no application to pending cases. The Court of Appeals was correct to take note of the legislative history when construing the statute, and we agree with its conclusion that the MCA deprives the federal courts of jurisdiction to entertain the habeas corpus actions now before us.

III

In deciding the constitutional questions now presented we must determine whether petitioners are barred from seeking the writ or invoking the protections of the Suspension Clause either because of their status, i.e., petitioners' designation by the Executive Branch as enemy combatants, or their physical location, i.e., their presence at Guantanamo Bay. The Government contends that noncitizens designated as enemy combatants and detained in territory located outside our Nation's borders have no constitutional rights and no privilege of habeas corpus. Petitioners contend they do have cognizable constitutional rights and that Congress, in seeking to eliminate recourse to habeas corpus as a means to assert those rights, acted in violation of the Suspension Clause.

We begin with a brief account of the history and origins of the writ. . . .

A

The Framers viewed freedom from unlawful restraint as a fundamental precept of liberty, and they understood the writ of habeas corpus as a vital instrument to secure that freedom. Experience taught, however, that the common-law writ all too often had been insufficient to guard against the abuse of monarchial power. That history counseled the necessity for specific language in the Constitution to secure the writ and ensure its place in our legal system.

. . . .

B

The broad historical narrative of the writ and its function is central to our analysis, but we seek guidance as well from founding-era authorities addressing the specific question before us: whether foreign nationals, apprehended and detained in distant countries during a time of serious threats to our Nation's security, may assert the privilege of the writ and seek its protection. The Court has been careful not to foreclose the possibility that the protections of the Suspension Clause have expanded along with post-1789 developments that define the present scope of the writ. But the analysis may begin with precedents as of 1789, for the Court has said that "at the absolute minimum" the Clause protects the writ as it existed when the Constitution was drafted and ratified.

. . . .

Each side in the present matter argues that the very lack of a precedent on point supports its position. The Government points out there is no evidence that a court sitting in England granted habeas relief to an enemy alien detained abroad; petitioners respond there is no evidence that a court refused to do so for lack of jurisdiction.

Both arguments are premised, however, upon the assumption that the historical record is complete and that the common law, if properly understood, yields a definite answer to the questions before us. There are reasons to doubt both assumptions. Recent scholarship points to the inherent shortcomings in the historical record. And given the unique status of Guantanamo Bay and the particular dangers of terrorism in the modern age, the common-law courts simply may not have confronted cases with close parallels to this one. We decline, therefore, to infer too much, one way or the other, from the lack of historical evidence on point.

IV

Drawing from its position that at common law the writ ran only to territories over which the Crown was sovereign, the Government says the

Suspension Clause affords petitioners no rights because the United States does not claim sovereignty over the place of detention.

Guantanamo Bay is not formally part of the United States. And under the terms of the lease between the United States and Cuba, Cuba retains "ultimate sovereignty" over the territory while the United States exercises "complete jurisdiction and control." Under the terms of the 1934 Treaty, however, Cuba effectively has no rights as a sovereign until the parties agree to modification of the 1903 Lease Agreement or the United States abandons the base.

The United States contends, nevertheless, that Guantanamo is not within its sovereign control. This was the Government's position well before the events of September 11, 2001. And in other contexts the Court has held that questions of sovereignty are for the political branches to decide. Even if this were a treaty interpretation case that did not involve a political question, the President's construction of the lease agreement would be entitled to great respect.

We therefore do not question the Government's position that Cuba, not the United States, maintains sovereignty, in the legal and technical sense of the term, over Guantanamo Bay. But this does not end the analysis. Our cases do not hold it is improper for us to inquire into the objective degree of control the Nation asserts over foreign territory. . . . When we have stated that sovereignty is a political question, we have referred not to sovereignty in the general, colloquial sense, meaning the exercise of dominion or power, but sovereignty in the narrow, legal sense of the term, meaning a claim of right. . . . Indeed, it is not altogether uncommon for a territory to be under the de jure sovereignty of one nation, while under the plenary control, or practical sovereignty, of another. This condition can occur when the territory is seized during war, as Guantanamo was during the Spanish-American War. Accordingly, for purposes of our analysis, we accept the Government's position that Cuba, and not the United States, retains de jure sovereignty over Guantanamo Bay. As we did in *Rasul*, however, we take notice of the obvious and uncontested fact that the United States, by virtue of its complete jurisdiction and control over the base, maintains de facto sovereignty over this territory.

Were we to hold that the present cases turn on the political question doctrine, we would be required first to accept the Government's premise that de jure sovereignty is the touchstone of habeas corpus jurisdiction. This premise, however, is unfounded. For the reasons indicated above, the history of common-law habeas corpus provides scant support for this proposition; and, for the reasons indicated below, that position would be inconsistent with our precedents and contrary to fundamental separation-of-powers principles.

A

The Court has discussed the issue of the Constitution's extraterritorial application on many occasions. These decisions undermine the Government's argument that, at least as applied to noncitizens, the Constitution necessarily stops where de jure sovereignty ends.

The Framers foresaw that the United States would expand and acquire new territories. . . . Save for a few notable (and notorious) exceptions, e.g., *Dred Scott v. Sandford* (1856), throughout most of our history there was little need to explore the outer boundaries of the Constitution's geographic reach. When Congress exercised its power to create new territories, it guaranteed constitutional protections to the inhabitants by statute.

. . . .

Fundamental questions regarding the Constitution's geographic scope first arose at the dawn of the 20th century when the Nation acquired noncontiguous Territories: Puerto Rico, Guam, and the Philippines— ceded to the United States by Spain at the conclusion of the Spanish- American War—and Hawaii—annexed by the United States in 1898. At this point Congress chose to discontinue its previous practice of extending constitutional rights to the territories by statute.

In a series of opinions later known as the *Insular Cases*, the Court addressed whether the Constitution, by its own force, applies in any territory that is not a State. The Court held that the Constitution has independent force in these territories, a force not contingent upon acts of legislative grace. Yet it took note of the difficulties inherent in that position.

Prior to their cession to the United States, the former Spanish colonies operated under a civil-law system, without experience in the various aspects of the Anglo-American legal tradition, for instance the use of grand and petit juries. At least with regard to the Philippines, a complete transformation of the prevailing legal culture would have been not only disruptive but also unnecessary, as the United States intended to grant independence to that Territory. . . .

These considerations resulted in the doctrine of territorial incorporation, under which the Constitution applies in full in incorporated Territories surely destined for statehood but only in part in unincorporated Territories. . . . But, as early as *Balzac* in 1922, the Court took for granted that even in unincorporated Territories the Government of the United States was bound to provide to noncitizen inhabitants "guaranties of certain fundamental personal rights declared in the Constitution." . . . Yet noting the inherent practical difficulties of enforcing all constitutional provisions "always and everywhere," the Court devised . . . a doctrine that allowed it to use its power sparingly and where it would be most needed. This century-old doctrine informs our analysis in the present matter.

. . . .

Practical considerations weighed heavily as well in *Johnson v. Eisentrager* (1950), where the Court addressed whether habeas corpus jurisdiction extended to enemy aliens who had been convicted of violating the laws of war. The prisoners were detained at Landsberg Prison in Germany during the Allied Powers' postwar occupation. The Court stressed the difficulties of ordering the Government to produce the prisoners in a habeas corpus proceeding. It "would require allocation of shipping space, guarding personnel, billeting and rations" and would damage the prestige of military commanders at a sensitive time. In considering these factors the Court sought to balance the constraints of military occupation with constitutional necessities.

True, the Court in *Eisentrager* denied access to the writ, and it noted the prisoners "at no relevant time were within any territory over which the United States is sovereign, and [that] the scenes of their offense, their capture, their trial and their punishment were all beyond the territorial jurisdiction of any court of the United States." The Government seizes upon this language as proof positive that the *Eisentrager* Court adopted a formalistic, sovereignty-based test for determining the reach of the Suspension Clause. We reject this reading for three reasons.

First, we do not accept the idea that the above-quoted passage from *Eisentrager* is the only authoritative language in the opinion and that all the rest is dicta. The Court's further determinations, based on practical considerations, were integral to Part II of its opinion and came before the decision announced its holding.

Second, because the United States lacked both de jure sovereignty and plenary control over Landsberg Prison, it is far from clear that the *Eisentrager* Court used the term sovereignty only in the narrow technical sense and not to connote the degree of control the military asserted over the facility. The Justices who decided *Eisentrager* would have understood sovereignty as a multifaceted concept. . . . In its principal brief in *Eisentrager*, the Government advocated a bright-line test for determining the scope of the writ, similar to the one it advocates in these cases. Yet the Court mentioned the concept of territorial sovereignty only twice in its opinion. That the Court devoted a significant portion of Part II to a discussion of practical barriers to the running of the writ suggests that the Court was not concerned exclusively with the formal legal status of Landsberg Prison but also with the objective degree of control the United States asserted over it. Even if we assume the *Eisentrager* Court considered the United States' lack of formal legal sovereignty over Landsberg Prison as the decisive factor in that case, its holding is not inconsistent with a functional approach to questions of extraterritoriality. The formal legal status of a given territory affects, at least to some extent, the political branches' control over that territory. De jure sovereignty is a factor that bears upon which constitutional guarantees apply there.

Third, if the Government's reading of *Eisentrager* were correct, the opinion would have marked not only a change in, but a complete repudiation of, the *Insular Cases'* . . . functional approach to questions of extraterritoriality. We cannot accept the Government's view. Nothing in *Eisentrager* says that de jure sovereignty is or has ever been the only relevant consideration in determining the geographic reach of the Constitution or of habeas corpus. Were that the case, there would be considerable tension between *Eisentrager*, on the one hand, and the *Insular Cases* . . . on the other. Our cases need not be read to conflict in this manner. A constricted reading of *Eisentrager* overlooks what we see as a common thread uniting [these cases]: the idea that questions of extraterritoriality turn on objective factors and practical concerns, not formalism.

B

The Government's formal sovereignty-based test raises troubling separation-of-powers concerns as well. The political history of Guantanamo illustrates the deficiencies of this approach. The United States has maintained complete and uninterrupted control of the bay for over 100 years. At the close of the Spanish-American War, Spain ceded control over the entire island of Cuba to the United States and specifically "relinquishe[d] all claim[s] of sovereignty . . . and title." See Treaty of Paris, Dec. 10, 1898. . . . From the date the treaty with Spain was signed until the Cuban Republic was established on May 20, 1902, the United States governed the territory "in trust" for the benefit of the Cuban people. And although it recognized, by entering into the 1903 Lease Agreement, that Cuba retained "ultimate sovereignty" over Guantanamo, the United States continued to maintain the same plenary control it had enjoyed since 1898. Yet the Government's view is that the Constitution had no effect there, at least as to noncitizens, because the United States disclaimed sovereignty in the formal sense of the term. The necessary implication of the argument is that by surrendering formal sovereignty over any unincorporated territory to a third party, while at the same time entering into a lease that grants total control over the territory back to the United States, it would be possible for the political branches to govern without legal constraint.

Our basic charter cannot be contracted away like this. The Constitution grants Congress and the President the power to acquire, dispose of, and govern territory, not the power to decide when and where its terms apply. Even when the United States acts outside its borders, its powers are not "absolute and unlimited" but are subject "to such restrictions as are expressed in the Constitution." Abstaining from questions involving formal sovereignty and territorial governance is one thing. To hold the political branches have the power to switch the Constitution on or off at will is quite another. The former position reflects this Court's recognition that certain matters requiring political judgments are best left to the political branches. The latter would permit a striking anomaly in our tripartite system of government, leading to a regime in which Congress and the President, not this Court, say "what the law is." *Marbury v. Madison* (1803).

These concerns have particular bearing upon the Suspension Clause question in the cases now before us, for the writ of habeas corpus is itself an indispensable mechanism for monitoring the separation of powers. The test for determining the scope of this provision must not be subject to manipulation by those whose power it is designed to restrain.

C

As we recognized in *Rasul*, the outlines of a framework for determining the reach of the Suspension Clause are suggested by the factors the Court relied upon in *Eisentrager*. In addition to the practical concerns discussed above, the *Eisentrager* Court found relevant that each petitioner:

> (a) is an enemy alien; (b) has never been or resided in the United States; (c) was captured outside of our territory and there held in military custody as a prisoner of war; (d) was tried and convicted by a Military Commission sitting outside the United States; (e) for offenses against laws of war committed outside the United States; (f) and is at all times imprisoned outside the United States.

Based on this language from *Eisentrager*, and the reasoning in our other extraterritoriality opinions, we conclude that at least three factors are relevant in determining the reach of the Suspension Clause: (1) the citizenship and status of the detainee and the adequacy of the process through which that status determination was made; (2) the nature of the sites where apprehension and then detention took place; and (3) the practical obstacles inherent in resolving the prisoner's entitlement to the writ.

Applying this framework, we note at the onset that the status of these detainees is a matter of dispute. The petitioners, like those in *Eisentrager*, are not American citizens. But the petitioners in *Eisentrager* did not contest, it seems, the Court's assertion that they were "enemy alien[s]." In the instant cases, by contrast, the detainees deny they are enemy combatants. They have been afforded some process in CSRT proceedings to determine their status; but, unlike in *Eisentrager*, there has been no trial by military commission for violations of the laws of war. The difference is not trivial. The records from the *Eisentrager* trials suggest that, well before the petitioners brought their case to this Court, there had been a rigorous adversarial process to test the legality of their detention. The *Eisentrager* petitioners were charged by a bill of particulars that made detailed factual allegations against them. To rebut the accusations, they were entitled to representation by counsel, allowed to introduce evidence on their own behalf, and permitted to cross-examine the prosecution's witnesses.

In comparison the procedural protections afforded to the detainees in the CSRT hearings are far more limited, and, we conclude, fall well short of the procedures and adversarial mechanisms that would eliminate the need for habeas corpus review. Although the detainee is assigned a "Personal Representative" to assist him during CSRT proceedings, the Secretary of the Navy's memorandum makes clear that person is not the detainee's lawyer or even his "advocate." The Government's evidence is accorded a presumption of validity. The detainee is allowed to present "reasonably available" evidence, but his ability to rebut the Government's evidence against him is limited by the circumstances of his confinement and his lack of counsel at this stage. And although the detainee can seek review of his status determination in the Court of Appeals, that review process cannot cure all defects in the earlier proceedings.

As to the second factor relevant to this analysis, the detainees here are similarly situated to the *Eisentrager* petitioners in that the sites of their apprehension and detention are technically outside the sovereign territory of the United States. As noted earlier, this is a factor that weighs against finding they have rights under the Suspension Clause. But there are critical differences between Landsberg Prison, circa 1950, and the United States Naval Station at Guantanamo Bay in 2008. Unlike its present control over the naval station, the United States' control over the prison in Germany was neither absolute nor indefinite. Like all parts of occupied Germany, the prison was under the jurisdiction of the combined Allied Forces. The United States was therefore answerable to its Allies for all activities occurring there. The Allies had not planned a long-term occupation of Germany, nor did they intend to displace all German institutions even during the period of occupation. The Court's holding in *Eisentrager* was thus consistent with the *Insular Cases*, where it had held there was no need to extend full constitutional protections to territories the United States did not intend to govern indefinitely. Guantanamo Bay, on the other hand, is no transient possession. In every practical sense Guantanamo is not abroad; it is within the constant jurisdiction of the United States.

As to the third factor, we recognize, as the Court did in *Eisentrager*, that there are costs to holding the Suspension Clause applicable in a case of military detention abroad. Habeas corpus proceedings may require expenditure of funds by the Government and may divert the attention of military personnel from other pressing tasks. While we are sensitive to these concerns, we do not find them dispositive. Compliance with any judicial process requires some incremental expenditure of resources. Yet civilian courts and the Armed Forces have functioned along side each other at various points in our history. The Government presents no credible arguments that the military mission at Guantanamo would be compromised if habeas corpus courts had jurisdiction to hear the detainees' claims. And in light of the plenary control the United States asserts over the base, none are apparent to us.

The situation in *Eisentrager* was far different, given the historical context and nature of the military's mission in post-War Germany. When hostilities in the European Theater came to an end, the United States became responsible for an occupation zone encompassing over 57,000 square miles with a population of 18 million. In addition to supervising massive reconstruction and aid efforts the American forces stationed in Germany faced potential security threats from a defeated enemy. In retrospect the post-War occupation may seem uneventful. But at the time *Eisentrager* was decided, the Court was right to be concerned about judicial interference with the military's efforts to contain "enemy elements, guerilla fighters, and 'were-wolves.'"

Similar threats are not apparent here; nor does the Government argue that they are. The United States Naval Station at Guantanamo Bay consists of 45 square miles of land and water. The base has been used, at various points, to house migrants and refugees temporarily. At present, however, other than the detainees themselves, the only long-term residents are American military personnel, their families, and a small number of workers. The detainees have been deemed enemies of the United States. At present, dangerous as they may be if released, they are contained in a secure prison facility located on an isolated and heavily fortified military base.

There is no indication, furthermore, that adjudicating a habeas corpus petition would cause friction with the host government. No Cuban court has jurisdiction over American military personnel at Guantanamo or the enemy combatants detained there. While obligated to abide by the terms of the lease, the United States is, for all practical purposes, answerable to no other sovereign for its acts on the base. Were that not the case, or if the detention facility were located in an active theater of war, arguments that issuing the writ would be "impracticable or anomalous" would have more weight. Under the facts presented here, however, there are few practical barriers to the running of the writ. To the extent barriers arise, habeas corpus procedures likely can be modified to address them.

It is true that before today the Court has never held that noncitizens detained by our Government in territory over which another country maintains de jure sovereignty have any rights under our Constitution. But the cases before us lack any precise historical parallel. They involve individuals detained by executive order for the duration of a conflict that, if measured from September 11, 2001, to the present, is already among the longest wars in American history. The detainees, moreover, are held in a territory that, while technically not part of the United States, is under the complete and total control of our Government. Under these circumstances the lack of a precedent on point is no barrier to our holding.

We hold that Art. I, §9, cl. 2, of the Constitution has full effect at Guantanamo Bay. If the privilege of habeas corpus is to be denied to the detainees now before us, Congress must act in accordance with the requirements of the Suspension Clause. This Court may not impose a de facto suspension by abstaining from these controversies. The MCA does not purport to be a formal suspension of the writ; and the Government, in its submissions to us, has not argued that it is. Petitioners, therefore, are entitled to the privilege of habeas corpus to challenge the legality of their detention.

V

In light of this holding the question becomes whether the statute stripping jurisdiction to issue the writ avoids the Suspension Clause mandate
because Congress has provided adequate substitute procedures for
habeas corpus. The Government submits there has been compliance
with the Suspension Clause because the DTA review process in the
Court of Appeals, see DTA §1005(e), provides an adequate substitute.
Congress has granted that court jurisdiction to consider

> (i) whether the status determination of the [CSRT] ... was consis-
> tent with the standards and procedures specified by the Secretary of
> Defense ... and (ii) to the extent the Constitution and laws of the
> United States are applicable, whether the use of such standards and
> procedures to make the determination is consistent with the Consti-
> tution and laws of the United States.

. . . .

A

Our case law does not contain extensive discussion of standards defining
suspension of the writ or of circumstances under which suspension has
occurred. This simply confirms the care Congress has taken throughout
our Nation's history to preserve the writ and its function. . . .

. . . .

. . . [H]ere we confront statutes, the DTA and the MCA, that were
intended to circumscribe habeas review. Congress' purpose is evident

not only from the unequivocal nature of MCA §7's jurisdiction-stripping language ... but also from a comparison of the DTA to ... statutes [previously considered]. ... When Congress has intended to replace traditional habeas corpus with habeas-like substitutes, ... it has granted to the courts broad remedial powers to secure the historic office of the writ. In the §2255 context, for example, Congress has granted to the reviewing court power to "determine the issues and make findings of fact and conclusions of law" with respect to whether "the judgment [of conviction] was rendered without jurisdiction, or ... the sentence imposed was not authorized by law or otherwise open to collateral attack."

In contrast the DTA's jurisdictional grant is quite limited. The Court of Appeals has jurisdiction not to inquire into the legality of the detention generally but only to assess whether the CSRT complied with the "standards and procedures specified by the Secretary of Defense" and whether those standards and procedures are lawful. ...

. . . .

To the extent any doubt remains about Congress' intent, the legislative history confirms what the plain text strongly suggests: In passing the DTA Congress did not intend to create a process that differs from traditional habeas corpus process in name only. It intended to create a more limited procedure. ...

It is against this background that we must interpret the DTA and assess its adequacy as a substitute for habeas corpus. The present cases thus test the limits of the Suspension Clause in ways that [previous cases] did not.

B

We do not endeavor to offer a comprehensive summary of the requisites for an adequate substitute for habeas corpus. We do consider it uncontroversial, however, that the privilege of habeas corpus entitles the prisoner to a meaningful opportunity to demonstrate that he is being held pursuant to "the erroneous application or interpretation" of relevant law. And the habeas court must have the power to order the conditional release of an individual unlawfully detained—though release need not be the exclusive remedy and is not the appropriate one in every case in which the writ is granted. These are the easily identified attributes of any constitutionally adequate/habeas corpus proceeding. But, depending on the circumstances, more may be required.

. . . .

Where a person is detained by executive order, rather than, say, after being tried and convicted in a court, the need for collateral review is most pressing. A criminal conviction in the usual course occurs after a judicial hearing before a tribunal disinterested in the outcome and committed to procedures designed to ensure its own independence. These dynamics are not inherent in executive detention orders or executive review procedures. In this context the need for habeas corpus is more urgent. The intended duration of the detention and the reasons for it bear upon the precise scope of the inquiry. Habeas corpus proceedings need not resemble a criminal trial, even when the detention is by executive order. But the writ must be effective. The habeas court must have sufficient authority to conduct a meaningful review of both the cause for detention and the Executive's power to detain.

To determine the necessary scope of habeas corpus review, therefore, we must assess the CSRT process, the mechanism through which petitioners' designation as enemy combatants became final. . . .

Petitioners identify what they see as myriad deficiencies in the CSRTs. The most relevant for our purposes are the constraints upon the detainee's ability to rebut the factual basis for the Government's assertion that he is an enemy combatant. . . .

. . . .

Although we make no judgment as to whether the CSRTs, as currently constituted, satisfy due process standards, we agree with petitioners that, even when all the parties involved in this process act with diligence and in good faith, there is considerable risk of error in the tribunal's findings of fact. . . .

C

. . . .

Under the DTA the Court of Appeals has the power to review CSRT determinations by assessing the legality of standards and procedures. This implies the power to inquire into what happened at the CSRT hearing and, perhaps, to remedy certain deficiencies in that proceeding. But should the Court of Appeals determine that the CSRT followed appropriate and lawful standards and procedures, it will have reached the limits of its jurisdiction. There is no language in the DTA that can be construed to allow the Court of Appeals to admit and consider newly discovered evidence that could not have been made part of the CSRT record because it was unavailable to either the Government or the detainee when the CSRT made its findings. This evidence, however, may be critical to the detainee's argument that he is not an enemy combatant and there is no cause to detain him.

. . . .

By foreclosing consideration of evidence not presented or reasonably available to the detainee at the CSRT proceedings, the DTA disadvantages the detainee by limiting the scope of collateral review to a record that may not be accurate or complete. . . .

. . . .

. . . Petitioners have met their burden of establishing that the DTA review process is, on its face, an inadequate substitute for habeas corpus.

. . . [T]he Government has not established that the detainees' access to the statutory review provisions at issue is an adequate substitute for the writ of habeas corpus. MCA §7 thus effects an unconstitutional suspension of the writ. In view of our holding we need not discuss the reach of the writ with respect to claims of unlawful conditions of treatment or confinement.

VI

A

In light of our conclusion that there is no jurisdictional bar to the District Court's entertaining petitioners' claims the question remains whether there are prudential barriers to habeas corpus review under these circumstances.

The Government argues petitioners must seek review of their CSRT determinations in the Court of Appeals before they can proceed with their habeas corpus actions in the District Court. As noted earlier, in other contexts and for prudential reasons this Court has required exhaustion of alternative remedies before a prisoner can seek federal habeas relief. . . .

. . . .

The cases before us, however, do not involve detainees who have been held for a short period of time while awaiting their CSRT determinations. . . . The first DTA review applications were filed over a year ago, but no decisions on the merits have been issued. While some delay in fashioning new procedures is unavoidable, the costs of delay can no longer be borne by those who are held in custody. The detainees in these cases are entitled to a prompt habeas corpus hearing.

Our decision today holds only that the petitioners before us are entitled to seek the writ; that the DTA review procedures are an inadequate substitute for habeas corpus; and that the petitioners in these cases need not exhaust the review procedures in the Court of Appeals before proceeding with their habeas actions in the District Court. The only law we identify as unconstitutional is MCA §7. Accordingly, both the DTA and the CSRT process remain intact. Our holding with regard to exhaustion should not be read to imply that a habeas court should intervene the moment an enemy combatant steps foot in a territory where the writ runs. The Executive is entitled to a reasonable period of time to determine a detainee's status before a court entertains that detainee's habeas corpus petition. The CSRT process is the mechanism Congress and the President set up to deal with these issues. Except in cases of undue delay, federal courts should refrain from entertaining an enemy combatant's habeas corpus petition at least until after the Department, acting via the CSRT, has had a chance to review his status.

B

Although we hold that the DTA is not an adequate and effective substitute for habeas corpus, it does not follow that a habeas corpus court may disregard the dangers the detention in these cases was intended to prevent. . . . In the DTA Congress sought to consolidate review of petitioners' claims in the Court of Appeals. Channeling future cases to one district court would no doubt reduce administrative burdens on the Government. . . . We recognize . . . that the Government has a legitimate interest in protecting sources and methods of intelligence gathering; and we expect that the District Court will use its discretion to accommodate this interest to the greatest extent possible.

These and the other remaining questions are within the expertise and competence of the District Court to address in the first instance.

. . . .

Officials charged with daily operational responsibility for our security may consider a judicial discourse on the history of the Habeas Corpus Act of 1679 and like matters to be far removed from the Nation's present, urgent concerns. Established legal doctrine, however, must be consulted for its teaching. Remote in time it may be; irrelevant to the present it is not. Security depends upon a sophisticated intelligence apparatus and the ability of our Armed Forces to act and to interdict. There are further considerations, however. Security subsists, too, in fidelity to freedom's first principles. Chief among these are freedom from arbitrary and unlawful restraint and the personal liberty that is secured by adherence to the separation of powers. It is from these principles that the judicial authority to consider petitions for habeas corpus relief derives.

Our opinion does not undermine the Executive's powers as Commander in Chief. On the contrary, the exercise of those powers is vindicated, not eroded, when confirmed by the Judicial Branch. Within the Constitution's separation-of-powers structure, few exercises of judicial power are as legitimate or as necessary as the responsibility to hear challenges to the authority of the Executive to imprison a person. Some of these petitioners have been in custody for six years with no definitive judicial determination as to the legality of their detention. Their access to the writ is a necessity to determine the lawfulness of their status, even if, in the end, they do not obtain the relief they seek.

Because our Nation's past military conflicts have been of limited duration, it has been possible to leave the outer boundaries of war powers undefined. If, as some fear, terrorism continues to pose dangerous threats to us for years to come, the Court might not have this luxury. This result is not inevitable, however. The political branches, consistent with their independent obligations to interpret and uphold the Constitution, can engage in a genuine debate about how best to preserve constitutional values while protecting the Nation from terrorism.

It bears repeating that our opinion does not address the content of the law that governs petitioners' detention. That is a matter yet to be determined. We hold that petitioners may invoke the fundamental procedural protections of habeas corpus. The laws and Constitution are designed to survive, and remain in force, in extraordinary times. Liberty and security can be reconciled; and in our system they are reconciled within the framework of the law. The Framers decided that habeas corpus, a right of first importance, must be a part of that framework, a part of that law.

The determination by the Court of Appeals that the Suspension Clause and its protections are inapplicable to petitioners was in error. The judgment of the Court of Appeals is reversed. The cases are remanded to the Court of Appeals with instructions that it remand the cases to the District Court for proceedings consistent with this opinion.

It is so ordered.

[Editors' Note: The concurring opinion of Justice Souter is omitted.]

Roberts, C. J., dissenting

Chief Justice Roberts, with whom Justice Scalia, Justice Thomas, and Justice Alito join, dissenting.

Today the Court strikes down as inadequate the most generous set of procedural protections ever afforded aliens detained by this country as enemy combatants. The political branches crafted these procedures amidst an ongoing military conflict, after much careful investigation and thorough debate. The Court rejects them today out of hand, without bothering to say what due process rights the detainees possess, without explaining how the statute fails to vindicate those rights, and before a single petitioner has even attempted to avail himself of the law's operation. And to what effect? The majority merely replaces a review system designed by the people's representatives with a set of shapeless procedures to be defined by federal courts at some future date. One cannot help but think, after surveying the modest practical results of the majority's ambitious opinion, that this decision is not really about the detainees at all, but about control of federal policy regarding enemy combatants.

The majority is adamant that the Guantanamo detainees are entitled to the protections of habeas corpus—its opinion begins by deciding that question. I regard the issue as a difficult one, primarily because of the unique and unusual jurisdictional status of Guantanamo Bay. I nonetheless agree with Justice Scalia's analysis of our precedents and the pertinent history of the writ, and accordingly join his dissent. The important point for me, however, is that the Court should have resolved these cases on other grounds. Habeas is most fundamentally a procedural right, a mechanism for contesting the legality of executive detention. The critical threshold question in these cases, prior to any inquiry about the writ's scope, is whether the system the political branches designed protects whatever rights the detainees may possess. If so, there is no need for any additional process, whether called "habeas" or something else.

Congress entrusted that threshold question in the first instance to the Court of Appeals for the District of Columbia Circuit, as the Constitution surely allows Congress to do. See Detainee Treatment Act of 2005 (DTA). But before the D. C. Circuit has addressed the issue, the Court cashiers the statute, and without answering this critical threshold question itself. The Court does eventually get around to asking whether review under the DTA is, as the Court frames it, an "adequate substitute" for habeas, but even then its opinion fails to determine what rights the detainees possess and whether the DTA system satisfies them. The majority instead compares the undefined DTA process to an equally undefined habeas right—one that is to be given shape only in the future by district courts on a case-by-case basis. This whole approach is misguided.

It is also fruitless. How the detainees' claims will be decided now that the DTA is gone is anybody's guess. But the habeas process the Court mandates will most likely end up looking a lot like the DTA system it replaces, as the district court judges shaping it will have to reconcile review of the prisoners' detention with the undoubted need to protect the American people from the terrorist threat—precisely the challenge Congress undertook in drafting the DTA. All that today's opinion has done is shift responsibility for those sensitive foreign policy and national security decisions from the elected branches to the Federal Judiciary.

I believe the system the political branches constructed adequately protects any constitutional rights aliens captured abroad and detained as enemy combatants may enjoy. I therefore would dismiss these cases on that ground. With all respect for the contrary views of the majority, I must dissent.

[Editors' Note: The remainder of Justice Roberts's dissenting opinion is omitted.]

Scalia, J., dissenting

Justice Scalia, with whom The Chief Justice, Justice Thomas, and Justice Alito join, dissenting.

Today, for the first time in our Nation's history, the Court confers a constitutional right to habeas corpus on alien enemies detained abroad by our military forces in the course of an ongoing war. The Chief Justice's dissent, which I join, shows that the procedures prescribed by Congress in the Detainee Treatment Act provide the essential protections that habeas corpus guarantees. . . . My problem with today's opinion is more fundamental still: The writ of habeas corpus does not, and never has, run in favor of aliens abroad; the Suspension Clause thus has no application, and the Court's intervention in this military matter is entirely ultra vires.

I shall devote most of what will be a lengthy opinion to the legal errors contained in the opinion of the Court. Contrary to my usual practice, however, I think it appropriate to begin with a description of the disastrous consequences of what the Court has done today.

I

America is at war with radical Islamists. The enemy began by killing Americans and American allies abroad: 241 at the Marine barracks in

Lebanon, 19 at the Khobar Towers in Dhahran, 224 at our embassies in Dar es Salaam and Nairobi, and 17 on the USS Cole in Yemen. On September 11, 2001, the enemy brought the battle to American soil, killing 2,749 at the Twin Towers in New York City, 184 at the Pentagon in Washington, D. C., and 40 in Pennsylvania. It has threatened further attacks against our homeland; one need only walk about buttressed and barricaded Washington, or board a plane anywhere in the country, to know that the threat is a serious one. Our Armed Forces are now in the field against the enemy, in Afghanistan and Iraq. . . .

The game of bait-and-switch that today's opinion plays upon the Nation's Commander in Chief will make the war harder on us. It will almost certainly cause more Americans to be killed. That consequence would be tolerable if necessary to preserve a time-honored legal principle vital to our constitutional Republic. But it is this Court's blatant abandonment of such a principle that produces the decision today. The President relied on our settled precedent in *Johnson v. Eisentrager* when he established the prison at Guantanamo Bay for enemy aliens. Citing that case, the President's Office of Legal Counsel advised him "that the great weight of legal authority indicates that a federal district court could not properly exercise habeas jurisdiction over an alien detained at [Guantanamo Bay]." Memorandum from Patrick F. Philbin and John C. Yoo, Deputy Assistant Attorneys General, Office of Legal Counsel, to William J. Haynes II, General Counsel, Dept. of Defense (Dec. 28, 2001). Had the law been otherwise, the military surely would not have transported prisoners there, but would have kept them in Afghanistan, transferred them to another of our foreign military bases, or turned them over to allies for detention. Those other facilities might well have been worse for the detainees themselves.

In the long term, then, the Court's decision today accomplishes little, except perhaps to reduce the well-being of enemy combatants that the Court ostensibly seeks to protect. In the short term, however, the decision is devastating. At least 30 of those prisoners hitherto released from Guantanamo Bay have returned to the battlefield. Some have been captured or killed. But others have succeeded in carrying on their atrocities against innocent civilians. In one case, a detainee released from Guantanamo Bay masterminded the kidnapping of two Chinese dam workers, one of whom was later shot to death when used as a human shield against Pakistani commandoes. Another former detainee promptly resumed his post as a senior Taliban commander and murdered a United Nations engineer and three Afghan soldiers. Still another murdered an Afghan judge. It was reported only last month that a released detainee carried out a suicide bombing against Iraqi soldiers in Mosul, Iraq.

These, mind you, were detainees whom the military had concluded were not enemy combatants. Their return to the kill illustrates the incredible difficulty of assessing who is and who is not an enemy combatant in a foreign theater of operations where the environment does not lend itself to rigorous evidence collection. Astoundingly, the Court today raises the bar, requiring military officials to appear before civilian courts and defend their decisions under procedural and evidentiary rules that go beyond what Congress has specified. As The Chief Justice's dissent makes clear, we have no idea what those procedural and evidentiary rules are, but they will be determined by civil courts. . . . If they impose a higher standard of proof (from foreign battlefields) than the current procedures require, the number of the enemy returned to combat will obviously increase.

But even when the military has evidence that it can bring forward, it is often foolhardy to release that evidence to the attorneys representing our enemies. And one escalation of procedures that the Court is clear about is affording the detainees increased access to witnesses (perhaps troops serving in Afghanistan?) and to classified information. During the 1995 prosecution of Omar Abdel Rahman, federal prosecutors gave the names of 200 unindicted co-conspirators to the "Blind Sheik's" defense lawyers; that information was in the hands of Osama Bin Laden within two weeks. . . .

And today it is not just the military that the Court elbows aside. A mere two Terms ago in *Hamdan v. Rumsfeld* when the Court held (quite amazingly) that the Detainee Treatment Act of 2005 had not stripped habeas jurisdiction over Guantanamo petitioners' claims, four Members of today's five-Justice majority joined an opinion saying the following:

> Nothing prevents the President from returning to Congress to seek the authority [for trial by military commission] he believes necessary.
>
> Where, as here, no emergency prevents consultation with Congress, judicial insistence upon that consultation does not weaken our Nation's ability to deal with danger. To the contrary, that insistence strengthens the Nation's ability to determine—through democratic means—how best to do so. The Constitution places its faith in those democratic means." (Breyer, J., concurring).

Turns out they were just kidding. For in response, Congress, at the President's request, quickly enacted the Military Commissions Act, emphatically reasserting that it did not want these prisoners filing habeas petitions. It is therefore clear that Congress and the Executive—both political branches—have determined that limiting the role of civilian courts in adjudicating whether prisoners captured abroad are properly detained is important to success in the war that some 190,000 of our men and women are now fighting. As the Solicitor General argued, "the Military Commissions Act and the Detainee Treatment Act . . . represent an effort by the political branches to strike an appropriate balance between the need to preserve liberty and the need to accommodate the weighty and sensitive governmental interests in ensuring that those who have in fact fought with the enemy during a war do not return to battle against the United States."

But it does not matter. The Court today decrees that no good reason to accept the judgment of the other two branches is "apparent." "The Government," it declares, "presents no credible arguments that the military mission at Guantanamo would be compromised if habeas corpus courts had jurisdiction to hear the detainees' claims." What competence does the Court have to second-guess the judgment of Congress and the President on such a point? None whatever. But the Court blunders in nonetheless. Henceforth, as today's opinion makes unnervingly clear, how to handle enemy prisoners in this war will ultimately lie with the branch that knows least about the national security concerns that the subject entails.

II

A

The Suspension Clause of the Constitution provides: "The Privilege of the Writ of Habeas Corpus shall not be suspended, unless when in Cases of Rebellion or Invasion the public Safety may require it." Art. I, §9, cl. 2. As a court of law operating under a written Constitution, our role is to determine whether there is a conflict between that Clause and the Military Commissions Act. A conflict arises only if the Suspension Clause preserves the privilege of the writ for aliens held by the United States military as enemy combatants at the base in Guantanamo Bay, located within the sovereign territory of Cuba.

403

We have frequently stated that we owe great deference to Congress's view that a law it has passed is constitutional. That is especially so in the area of foreign and military affairs. . . . Indeed, we accord great deference even when the President acts alone in this area.

In light of those principles of deference, the Court's conclusion that "the common law [does not] yiel[d] a definite answer to the questions before us," leaves it no choice but to affirm the Court of Appeals. The writ as preserved in the Constitution could not possibly extend farther than the common law provided when that Clause was written. See Part III, *infra*. The Court admits that it cannot determine whether the writ historically extended to aliens held abroad, and it concedes (necessarily) that Guantanamo Bay lies outside the sovereign territory of the United States. Together, these two concessions establish that it is (in the Court's view) perfectly ambiguous whether the common-law writ would have provided a remedy for these petitioners. If that is so, the Court has no basis to strike down the Military Commissions Act, and must leave undisturbed the considered judgment of the coequal branches.

How, then, does the Court weave a clear constitutional prohibition out of pure interpretive equipoise? The Court resorts to "fundamental separation-of-powers principles" to interpret the Suspension Clause. According to the Court, because "the writ of habeas corpus is itself an indispensable mechanism for monitoring the separation of powers," the test of its extraterritorial reach "must not be subject to manipulation by those whose power it is designed to restrain."

That approach distorts the nature of the separation of powers and its role in the constitutional structure. The "fundamental separation-of-powers principles" that the Constitution embodies are to be derived not from some judicially imagined matrix, but from the sum total of the individual separation-of-powers provisions that the Constitution sets forth. . . .

B

The Court purports to derive from our precedents a "functional" test for the extraterritorial reach of the writ which shows that the Military Commissions Act unconstitutionally restricts the scope of habeas. That is remarkable because the most pertinent of those precedents, *Johnson v. Eisentrager*, conclusively establishes the opposite. There we were confronted with the claims of 21 Germans held at Landsberg Prison, an American military facility located in the American Zone of occupation in postwar Germany. They had been captured in China, and an American military commission sitting there had convicted them of war crimes—collaborating with the Japanese after Germany's surrender. Like the petitioners here, the Germans claimed that their detentions violated the Constitution and international law, and sought a writ of habeas corpus. Writing for the Court, Justice Jackson held that American courts lacked habeas jurisdiction:

"We are cited to [*sic*] no instance where a court, in this or any other country where the writ is known, has issued it on behalf of an alien enemy who, at no relevant time and in no stage of his captivity, has been within its territorial jurisdiction. Nothing in the text of the Constitution extends such a right, nor does anything in our statutes."

Justice Jackson then elaborated on the historical scope of the writ:

The alien, to whom the United States has been traditionally hospitable, has been accorded a generous and ascending scale of rights as he increases his identity with our society. . . .

But, in extending constitutional protections beyond the citizenry, the Court has been at pains to point out that it was the alien's presence within its territorial jurisdiction that gave the Judiciary power to act.

Lest there be any doubt about the primacy of territorial sovereignty in determining the jurisdiction of a habeas court over an alien, Justice Jackson distinguished two cases in which aliens had been permitted to seek habeas relief, on the ground that the prisoners in those cases were in custody within the sovereign territory of the United States. [*Eisentrager*] (discussing *Ex parte Quirin* [1942], and *In re Yamashita* [1946]). "By reason of our sovereignty at that time over [the Philippines]," Jackson wrote, "Yamashita stood much as did Quirin before American courts."

Eisentrager thus held—held beyond any doubt—that the Constitution does not ensure habeas for aliens held by the United States in areas over which our Government is not sovereign.

The Court would have us believe that *Eisentrager* rested on "[p]ractical considerations," such as the "difficulties of ordering the Government to produce the prisoners in a habeas corpus proceeding." Formal sovereignty, says the Court, is merely one consideration "that bears upon which constitutional guarantees apply" in a given location. This is a sheer rewriting of the case. *Eisentrager* mentioned practical concerns, to be sure—but not for the purpose of determining under what circumstances American courts could issue writs of habeas corpus for aliens abroad. It cited them to support its holding that the Constitution does not empower courts to issue writs of habeas corpus to aliens abroad in any circumstances. As Justice Black accurately said in dissent, "the Court's opinion inescapably denies courts power to afford the least bit of protection for any alien who is subject to our occupation government abroad, even if he is neither enemy nor belligerent and even after peace is officially declared."

The Court also tries to change *Eisentrager* into a "functional" test by quoting a paragraph that lists the characteristics of the German petitioners. . . . [T]he characteristics of the German prisoners were set forth, not in application of some "functional" test, but to show that the case before the Court represented an a fortiori application of the ordinary rule. That is reaffirmed by the sentences that immediately follow the listing of the Germans' characteristics:

> We have pointed out that the privilege of litigation has been extended to aliens, whether friendly or enemy, only because permitting their presence in the country implied protection. No such basis can be invoked here, for these prisoners at no relevant time were within any territory over which the United States is sovereign, and the scenes of their offense, their capture, their trial and their punishment were all beyond the territorial jurisdiction of any court of the United States.

Eisentrager nowhere mentions a "functional" test, and the notion that it is based upon such a principle is patently false.

The Court also reasons that *Eisentrager* must be read as a "functional" opinion because of our prior decisions in the *Insular Cases*.... The *Insular Cases* all concerned territories acquired by Congress under its Article IV authority and indisputably part of the sovereign territory of the United States. None of the *Insular Cases* stands for the proposition that aliens located outside U. S. sovereign territory have constitutional rights, and *Eisentrager* held just the opposite with respect to habeas corpus....

. . . .

The Court tries to reconcile *Eisentrager* with its holding today by pointing out that in postwar Germany, the United States was "answerable to its Allies" and did not "pla[n] a long-term occupation." Those factors were not mentioned in *Eisentrager*. Worse still, it is impossible to see how they relate to the Court's asserted purpose in creating this "functional" test—namely, to ensure a judicial inquiry into detention and prevent the political branches from acting with impunity. Can it possibly be that the Court trusts the political branches more when they are beholden to foreign powers than when they act alone?

After transforming the a fortiori elements discussed above into a "functional" test, the Court is still left with the difficulty that most of those elements exist here as well with regard to all the detainees. To make the application of the newly crafted "functional" test produce a different result in the present cases, the Court must rely upon factors (d) and (e): The Germans had been tried by a military commission for violations of the laws of war; the present petitioners, by contrast, have been tried by a Combatant Status Review Tribunal (CSRT) whose procedural protections, according to the Court's ipse dixit, "fall well short of the procedures and adversarial mechanisms that would eliminate the need for habeas corpus review." But no one looking for "functional" equivalents would put *Eisentrager* and the present cases in the same category, much less place the present cases in a preferred category. The difference between them cries out for lesser procedures in the present cases. The prisoners in *Eisentrager* were prosecuted for crimes after the cessation of hostilities; the prisoners here are enemy combatants detained during an ongoing conflict.

The category of prisoner comparable to these detainees are not the *Eisentrager* criminal defendants, but the more than 400,000 prisoners of war detained in the United States alone during World War II. Not a single one was accorded the right to have his detention validated by a habeas corpus action in federal court—and that despite the fact that they were present on U.S. soil. The Court's analysis produces a crazy result: Whereas those convicted and sentenced to death for war crimes are without judicial remedy, all enemy combatants detained during a war, at least insofar as they are confined in an area away from the battlefield over which the United States exercises "absolute and indefinite" control, may seek a writ of habeas corpus in federal court. And, as an even more bizarre implication from the Court's reasoning, those prisoners whom the military plans to try by full-dress Commission at a future date may file habeas petitions and secure release before their trials take place.

There is simply no support for the Court's assertion that constitutional rights extend to aliens held outside U.S. sovereign territory, and *Eisentrager* could not be clearer that the privilege of habeas corpus does not extend to aliens abroad. By blatantly distorting *Eisentrager*, the Court avoids the difficulty of explaining why it should be overruled. The rule that aliens abroad are not constitutionally entitled to habeas corpus has not proved unworkable in practice; if anything, it is the Court's "functional" test that does not (and never will) provide clear guidance for the future. *Eisentrager* forms a coherent whole with the accepted proposition that aliens abroad have no substantive rights under our Constitution. Since it was announced, no relevant factual premises have changed. It has engendered considerable reliance on the part of our military. And, as the Court acknowledges, text and history do not clearly compel a contrary ruling. It is a sad day for the rule of law when such an important constitutional precedent is discarded without an apologia, much less an apology.

C

What drives today's decision is neither the meaning of the Suspension Clause, nor the principles of our precedents, but rather an inflated notion of judicial supremacy....

III

Putting aside the conclusive precedent of *Eisentrager*, it is clear that the original understanding of the Suspension Clause was that habeas corpus was not available to aliens abroad, as Judge Randolph's thorough opinion for the court below detailed.

. . . .

In sum, all available historical evidence points to the conclusion that the writ would not have been available at common law for aliens captured and held outside the sovereign territory of the Crown. Despite three opening briefs, three reply briefs, and support from a legion of amici, petitioners have failed to identify a single case in the history of Anglo-American law that supports their claim to jurisdiction. The Court finds it significant that there is no recorded case denying jurisdiction to such prisoners either. But a case standing for the remarkable proposition that the writ could issue to a foreign land would surely have been reported, whereas a case denying such a writ for lack of jurisdiction would likely not. At a minimum, the absence of a reported case either way leaves unrefuted the voluminous commentary stating that habeas was confined to the dominions of the Crown.

. . . .

In sum, because I conclude that the text and history of the Suspension Clause provide no basis for our jurisdiction, I would affirm the Court of Appeals even if *Eisentrager* did not govern these cases.

. . . .

Today the Court warps our Constitution in a way that goes beyond the narrow issue of the reach of the Suspension Clause, invoking judicially brainstormed separation-of-powers principles to establish a manipulable "functional" test for the extraterritorial reach of habeas corpus (and, no doubt, for the extraterritorial reach of other constitutional protections as well). It blatantly misdescribes important precedents, most conspicuously Justice Jackson's opinion for the Court in *Johnson v. Eisentrager*. It breaks a chain of precedent as old as the common law that prohibits judicial inquiry into detentions of aliens abroad absent statutory authorization. And, most tragically, it sets our military commanders the impossible task of proving to a civilian court, under whatever standards this Court devises in the future, that evidence supports the confinement of each and every enemy prisoner.

The Nation will live to regret what the Court has done today. I dissent.

29

BOUMEDIENE V. BUSH AND GUANTÁNAMO, CUBA
Does the "Empire Strike Back"? cont.
(2009)

Ernesto Hernández-López

[Editors' Note: As developed in the earlier part of this article a post-colonial approach focuses on historical appreciation of how norms developed.]

. . . .

In a highly preliminary fashion, this part extends the article's analysis to post-*Boumediene* events.

While a recent executive order ends Guantánamo detentions by January 22, 2010 and *Boumediene* affirms significant constitutional rights protections, legal anomaly appears to characterize the release of Guantánamo detainees and judicial review for detainees under US control in Afghanistan. These two facts, legal challenges for release and alternative detention locations, point to this article's three central claims. Specifically for these detention developments, anomaly is not an aberration but a precise objective; postcolonial analysis of foreign relations history describe how the law creates and facilitates anomaly, and four objectives characterize anomaly, i.e., the United States avoids sovereign authority overseas, limits sovereign authority for other states, seeks to avoid constitutional limitation abroad, and protects strategic interests. Accordingly, this part proceeds with preliminary identifications of anomaly in the January 22, 2009 Executive Order, habeas corpus efforts to release base detainees, and recent legal challenges to detentions in the US Bagram Airfield in Afghanistan.

A. Guantánamo Detention Ends, Avoiding New Rights and Spurring Relocation

In his first week in office, President Obama issued an executive order ending the Guantánamo detention program by January 22, 2010. It requires that all remaining detentions be subject to reviews, coordinated by the attorney general with cooperation and participation from foreign relations, defense, homeland security, intelligence, and counterterrorism agencies. Regarding these detainees, it stays military commission proceedings which have not reached judgment and bars any new charges from being sworn. Similarly, it requires detainee custody be under humane standards, described as confirming with "all applicable laws governing such confinement, including Common Article 3 of the Geneva Conventions." The secretary of defense will review these conditions to ensure full compliance by February 22.

[Editors' Note: Guantánamo detentions did not, of course, end on January 22, 2010. In addition, since this article was written, military commissions were poised to resume.]

While . . . much policy remains to be implemented, the order disposing detainees and closing the detention facilities points to elements of anomaly on two fronts. Specifically, the order states: 1) it does not create any rights, and 2) detainees may be transferred to other US detention facilities or third countries. The order does affirm that these detentions are governed by the Geneva Conventions and that detainees have the constitutional writ of habeas corpus. But it does not give any indication whether detainees in Guantánamo or in other locations have constitutional rights beyond habeas challenges of unlawful detention. For instance, due process rights are not mentioned. Accordingly, the order potentially leaves detainees on the base with district court jurisdiction to claim unlawful detention, but without any clear determination of what substantive rights do or do not apply to this nonsovereign space. This anomaly is compounded with the prudential concerns and Constitution-light approaches affirmed by the slim *Boumediene* majority.

This anomaly, i.e., unclear state of what rights check detention authority, is reified in the order's last subsection. After announcing dramatic changes in detention policy, the order states it does not intend to and "does not, create any right or benefit, substantive or procedural, enforceable at law or in equity. . . ." As such in legal terms, the order leaves things as they were after *Boumediene*, but clearly states that no right (procedural, substantive, or in equity) exists to seek the order's objectives.

Second, the order opens the door for detainees to be transferred to locations where constitutional habeas and/or other individual rights do not extend. For remaining Guantánamo detainees, it provides they may be "returned to their home country, released, transferred to a third country, or transferred to another" US detention facility. Here, the concern is detainees may be relocated to third countries where they may [be] tortured. Alternatively, they may be placed in US detention facilities with even less jurisdiction or constitutional rights than Guantánamo. As explained below, the detention example in Afghanistan has quickly developed.

B. Anomaly Amidst Habeas Proceedings For Detainees

Habeas proceedings since *Boumediene* suggest anomaly appears when courts start examining what makes detention unlawful. Anomaly exists because the location of detention produces a situation where it is unclear what legal norms, sources of law, or jurisdiction apply. This develops from situations created by US foreign relations to have control of base territory without de jure sovereignty. Here, the puzzle develops from constitutional habeas rights affirmed by *Boumediene*, providing a judicial method to contest detention, but it is not entirely clear what makes detention illegal. Many substantive rights in constitutional or international law remain unconfirmed if they extend, by case law or statute, to the base or to noncitizens there. In theory, a clear determination that these rights exist or apply would ease the release of Guantánamo detainees after *Boumediene*. Meanwhile some detainees remain in custody seven years after detentions began.

While habeas proceedings since June 2008 have been numerous and their full examination beyond this article's scope, preliminary developments suggest anomaly may cloud these proceedings. . . .

[Editors' Note: On April 1, 2010, district court judge Thomas F. Hogan dismissed 105 habeas claims as moot because the detainees had been released or transferred to foreign countries. The Center for Constitutional Rights reports that as of September 27, 2010, the district court has decided 54 habeas cases for base detainees, resulting in 37 granted and 17 denied habeas petitions. Of the 37 detainess whose habeas petitions have been granted, the government has released 23, leaving 14 still detained.]

VI. CONCLUSION

In conclusion, this article has described how Guantánamo's legally anomalous status exerted enormous influence in recent determinations made by the Supreme Court in *Boumediene*. Legal anomaly is evident as an unclear state of what rights check detention authority. Legal anomaly exists because the base's territory is not clearly within American or Cuban sovereignty. This ambiguity unclearly guides what law (if any) checks detention authority on the base. This is apparent when litigation confronts how detention location produces a situation where it is unclear what legal norms, sources of law, or jurisdiction exists.

Historic agreements with Cuba in 1903 specifically created Guantánamo's legal anomaly, while American foreign relations practices, at the time and since, perpetuate it. This decision continues a discourse of normative anomaly on the base. This legal anomaly has facilitated detention policies in which the United States tries to avoid individual rights protections for "War on Terror" detainees on the base since 2002. Just in June of 2008, after a second Supreme Court case on the writ and the base, may habeas proceedings possibly release persons from detention. Trying to paint this legal anomaly as an accident or unintended, recent Supreme Court opinions refer to this anomaly by labeling base jurisdiction as "quirky" or "unusual."

An analysis of US-Cuba relations since 1898 shows that the base's legally anomalous status was a precise US foreign policy objective. This legal anomaly develops from the United States avoiding sovereignty overseas while reserving the authority to exercise significant influence abroad. Specific to the base at Guantánamo, US-Cuba agreements in 1903 and 1934 crafted this legal anomaly. They affirm that the US lacks sovereignty over Guantánamo, but retains "complete jurisdiction and control" for an indefinite period, while Cuba has "ultimate sovereignty" with no ability to end US occupation. Wavering between the concepts of sovereignty and jurisdiction, this legal anomaly clouds legal challenges to base detention. This is achieved by arguing that the base is not within US sovereignty, thus the Constitution cannot check base authority, and by arguing that Cuban sovereignty prohibits extending constitutional protections in American law.

Boumediene addressed this legal anomaly with its examination concerning whether the Constitution's suspension clause applies on the base. By a slim majority, the Court held that it does apply to this nonsovereign territory under US control. Importantly, this holding extends the privilege of the writ of habeas corpus to base detainees. To do this, the Court found that the United States has de facto sovereignty on the base and the Constitution applies extraterritorially. Highlighting these findings, this article raises two general points regarding the legal analysis of base detention.

First, while the base's legally anomalous status effectively endorses detention, four legal objectives in US foreign relations shape this anomalous status. Any legal continuation or limitation to this overseas authority must address these objectives. These objectives are that the United States avoids sovereignty abroad, limits incidents of sovereignty for foreign states, avoids constitutional limits for its overseas authority, and protects strategic overseas interests (geopolitical, economic, and legal). These objectives craft the legal anomaly evident in base occupation since 1898 and in base detention litigation since 2002. Specific to the base, lease agreements in 1903 and a bilateral treaty in 1934 provide the United States with nonsovereign control and protection of overseas interests, such as a strategically placed base, an effectively indefinite term of occupation, and military authority free from constitutional restraints. These objectives also appear in the Treaty of Paris of 1898 and in the Platt Amendment of 1901. The Platt Amendment is significant to the base for two reasons. It required that Cuba lease or sell lands to the United States for coaling or naval stations. This provides the United States legal occupancy of Guantánamo, which it had physically occupied since 1898. Also, the amendment set the terms for the United States to avoid sovereignty over Cuba, but to retain enormous influence over the island state. The amendment limited Cuban sovereignty with a "right of intervention" for the United States, limitations on Cuban foreign relations and economic powers, and a base for the US military on Cuban soil. The United States moved to include these amendment provisions in military appropriations, the Cuban Constitution of 1901, and a bilateral treaty in 1902.

These legal objectives similarly characterize how the Court in *Boumediene* recently addressed this legal anomaly regarding detainee access to the writ of habeas corpus. The Court addressed whether base detainees benefit from the writ in the Constitution's suspension clause, whether the MCA and DTA legally suspend the writ, and whether the MCA and DTA offer an adequate substitute for habeas proceedings. The Court found that the constitutional writ extends to the base and to alien detainees, the MCA and DTA unconstitutionally suspend the writ, and the DTA and MCA provide an inadequate substitute for habeas proceedings.

To reach these holdings, the Court confronted each of the four legal objectives regarding this legal anomaly. For instance, its finding that the United States exercises de facto sovereignty over the base tempers the objective of avoiding sovereignty for the United States. Next, the Court regarded formal or de jure sovereignty over the base, belonging to Cuba, as irrelevant to "practical" considerations governing the base. In this regard, the Court does not find a formal determination of Cuban sovereignty, termed "ultimate sovereignty" in the agreements, as a bar to finding the writ is applicable. These sovereignty findings essentially provide a slight and nuanced distancing from the two objectives of avoiding US sovereignty and limiting Cuban sovereignty. This is achieved by the Court focusing less on sovereignty as a categorical determination, but more on prudential or practical concerns regarding base authority. Here, the Court is motivated by practical concerns, for example, that US authority on the base is over a century old, capable of following court orders, and answerable to no other sovereign. The next two objectives, avoiding constitutional limitations overseas and protecting strategic overseas interests, appear in the *Boumediene* opinions as well. With examples from the *Insular Cases*, the Court suggests a Constitution-light for the base. It affirms the doctrine that not all of the Constitution's provisions apply to overseas authority under US sovereignty. This doctrine historically endorsed an informal empire for the United States. Similarly, the opinions identify strategic overseas interests, such as national security, deference to the political branches in foreign relations, and the ability to hold individual detainees for six years without any court proceedings

Second, *Boumediene* provides an example of how the law addresses postcolonial circumstances. In identifying history's present influence, this article contextualizes future and deeper examinations of what legal checks (if any) apply to US authority overseas. The law used to support historic imperial control, such as the Incorporation Doctrine and base agreements, currently governs overseas authority. Specific to Guantánamo, base occupation and legal anomaly on the base are products from US influence over Cuba since its independence from Spain in 1898. Here, the relevant legal instruments are the Treaty of Paris from 1898, the Platt Amendment process initiated in 1901, base lease agreements in 1903, and a bilateral treaty in 1934. This article highlighted the following three points from postcolonial legal analysis relevant to Guantánamo: (1) that legal narratives deny sovereignty to certain populations in order to exert overseas control; (2) that American constitutional law excludes various individual rights protections overseas; and (3) that American constitutional law creates ambiguities and ambivalences in the rule of law overseas.

Sovereignty continues to be the reference point for legal approaches to overseas authority. This is obvious whether sovereignty is checked in the Platt Amendment in 1901 or found to be de facto by the *Boumediene* Court. Likewise, individual rights protections are potentially excluded when US authority extends abroad. This occurs whether in the fundamental rights distinction of the *Insular Cases* (1901–1920) or more recently in MCA and DTA efforts to deny the writ to Guantánamo detainees. Developed from informal and formal colonial encounters, American law regarding overseas authority purposefully created ambivalences and ambiguities in the law. These legal anomalies currently have normative and doctrinal impacts. The most vivid and applicable example exists in the United States having "complete jurisdiction and control" over the base and Cuba having "ultimate sovereignty." This lack of clarity suited US needs to occupy a base over a century ago, but it has been used for over seventeen years to detain foreign civilians. This legal anomaly also permits US authority to escape limits in constitutional and international law because detention occurs on territory that is neither fully within a foreign sovereign jurisdiction nor clearly within domestic US jurisdiction.

A preliminary analysis of developments since *Boumediene* suggests similar anomalous situations are emerging. Briefly, this article has examined a recent executive order to end the Guantánamo detentions and dispose detainees to other locations, initial habeas proceedings to release detainees, and legal challenges to detention by the United States in Afghanistan. In each of these situations, individual rights are clouded by anomaly. The parameters of detention authority get lost amidst determinations of sovereignty and territorial distinctions of foreign versus domestic. Similar to Guantánamo, anomaly is shaped by policy objectives seeking to avoid sovereign authority overseas, limit sovereignty authority for other states, avoid constitutional limitation abroad, and protect strategic interests. Here, the interests are intelligence gathering and detention during the War on Terror. Checks to detention authority are avoided by mitigating sovereign authority with agreements to lease bases, transfers of custody authority, or claims of judicial immunity over immigration authority. While this analysis is extremely preliminary, it suggests postcolonial approaches to examining the law of overseas authority should not be limited to habeas rights and a base in Cuba.

Taking these suggestions on the doctrine and theory of overseas detention at Guantánamo, it appears that the "empire strikes back." The legal legacy of imperial influence is not limited to history in 1898, old European practices, or "a long time ago in a galaxy far, far away . . ." (as the *Star Wars* movies explain). Instead, these legacies have current legal currency in base occupation and base detention on Guantánamo, Cuba. Postcolonial legal theory suggests that the "empire strikes back" with legal ambivalences shaped by objectives to avoid sovereignty, limit sovereign powers for foreign states, avoid constitutional protections abroad, and protect strategic overseas interests. With doctrinal narratives, we see sovereignty is manipulated and the Constitution is severed to endorse overseas authority. The narratives are both historic and present. Within this discourse, legal goals of indefinite detention and protecting individual rights ambiguously coexist. Whether these goals belong to Lord Darth Vader in a fictional story, US General Leonard Wood in Cuba in 1902, Guantánamo detainees since 2002, or US base authority since 1898, they seek normative doctrinal force.

30

AL MAQALEH V. GATES

US Court of Appeals,
DC Circuit
Fadi AL MAQALEH, Detainee and Ahmad Al Maqaleh,
as Next Friend of Fadi Al Maqaleh, Appellees
v.
Robert M. GATES, Secretary, United States Department of Defense,
et al., Appellants.

Argued Jan. 7, 2010.
Decided May 21, 2010.

SENTELLE, Chief Judge:

Three detainees at Bagram Air Force Base in Afghanistan petitioned the district court for habeas corpus relief from their confinement by the United States military. Appellants (collectively "the United States" or "the government") moved to dismiss for lack of jurisdiction based on § 7(a) of the Military Commissions Act of 2006 ("MCA"). The district court [a]greed with the United States that § 7(a) of the MCA purported to deprive the court of jurisdiction, but held that this section could not constitutionally be applied to deprive the court of jurisdiction under the Supreme Court's test articulated in *Boumediene v.*

Bush (2008). The court therefore denied the motion to dismiss but certified the three habeas cases for interlocutory appeal. Pursuant to that certification, the government filed a petition to this court for interlocutory appeal. We granted the petition and now consider the jurisdictional question. Upon review, and applying the Supreme Court decision in *Boumediene*, we determine that the district court did not have jurisdiction to consider the petitions for habeas corpus. We therefore reverse the order of the district court and order that the petitions be dismissed.

I. BACKGROUND

A. The Petitioners

All three petitioners are being held as unlawful enemy combatants at the Bagram Theater Internment Facility on the Bagram Airfield Military Base in Afghanistan. Petitioner Fadi Al-Maqaleh is a Yemeni citizen who alleges he was taken into custody in 2003. While Al-Maqaleh's petition asserts "on information and belief" that he was captured beyond Afghan borders, a sworn declaration from Colonel James W. Gray, Commander of Detention Operations, states that Al-Maqaleh was captured in Zabul, Afghanistan. Redha Al-Najar is a Tunisian citizen who alleges he was captured in Pakistan in 2002. Amin Al-Bakri is a Yemeni citizen who alleges he was captured in Thailand in 2002. Both Al-Najar and Al-Bakri allege they were first held in some other unknown location before being moved to Bagram.

B. The Place of Confinement

Bagram Airfield Military Base is the largest military facility in Afghanistan occupied by United States and coalition forces. The United

423

States entered into an "Accommodation Consignment Agreement for Lands and Facilities at Bagram Airfield" with the Islamic Republic of Afghanistan in 2006, which "consigns all facilities and land located at Bagram Airfield . . . owned by [Afghanistan,] or Parwan Province, or private individuals, or others, for use by the United States and coalition forces for military purposes." (Accommodation and Consignment Agreement for Lands and Facilities at Bagram Airfield Between the Islamic Republic of Afghanistan and the United States of America) (internal capitalization altered [in original]). The Agreement refers to Afghanistan as the "host nation" and the United States "as the lessee." The leasehold created by the agreement is to continue "until the United States or its successors determine that the premises are no longer required for its use." *Id.* (internal capitalization altered [in original]).

Afghanistan remains a theater of active military combat. The United States and coalition forces conduct "an ongoing military campaign against al Qaeda, the Taliban regime, and their affiliates and supporters in Afghanistan." These operations are conducted in part from Bagram Airfield. Bagram has been subject to repeated attacks from the Taliban and al Qaeda, including a March 2009 suicide bombing striking the gates of the facility, and Taliban rocket attacks in June of 2009 resulting in death and injury to United States service members and other personnel.

While the United States provides overall security to Bagram, numerous other nations have compounds on the base. Some of the other nations control access to their respective compounds. The troops of the other nations are present at Bagram both as part of the American-led military coalition in Afghanistan and as members of the International Security Assistance Force (ISAF) of the North Atlantic Treaty Organization. The mission of the ISAF is to support the Afghan government in the maintenance of security in Afghanistan. According to the United

States, as of February 1, 2010, approximately 38,000 non-United States troops were serving in Afghanistan as part of the ISAF, representing 42 other countries.

C. The Litigation

Appellees in this action, three detainees at Bagram, filed habeas petitions against the President of the United States and the Secretary of Defense in the district court. The government moved to dismiss for lack of jurisdiction, relying principally upon § 7(a) of the Military Commissions Act of 2006. The district court consolidated these three cases and a fourth case, not a part of these proceedings, for argument. After the change in presidential administrations on January 22, 2009, the court invited the government to express any change in its position on the jurisdictional question. The government informed the district court that it "adheres to its previously articulated position."

The district court, recognizing that the issue of whether the court had jurisdiction presented a controlling question of law as to which there were substantial grounds for difference of opinion, certified the question for interlocutory appeal. We accepted the case for interlocutory review, bringing the jurisdictional issue before us in the present appeal.

II. ANALYSIS

A. The Legal Framework

While we will discuss specific points of law in more detail below, for a full understanding, we must first set forth some of the legal history underlying the controversy over the availability of the writ of habeas corpus and the constitutional protections it effectuates to noncitizens of the United States held beyond the sovereign territory of the United States. The Supreme Court first addressed this issue in *Johnson v. Eisentrager* (1950). In *Eisentrager* 21 German nationals petitioned the district court for writs of habeas corpus. The *Eisentrager* petitioners had been convicted by a military commission in China of "engaging in, permitting or ordering continued military activity against the United States after surrender of Germany and before surrender of Japan." Because, during that period, the United States and Germany were no longer at war, hostile acts against the United States by German citizens were violations of the law of war. Petitioners were captured in China, tried in China, and repatriated to Germany to serve their sentences in Landsberg Prison, a facility under the control of the United States as part of the Allied Powers' post-war occupation. None ever entered the United States, nor were any held in the United States.

Petitioners sought habeas relief, alleging that their confinement was in violation of the Constitution and laws of the United States and the Geneva Convention. . . .

. . . .

. . . The Supreme Court [ultimately] granted review. . . . [T]he Court noted that "[w]e are cited to no instance where a court, in this or any other country where the writ is known, has issued it on behalf of an alien enemy who, at no relevant time and in no stage of his captivity, has been within its territorial jurisdiction."

The Court went on to hold that the writ was unavailable to the enemy aliens beyond the sovereign territory of the United States. The Court did not end its discussion with the language concerning sovereignty, however. It noted that trial of the writ "would hamper the war effort and bring aid and comfort to the enemy." The Court further noted that such trial would constitute "effective fettering of a field commander," by allowing "the very enemies he is ordered to reduce to submission to call him to account in his own civil courts and divert his efforts and attention from the military offensive abroad to the legal defensive at home."

The *Eisentrager* case remained the governing precedent concerning the jurisdiction of United States courts over habeas petitions on behalf of aliens held outside the sovereign territory of the United States until the Court revisited the question in *Rasul v. Bush* (2004). In *Rasul* the petitioners were aliens (not from enemy nations) who were captured abroad during hostilities between the United States and the Taliban. The United States transported them to the naval base at Guantanamo Bay, Cuba, which the United States holds under a 1903 lease agreement specifying that: "the United States recognizes the continuance of the ultimate sovereignty of the Republic of Cuba over the [leased areas]." Thus, the habeas corpus petitioners were foreign nationals, not from nations currently in a state of war with the United States, taken by the United States military, and transported to locations outside the sovereign territory of the United States. . . .

. . . .

The Supreme Court in *Rasul* reasoned that because [a later case] overruled the statutory predicate to *Eisentrager*'s holding, *Eisentrager* did not compel a holding that the courts lack jurisdiction to issue the writ. The *Rasul* Court then held that the habeas statute did extend geographically to the base at which the petitioners were held in Guantanamo. "At common law, courts exercised habeas jurisdiction over the claims of aliens detained within sovereign territory of the realm. . . ."

Citing Lord Mansfield from 1759, the *Rasul* majority stated that "there was 'no doubt' as to the court's power to issue writs of habeas corpus if the territory was 'under the subjection of the Crown.'" The Court noted that no one questioned the district court's jurisdiction over the custodians of the petitioners and "therefore [held] that § 2241 confers on the district court jurisdiction to hear petitioners' habeas corpus challenges to the legality of their detention at the Guantanamo Bay Naval Base." Finally, the Court concluded that

> [w]hat is presently at stake is . . . whether the federal courts have jurisdiction to determine the legality of the Executive's potentially indefinite detention of individuals who claim to be wholly innocent of wrongdoing.

The Court "[a]nswer[ed] that question in the affirmative, . . . reverse[d] the judgment of the Court of Appeals and remand[ed] the [ ] cases for the district court to consider in the first instance the merits of the petitioners' claims."

Responding to the *Rasul* decision, Congress passed the Detainee Treatment Act of 2005 (DTA), which President Bush signed into law on December 30 of that year. Among other things, that Act added a new provision to the Habeas Act which provided that:

> Except as provided in section 1005 of the [DTA] no court, justice, or judge shall have jurisdiction to hear or consider—
>
> (1) an application for a writ of habeas corpus filed by or on behalf of an alien detained by the Department of Defense at Guantanamo Bay, Cuba; or
>
> (2) any other action against the United States or its agents relating to any aspect of the detention by the Department of Defense of an alien at Guantanamo Bay, Cuba, who

(A)   is currently in military custody; or

(B)   has been determined by the United States Court of Appeals for the District of Columbia Circuit ... to have been properly detained as an enemy combatant.

In June of 2006, the Supreme Court decided *Hamdan v. Rumsfeld.* ... In *Hamdan*, the Supreme Court held that the DTA did not operate to strip the federal courts of jurisdiction to hear petitions for writs of habeas corpus on behalf of Guantanamo detainees that were pending at the time of the DTA's enactment. Therefore, the Supreme Court reversed this court's dismissal of the petitions and remanded again for further proceedings.

In October of 2006, in response to the *Hamdan* decision, Congress passed the Military Commissions Act of 2006 (MCA). That Act, among many other things, included a further amendment to the habeas statute. The new amendment reads:

(1) No court, justice, or judge shall have jurisdiction to hear or consider an application for a writ of habeas corpus filed by or on behalf of an alien detained by the United States who has been determined by the United States to have been properly detained as an enemy combatant or is awaiting such determination.

(2) Except as provided in [section 1005(e)(2) and (e)(3) of the DTA], no court, justice, or judge shall have jurisdiction to hear or consider any other action against the United States or its agents relating to any aspect of the detention, transfer, treatment, trial, or conditions of confinement of an alien who is or was detained by the United States and has been determined by the United States to have been properly detained as an enemy combatant or is awaiting such determination.

Congress went on to explicitly state:

> The amendment made by subsection (a) shall take effect on the date
> of the enactment of this Act, and shall apply to all cases, without
> exception, pending on or after the date of the enactment of this Act
> which relate to any aspect of the detention, transfer, treatment, trial,
> or conditions of detention of an alien detained by the United States
> since September 11, 2001.

This clearer statement of congressional intent to strip the courts of
habeas jurisdiction set the stage for an inevitable determination of the
constitutionality of such a stripping in light of the Suspension Clause,
U.S. CONST. Art. I, § 9, cl. 2.... [That case was decided by the
Supreme Court in *Boumediene v. Bush* (2008).]

. . . .

At the outset, the Supreme Court [found] that the Military Commissions Act did in fact "deprive [ ] the federal courts of jurisdiction to
entertain the habeas corpus actions" by the detainees held at Guantanamo Bay. The Court therefore faced the constitutional questions

> whether petitioners are barred from seeking the writ or invoking the
> protections of the Suspension Clause either because of their status, . . .
> designation by the Executive Branch as enemy combatants, or their
> physical location . . . at Guantanamo Bay.

In a thorough and detailed opinion, the Court undertook its
inquiry into the constitutional questions on two levels. First, it explored
the breadth of the Court's holding in *Eisentrager* (still not overruled) in
response to the argument by the United States that constitutional rights

protected by the writ of habeas corpus under the Suspension Clause extended only to territories over which the United States held *de jure* sovereignty. Second, it explored the more general question of extension of constitutional rights and the concomitant constitutional restrictions on governmental power exercised extraterritorially and with respect to noncitizens. In so doing, the Court set forth a "broad historical narrative of the writ [of habeas corpus] and its function...." While the Court concluded that the historical record did not provide a clear answer, it accepted the government's position that the United States did not exercise *de jure* sovereignty over Guantanamo Bay, but took notice of "the obvious and uncontested fact that the United States, by virtue of its complete jurisdiction and control over the base, maintains *de facto* sovereignty over this territory." However, the Court further concluded that "the Government's premise that *de jure* sovereignty is the touchstone of habeas jurisdiction . . . is unfounded."

The Court reasoned that the adoption of a bright-line rule based on *de jure* sovereignty would be inconsistent with a long line of Supreme Court cases exploring "the Constitution's geographic scope." In explaining this proposition, the Court explored the series of opinions known as the "*Insular Cases*," in which the Court had "addressed whether the Constitution, by its own force, applies in any territory that is not a state." The *Boumediene* Court recalled the practical doctrine drawn from the *Insular Cases* and applied in . . . later decisions . . . , applying the Constitution by its own force in territories which were destined for apparent statehood, but recognizing a more practical and selective application of constitutional protection of rights in territories temporarily held by the United States, or in acts by the United States government outside United States territory altogether.

More directly pertinent to the issue before us today, the Court stated that "nothing in *Eisentrager* says that *de jure* sovereignty is or has ever been the only relevant consideration in determining the geographic reach of the Constitution or of habeas corpus." The Court explained that such a holding would have been inconsistent with the *Insular Cases* and [the later case of *Reid v. Covert* (1957)]. Seeing no need to create such a conflict between its holdings, the Court found what it called "a common thread uniting the *Insular Cases*, *Eisentrager*, and *Reid*: the idea that questions of extraterritoriality turn on objective factors and practical concerns, not formalism."

Applying the "common thread" to the question of the jurisdiction of United States courts to consider habeas petitions from detainees in Guantanamo, the Court concluded that "at least three factors are relevant in determining the reach of the Suspension Clause." Those three factors, which we must apply today in answering the same question as to detainees at Bagram, are:

> (1) the citizenship and status of the detainee and the adequacy of the process through which that status determination was made; (2) the nature of the sites where apprehension and then detention took place; and (3) the practical obstacles inherent in resolving the prisoner's entitlement to the writ.

Applying these factors to the detainees at Guantanamo, the Court held that the petitioners had the protection of the Suspension Clause.

B. Application to the Bagram Petitioners

Our duty, as explained above, is to determine the reach of the right to habeas corpus and therefore of the Suspension Clause to the factual context underlying the petitions we consider in the present appeal. In doing so, we are controlled by the Supreme Court's interpretation of the Constitution in *Eisentrager* as construed and explained in the Court's more recent opinion in *Boumediene*. This is not an easy task, as illustrated by the thorough and careful opinion of the district court. While we are properly respectful of the district court's careful undertaking of this difficult task, as we review rulings on motions to dismiss under Federal Rule of Civil Procedure 12 *de novo,* we reexamine the issue and ultimately reach a different conclusion.

At the outset, we note that each of the parties has asserted both an extreme understanding of the law after *Boumediene* and a more nuanced set of arguments upon which each relies in anticipation of the possible rejection of the bright-line arguments. The United States would like us to hold that the *Boumediene* analysis has no application beyond territories that are, like Guantanamo, outside the *de jure* sovereignty of the United States but are subject to its *de facto* sovereignty. As the government puts it in its reply brief, "[t]he real question before this Court, therefore, is whether Bagram may be considered effectively part of the United States in light of the nature and history of the U.S. presence there." We disagree.

[Editors' Note: The court then discussed its rejection of that government argument.]

. . . .

For similar reasons, we reject the most extreme position offered by the petitioners. At various points, the petitioners seem to be arguing that the fact of United States control of Bagram under the lease of the military base is sufficient to trigger the extraterritorial application of the Suspension Clause, or at least satisfy the second factor of the three set forth in *Boumediene*. Again, we reject this extreme understanding. Such an interpretation would seem to create the potential for the extraterritorial extension of the Suspension Clause to noncitizens held in any United States military facility in the world, and perhaps to an undeterminable number of other United States-leased facilities as well. Significantly, the court engaged in an extended dialog with counsel for the petitioners in which we repeatedly sought some limiting principle that would distinguish Bagram from any other military installation. Counsel was able to produce no such distinction. Again, such an extended application is not a tenable interpretation of *Boumediene*. If it were the Supreme Court's intention to declare such a sweeping application, it would surely have said so. Just as we reject the extreme argument of the United States that would render most of the decision in *Boumediene* dicta, we reject the first line of argument offered by petitioners. Having rejected the bright-line arguments of both parties, we must proceed to their more nuanced arguments, and reach a conclusion based on the application of the Supreme Court's enumerated factors to the case before us.

The first of the enumerated factors is "the citizenship and status of the detainee and the adequacy of the process through which that status determination was made." Citizenship is, of course, an important factor in determining the constitutional rights of persons before the court. It is well established that there are "constitutional decisions of [the Supreme] Court expressly according differing protection to aliens than to citizens." *United States v. Verdugo-Urquidez* (1990). However, clearly the alien citizenship of the petitioners in this case does not weigh against their claim to protection of the right of habeas corpus under the Suspension Clause. So far as citizenship is concerned, they differ in no material respect from the petitioners at Guantanamo who prevailed in *Boumediene*. As to status, the petitioners before us are held as enemy aliens. But so were the *Boumediene* petitioners. While the *Eisentrager* petitioners were in a weaker position by having the status of war criminals, that is immaterial to the question before us. This question is governed by *Boumediene* and the status of the petitioners before us again is the same as the Guantanamo detainees, so this factor supports their argument for the extension of the availability of the writ.

So far as the adequacy of the process through which that status determination was made, the petitioners are in a stronger position for the availability of the writ than were either the *Eisentrager* or *Boumediene* petitioners. As the Supreme Court noted, the *Boumediene* petitioners were in a very different posture than those in *Eisentrager* in that "there ha[d] been no trial by military commission for violations of the laws of war." Unlike the *Boumediene* petitioners or those before us, "[t]he *Eisentrager* petitioners were charged by a bill of particulars that made detailed factual allegations against them." The *Eisentrager* detainees were "entitled to representation by counsel, allowed to introduce evidence on their own behalf, and permitted to cross-examine the prosecution's witnesses" in an adversarial proceeding. The status of the *Boumediene* petitioners was determined by Combatant Status Review Tribunals (CSRTs) affording far less protection. Under the CSRT proceeding, the detainee, rather than being represented by an attorney, was advised by a "Personal Representative" who was "not the detainee's lawyer or even his 'advocate.'" The CSRT proceeding was less protective than the military tribunal procedures in *Eisentrager* in other particulars as well, and the Supreme Court clearly stated that "[t]he difference is not trivial."

The status of the Bagram detainees is determined not by a Combatant Status Review Tribunal but by an "Unlawful Enemy Combatant Review Board" (UECRB). As the district court correctly noted, proceedings before the UECRB afford even less protection to the rights of detainees in the determination of status than was the case with the CSRT. Therefore, as the district court noted, "while the important adequacy of process factor strongly supported the extension of the Suspension Clause and habeas rights in *Boumediene*, it even more strongly favors petitioners here." Therefore, examining only the first of the Supreme Court's three enumerated factors, petitioners have made a strong argument that the right to habeas relief and the Suspension Clause apply in Bagram as in Guantanamo. However, we do not stop with the first factor.

The second factor, "the nature of the sites where apprehension and then detention took place," weighs heavily in favor of the United States. Like all petitioners in both *Eisentrager* and *Boumediene*, the petitioners here were apprehended abroad. While this in itself would appear to weigh against the extension of the writ, it obviously would not be sufficient, otherwise *Boumediene* would not have been decided as it was. However, the nature of the place where the detention takes place weighs more strongly in favor of the position argued by the United States and against the extension of habeas jurisdiction than was the case in either *Boumediene* or *Eisentrager*. In the first place, while *de facto* sovereignty is not determinative, for the reasons discussed above, the very fact that it was the subject of much discussion in *Boumediene* makes it obvious that it is not without relevance. As the Supreme Court set forth, Guantanamo Bay is "a territory that, while technically not part of the United States, is under the complete and total control of our Government." While it is true that the United States holds a leasehold interest in Bagram, and held a leasehold interest in Guantanamo, the surrounding circumstances are hardly the same. The United States has maintained its total control of Guantanamo Bay for over a century, even in the face of a hostile government maintaining *de jure* sovereignty over the property. In Bagram, while the United States has options as to duration of the lease agreement, there is no indication of any intent to occupy the base with permanence, nor is there hostility on the part of the "host" country.

Therefore, the notion that *de facto* sovereignty extends to Bagram is no more real than would have been the same claim with respect to Lands-berg in the *Eisentrager* case. While it is certainly realistic to assert that the United States has *de facto* sovereignty over Guantanamo, the same simply is not true with respect to Bagram. Though the site of detention analysis weighs in favor of the United States and against the petitioners, it is not determinative.

But we hold that the third factor, that is "the practical obstacles inherent in resolving the prisoner's entitlement to the writ," particularly when considered along with the second factor, weighs overwhelmingly in favor of the position of the United States. It is undisputed that Bagram, indeed the entire nation of Afghanistan, remains a theater of war. Not only does this suggest that the detention at Bagram is more like the detention at Landsberg than Guantanamo, the position of the United States is even stronger in this case than it was in *Eisentrager*. As the Supreme Court recognized in *Boumediene*, even though the active hostilities in the European theater had "c[o]me to an end," at the time of the *Eisentrager* decision, many of the problems of a theater of war remained:

> In addition to supervising massive reconstruction and aid efforts the American forces stationed in Germany faced potential security threats from a defeated enemy. In retrospect the post-War occupation may seem uneventful. But at the time *Eisentrager* was decided, the Court was right to be concerned about judicial interference with the military's efforts to contain "enemy elements, guerilla fighters, and 'were-wolves.'"

In ruling for the extension of the writ to Guantanamo, the Supreme Court expressly noted that "[s]imilar threats are not apparent here." In the case before us, similar, if not greater, threats are indeed apparent. The United States asserts, and petitioners cannot credibly dispute, that all of the attributes of a facility exposed to the vagaries of war are present in Bagram. The Supreme Court expressly stated in *Boumediene* that at Guantanamo, "[w]hile obligated to abide by the terms of the lease, the United States is, for all practical purposes, answerable to no other sovereign for its acts on the base. Were that not the case, *or if the detention facility were located in an active theater of war*, arguments that issuing the writ would be 'impractical or anomalous' would have more weight." Indeed, the Supreme Court supported this proposition with reference to the separate opinion of Justice Harlan in *Reid*, where the Justice expressed his doubts that "every provision of the Constitution must always be deemed automatically applicable to United States citizens in every part of the world." (Harlan, J., concurring in the result). We therefore conclude that under both *Eisentrager* and *Boumediene*, the writ does not extend to the Bagram confinement in an active theater of war in a territory under neither the *de facto* nor *de jure* sovereignty of the United States and within the territory of another *de jure* sovereign.

We are supported in this conclusion by the rationale of *Eisentrager*, which was not only not overruled, but reinforced by the language and reasoning just referenced from *Boumediene*. As we referenced in the background discussion of this opinion, we set forth more fully now concerns expressed by the Supreme Court in reaching its decision in *Eisentrager*:

> Such trials would hamper the war effort and bring aid and comfort to the enemy. They would diminish the prestige of our commanders, not only with enemies but with wavering neutrals. It would be difficult to devise more effective fettering of a field commander than to allow the very enemies he is ordered to reduce to submission to call him to account in his own civil courts and divert his efforts and attention

from the military offensive abroad to the legal defensive at home. Nor is it unlikely that the result of such enemy litigiousness would be a conflict between judicial and military opinion highly comforting to enemies of the United States.

Those factors are more relevant to the situation at Bagram than they were at Landsberg. While it is true, as the Supreme Court noted in *Boumediene*, that the United States forces in Germany in 1950 faced the possibility of unrest and guerilla warfare, operations in the European theater had ended with the surrender of Germany and Italy years earlier. Bagram remains in a theater of war. We cannot, consistent with *Eisentrager* as elucidated by *Boumediene*, hold that the right to the writ of habeas corpus and the constitutional protections of the Suspension Clause extend to Bagram detention facility in Afghanistan, and we therefore must reverse the decision of the district court denying the motion of the United States to dismiss the petitions.

We do not ignore the arguments of the detainees that the United States chose the place of detention and might be able "to evade judicial review of Executive detention decisions by transferring detainees into active conflict zones, thereby granting the Executive the power to switch the Constitution on or off at will." However, that is not what happened here. Indeed, without dismissing the legitimacy or sincerity of appellees' concerns, we doubt that this fact goes to either the second or third of the Supreme Court's enumerated factors. We need make no determination on the importance of this possibility, given that it remains only a possibility; its resolution can await a case in which the claim is a reality rather than a speculation. In so stating, we note that the Supreme Court did not dictate that the three enumerated factors are exhaustive. It only told us that "*at least* three factors" are relevant. Perhaps such manipulation by the Executive might constitute an additional factor in some case in which it is in fact present. However, the notion that the United States deliberately confined the detainees in the theater of war rather than at, for example, Guantanamo, is not only unsupported by the evidence, it is not supported by reason. To have made such a deliberate decision to "turn off the Constitution" would have required the military commanders or other Executive officials making the situs determination to anticipate the complex litigation history set forth above and predict the *Boumediene* decision long before it came down.

Also supportive of our decision that the third factor weighs heavily in favor of the United States, as the district court recognized, is the fact that the detention is within the sovereign territory of another nation, which itself creates practical difficulties. Indeed, it was on this factor that the district court relied in dismissing the fourth petition, which was filed by an Afghan citizen detainee. While that factor certainly weighed more heavily with respect to an Afghan citizen, it is not without force with respect to detainees who are alien to both the United States and Afghanistan. The United States holds the detainees pursuant to a cooperative arrangement with Afghanistan on territory as to which Afghanistan is sovereign. While we cannot say that extending our constitutional protections to the detainees would be in any way disruptive of that relationship, neither can we say with certainty what the reaction of the Afghan government would be.

In sum, taken together, the second and especially the third factors compel us to hold that the petitions should have been dismissed.

CONCLUSION

For the reasons set forth above, we hold that the jurisdiction of the courts to afford the right to habeas relief and the protection of the Suspension Clause does not extend to aliens held in Executive detention in the Bagram detention facility in the Afghan theater of war. We therefore reverse the order of the district court denying the motion for dismissal of the United States and order that the petitions be dismissed for lack of jurisdiction.

So ordered.

WORST-CASE JUSTICE
We're Holding Terrorism Suspects without Trial, But Should We?
A Task Force Gives Recommendations

Editorial, Los Angeles Times, *June 15, 2010*

Even as it plans civilian trials for some detainees at Guantanamo Bay, the Obama administration has reserved the right to hold others without trial under the Authorization for Use of Military Force approved by Congress after 9/11. As President Obama put it: "I am not going to release individuals who endanger the American people."

Imprisonment without trial violates the most fundamental principles of American due process and can be countenanced only under our traditionally accepted practice of holding enemy combatants as prisoners of war until a cessation of hostilities. Such cases should be exceedingly rare and subject to stringent outside review. The recommendations of an interagency task force convened by Obama that were recently made public fail to meet that standard.

The task force recommends that the administration detain forty-eight prisoners without trial. And although those inmates have the right to challenge their confinement in federal court, judges lack guidance about whether and on what grounds they should order any prisoner's release.

The task force's report confirms the popular assumption that some suspects can't be put on trial even if they have committed terrorist acts, because evidence was gathered on a battlefield and "was neither garnered nor preserved with an eye toward prosecuting them." Others, while active in al Qaeda, couldn't be tied to specific plots. The report says that the principal obstacles to prosecution are not tainted evidence (presumably obtained by torture) or a desire to protect sources.

The report cites four grounds for holding a detainee without trial: a significant organizational role in al Qaeda, the Taliban, or "associated forces"; advanced training or combat experience with forces targeted by the Authorization for Use of Military Force; an expression by the prisoner of an intention to "reengage in extremist activity upon release"; and a history of association with extremist activity or "strong ties (either directly or through family members) to extremist organizations."

Of these criteria, only the first and second strike us as even vaguely justified by the fact that Congress has approved the equivalent of a declaration of war against al Qaeda and the Taliban. None of them, without further explanation, distinguishes between authentic preventive detention and imprisonment without trial for criminal punishment or political expediency. As the history of Guantánamo demonstrates, there is the possibility of error, exaggeration, or mistaken identity. What's more, in a conflict that, unlike past wars, is open-ended, we're concerned that people could end up being held for years, theoretically even for life, under this plan. The task force notes that there will be periodic reviews by the executive branch, but we believe that there must be oversight of detention decisions by an independent body. And the burden should rest on the government to demonstrate that there is a high risk of imminent harm to Americans that the detention is meant to prevent.

The report notes that judicial review is already assured by a 2008 Supreme Court decision holding that Guantanamo inmates have a constitutional right to challenge their confinement by seeking writs of habeas corpus. But the justices didn't provide detailed guidance to lower courts about how to evaluate such claims. As a result, according to a Brookings Institution report, judges "disagree about what the government needs to prove to a court to sign off on a detention, about what evidence it may employ in doing so."

One remedy to that would be legislation providing guidance to the courts—including, perhaps, a new, specialized tribunal that, to the extent possible, would function in public while allowing judges to consider classified information when necessary. Alternatively, the Supreme Court could agree to review a case that would allow it to provide detailed instructions to lower courts about what level of threat justifies detention without trial and what showing the government must make. Either way, this and future administrations must be put on notice that they will be able to detain indefinitely only the "worst of the worst," and only if it's absolutely impossible to prosecute them for past acts. (Those standards should apply not only to inmates now held at Guantanamo but also to detainees captured away from a battlefield in the future.)

Obama's decision to hold some prisoners without trial creates a dilemma for those who oppose preventive detention: Allowing the status quo to continue is unsatisfactory, but action by Congress or the high court to provide judicial review would institutionalize a practice abhorrent to fundamental American principles. We uneasily would choose the second course, but only if the courts subject the executive branch's decisions to searching and sustained scrutiny.

AUTHORS OF SELECTIONS

JENNIFER CHACÓN, Professor of Law and Senior Associate Dean for Academic Affairs, University of California, Irvine School of Law.

ERWIN CHEMERINSKY, current and founding Dean, Professor of Law, University of California, Irvine School of Law.

MARJORIE COHN, Professor of Law, Thomas Jefferson School of Law; former president of the National Lawyers Guild.

DAVID COLE, John Carroll Research Professor of Law, Georgetown University Law Center.

M. KATHERINE BAIRD DARMER, Professor of Law, Chapman University School of Law.

RICHARD D. FYBEL, Associate Justice, California Court of Appeal, District Four, Division Three (Santa Ana).

ERNESTO HERNÁNDEZ-LÓPEZ, Associate Professor of Law, Chapman University School of Law.

WENDY KAMINER, author, lawyer, senior correspondent for the *American Prospect*, contributing writer for the *Atlantic*, the *New York Times*,

AUTHORS OF SELECTIONS

the *Wall Street Journal*, *Newsweek*, *Dissent*, the *Nation*, the *Wilson Quarterly*, and *Free Inquiry*.

ORIN KERR, Professor of Law, The George Washington University Law School.

JOHN T. PARRY, Professor of Law, Lewis & Clark Law School.

ROBERT J. PUSHAW JR., James Wilson Endowed Professor of Law, Pepperdine University School of Law.

WILLIAM H. REHNQUIST, former chief justice, United States Supreme Court.

SUDHA SETTY, Professor of Law, Western New England College School of Law

STUART TAYLOR JR., columnist for *National Journal*, contributing editor at *Newsweek*.

JOHN TEHRANIAN, Professor of Law, Chapman University School of Law.

JEREMY WALDRON, University Professor, New York University School of Law.

WELSH S. WHITE, former Professor of Law, University of Pittsburgh.

TUNG YIN, Professor of Law, Lewis & Clark Law School.

NOTES

INTRODUCTION

1. Portions of this introduction are adapted from the precursor volume.

CHAPTER 1

1. I am indebted to Professor Michael Bazyler of Chapman Law School for sharing his vast knowledge of Holocaust legal issues. Professor Bazyler accurately describes the German legal system as "legal barbarism." I am also grateful to Dr. Marilyn Harran, Stern Chair in Holocaust History and the Director of Chapman's Rodgers Center for Holocaust Education. She recommended key books and other resources for my research.

2. The sources for this chronology are United States Holocaust Memorial Museum, "The Anti-Jewish Legislation of Nazi Germany from 1933–1945," in "The Holocaust, Genocide, and the Law," ed. Michael J. Bazyler, http://www.michael balyzer.com/downloads/HolocaustReaderFall%202008 aChapman.doc (accessed February 8, 2011); and Diemut Majer, "Non-Germans" under the Third Reich: The Nazi Judicial and Administrative System in Germany and Occupied Eastern Europe, with Special Regard to Occupied Poland, 1939–1945, trans. Peter Thomas Hill, Edward Vance, and Brian Levin (Baltimore, MD: Johns Hopkins University Press, 2003).

3. Majer, "Non-Germans" under the Third Reich, p. 6.

4. William F. Meinecke Jr. and Alexandra Zapruder, Law, Justice, and the

Holocaust (Washington, DC: United States Holocaust Memorial Museum, 2009), pp. 8–10.

5. Richard J. Evans, *The Third Reich in Power: 1933–1939* (New York: Penguin Books, 2005), p. 42.

6. As of August 20, 1934, the oath became: "I swear I will be true and obedient to the Führer of the German Reich and people, Adolf Hitler, observe the law, and conscientiously fulfill the duties of my office, so help me God." Before this change, the oath read: "I swear loyalty to the Constitution, obedience to the law, and conscientious fulfillment of the duties of my office, so help me God" (Meinecke and Zapruder, *Law, Justice, and the Holocaust*, p. 20).

7. Eva Fogelman, *Conscience & Courage: Rescuers of Jews during the Holocaust* (New York: Anchor Books, 1994), p. 24.

8. Meinecke and Zapruder, *Law, Justice, and the Holocaust*, pp. 32–34.

9. Martin Gilbert, *Kristallnacht: Prelude to Destruction* (New York: HarperCollins, 2006), p. 13.

10. Ibid.

11. Ibid.

12. Ibid., p. 33.

13. H. W. Koch, *In the Name of the Volk: Political Justice in Hitler's Germany* (New York: I. B. Tauris, 1997), p. 4.

14. Ingo Müller, *Hitler's Justice: The Courts of the Third Reich* (Cambridge, MA: Harvard University Press, 1994), p. 141.

15. Majer, *"Non-Germans" under the Third Reich*, p. 360, n. 100.

16. Müller, *Hitler's Justice*, p. 141.

17. Koch, *In the Name of the Volk*, p. 5.

18. Ibid., p. 57.

19. Majer, *"Non-Germans" under the Third Reich*, p. 350.

20. Ibid., p. 351.

21. Ibid., p. 361.

22. Koch, *In the Name of the Volk*, p. 5; Majer, *"Non-Germans" under the Third Reich*, p. 365.

23. Majer, *"Non-Germans" under the Third Reich*, p. 10.

24. Evans, *The Third Reich in Power*, p. 73.

25. Koch, *In the Name of the Volk*, p. 84.

26. Ibid., p. 119.

27. Ibid., p. 120.

28. Evans, *The Third Reich in Power*, p. 73.

29. Koch, *In the Name of the Volk*, p. 119.

30. Ibid., p. 119. According to a presentation prepared by the United States Holocaust Memorial Museum, an attorney prosecutor resigned instead of taking the oath to Hitler. In August 1934, prosecutor Martin Gauger submitted his resignation, stating: "After careful consideration I find, in good conscience, that I am not able to swear the loyalty oath to the Reich Chancellor and Führer, Adolf Hitler. . . ." After resigning, Gauger became an attorney for the Confessing Church.

31. Dr. Luther Kreyssig, judge of the Court of Guardianship in Brandenburg on the Havel (Müller, *Hitler's Justice*, pp. 193–95).

32. Fogelman, *Conscience & Courage*, pp. 23–24.

33. Dr. Karl Sack, a general staff judge, and Dr. Johann von Dohnanyi, formerly a supreme court judge, were conspirators in a failed plot to kill Hitler (Müller, *Hitler's Justice*, pp. 192–93).

34. Ibid., p. 192.

35. Majer, *"Non-Germans" under the Third Reich*, p. 352.

36. Ibid.

37. Ibid., p. 361.

38. Claudia Koonz, *The Nazi Conscience* (Cambridge: Belknap Press of Harvard University Press, 2005), p. 168.

39. Ibid., pp. 1–2.

40. Ibid., p. 2.

41. Ibid.

42. Ibid., p. 3.

43. Ibid.

44. Majer, *"Non-Germans" under the Third Reich*, p. 351.

45. Ibid., p. 23.

NOTES

46. American Bar Association, ABA Model Code of Judicial Conduct (2007 ed.), http://www.americanbar.org/content/dam/aba/migrated/judicialethics/ABA_MCJC_approved.authcheckdam.pdf (accessed February 8, 2011).

47. Koch, *In the Name of the Volk*, p. 120.

48. Ibid., p. 120.

49. Ibid.

50. Christopher J. Dodd, *Letters from Nuremberg: My Father's Narrative of a Quest for Justice* (New York: Three Rivers Press, 2007), p. 39.

51. Diane Ackerman, *The Zookeeper's Wife: A War Story* (New York: W. W. Norton & Co., 2007), p. 69.

52. Whitney R. Harris, *Tyranny on Trial: The Trial of the Major German War Criminals at the End of World War II at Nuremberg, Germany, 1945–1946* (Dallas, TX: Southern Methodist University Press), pp. 479, 486.

53. N. Ehrenfreund, *The Nuremberg Legacy: How the Nazi War Trials Changed the Court of History* (New York: Palgrave Macmillan, 2007), p. 96.

54. Harris, *Tyranny on Trial*, p. 551.

55. Meinecke and Zapruder, *Law, Justice, and the Holocaust*, p. 51.

56. Harris, *Tyranny on Trial*, p. 551.

57. Evans, *The Third Reich in Power*, p. 96.

58. Ibid., p. 659.

59. Majer, *"Non-Germans" under the Third Reich*, pp. 556–61.

60. Ibid.

CHAPTER 2

1. *The Prize Cases*, 67 US 635 (1863).

2. *Youngstown Sheet and Tool Company v. Sawyer*, 343 US 579, 635–36 (1952).

3. *Ex Parte Quirin*, 317 US 1 (1942).

4. *Ex Parte Milligan*, 71 US 2 (1866).

5. *Ex Parte Endo*, 323 US 283 (1944).

NOTES

6. *Duncan v. Kahanamoku*, 327 US 304 (1946).

7. Learned Hand, *The Spirit of Liberty* (New York: Alfred A. Knopf, 1952), p. 191.

8. Francis Biddle, *In Brief Authority* (Garden City, NY: Doubleday, 1962), p. 219.

CHAPTER 3

1. Gerald L. Neuman, "Anomalous Zones," *Stanford Law Review* 48 (1996): 1197, 1201.

2. Salman Rushdie, "The Empire Writes Back with a Vengeance," *London Times*, July 3, 1982.

3. See generally Bill Ashcroft, Gareth Griffiths, and Helen Tiffin, *The Empire Writes Back: Theory and Practice in Post-Colonial Literatures* (London: Routledge, 1989).

4. Bill Ashcroft, Gareth Griffiths, and Helen Tiffin, *Post-Colonial Studies: The Key Concepts* (London: Routledge, 2000), p. 186.

5. Edward Said, *Culture and Imperialism* (New York: Knopf, 1993), p. 9.

6. Michael W. Doyle, *Empires* (Ithaca, NY: Cornell University Press, 1986), p. 45.

7. The Insular Cases refer to a series of Supreme Court cases from 1901 to 1922 determining how the US Constitution and international law checked political authority over territorial possessions that were not states in the Union but that lacked international sovereignty, which Spain ceded to the United States in the Treaty of Paris. While including many cases, the most common ones are *Downes v. Bidwell*, 182 US 244 (1901), *Dorr v. United States*, 195 US 138 (1904), and *Balzac v. Porto Rico*, 258 US 298 (1922).

8. Edward Said, *Orientalism* (New York: Vintage Books, 1979).

9. Anthony Anghie, *Imperialism, Sovereignty, and the Making of International Law* (New York: Cambridge University Press, 2004), pp. 3, 4, 10, 103.

10. Peter Fitzpatrick and Eve Darian-Smith, "Laws of the Postcolonial: An

Insistent Introduction," in *Laws of the Postcolonial*, ed. Eve Darian-Smith and Peter Fitzpatrick (Ann Arbor: University of Michigan Press, 1999), pp. 2, 4.

11. See generally Phillip C. Jessup, *Elihu Root* (New York: Dodd, Mead & Company, 1938), p. 348; Bartholomew H. Sparrow, *The Insular Cases and the Emergence of American Empire* (Lawrence: University Press of Kansas, 2006).

12. Walter LaFeber, *The New Empire: An Interpretation of American Expansion 1860–1898* (Ithaca, NY: Cornell University Press, 1963), p. 416.

13. Karl Raustiala, "The Geography of Justice," *Fordham Law Review* 73 (2005): 2501, 2540–42.

CHAPTER 4

1. Benjamin Franklin, *Memoirs of the Life and Writings of Benjamin Franklin* (1818), p. 270.

2. Abraham Lincoln, "To Erastus Corning and Others," in *Abraham Lincoln, Speeches and Writings, 1859–1865* (New York: Library of America, 1989), p. 458.

3. J. G. Randall, *Lincoln the Liberal Statesman* (New York: Dodd, Mead & Co., 1947), p. 123.

4. James Madison, *The Federalist*, no. 47, p. 261, ed. J. R. Pole (2005).

5. Attorney General John Ashcroft, testimony at Anti-Terrorism Policy Review Hearing before Senate Committee on the Judiciary, 108th Cong. (2001).

6. Michael Kent Curtis, "Lincoln, the Constitution of Necessity, and the Necessity of Constitutions: A Reply to Professor Paulsen," *Maine Law Review* 59, no. 1 (2007): 30.

7. Geoffrey R. Stone, *Perilous Times: Free Speech in Wartime from the Sedition Act of 1798 to the War on Terrorism* (New York: W. W. Norton & Co., 2004), p. 494.

8. Dorothy Ehrlich, "Taking Liberties: The Growing Scope of Government Power," *Los Angeles Daily Journal*, February 26, 2002.

9. Intelligence Activities and the Rights of Americans, Final Report of the

NOTES

Senate Committee to Study Governmental Operations with respect to Intelligence Activities, Book II (1976), http://www.icdc.com/~paulwolf/cointel pro/churchfinalreportIId.htm (accessed February 23, 2011).

10. Ibid.

11. Kim Zetter, "Whistleblower: NSA Targeted Journalists, Snooped on All U.S. Communications," Wired Blog Network, http://www.wired.com/threatlevel/2009/01/nsa-whistleblow-2/ (accessed February 23, 2011).

12. Editorial, "Closely Watched Judges: Judicial Spat Highlights Workplace Privacy," *Sacramento Bee*, September 11, 2001, p. B6.

13. Marjorie Cohn, "Bush's War on Democracy," Truthout, August 31, 2004, http://www.uncle-scam.com/Breaking/aug-04/to-8-31.pdf (accessed February 23, 2011).

14. Letter from Rabih Haddad to Mr. Thayer (January 27, 2002), American Immigration Lawyers Association, http://www.aila.org/content/default .aspx?docid=2051 (accessed February 23, 2011).

15. *Korematsu v. United States*, 323 US 214, 246 (1944) (Jackson, dissenting).

16. *Olmstead v. United States*, 277 US 438, 479 (1928) (Brandeis, J., dissenting).

17. Scott Higham, "No Welcome in Guantanamo as Rights Groups Land," *Washington Post*, August 24, 2004, p. A5.

18. Daphne Eviatar, "Those 61 Gitmo Recidivists Keep Popping Back Up . . . ," *Washington Independent*, January 23, 2009, http://washington independent.com/26969/those-61-gitmo-recidivists-keep-popping-back-up (accessed February 23, 2011); Mark Denbeaux et al., "Justice Scalia, the Department of Defense, and the Perpetuation of an Urban Legend: The Truth about the Alleged Recidivism of Released Guantánamo Detainees," http:// law.shu.edu/publications/guantanamoReports/urban_legend_final_63008.p df (accessed February 23, 2011).

CHAPTER 5

1. See Alexander Hamilton (no. 23, p. 147) and James Madison (no. 41, p. 270), in *The Federalist*, ed. Jacob E. Cooke (Middletown, CT: Wesleyan University Press, 1961) (original emphasis omitted, new emphasis added).

2. See Michael Stokes Paulsen's book review quoting Lincoln and defending his theory of the Constitution during wartime, "The Civil War as Constitutional Interpretation," *University of Chicago Law Review* 71 (2004): 691, 721.

3. *Korematsu v. United States*, 323 US 214, 248 (1944).

CHAPTER 6

1. Ian Elsner and Arthur Spiegelman, "US Vows Revenge on 'Acts of War,' FBI Looks to Middle East for Suspects," *Cairns Post* (Australia) September 13, 2001.

2. See, for example, Jane Mayer, *The Dark Side: The Inside Story of How the War on Terror Turned into a War on American Ideals* (New York: Doubleday, 2008), p. 8.

3. *Ex Parte Quirin*, 317 US 1 (1942).

CHAPTER 7

1. 297 US 278 (1936).

2. Cpt. Chase Jay Nielsen, Trial Record, *United States v. Sawada*, 5 L. Rep. Trials of War Criminals 1 (1948), p. 55, quoted in Evan Wallach, "Drop by Drop: Forgetting the History of Water Torture in US Courts," *Columbia Journal of Transnational Law* 45 (2007): 468, 476.

3. Christopher Hitchens, "Believe Me, It's Torture," *Vanity Fair*, August 2008.

NOTES

4. Laurie Magid, "Deceptive Police Interrogation Practices: How Far Is Too Far? *Michigan Law Review* 99 (2001): 1168, 1173.

5. Arnold H. Loewy, "Police-Obtained Evidence and the Constitution: Distinguishing Unconstitutionally Obtained Evidence from Unconstitutionally Used Evidence," *Michigan Law Review* 87 (1989): 907, 933–34.

6. Magid, "Deceptive Police Interrogation Practices," p. 1174.

7. 538 US 760 (2003).

8. 467 US 649 (1984).

9. M. K. B. Darmer, "Beyond Bin Laden and Lindh: Confessions Law in an Age of Terrorism," *Cornell Journal of Law and Public Policy* 12 (2003): 319, 357.

10. 479 US 157 (2003).

11. Personal conversation between Lawrence Herman and Yale Kamisar, recounted in Lawrence Herman, "The Unexplained Relationship between the Privilege against Compulsory Self-Incrimination and the Involuntary Confessions Rule (Part II)," *Ohio State Law Journal* 53 (1992): 497 n. 647.

12. Mark A. Godsey, "Reliability Lost, False Confessions Discovered," *Chapman Law Review* (2007): 623, 627 n. 30.

13. See Richard Cohen, "A Plunge from the Moral Heights," in *Civil Liberties vs. National Security in a Post-9/11 World*, ed. M. Katherine B. Darmer, Robert M. Baird, and Stuart E. Rosenbaum (Amherst, NY: Prometheus Books, 2004), pp. 317–19.

CHAPTER 9

1. Alan M. Dershowitz, *Why Terrorism Works: Understanding the Threat, Responding to the Challenge* (New Haven, CT: Yale University Press, 2002), p. 144.

2. Seth F. Kreimer, "Too Close to the Rack and the Screw: Constitutional Constraints on Torture in the War on Terror," *University of Pennsylvania Journal of Constitutional Law* 6 (2003): 278, 306.

3. Ibid.

CHAPTER 10

1. Walter Pincus, "Silence of 4 Terror Probe Suspects Poses a Dilemma for FBI," *Washington Post*, October 21, 2001.

2. Ibid.

3. Ibid.

4. See Alan M. Dershowitz, "Is There a Torturous Road to Justice?" *Los Angeles Times*, November 8, 2001. See also Alan M. Dershowitz, *Shouting Fire: Civil Liberties in a Turbulent Age* (Boston: Little, Brown, 2002), p. 477; Alan M. Dershowitz, "Is It Necessary to Apply 'Physical Pressure' to Terrorists— And to Lie About It?" *Israel Law Review* 23 (1989): 192; Alan M. Dershowitz, "Want to Torture? Get a Warrant," *San Francisco Chronicle*, January 22, 2002.

5. Dershowitz, "Is There a Torturous Road to Justice?"

6. Ibid.

7. *United States v. Schoon*, 971 F.2d 193, 200 (9th Cir. 1991) (Fernandez, J. concurring).

CHAPTER 11

1. Richard Cohen, "A Plunge from the Moral Heights," in *Civil Liberties vs. National Security in a Post-9/11 World*, ed. M. Katherine B. Darmer, Robert M. Baird, and Stuart E. Rosenbaum (Amherst, NY: Prometheus Books, 2004), p. 319.

2. E-mail to author from Kurt Eggert dated March 11, 2009 (on file with author).

3. John Yoo, "Obama Made a Rash Decision on Gitmo," *Wall Street Journal*, January 29, 2009.

4. Professor Marjorie Cohn of Thomas Jefferson and Robert J. Pushaw Jr. of Pepperdine appeared on the same panel, and excerpts from their contributions are also included in this volume (see chapters 4, 5, 26, and 27).

5. Yoo, "Obama Made a Rash Decision on Gitmo."

NOTES

6. Cohen, "A Plunge from the Moral Heights."

7. As an aside, there is something unsettling about the degree of opprobrium faced by Professor Yoo when contrasted with the relative quiet regarding Judge Bybee. I have read no reports of protests at the Court of Appeals where Judge Bybee sits, whereas Yoo has been the target of a number of protests (including a very loud one outside the building where this is being written). I also note that Alberto Gonzalez seems to have faced more vilification than others equally complicit in the failings at the Justice Department.

8. Peter Margulies, "True Believers at Law: National Security Agendas, the Regulation of Lawyers, and the Separation of Powers," *Maryland Law Review* 68, no. 1 (2008): 37–40.

9. David Glenn, "'Torture Memos' vs. Academic Freedom," *Chronicle of Higher Education*, March 20, 2009; citing Jack L. Goldsmith, *The Terror Presidency: Law and Judgment Inside the Bush Administration* (New York: W. W. Norton & Co., Inc., 2007).

10. See Trevor W. Morrison, "Constitutional Avoidance in the Executive Branch," *Columbia Law Review* 106 (2006): 1189, 1231, n. 182. "In the two years since it was leaked to the public, the Bybee Memorandum has been withered by criticism for the poor quality of its legal analysis" (citing sources of criticism, including statement by Yale Law School dean Harold Hongju Koh that it was "perhaps the most clearly erroneous legal opinion I have ever read").

11. Margulies, "True Believers at Law," p. 41 (citing Memorandum from Acting Assistant Attorney General Daniel Levin to Deputy Attorney General James B. Comey, December 30, 2004).

12. Evan Wallach, "Drop by Drop: Forgetting the History of Water Torture in US Courts," *Columbia Journal of Transnational Law* 45 (2007): 468.

13. Ibid., p. 502.

14. Ibid., p. 504.

15. Ibid., p. 474.

16. Hitchens's experience is detailed in Darmer, "Reliability, Waterboarded Confessions and Reclaiming the Lessons of *Brown v. Mississippi* in the Terrorism Cases," chapter 7.

17. Christopher Hitchens, "Believe Me, It's Torture," *Vanity Fair*, August 2008.

18. Eyal Press, "In Torture We Trust?" in *Civil Liberties vs. National Security in a Post-9/11 World*, ed. M. Katherine B. Darmer, Robert M. Baird, and Stuart E. Rosenbaum (Amherst, NY: Prometheus Books, 2004), p. 228.

19. Philip H. Heymann, "Torture Should Not be Authorized," in *Civil Liberties vs. National Security in a Post-9/11 World*, ed. M. Katherine B. Darmer, Robert M. Baird, and Stuart E. Rosenbaum (Amherst, NY: Prometheus Books, 2004), p. 217.

20. Yoo, "Obama Made a Rash Decision on Gitmo."

21. Alan Clarke, "Creating a Torture Culture," *Suffolk Transnational Law Review* 32 (2008): 18.

22. Press, "In Torture We Trust?" pp. 223–24.

23. Clarke, "Creating a Torture Culture," p. 24.

24. Ibid., p. 13.

25. Ibid.

26. Yoo, "Obama Made a Rash Decision on Gitmo."

27. Clarke, "Creating a Torture Culture," p. 3.

28. Yoo, "Obama Made a Rash Decision on Gitmo."

29. Press, "In Torture We Trust?" p. 219.

CHAPTER 13

1. 132 F. Supp. 2d 168 (S.D.N.Y. 2001).

2. Mark Godsey, "The New Frontier of Constitutional Confession Law— The International Arena: Exploring the Admissibility of Confessions Taken by US Investigators from Non-Americans Abroad, *Georgetown Law Journal* 91 (2003): 851, 877.

3. *United States v. Welch*, 455 F.2d 211, 213 (2d Cir. 1972).

4. George C. Thomas III, "Separated at Birth but Siblings Nonetheless: Miranda and the Due Process Notice Cases, *Michigan Law Review* 99 (2001): 1081, 1085.

NOTES

CHAPTER 17

1. Mae M. Ngai, *Impossible Subjects: Illegal Aliens and the Making of Modern America* (Princeton, NJ: Princeton University Press, 2004), p. 27.

2. Eric Schmitt, "Senate Votes Bill to Reduce Influx of Illegal Aliens," *New York Times*, May 3, 1996.

3. 142 CONG. REC. S11, 505 (daily ed. September 27, 1996) (statement of Sen. Hatch).

4. President George W. Bush, Address to the Nation on Immigration Reform (May 15, 2006), available at http://www.whitehouse.gov/news/releases/2006/05/20060515-8.html (emphasis added).

5. Joseph Nevins, *Operation Gatekeeper: The Rise of the "Illegal Alien" and the Making of the US-Mexico Boundary* (New York: Routledge, 2002), pp. 88–89 (quoting President William Jefferson Clinton, Press Conference, July 27, 1993).

6. Donald Kerwin, "Revisiting the Need for Appointed Counsel," *Insight* 4 (2004): 1, 4, available at http://www.migrationpolicy.org/insight/Insight _Kerwin.pdf.

7. See George Rusche and Otto Kirchheimer, *Punishment and Social Structure* (New York: Columbia University Press, 1939), p. 66.

8. Rubén G. Rumbaut and others, "Debunking the Myth of Immigrant Criminality: Imprisonment among First- and Second-Generation Young Men," Migration Information Source, June 1, 2006, http://www.migration information.org/Feature/display.cfm?id=403 (accessed February 25, 2007).

9. Ibid.

10. Eyal Press, "Do Immigrants Make Us Safer?" *New York Times Magazine*, December 3, 2006, p. 24 (quoting John Mollenkopf, political scientist and professor of political science and sociology at the CUNY Graduate Center).

CHAPTER 19

1. Michael Luo, "For Exercise in New York Futility, Push Button," *New York Times*, February 27, 2004.

2. David Cole, "Enemy Aliens," *Stanford Law Review* 54 (2002): 953, 976.

3. *Parents Involved in Community Schools v. Seattle School District*, 127 S. Ct. 2738, 2768 (2007).

4. See Adam Litpak, "Impressions of Terrorism, Drawn from Court Files," *New York Times*, February 19, 2008.

5. Dan Ouimette, Captain, US Navy, America WAKE UP! (February 19, 2003), http://www.versagivoice.com/World_affairs/wakeup.htm (accessed October 4, 2008).

6. Leti Volpp, "The Citizen and the Terrorist," *UCLA Law Review* 49 (2002): 1575, 1585.

7. Susan M. Akram and Maritza Karmely, "Immigration and Constitutional Consequences of Post-9/11 Policies Involving Arabs and Muslims in the United States: Is Alienage a Distinction without a Difference?" *U.C. Davis Law Review* 38 (2005): 609, 669.

8. Cole, "Enemy Aliens," p. 976.

9. Ibid., p. 3.

10. Duncan Campbell, "From Hot Tub to Hot Water," *Guardian Unlimited*, July 16, 2002, available at http://www.guardian.co.uk/world/2002/jul/16/worlddispatch.usa.

CHAPTER 20

1. Press Release, Office of US Senator Edward M. Kennedy, "Kennedy Introduces State Secrets Protection Act" (January 22, 2008) (internal quotation marks omitted), available at http://kennedy.senate.gov/newsroom/press_release.cfm?id=C56BD1D0-7AD3-46EA-9D30-A77317F28B70; see also

NOTES

William G. Weaver and Danielle Escontrias, "Origins of the State Secrets Privilege" (February 10, 2008) (unpublished paper, available at http://ssrn.com/abstract=1079364), pp. 3–4.

2. 154 CONG. REC. S93 (daily ed. Jan. 22, 2008) (introduction by Senator Ted Kennedy).

3. State Secrets Protection Act of 2008, H.R. 5607, 110th Cong. (2d Sess. 2008).

4. State Secrets Protection Act of 2008: Hearing on H.R. 5607 Before the Subcomm. on the Constitution, Civil Rights, and Civil Liberties of the H. Comm. on the Judiciary, 110th Cong. 77 (2008) (statement of Rep. Jerrold Nadler, Chairman, H. Comm. on the Judiciary).

5. John Henry Wigmore, *Evidence in Trials at Common Law*, vol. 8 (Boston: Little, Brown, 1940), section 2212a(4); see also *Reynolds*, 345 US, pp. 6–7.

6. Complaint at paragraph 40. 44, *El-Masri v. Tenet*, 437 F. Supp. 2d 530 (E.D. Va. 2006) (No. 1:05cv1417), available at http://www.aclu.org/images/extraordinaryrendition/asset_upload_file829_22211.pdf.

7. *In re United States*, 872 F.2d 472, 474 (D.C. Cir. 1989); *In re NSA Telecomm. Records Litig.*, 564 F. Supp. 2d 1109, 1118 (N.D. Cal. 2008); *Hepting v. AT&T Corp.*, 439 F. Supp. 2d 974, 980–85 (N.D. Cal. 2006); see also *Al-Haramain Islamic Found. v. Bush*, 507 F.3d 1190, 1196 (9th Cir. 2007) ("The state secrets privilege is a common law evidentiary privilege that permits the government to bar the disclosure of information if 'there is a reasonable danger' that disclosure will 'expose military matters which, in the interest of national security, should not be divulged.'" [quoting Reynolds, 345 US, p. 10]).

CHAPTER 21

1. FISA is inapplicable to surveillance of communications collected outside the United States and not targeted at US citizens or permanent resident

aliens (collectively referred to as "U.S. persons") within the United States. See 50 U.S.C. 1801(f)(1)-(2) (defining "electronic surveillance"). Thus, FISA does not impose any limits on wiretapping of calls between foreign nationals outside the United States—whether or not they are associated with al Qaeda—and persons within the United States, as long as the calls are not intercepted domestically, and the tap is not "targeted" at a US person within the country. If international surveillance is targeted at US persons abroad, the Fourth Amendment might impose some limits. See also Exec. Order No. 12,333 § 2.5, 46 Fed. Reg. 59,941 (Dec. 4, 1981) (delegating to the attorney general the power to approve the use for intelligence purposes, within the United States or against a United States person abroad, of any technique for which a warrant would be required if undertaken for law enforcement purposes, "provided that such techniques shall not be undertaken unless the Attorney General has determined in each case that there is probable cause to believe that the technique is directed against a foreign power or an agent of a foreign power"). (But FISA as such does not regulate such surveillance.)

2. Where FISA applies—i.e., where the calls are intercepted domestically, or where the surveillance targets a US person in the United States—the statute merely requires that certain criteria for such surveillance be demonstrated to the satisfaction of a neutral judge on the Foreign Intelligence Surveillance Court. The FISA Court is required to issue an *ex parte* order approving such surveillance if the statutory criteria are satisfied—the most significant of which are that there is probable cause to believe (i) that the target of the electronic surveillance is a foreign power or an agent of a foreign power, and (ii) that each of the facilities or places at which the electronic surveillance is directed is being used, or is about to be used, by a foreign power or an agent of a foreign power. 50 U.S.C. 1805(a)(3). Under the statute, "agents of a foreign power" includes persons who knowingly engage in, or aid and abet, or conspire to commit, sabotage or international terrorism (or activities in preparation for such terrorism), for or on behalf of a foreign power (including al Qaeda), as well as other non-US persons who act in the United States as officers or employees of a foreign power. 50 U.S.C. 1801(b).

3. The NSA program apparently includes surveillance that is acquired within the United States and/or targeted at US persons, because the Bush administration has conceded that its wiretaps include "electronic surveillance" covered by FISA. See Press Briefing by Attorney General Alberto Gonzales and General Michael Hayden, Principal Deputy Director for National Intelligence (Dec. 19, 2005), http://www.whitehouse.gov/news/releases/2005/12/20051219-1.html) (stating that NSA is engaged in "electronic surveillance" and that FISA "requires a court order before engaging in this kind of surveillance"); White Paper, p. 17 n. 5, infra at 1390 (assuming arguendo that the NSA program involves "electronic surveillance" as defined in FISA).

4. As of the time of this writing [the article's original publication] it appears that the NSA program collects surveillance that would not be approved under FISA if the administration were to seek authorization by a FISA court under the statute. According to the administration, under the program the NSA must only find "reasonable grounds to believe" that at least one party to the communication is a member or agent of al Qaeda or an "affiliated terrorist organization"—a standard that could permit wiretaps of the phones of US persons in the United States who are not themselves al Qaeda agents. Thus, it appears that NSA does *not* require in every case that there be probable cause to believe that the *target* of the electronic surveillance is a foreign power or an agent of a foreign power. Under FISA as currently written, the FISA court could not approve such surveillance, and the leading judicial precedent indicates that *without* judicial approval such surveillance of US persons would likely violate the Fourth Amendment. See *Zweibon v. Mitchell*, 516 F.2d 594, 614 (D.C. Cir. 1975) (en banc) (plurality opinion) ("[W]e hold today ... that a warrant must be obtained before a wiretap is installed on a domestic organization that is neither the agent of nor acting in collaboration with a foreign power, even if the surveillance is installed under presidential directive in the name of foreign intelligence gathering for protection of the national security."); id. at 689 (Wilkey, J., concurring in pertinent part, agreeing with plurality that if an exemption from the Fourth Amendment's warrant requirement exists, "it exists only for a narrow category of wiretaps on foreign agents or collaborators with a foreign power.")

NOTES

CHAPTER 26

1. Reply to Opp'n of Petition for Rehearing, *Al Odah v. United States*, 128 S. Ct. 1923 (2008), p. 4 and appendix 1–3, 5, 6, 7.

2. John Yoo, "Obama Made a Rash Decision on Gitmo," *Wall Street Journal*, January 29, 2009.

SOURCES AND PERMISSIONS

CHAPTER 2

"Inter Arma Silent Leges"

Reprinted from *All the Laws but One* by William H. Rehnquist. Copyright ©
1998 by William H. Rehnquist. Used by permission of Alfred A. Knopf, a
division of Random House, Inc.

CHAPTER 3

"*Boumediene v. Bush* and Guantánamo, Cuba: Does the 'Empire Strike Back'?"

Originally appeared in Vol. 62, No. 1 of the *SMU Law Review*. Reprinted with
permission from the *SMU Law Review* and the Southern Methodist University Dedman School of Law, and Ernesto Hernández-López.

CHAPTER 4

"Trading Civil Liberties for Apparent Security Is a Bad Deal"

Chapman Law Review 12 (2009): 615. Reprinted by permission of the
Chapman Law Review and Marjorie Cohn.

SOURCES AND PERMISSIONS

CHAPTER 5

"Justifying Wartime Limits on Civil Rights and Liberties"

Chapman Law Review 12 (2009): 675. Reprinted by permission of the
Chapman Law Review and Robert J. Pushaw Jr.

CHAPTER 6

"Broken Promises or Unrealistic Expectations?:
Comparing the Bush and Obama Administrations on Counterterrorism"

Forthcoming in *Transnational Law and Contemporary Problems* 20 (2011).
Used by permission of *Transnational Law and Contemporary Problems*
and Tung Yin.

CHAPTER 7

"Reliability, Waterboarded Confessions and Reclaiming the
Lessons of *Brown v. Mississippi* in the Terrorism Cases"

Modified from an earlier version published in the *Guild Practitioner* 66
(2009): 18. Used by permission of the *Guild Practitioner* and M. Katherine
B. Darmer.

SOURCES AND PERMISSIONS

CHAPTER 9

"Torture and Positive Law: Jurisprudence for the White House"

Columbia Law Review 105 (2005): 1681. Copyright © 2005 by Columbia Law Review Association, Inc. Reproduced with permission of Columbia Law Review Association, Inc., via Copyright Clearance Center, and Jeremy Waldron.

CHAPTER 10

"Interrogating Suspected Terrorists: Should Torture Be an Option?"

University of Pittsburgh Law Review 63 (Summer 2002): 743. Reprinted with permission from John T. Parry and the *University of Pittsburgh Law Review*.

CHAPTER 11

"Waterboarding and the Legacy of the Bybee-Yoo 'Torture and Power' Memorandum: Reflections from a Temporary Yoo Colleague and Erstwhile Bush Administration Apologist"

Originally appeared in *Chapman Law Review* 12 (2009): 639. Copyright © 2009 M. Katherine B. Darmer. Reprinted with permission.

SOURCES AND PERMISSIONS

CHAPTER 12

"Torture"

From the *New York Times*, April 1, 2010, issue © 2010 The New York Times. All rights reserved. Used by permission and protected by Copyright Laws of the United States. The printing, copying, and redistribution, or retransmission of this Content without express written permission is prohibited.

CHAPTER 13

"Beyond *Bin Laden* and *Lindh*: Confessions Law in an Age of Terrorism"

Cornell Journal of Law and Public Policy 12 (2003): 313. Reprinted with permission from *Cornell Journal of Law and Public Policy*. Copyright © 2003 Cornell University.

CHAPTER 14

"Holder's Promising Interrogation Plan"

National Journal, May 22, 2010. Reprinted with permission from *National Journal*, May 22, 2010. Copyright © 2011 by National Journal Group, Inc. All rights reserved.

SOURCES AND PERMISSIONS

CHAPTER 15

"*Miranda* and 'Enhanced Interrogations'"

Copyright Wendy Kaminer, 2010. This article first appeared at theatlantic.com, May 10, 2010.

CHAPTER 16

"Shahzad and *Miranda* Rights"

Reprinted courtesy of Orin Kerr. Originally published at the Volokh Conspiracy blog, volokh.com, May 5, 2010.

CHAPTER 17

"Unsecured Borders: Immigration Restrictions, Crime Control, and National Security"

Connecticut Law Review 39, no. 5 (2007). Reprinted courtesy of the *Connecticut Law Review*, copyright © 2009 *Connecticut Law Review*, and Jennifer M. Chacón.

CHAPTER 18

"The Skies Won't Be Safe Until We Use Commonsense Profiling"

National Journal, March 16, 2002. Reprinted with permission from *National Journal*, copyright 2011 by National Journal Group, Inc. All rights reserved.

SOURCES AND PERMISSIONS

CHAPTER 19

"The Last Minstrel Show? Racial Profiling, the War on Terrorism, and the Mass Media"

Connecticut Law Review 41, no. 3 (2009). Reprinted courtesy of the *Connecticut Law Review*, copyright © 2009 *Connecticut Law Review*, and John Tehranian.

CHAPTER 20

"Litigating Secrets: Comparative Perspectives on the State Secrets Privilege"

Brooklyn Law Review 75 (2009): 201. Reprinted courtesy of the *Brooklyn Law Review*. Copyright © 2009 *Brooklyn Law Review*; Sudha Setty.

CHAPTER 21

"The National Security Agency's Domestic Spying Program: Framing the Debate"

Indiana Law Journal 81 (2006): 1355. Reprinted courtesy of the *Indiana Law Journal*. Copyright © 2006 by the trustees of Indiana University; David Cole, Martin S. Lederman.

SOURCES AND PERMISSIONS

CHAPTER 23

"Foreign Intelligence Surveillance Act (FISA)"

From the *New York Times*, April 1, 2010, issue, © 2010 The New York Times.
All rights reserved. Used by permission and protected by Copyright Laws
of the United States. The printing, copying, and redistribution, or retransmission of this Content without express written permission is prohibited.

CHAPTER 24

"Wrong in All Aspects"

Los Angeles Daily Journal, September 15, 2010. Reprinted with the permission
of Daily Journal Corp. (2011).

CHAPTER 26

"Trading Civil Liberties for Apparent Security Is a Bad Deal"

Chapman Law Review 12 (2009): 615. Reprinted by permission of the
Chapman Law Review and Marjorie Cohn.

SOURCES AND PERMISSIONS

CHAPTER 27

"Justifying Wartime Limits on Civil Rights and Liberties"

Chapman Law Review 12 (2009): 675. Reprinted by permission of the *Chapman Law Review* and Robert J. Pushaw Jr.

CHAPTER 29

"*Boumediene v. Bush* and Guantánamo, Cuba: Does the 'Empire Strike Back'?"

Originally appeared in Vol. 62, No. 1 of the *SMU Law Review*. Reprinted with permission from the *SMU Law Review* and the Southern Methodist University Dedman School of Law, and Ernesto Hernández-López.

CHAPTER 31

"Worst-Case Justice; We're Holding Terrorism Suspects Without Trial, But Should We? A Task Force Gives Recommendations"

Editorial, *Los Angeles Times*, June 15, 2010. Used by permission of the *Los Angeles Times*.